OVID'S FASTI

OVID'S FASTI

WITH AN ENGLISH TRANSLATION BY

SIR JAMES GEORGE FRAZER

FELLOW OF TRINITY COLLEGE, CAMBRIDGE

CAMBRIDGE, MASSACHUSETTS

HARVARD UNIVERSITY PRESS

LONDON

WILLIAM HEINEMANN LTD

MCMLXVII

First printed 1931
Reprinted 1931, 1959, 1967

Printed in Great Britain

CONTENTS

INTRODUCTION

§ 1. The Life of Ovid

On the life of Ovid we have more authentic information than on that of most ancient writers, for not only has he interspersed many allusions to it in his poems but in one of them he has given us a formal autobiography,[a] a species of composition to which the ancients were not addicted. Indeed, even the art of biography was little cultivated in antiquity, and were it not for the splendid portrait gallery which Plutarch has bequeathed to us in his *Lives* our knowledge of the personal character and fortunes of the great men of Greece and Rome would be for the most part but slight and fragmentary, and for us they might have stalked like masked figures, looming vast and dim through the mist, across the stage of history.

Ovid was born in 43 B.C., the year in which the two consuls, Hirtius and Pansa, fell in battle during the civil war which followed the assassination of Caesar. His birthplace was Sulmo, the modern Solmona, a town situated in a well-watered valley of the Apennines, in the land of the Paelignians, about ninety miles to the east of Rome. He has himself described the happy vale, rich in corn and vines, dotted here

[a] *Tristia*, iv. 10.

and there with grey olive-groves and traversed by winding streams, the ground everywhere kept fresh and green even in the baking heat of summer by the springs that bubbled up through the grassy turf.[a] No wonder that in his dreary exile on the dismal shore of the Black Sea the memory of his sweet native dale should have come back on him with many a pang of fond regret.[b]

The poet came of an old equestrian or knightly family and prided himself on being a knight by birth and not by the gift of fortune or, like a multitude of newly dubbed knights in that age of civil war, in virtue of military service.[c] He had a brother a year older than himself, who died at the age of twenty. Together the boys were sent at an early age by their father to be educated at Rome, where they were placed under the care of eminent masters. His brother displayed a taste for rhetoric and looked forward to the profession of a pleader in the courts.[d] Ovid's own bent from childhood was all for poetry. In this he received no encouragement from his father, who endeavoured to dissuade him from so unprofitable a course of life, holding up to him, as an awful warning, the fate of Homer, who had died a poor man.[e] Clearly the old gentleman thought that there was no money in the poetical business, and substantially he was doubtless right. Gold is not the guerdon which the Muses dangle before the eyes of their votaries, luring them on " to scorn delights and live laborious days." For a time the youthful poet

[a] *Amores*, ii. 16. 1-10.   [b] *Fasti*, iv. 81 *sqq.*
[c] *Amores*, iii. 15. 5 *sq.* ; *Tristia*, iv. 10. 7 *sq.*
[d] *Tristia*, iv. 10. 9-18.
[e] *Tristia*, iv. 10. 19-22.

endeavoured to comply with the paternal injunction. He turned his back on the Muses' hill and struggled to write prose instead of poetry, but do what he would all that he wrote fell naturally and inevitably into verse.[a]

On attaining to manhood he exchanged the broad purple stripe, which as a noble youth he had worn on his tunic, for the narrow purple edge which was the badge of a Roman knight. At the same time he renounced all intention of aspiring to the rank of senator, which would have entitled him to flaunt for life the broad purple on his tunic. However, he set his foot on the first rung of the official ladder by accepting a place on the board of minor magistrates charged with the duty of inspecting prisons and superintending executions—duties which can have been but little to the taste of the poet's gentle and sensitive nature.[b] But in the company of poets he found a society more congenial than that of gaol-birds and hangmen. For Rome was then at the very zenith of its poetical activity and fame. Virgil and Horace, Propertius and Tibullus, were all alive and singing when Ovid was a young man at Rome, and in the poetical heaven shone lesser stars whose light has long been quenched. Among them Ovid sat entranced, looking on every poet as a god. He was an intimate friend of Propertius and listened to the bard pouring out his fiery elegiacs. He heard Horace chanting his melodious lays to the music of the Ausonian lyre.[c] He lived to mourn the early death of Tibullus.[d] Virgil our author appears to have seen

---

[a] *Tristia*, iv. 10. 23-26.
[b] *Tristia*, iv. 10. 27-36.
[c] *Tristia*, iv. 10. 41-54.   [d] *Amores*, iii. 9.

only once without obtaining speech of him,[a] in which he was less fortunate than the nobody, recorded by Browning, who once had the good fortune to see Shelley :

> And did you once see Shelley plain ?
> And did he stop and speak to you ?

But even in the society of poets Ovid was not content to pass all his life in the smoke and din of Rome. He travelled widely to see for himself the places of which he had read in story. As a student he visited Athens,[b] and in the company of his friend Macer he roamed among the splendid cities of Asia and spent the greater part of a year in Sicily, where he beheld the famous fountain of Arethuse, the lakes of Enna, and the sky ablaze with the flames of Aetna ; and in a letter to his friend, written in exile, he recalls the happy time they had passed together driving in a light car or floating in a painted skiff on the blue water, when even the long hours of a summer day seemed too short for their talk.[c]

Ovid was thrice married. His first marriage, contracted in early youth, was brief and unhappy : his second was also brief ; but his third wife proved a faithful helpmeet to him in his later years and stood by him in the last great trial of his life, his exile, though she was not allowed to share it.[d] In a letter addressed to her from his place of banishment he speaks of her as the model of a good wife.[e] By one

---

[a] *Tristia*, iv. 10. 51 " Vergilium vidi tantum." Among the intimate friends of Ovid was the grammarian C. Julius Hyginus, the head of the Palatine library. See Suetonius, *De grammaticis*, 20.

[b] *Tristia*, i. 2. 77.

[c] *Ex Ponto*, ii. 10. 21-44.

[d] *Tristia*, iv. 10. 69-74.

[e] *Ex Ponto*, iii. 1. 43 *sq.*

of his wives Ovid had a daughter to whom he was tenderly attached, and who made him twice a grand-father, though by different husbands.[a] When he was about to give her in marriage, the poet consulted no less a personage than the High Priestess of Jupiter (the Flaminica Dialis) as to a lucky day for the wed-ding, and was warned by her not to let his daughter wed in the first half of June or, to be more exact, not until the Ides (the thirteenth day of the month) should be past.[b]

Meantime his poems had made him famous : his acquaintance was sought by younger bards, as he himself had courted that of their elders [c] ; and in the noble epilogue to his greatest work, the *Metamor-phoses*, the poet anticipated, not unjustly, for his works a deathless renown.[d]

It was when he was thus in the full enjoyment of domestic happiness and literary fame that the sen-tence of banishment, pronounced by Augustus, fell on Ovid like a bolt from the blue. His fiftieth year was past and his hair was already grisled ; we may suppose that it was the year 8 of our era.[e] The place of his exile was to be Tomi on the bleak western shore of the Black Sea, where the land of the barbarous Getae bordered on the land of the barbarous Sarma-tians.[f] The alleged reason for the sentence was the immoral tendency of his poem *The Art of Love*,[g] but that can hardly have been the Emperor's real motive, since the offending poem had been published many

[a] *Tristia*, iv. 10. 75 *sq.*   [b] *Fasti*, vi. 219-234.
[c] *Tristia*, iv. 10. 53 *sqq.*
[d] *Metamorphoses*, xv. 871-879.
[e] *Tristia*, iv. 8. 33, iv. 10. 93-98.
[f] *Tristia*, iv. 10. 97 *sq.*, 109 *sqq.*
[g] *Tristia*, ii. 207, 211 *sq.*

years before, apparently without creating a scandal at the time. The real motive, as the poet plainly implies, was a deep offence which he had given to Augustus and which the Emperor never forgave.[a] To this the poet alludes again and again, but always in veiled language; he never revealed the exact nature of the offence. He protests over and over again that the cause of his ruin was an error, not a crime.[b] The nearest he comes to lifting the veil is a passage in which he asks, in grief and remorse, why had he seen something? why had he made his eyes culpable? why had he been accidentally privy to a guilty secret? and compares his case to that of Actaeon who was punished for unwittingly coming on Diana naked.[c] On the strength of this passage some modern writers have suggested that Ovid may have accidentally witnessed an escapade of the Emperor's profligate granddaughter Julia, who was banished by Augustus in the same year as the poet.[d] But this is a mere conjecture. Ovid kept the fatal secret locked up in his breast, and we shall never know it.

He has described in pathetic language the last night he passed in Rome—the passionate grief of his weeping wife, now clasping him in her arms, now prostrating herself in prayer before the household gods at the hearth where the fire was dead as her hopes; the tears and sighs of the grief-stricken household, the last farewell to friends; till, as the night

---

[a] *Tristia*, ii. 207-210.

[b] *Tristia*, i. 3. 37 *sq.*, iii. 1. 51 *sq.*, iii. 6. 25 *sq.*, iv. 10. 89 *sq.*

[c] *Tristia*, ii. 103-106; compare *Tristia*, iii. 5. 49 *sq.*,

> Inscia quod crimen viderunt lumina plector,
> peccatumque oculos est habuisse meum.

[d] Suetonius, *Augustus*, 65. 1.

INTRODUCTION

grew late, the sounds of lamentation died away into silence in the house, while outside the moonlight slept white on the marble fanes of the Capitol close at hand. But with break of day the parting hour was come, and the Morning Star gave the signal for departure.[a]

The long and difficult journey to Tomi would seem to have been compulsorily undertaken in winter, for the poet tells us that in chill December he was shivering on the Adriatic, while he wrote versified epistles on shipboard to the friends he had left behind him.[b] Here the ship encountered a storm that threatened to drive her back to the port from which she had sailed, and the exiled bard was tantalized by seeing, across the heaving waters, the distant coast of Italy on which he might never set foot again.[c] He crossed the Isthmus of Corinth and took ship again at the port of Cenchreae, only to be again tempest-tossed on the Aegean as he had been on the Adriatic, and again to scribble verses in the height of the storm, to the astonishment, as the poet imagined, of the very Cyclades themselves. After touching at the island of Samothrace he landed in Thrace and made his way on foot through the country of the Bistones to Tomi.[d] It was doubtless on this land journey through the snowy Thracian mountains that our author beheld the Sapaeans and other wild highlanders offering the entrails of dogs in sacrifice to a barbarous deity whom he identified with Diana.[e]

At Tomi our author sought to while away the tedious hours of exile by inditing poetical epistles to

---

[a] *Tristia*, i. 3.   [b] *Tristia*, i. 11. 3 *sq.*
[c] *Tristia*, i. 4. 1-20.   [d] *Tristia*, i. 10. 9-23, i. 11. 1-10.
[e] *Fasti*, i. 389 *sq.*

his family, his friends and patrons in Rome, entreating them to use their influence with the Emperor to ensure his pardon or at least his removal to a less distant and less barbarous place of banishment. He even addressed himself to Augustus direct in the longest of these poems,[a] beseeching him for mercy, but all in vain. And after the death of Augustus the unhappy poet turned to the popular prince Germanicus the stream of his mingled flattery and prayer in the hope of touching his clement heart and obtaining at least a mitigation of his sentence.[b] But all his entreaties fell on deaf ears.

The neighbouring barbarians did not add to the amenities of life in the frontier town by the random flights of poisoned arrows which from time to time they sent whizzing over the walls in the hope of picking off some fat pursy citizen as he went about his peaceful business in the streets. Ovid often alludes to these missiles[c] and even contemplated the possibility of his blood dyeing a Scythian arrow or a Getic sword,[d] but we have no reason to suppose that his life was thus brought to an untimely end, although, when the watchman on the battlements gave the signal of an approaching raid, and the hostile cavalry were circling at full gallop round the walls, the stouthearted bard used to clap a helmet on his grey head and, grasping sword and shield in his tremulous hands, hurry to the gate to meet the foe.[e]

However, the valiant poet returned good for evil by learning the languages of both the barbarous

---

[a] *Tristia*, ii.   [b] *Ex Ponto*, ii. 1, iv. 8. 21 *sqq.*

[c] *Tristia*, iii. 10. 63 *sq.*, iv. 1. 77, 84, v. 7. 15 *sq.*; *Ex Ponto*, i. 2. 15 *sq.*, iii. 1. 25 *sq.*, iv. 7. 11 *sq.*, 36, iv. 9. 83, iv. 10. 31.

[d] *Ex Ponto*, ii. 1. 65 *sq.*   [e] *Tristia*, iv. 1. 73 *sqq.*

tribes, the Getae and the Sarmatians,[a] who infested
the bleak, treeless, birdless plains that stretched away
to the horizon from the walls of Tomi—plains where
spring brought no vernal flowers and autumn no cheer-
ful reapers, and the only crop that broke the dreary
prospect was here and there a patch of bitter worm-
wood.[b] But Ovid did more than learn the language
of his enemies. He composed a poem in the Getic
language in which he paid high, not to say fulsome,
compliments to the memory of the deceased Augustus,
to his surviving widow, to his sons, and to his successor on the throne, the Emperor Tiberius ; and this
precious effusion he professes to have recited to a
circle of Getic hearers, who received it with murmurs
of applause, which they emphasized appropriately by
rattling their quivers.[c] The poet even expressed a
fear that his study of the Getic language had corrupted his Latin style.[d] In the interest of science, if
not of literature, it is much to be regretted that the
poem has perished ; had it survived it would have
been of priceless value as a unique example of a barbarous language preserved for us by the care and
diligence of a classical writer.

Among the poet's murmurs at his fate are naturally
many references to the rigorous climate of his place
of banishment in the far north, on the very edge of
the Roman world. He says that winter there was
almost continuous,[e] that the sea froze, that the wine
turned to blocks of ice, and that the barbarians drove

---

[a] *Ex Ponto*, iii. 2. 40.

[b] As to the scenery of the country round Tomi see *Ex
Ponto*, i. 2. 23, iii. 1. 5-24.

[c] *Ex Ponto*, iv. 13. 19-38.   [d] *Ex Ponto*, iv. 13. 17 *sq.*

[e] *Ex Ponto*, i. 2. 24.

INTRODUCTION

their creaking ox-drawn wains over the frozen Danube.[a] Of the society of the place he does not paint a flattering portrait. He admits that there was a tincture of Greek blood and a smatch of Greek culture in them, but adds that in their composition there was more of the Getic barbarian, which came out in their harsh voices, grim faces, and shaggy unkempt hair and beard ; every man carried a bow and wore a knife at his side, with which he was ready to stab at the smallest provocation.[b] However, a residence of nine or ten years at this end of the world would seem to have in some measure reconciled the poet to his lot. In one of his last letters, written to a friend from Tomi, he tells him that he keeps all his old serenity of mind ; that he had won the goodwill of the people of Tomi, who for their own sakes would gladly keep him with them, though for his sake they would willingly let him depart ; and that they and the inhabitants of neighbouring towns had publicly testified to their friendship by passing decrees in his honour and granting him immunity from taxes.[c] And in almost the last letter of all he addresses the people of Tomi, telling them that not even the folk of his dear native vale among the Apennines could have been kinder to him in his misfortune and sorrow than they had been, and he even adds that Tomi had grown as dear to him as Delos to Diana when she stayed the wandering island and found in it a place of rest and peace.[d] So the curtain falls gently, almost tenderly, on the exiled poet. He died at the age of sixty in the year A.D. 17 or 18, and was buried at

[a] *Ex Ponto*, iv. 7. 7-10, iv. 9. 85 *sq.*
[b] *Tristia*, v. 7. 9-20.   [c] *Ex Ponto*, iv. 9. 87-104.
[d] *Ex Ponto*, iv. 14. 47-62.

Tomi,[a] among the people whom he had made his friends.

§ 2. THE *FASTI*

The *Fasti* may rank next to the *Metamorphoses* as the most elaborate and important of Ovid's works. It is a poetical treatise on the Roman calendar, which it discusses in strictly chronological order, beginning with the first day of January and ending with the last day of June, where it stops abruptly. But repeated references in the poem to later dates in the year, of which he purposed to speak,[b] suffice to prove that the poet intended to continue his work on the same plan to the end of December, no doubt devoting to each of the last six months a separate book, as he has done with the first six months of the year in the poem as we possess it. Indeed, in one of his poems written in exile and addressed to Augustus, he expressly says that he had written the *Fasti* in twelve books, each book dealing with a separate month, and that he had dedicated the whole work to the Emperor, though his fate, by which he means his exile, had interrupted it.[c] We have no reason to reject such a definite statement addressed by the author to the man whom of

---

[a] Jerome, in Eusebius, *Chronic.*, ed. A. Schoene, vol. ii. (Berlin, 1866), p. 147, under the year of Abraham 2033, " Ovidius poeta in exilio diem obiit et iuxta oppidum Tomos sepelitur."

[b] *Fasti*, iii. 57 *sq.*, 199 *sq.*, v. 147 *sq.*

[c] *Tristia*, ii. 549 *sqq.* :

> Sex ego Fastorum scripsi totidemque libellos,
>   cumque suo finem mense volumen habet,
> idque tuo nuper scriptum sub nomine, Caesar,
>   et tibi sacratum sors mea rupit opus.

all others he least dared to deceive. But the last six books of the poem have disappeared without leaving a trace ; for no ancient writer cites or refers to them, and the four doggerel verses which a few manuscripts insert at the end of the sixth book, purporting to explain the old name of July (*Quintilis*), are clearly the interpolation of a clumsy scribe. It is true that in the seventeenth century the great scholar Nicolaus Heinsius mentioned, on the authority of Gronovius, a rumour that the last six books of the *Fasti* were preserved by a presbyter in a village near Ulm, but the rumour was probably no better founded than the reports of the discovery of the lost books of Livy, which occasionally startle the more credulous portion of the learned world. We can only apparently conclude, either that the last six books of the *Fasti* were lost, possibly in the post, which can hardly have been very regular or secure at Tomi, or that the poet left them in so rough and unfinished a state that his literary executors, in justice to the author's reputation, deemed it prudent to suppress them. Of the two alternative suppositions the latter is perhaps the more probable, since Ovid's own words seem to imply that his exile interrupted his work on the poem and prevented him from putting the final touches to it. The same conclusion is reinforced by another consideration. In the poem addressed to Augustus, as we have just seen, our author expressly affirms that he had dedicated the *Fasti* to Augustus, but in that work, as we have it, the dedication is not to Augustus but to Germanicus. The only reasonable explanation of this anomaly, as modern editors have seen, appears to be that after the death of Augustus the author cancelled the original dedication and substituted a

INTRODUCTION

dedication to Germanicus in the hope that the clement and popular prince, himself a poet, would be moved by the compliment to intercede with the reigning Emperor Tiberius in order to procure the poet's pardon, or at least a mitigation of his sentence. Whatever the motive, the change of dedication suffices to prove that during the later years of his exile Ovid was engaged in the revision of the *Fasti*; but, so far as the substitution of Germanicus for Augustus in the place of honour is concerned, the revision appears not to have extended beyond the first book, for in the remaining five books it is the dead emperor and not the living prince at whom the poet aims the shafts of his flattery and praise. But other traces of revision may be seen in the veiled allusions to his exile which Ovid has let fall in some of the later books of the *Fasti*.[a]

While the poet was thus filing and polishing the *Fasti* down to near the end of his life, we have no direct evidence as to the time when the work was begun. However, the author's own declaration to Augustus, quoted above, seems clearly to imply that the poem was nearly completed at the date of the writer's exile in A.D. 8 when he was about fifty years of age. We may conclude, then, that the *Fasti* was a work of Ovid's maturity, when the poet was at the height of his intellectual powers and a passed master of his art. The subject was happily chosen, for it offered him full scope for the display not merely of his fancy and eloquence but of his learning, which was very considerable. The matter of the poem falls, roughly speaking, into three sections, the historical, the astronomical, and the religious, which form, if

---

[a] *Fasti*, iv. 81 *sqq.*, vi. 666.

we may say so, the three threads out of which the
artist has woven the web of the *Fasti*.

The historical section comprises a considerable portion of the legends and annals of Rome, so far as these
were attached to definite dates in the calendar. Thus,
for example, the author seizes the traditional date of
the foundation of Rome on the twenty-first of April
as a peg on which to hang the legend of that momen-
tous event in the history of the world[a]; the Ides of
February recalls the march out and final destruction
of the three hundred heroic Fabii, which the poet
recounts at full length[b]; the notice of the foundation
of the temple of Fortune on the eleventh of June
furnishes the author with an opportunity of telling
the story of the foul murder of the popular king
Servius Tullius and the infamous conduct of his unnatural daughter[c]; the Flight of the King, which
the calendar placed on the twenty-fourth of February,
allows the poet to relate in graphic detail the crime
which led to the downfall of Tarquin the Proud and
the expulsion of the kings from Rome.[d] And so on
with page after page of legend and story; in a
sense the Roman calendar was an epitome of Roman
history, and Ovid's poem is an illuminated edition of
that epitome, in which the bare mention of an event is
often expanded into a beautiful picture aglow with
all the rich colours of poetic fancy.

The astronomical section of the poem, which the
author puts prominently forward in his exordium, is
much less valuable than the historical. The notices of
the rising and setting of the constellations, which were
the hinges whereon the ancient calendars revolved,

[a] *Fasti*, iv. 807 *sqq.*
[b] *Fasti*, ii. 193 *sqq.*
[c] *Fasti*, vi. 569 *sqq.*
[d] *Fasti*, ii. 685 *sqq.*

are often very inaccurate in the *Fasti*, and while
Ovid pays a warm tribute to the genius and lofty
character of the ancient astronomers,[a] he seems not
to have learned even the elements of their science.
Indeed, he has fallen into the strange mistake of men-
tioning an entirely fictitious constellation, that of the
Kite,[b] which seems to have owed its imaginary existence to the blunder of some ignorant Roman calendar-
maker, who, finding in a Greek calendar the notice
of the arrival of the kite in spring, converted the first
appearance of that migratory bird into the rising of
a constellation of the same name. However, the
mention of the constellations furnishes our author
with a reason, or an excuse, for relating some of their
myths in his usual agreeable style.[c]

The religious section of the poem embraces the
notices and explanations of those fixed festivals and
sacred rites which were recorded in the calendar.
This is for us moderns by far the most interesting and
valuable part of the work, for our knowledge of Roman
religion is comparatively meagre and fragmentary,
and in the absence of more detailed and authoritative
expositions, such as were doubtless to be found in
some of the lost books of Varro, the *Fasti* of Ovid must
always rank as a document of the first importance.
To note only a few of the festivals on which the poet has
thrown light that we could ill afford to spare, we may
mention the quaint ritual of the Festival of the Dead
(the Lemuria) in May [d]; the no less curious rites in
honour of the God of Boundaries [e] and of the Goddess

[a] *Fasti*, i. 297 *sqq.*   [b] *Fasti*, iii. 793 *sqq.*
[c] See for example *Fasti*, ii. 79 *sqq.* (the Dolphin); ii. 153
sqq. (the Bear); v. 493 *sqq.* (Orion).
[d] *Fasti*, v. 421 *sqq.*   [e] *Fasti*, ii. 639 *sqq.*

INTRODUCTION

Mildew [a]; the Shepherds' Festival of the Parilia, with its leaps over three fires and the driving of the flocks through the smoke and flames [b]; the enigmatic rites of the Lupercalia with its strange mode of conferring the blessing of offspring on women [c]; the merry revels in the flower-decked boats floating down the Tiber on Midsummer Eve [d]; and the very different rite in the month of May when Father Tiber received those rush-made effigies of men which were cast from the old wooden bridge into his yellow stream, apparently as a toll to compensate the river-god for the loss of the human beings who now passed dryshod over the bridge instead of being drowned at the ford. [e] These and many other sacred rites are described by Ovid in the *Fasti*, and if we cannot always accept his explanations of them, we ought always to be grateful to him for having recorded the facts.

A work embracing such a mass of varied information must have entailed a considerable amount of research, but Ovid mentions none of his authorities by name, contenting himself with saying briefly that he had drawn his materials "from annals old." [f] He had probably read some of the early Roman historians, such as the poet Ennius and the old annalist Quintus Fabius Pictor, and it is possible that he may have inspected the official *Annales Maximi* compiled by the pontiffs, which formed the real basis of authentic Roman history. He must certainly have known and used, though he does not mention, the great work of his contemporary the historian Livy, as his narratives

[a] *Fasti*, iv. 905 *sqq.*   [b] *Fasti*, iv. 721 *sqq.*
[c] *Fasti*, ii. 267 *sqq.*   [d] *Fasti*, vi. 773-790.
[e] *Fasti*, v. 621 *sqq.*   [f] *Fasti*, i. 7, iv. 11.

of the tragedy of Lucretia and of the defeat and death of the Fabii suffice to prove. He naturally also consulted the official Roman calendar, of which a number of versions, for the most part fragmentary, have come down to us and afford invaluable help to a commentator on the *Fasti* by enabling him to check and control the statements of his author as to the dates of festivals and the foundation of temples.[a] For the most part the records of these calendars confirm the poet's evidence and strengthen our confidence in the general accuracy of his testimony on matters for which other witnesses are lacking. He seems to have had some knowledge also of the local calendars of various Latin and Sabine towns, to which he repeatedly refers.[b] On questions of Roman antiquities and religion we cannot doubt that he conned and drew freely on the vast stores of the great antiquary Varro, whose existing works, scanty and fragmentary as they are, often serve to illustrate the topics treated of by Ovid in his poem. He may also have known the writings of the learned grammarian Verrius Flaccus, whose treatise on the signification of words, though it survives only in the abridgements of Festus and Paulus

---

[a] The remains of these ancient Roman calendars, whether preserved in inscriptions or in manuscript, have been collected and published, with valuable commentaries by Theodor Mommsen and Christian Huelsen, in the second edition of the first part of the first volume of the great *Corpus Inscriptionum Latinarum*. For the sake of brevity the volume is commonly referred to as *C.I.L.* i². It is indispensable to the serious student of the *Fasti*. The English student should not fail to consult the late Mr. W. Warde Fowler's learned and suggestive work *Roman Festivals of the Period of the Republic*, which is itself almost a commentary on Ovid's poem.

[b] *Fasti*, iii. 87 sqq., vi. 57 sqq.

Diaconus, is of itself almost a commentary on the
Fasti.[a]

It has been suggested that Ovid may have
borrowed the idea of writing the *Fasti* from the
Aitia or " Causes " of Callimachus, an elegiac poem
in four books, in which the learned Alexandrian
poet set forth many myths and legends explanatory
of Greek customs and rites. The *Aitia* as a whole is
lost, but in recent years some considerable fragments
of it have been recovered from Egyptian papyri.[b]
The last book of the elegies of Propertius, in which
that poet relates a number of Roman legends, may
have served as the immediate model of the *Fasti.*

§ 3. EDITIONS OF THE *FASTI*

Of the older editions of the *Fasti* the most valuable
is still that of the Dutch scholar, Pieter Burman, published at Amsterdam in 1727 and forming part of the
third volume of his complete edition of Ovid's works ;
it contains entire the learned commentaries of the
early editors, above all the commentary of the great
scholar, Nicolaus Heinsius, who, by collating many
manuscripts and correcting many of their errors with
the help of his wide learning and critical acumen,
placed the text of the *Fasti* on a sound basis. Many
of his conjectural emendations have been accepted

---

[a] This valuable work is now accessible to students in a
handy edition accurately edited by Professor W. M. Lindsay
(Leipzig, 1913, in the Teubner series of classical texts).

[b] See A. W. Mair's edition of Callimachus (London, 1921),
pp. 183 *sqq.* (in the Loeb Classical Library). As to the
Aitia see further A. Couat, *Alexandrian Poetry under the
first three Ptolemies*, translated by James Loeb (London,
1931), pp. 127 *sqq.*, 549 *sqq.*

by later editors and are reproduced in the text of the present edition.

Of editions published in the nineteenth century the most important for the constitution of the text is that of R. Merkel (Berlin, 1841), which contains a copious critical apparatus drawn partly from the collections of Heinsius, partly from the editor's own examination of manuscripts or from collations made for him by others. In learned Latin prolegomena prefixed to his edition Merkel discusses many questions concerning the sources, the successive recensions, and the manuscripts of the *Fasti*. He subsequently edited two editions for the Teubner series in which he made many changes in the text. The critical edition of A. Riese (Leipzig, 1874) contains a full collation of the important Vatican manuscript *Codex Reginensis* which was made for the editor by H. Keil.

Of explanatory editions of the *Fasti* published in the nineteenth century the most useful are those of G. E. Gierig with a Latin commentary (Leipzig, 1812) ; Thomas Keightly, with English notes (First Edition, London, 1839 ; Second Edition, London, 1848) ; F. A. Paley, with an English commentary (London, no date) ; and Hermann Peter, with a concise but adequate and judicious German commentary (Second Edition, Leipzig, 1879 ; Third Edition, Leipzig, 1889 ; Fourth Edition, Leipzig, 1907). Peter's edition has a critical as well as an exegetical value, for he collated several manuscripts, including the important Munich manuscript *Codex Mallersdorfiensis* ; the principal results of his collations are contained in his dissertation *De P. Ovidi Nasonis fastis disputatio critica* (Meissen, 1877). An edition of the *Fasti* adapted for use in schools was published by

INTRODUCTION

Mr. G. H. Hallam at London in 1881 and has often been reprinted. A separate edition of the Third Book with an Introduction and Commentary has been published by Mr. Cyril Bailey (Oxford, at the Clarendon Press, 1921). A critical recension of the text by R. Ehwald and F. W. Levy appeared at Leipzig in the Teubner series in 1924. Another critical edition of the *Fasti* is that published in the *Corpus Scriptorum Latinorum Paravianum* (Turin, Milan, etc., 1928) under the editorship of the Italian scholar, C. Landi, who for the purpose of this edition has collated afresh the two chief Vatican codices (*A* and *U*) and many inferior Italian manuscripts. In 1957–1958 appeared Börner's text and commentary of Vol. I and commentary for Vol. II, Heidelberg.

The text and translation of the present edition are reproduced from the large edition in five volumes which I published with a commentary and illustrations in 1929 (Macmillan & Co., London). The notes have been specially written for this Loeb edition by my friend, Dr. W. H. D. Rouse, who has also selected and abridged from my commentary the passages which are printed as an Appendix to the present volume. I thank him for kindly sparing me the labour of reducing my large edition to a scale more commensurate with the needs of readers of the Loeb Classical Library, for whose use the book was originally intended. At the same time I take this opportunity of renewing my grateful thanks to my friend, Dr. James Loeb, for the ready and generous permission he gave me to transfer the publication of the complete edition to Messrs. Macmillan & Co. so soon as it appeared that in the process of composition the work had outgrown the limits imposed by the plan of the

INTRODUCTION

Loeb Classical Library. I desire also to thank
Messrs. Macmillan & Co. for their courtesy in giving
leave to reproduce the selections from my commentary which are printed at the end of this volume.

§ 4. MANUSCRIPTS OF THE *FASTI*

Manuscripts of the *Fasti* are very numerous; the
British Museum alone possesses fifteen of them, of
which the oldest is believed to date from the twelfth
or early thirteenth century.

The text of this as of my large edition is based
mainly on the evidence of six manuscripts, of which
I append a list, with the symbols by which I designate
them. Of all six manuscripts I procured complete
photographs (rotographs), which are now preserved
in the library of Trinity College, Cambridge. My
collations of the manuscripts, made chiefly from the
photographs, are printed in full in my large edition,
to which I must refer readers desirous of detailed information on the subject. In the present edition the
evidence of the manuscripts is cited only in a few
passages of special difficulty. The six manuscripts
are as follows :

A = the Vatican manuscript, No. 1709, known as
Codex Reginensis sive Petavianus. This is a manuscript
of the tenth century written in the Carolingian script:
it contains the first four books of the *Fasti*, but the
last two books are wanting, with the exception of the
first twenty-four lines of the Fifth Book. It is generally esteemed the oldest of the existing manuscripts
of the *Fasti*, and is usually taken as the basis of the
text, so far as it exists. But it is the work of a very

careless and ignorant scribe and swarms with gross and palpable blunders, many of which have been corrected by a later hand. A full and generally accurate collation of the manuscript is published, as we have seen, in A. Riese's edition of the *Fasti*.

U = the Vatican manuscript, No. 3262, known as *Codex Ursinianus*. This manuscript was written in the eleventh century at the monastery of Monte Cassino ; the script is that called Lombard. It contains the six books of the *Fasti*, with the curious exception of the last twelve lines of the Second Book, which are omitted without any sign of a lacuna. The manuscript as a whole is much more correctly written than *A*, but it has been to a considerable extent corrected and even rewritten by two later hands. A careful and generally accurate, but by no means complete, collation of the manuscript has been published by Mr. Gordon J. Laing, who distinguishes the readings of the three different hands.[a]

D = the Munich manuscript, No. 8122, of the Royal Library at Munich, known as *Codex Mallersdorfiensis sive Monacensis*. This is a manuscript of the twelfth or, according to Halm, of the thirteenth century ; it contains the six books, except that the first seventy lines of the First Book are wanting. The manuscript abounds in abbreviations which often create a difficulty, for the scribe uses the same abbreviation in different senses, with a resulting ambiguity which can only be resolved by a comparison with other manuscripts. A full collation of this manuscript is

[a] Gordon J. Laing, " The three principal manuscripts of the *Fasti* of Ovid, Reginensis 1709 (or Petavianus), Vaticanus 3262 (or Ursinianus), and Monacensis 8122 (or Mallerstorfiensis N. 2)," *American Journal of Archaeology*, Second Series, vol. iii. (1899, Norwood, Mass.), pp. 212-228.

given by R. Merkel in his edition of 1841, and the codex has since been again collated by H. Peter and R. Ehwald.

X = the Brussels manuscript, *Codex Bruxellensis sive Gemblacensis*, No. 5369 in the Royal Library at Brussels. It was brought to Brussels from the abbey of Gembloux at the time of the French Revolution in 1794. The manuscript has been assigned to the eleventh or possibly to the end of the tenth century. The writing is a round minuscule, large, bold and clear, with comparatively few abbreviations. The first 504 verses of the First Book are wanting in the manuscript, but otherwise, with the exception of a few verses (v. 365-366 and the doubtful lines vi. 271-276, 739-740), the poem is complete. The manuscript is undoubtedly one of the oldest and best codices of the *Fasti*, but its value and importance were ignored till Mr. E. H. Alton called attention to it in 1926.[a] My own attention was first drawn to this important manuscript by Professor M. A. Kugener of the University of Brussels, who has made a special study of it. I collated many of the readings at Brussels in January 1928 and have given a fairly full collation of the manuscript from the photograph in my large edition of the *Fasti*. The manuscript has a number of notes written in the margin which contain excerpts from ancient authors, such as Gellius, Valerius Maximus, Servius, Hyginus, and Macrobius. These have been edited and their authorities identified by Mr. E. H. Alton.[b]

[a] E. H. Alton, " The Zulichemianus, Mazarinianus, and other MSS. of the *Fasti* of Ovid," *Hermathena*, No. xliv. (Dublin and London, 1926), pp. 301 *sqq.*

[b] E. H. Alton, " The mediaeval commentaries on Ovid's *Fasti*," *Hermathena*, No. xliv. (1926), pp. 128-151.

INTRODUCTION

M = the Paris manuscript, *Codex Gallicus Mazarinianus*, No. 7992 in the National Library at Paris. It is a manuscript of the fifteenth or sixteenth century and contains the whole of the six books of the *Fasti* beautifully written in a large, clear Italian hand, with few abbreviations, very few erasures, and no corrections by a later hand. The variants written in the margin or between the lines appear to be all in the handwriting of the original scribe. The reputation of this manuscript seems not to stand high, perhaps on account of its late date, but I have found it excellent, generally in agreement with the best tradition and possessing the rare merit of being almost everywhere perfectly legible. In his critical edition of 1841 Merkel cites this manuscript under the symbol *g*, but he seems to have known little or nothing about it ; there are no such lacunae in it as he speaks of.

m = the Oxford manuscript, *Codex Oxoniensis sive Mazarinianus*, Auct. F. 4. 25, in the Bodleian Library. It belongs to the early fifteenth century and contains the whole of the six books of the *Fasti* ; there are many variants written in the margin or between the lines ; some of them are by the hand of Nicolaus Heinsius. There seems to be a special relation between this Oxford manuscript and the Brussels manuscript (*X*) ; for not only do the readings of the two manuscripts often agree, but in both of them the same long passage (vi. 33-294) has suffered a curious displacement of several hundred lines, without the least sign that the copyist was aware of the disorder. Mr. E. H. Alton inclines to believe that this Oxford manuscript is " a copy of a comparatively early (possibly ninth or tenth century) minuscule original." [a]

[a] E. H. Alton, " The Zulichemianus, Mazarinianus, and

INTRODUCTION

Besides these six manuscripts I have sometimes in my large edition referred to the readings of a few others, for a knowledge of which I am dependent chiefly on the collections of Merkel in his large critical edition of 1841, whose notation of them I follow. They are as follows :

F=the Cambridge manuscript, No. 280, in the library of Pembroke College, Cambridge, to which it came from Dover Priory. According to Dr. M. R. James, the manuscript dates from the twelfth century and the writing closely resembles that of Christ Church, Canterbury.[a] It is a small volume in vellum, with many interlineal and marginal notes. I inspected it in the library of Pembroke College, and through the kindness of Mr. Attwater, the librarian, procured a complete photograph of the manuscript. Circumstances have, to my regret, prevented me from making any use of the photograph, but it is now kept, with the other photographs of Ovid manuscripts used by me, in the library of Trinity College, Cambridge.

G=a manuscript at Göttingen, thought by Schneidewin to be not later than the twelfth century. Heinsius judged it to be older, but of little value. Merkel used a collation of it made for him by W. Müller and E. von Leutsch, and found a few good readings in it.

B=a manuscript at Leyden, *Codex Vossianus sive Arundelianus*, of the thirteenth century. It contains all six books. Heinsius assigned it to the tenth century. It has been collated by H. Peter and R. Ehwald.

other MSS. of the *Fasti of Ovid*," *Hermathena*, No. xliv. (1926), p. 105.

[a] M. R. James, *Catalogue of Manuscripts in the Library of Pembroke College, Cambridge* (Cambridge, 1905), p. 255.

INTRODUCTION

C = the collation of a lost manuscript (*Codex Vossianus*) inserted by Isaac Voss in an edition of the *Fasti* published at Amsterdam in 1630. The volume is in the library at Leyden. H. Peter examined it and made a copy of Voss's collation.[a]

My references to other manuscripts, designated by the general symbol ϛ, are derived from Merkel's edition of 1841 and from the Ehwald-Levy edition of 1924.

J. G. FRAZER

April 1931

[a] H. Peter, *De P. Ovidi Nasonis fastis disputatio critica* (Meissen, 1877), p. 5.

OVID'S FASTI

FASTORUM LIBER PRIMUS

Tempora cum causis Latium digesta per annum
    lapsaque sub terras ortaque signa canam.
excipe pacato, Caesar Germanice, voltu
    hoc opus et timidae dirige navis iter ;
5 officioque, levem non aversatus honorem,
    en tibi devoto numine dexter ades.
sacra recognosces annalibus eruta priscis,
    et quo sit merito quaeque notata dies.
invenies illic et festa domestica vobis :
10   saepe tibi pater est, saepe legendus avus ;
quaeque ferunt illi pictos signantia fastos,
    tu quoque cum Druso praemia fratre feres.
Caesaris arma canant alii : nos Caesaris aras,
    et quoscumque sacris addidit ille dies.
15 adnue conanti per laudes ire tuorum,
    deque meo pavidos excute corde metus.
da mihi te placidum, dederis in carmina viris ᵃ
    ingenium voltu statque caditque tuo.
pagina iudicium docti subitura movetur
20   principis, ut Clario missa legenda deo.
quae sit enim culti facundia sensimus oris,
    civica pro trepidis cum tulit arma reis ;

ᵃ Son of Drusus the brother of Tiberius, who adopted his
nephew A.D. 4. Thus his *pater* (l. 10) is Tiberius, his *avus*
Augustus. Drusus, called his brother (l. 12), was his first cousin,
the son of Tiberius. By Caesar (l. 13) is meant Augustus.

2

OVID'S FASTI—BOOK I

THE order of the calendar throughout the Latin year, its causes, and the starry signs that set beneath the earth and rise again, of these I'll sing. Caesar Germanicus,[a] accept with brow serene this work and steer the passage of my timid bark. Spurn not the honour slight, but come propitious as a god to take the homage vowed to thee. Here shalt thou read afresh of holy rites unearthed from annals old, and learn how every day has earned its own peculiar mark. There too shalt thou find the festivals pertaining to thy house ; often the names of thy sire and grandsire will meet thee on the page. The laurels that are theirs and that adorn the painted calendar, thou too shalt win in company with thy brother Drusus. Let others sing of Caesar's wars; my theme be Caesar's altars and the days he added to the sacred roll. Approve my effort to rehearse the praises of thy kin, and cast out quaking terrors from my heart. Show thyself mild to me ; so shalt thou lend vigour to my song ; at thy look my Muse must stand or fall. Submitted to the judgement of a learned prince my page doth shiver, even as if sent to the Clarian god [b] to read. On thy accomplished lips what eloquence attends, we have seen, when it took civic arms in defence of trembling prisoners at

[b] Apollo of Claros in Ionia, where he had an oracle.

scimus et, ad nostras cum se tulit impetus artes,
    ingenii currant flumina quanta tui.
25 si licet et fas est, vates rege vatis habenas,
    auspice te felix totus ut annus eat.
tempora digereret cum conditor urbis, in anno
    constituit menses quinque bis esse suo.
scilicet arma magis quam sidera, Romule, noras,
30   curaque finitimos vincere maior erat.
est tamen et ratio, Caesar, quae moverit illum,
    erroremque suum quo tueatur, habet.
quod satis est, utero matris dum prodeat infans,
    hoc anno statuit temporis esse satis.
35 per totidem menses a funere coniugis uxor
    sustinet in vidua tristia signa domo.
haec igitur vidit trabeati cura Quirini,
    cum rudibus populis annua iura daret.
Martis erat primus mensis, Venerisque secundus :
40   haec generis princeps, ipsius ille pater.
tertius a senibus, iuvenum de nomine quartus,
    quae sequitur, numero turba notata fuit.
at Numa nec Ianum nec avitas praeterit umbras,
    mensibus antiquis praeposuitque duos.
45 ne tamen ignores variorum iura dierum,
    non habet officii Lucifer omnis idem.
ille nefastus erit, per quem tria verba silentur :
    fastus erit, per quem lege licebit agi.

---

    ^a His translation of the *Phaenomena* of Aratus survives
in part (*Poet. Lat. Minores*, i. p. 142).
    ^b *Maius* from *maiores*, *Iunius* from *iuvenes*. The rest
are *Quintilis*, *Sextilis* (August), *September*, etc. See Appendix, p. 385.
    ^c *Do, dico, addico* the praetor's formula, " Do bonorum
possessionem, dico ius, addico id de quo ambigitur." In
the calendars, lawful days were marked by F (*fastus*),

the bar. And when to poetry thy fancy turns,[a] we know how broad the current of thy genius flows. If it is right and lawful, guide a poet's reins, thyself a poet, that under thy auspices the year may run its entire course happy.

27 When the founder of the city was setting the calendar in order, he ordained that there should be twice five months in his year. To be sure, Romulus, thou wert better versed in swords than stars, and to conquer thy neighbours was thy main concern. Yet, Caesar, there is a reason that may have moved him, and for his error he might urge a plea. The time that suffices for a child to come forth from its mother's womb, he deemed sufficient for a year. For just so many months after her husband's funeral a wife supports the signs of sorrow in her widowed home. These things, then, Quirinus in his striped gown had in view, when to the simple folk he gave his laws to regulate the year. The month of Mars was the first, and that of Venus the second; she was the author of the race, and he his sire. The third month took its name from the old, and the fourth from the young[b]; the months that trooped after were distinguished by numbers. But Numa overlooked not Janus and the ancestral shades, and so to the ancient months he prefixed two.

45 But that you may not be unversed in the rules of the different days, not every morning brings the same round of duty. That day is unlawful on which the three words may not be spoken[c]; that day is lawful on which the courts of law are open. But

unlawful by N (*nefastus*), the half-days NP (*nefastus parte*), or EN (*endotercisi, intercisi*) where the business-part came in the middle.

nec toto perstare die sua iura putaris :
50　qui iam fastus erit, mane nefastus erat ;
nam simul exta deo data sunt, licet omnia fari,
　　verbaque honoratus libera praetor habet.
est quoque, quo populum ius est includere saeptis :
　　est quoque, qui nono semper ab orbe redit.
55 vindicat Ausonias Iunonis cura Kalendas,
　　Idibus alba Iovi grandior agna cadit ;
Nonarum tutela deo caret.　omnibus istis
　　(ne fallare cave !) proximus ater erit.
omen ab eventu est, illis nam Roma diebus
60　damna sub averso tristia Marte tulit.
haec mihi dicta semel, totis haerentia fastis,
　　ne seriem rerum scindere cogar, erunt.

1. A · K · IAN · F

Ecce tibi faustum, Germanice, nuntiat annum
　　inque meo primus carmine Ianus adest.
65 Iane biceps, anni tacite labentis origo,
　　solus de superis qui tua terga vides,
dexter ades ducibus, quorum secura labore
　　otia terra ferax, otia pontus habet :
dexter ades patribusque tuis populoque Quirini,
70　et resera nutu candida templa tuo.
prospera lux oritur : linguis animisque favete !
　　nunc dicenda bona sunt bona verba die.

ᵃ Called *comitiales*, marked C in the calendar.

ᵇ The *nundinae*, or market-days.　The week was of eight
days, and the eighth was the *nundinae*, counting from the
last *nundinae* inclusively.　The whole week was called *inter-
nundinum*.　Similarly, the *Nones* were eight (not nine) days
before the Ides.　The eight days of the Roman week were
marked in the calendar with the letters A to H ; but Jan. 1
was always marked A, and the other days followed in order,
whenever *nundinae* might fall.

you must not suppose that every day keeps its
rules throughout its whole length: a lawful day
may have been unlawful in the morning; for as
soon as the inwards have been offered to the god,
all words may lawfully be spoken, and the honoured
praetor enjoys free speech. There are days, too,
on which the people may lawfully be penned in
the polling-booths [a]; there are also days that come
round ever in a cycle of nine.[b] The worship of
Juno claims Ausonia's Calends: on the Ides a bigger
white ewe-lamb falls to Jupiter: the Nones lack a
guardian god. The day next after all these days—
make no mistake—is black.[c] The omen is drawn
from the event; for on those days Rome suffered
grievous losses under the frown of Mars. These
remarks apply to the whole calendar; I have made
them once for all, that I may not be forced to break
the thread of my discourse.

KAL. IAN. 1st

63 See Janus comes, Germanicus, the herald of a
lucky year to thee,[d] and in my song takes precedence.
Two-headed Janus, opener of the softly gliding year,
thou who alone of the celestials dost behold thy back,
O come propitious to the chiefs whose toil ensures
peace to the fruitful earth, peace to the sea. And
come propitious to thy senators and to the people
of Quirinus, and by thy nod unbar the temples white.
A happy morning dawns. Fair speech, fair thoughts
I crave! Now must good words be spoken on a

[c] Ill-omened; a day on which no action should be taken;
much stronger than *nefastus*.

[d] Probably A.D. 15, 16, or 17, when he was campaigning
in Germany.

7

lite vacent aures, insanaque protinus absint
    iurgia ; differ opus, livida lingua, tuum !
75 cernis, odoratis ut luceat ignibus aether,
    et sonet accensis spica Cilissa focis ?
flamma nitore suo templorum verberat aurum
    et tremulum summa spargit in aede iubar.
vestibus intactis Tarpeias itur in arces,
80   et populus festo concolor ipse suo est,
iamque novi praeeunt fasces, nova purpura fulget,
    et nova conspicuum pondera sentit ebur.
colla rudes operum praebent ferienda iuvenci,
    quos aluit campis herba Falisca suis.
85 Iuppiter arce sua totum cum spectat in orbem,
    nil nisi Romanum, quod tueatur, habet.
salve, laeta dies, meliorque revertere semper,
    a populo rerum digna potente coli.
quem tamen esse deum te dicam, Iane biformis ?
90   nam tibi par nullum Graecia numen habet.
ede simul causam, cur de caelestibus unus,
    sitque quod a tergo, sitque quod ante, vides ?
haec ego cum sumptis agitarem mente tabellis,
    lucidior visa est, quam fuit ante, domus.
95 tunc sacer ancipiti mirandus imagine Ianus
    bina repens oculis obtulit ora meis.
extimui sensique metu riguisse capillos,
    et gelidum subito frigore pectus erat.
ille tenens baculum dextra clavemque sinistra
100   edidit hos nobis ore priore sonos :
" disce metu posito, vates operose dierum,
    quod petis, et voces percipe mente meas.
me Chaos antiqui (nam sum res prisca) vocabant :

---

      a The new consuls go in procession to the Capitol.
        b See Appendix, p. 387.
     c Some derived Janus from *hiare*, as χάος from χάσκειν.

good day. Let ears be rid of suits, and banish mad disputes forthwith! Thou rancorous tongue, adjourn thy wagging! Dost mark how the sky sparkles with fragrant fires, and how Cilician saffron crackles on the kindled hearths? The flame with its own splendour beats upon the temples' gold and spreads a flickering radiance on the hallowed roof. In spotless garments the procession wends to the Tarpeian towers [a] : the people wear the colour of the festal day; and now new rods of office lead the way, new purple gleams, and a new weight is felt by the far-seen ivory chair. Heifers, unbroken to the yoke, offer their necks to the axe, heifers that cropped the sward on the true Faliscan plains. When from his citadel Jupiter looks abroad on the whole globe, naught but the Roman empire meets his eye. Hail, happy day! and evermore return still happier, day worthy to be kept holy by a people the masters of the world.

[89] But what god am I to say thou art, Janus [b] of double shape? for Greece hath no divinity like thee. The reason, too, unfold why alone of all the heavenly ones thou dost see both back and front. While thus I mused, the tablets in my hand, methought the house grew brighter than it was before. Then of a sudden sacred Janus, in his two-headed shape, offered his double visage to my wondering eyes. A terror seized me, I felt my hair stiffen with fear, and with a sudden chill my bosom froze. He, holding in his right hand his staff and in his left the key, to me these accents uttered from his front mouth : " Dismiss thy fear, thy answer take, laborious singer of the days, and mark my words. The ancients called me Chaos,[c] for a being from of

9

aspice, quam longi temporis acta canam.
105 lucidus hic aer et quae tria corpora restant,
    ignis, aqua et tellus, unus acervus erat.
ut semel haec rerum secessit lite suarum
    inque novas abiit massa soluta domos,
flamma petit altum, propior locus aëra cepit,
110   sederunt medio terra fretumque solo.
tunc ego, qui fueram globus et sine imagine moles,
    in faciem redii dignaque membra deo.
nunc quoque, confusae quondam nota parva figurae
    ante quod est in me postque, videtur idem.
115 accipe, quaesitae quae causa sit altera formae,
    hanc simul ut noris officiumque meum.
quicquid ubique vides, caelum, mare, nubila, terras,
    omnia sunt nostra clausa patentque manu.
me penes est unum vasti custodia mundi,
120   et ius vertendi cardinis omne meum est.
cum libuit Pacem placidis emittere tectis,
    libera perpetuas ambulat illa vias :
sanguine letifero totus miscebitur orbis,
    ni teneant rigidae condita bella serae.
125 praesideo foribus caeli cum mitibus Horis :
    it, redit officio Iuppiter ipse meo.
inde vocor Ianus. cui cum Ceriale sacerdos
    imponit libum mixtaque farra sale,
nomina ridebis ; modo namque Patulcius idem
130   et modo sacrifico Clusius ore vocor.
scilicet alterno voluit rudis illa vetustas
    nomine diversas significare vices.
vis mea narrata est. causam nunc disce figurae :
    iam tamen hanc aliqua tu quoque parte vides.

ª As from *eo* ; so Cicero suggests, for Eanus (*Nat. D.* ii.
27. 1). Ovid has a craze for derivations, which are mostly
wrong.

old am I; observe the long, long ages of which my
song shall tell. Yon lucid air and the three other
bodies, fire, water, earth, were huddled all in one.
When once, through the discord of its elements, the
mass parted, dissolved, and went in diverse ways to
seek new homes, flame sought the height, air filled
the nearer space, while earth and sea sank in the
middle deep. 'Twas then that I, till that time a
mere ball, a shapeless lump, assumed the face and
members of a god. And even now, small index of
my erst chaotic state, my front and back look just
the same. Now hear the other reason for the shape
you ask about, that you may know it and my office
too. Whate'er you see anywhere—sky, sea, clouds,
earth—all things are closed and opened by my hand.
The guardianship of this vast universe is in my hands
alone, and none but me may rule the wheeling pole.
When I choose to send forth peace from tranquil
halls, she freely walks the ways unhindered. But
with blood and slaughter the whole world would
welter, did not the bars unbending hold the barri-
cadoed wars. I sit at heaven's gate with the gentle
Hours; my office regulates the goings and the comings
of Jupiter himself. Hence Janus is my name [a]; but
when the priest offers me a barley cake and spelt
mingled with salt, you would laugh to hear the
names he gives me, for on his sacrificial lips I'm
now Patulcius and now Clusius called.[b] Thus rude
antiquity made shift to mark my changing functions
with the change of name. My business I have told.
Now learn the reason of my shape, though already
you perceive it in part. Every door has two fronts,

[b] As from *pateo* and *claudo* (*cludo*).

135 omnis habet geminas, hinc atque hinc, ianua frontis,
    e quibus haec populum spectat, at illa larem;
  utque sedens primi vester prope limina tecti
    ianitor egressus introitusque videt,
  sic ego perspicio caelestis ianitor aulae
140   Eoas partes Hesperiasque simul.
  ora vides Hecates in tres vertentia partes,
    servet ut in ternas compita secta vias;
  et mihi, ne flexu cervicis tempora perdam,
    cernere non moto corpore bina licet."
145 dixerat et voltu, si plura requirere vellem,
    difficilem mihi se non fore fassus erat.
  sumpsi animum gratesque deo non territus egi
    verbaque sum spectans pauca locutus humum:
  " dic, age, frigoribus quare novus incipit annus,
150   qui melius per ver incipiendus erat?
  omnia tunc florent, tunc est nova temporis aetas,
    et nova de gravido palmite gemma tumet,
  et modo formatis operitur frondibus arbor,
    prodit et in summum seminis herba solum,
155 et tepidum volucres concentibus aëra mulcent,
    ludit et in pratis luxuriatque pecus.
  tum blandi soles, ignotaque prodit hirundo
    et luteum celsa sub trabe figit opus:
  tum patitur cultus ager et renovatur aratro.
160   haec anni novitas iure vocanda fuit."
  quaesieram multis: non multis ille moratus
    contulit in versus sic sua verba duos:
  " bruma novi prima est veterisque novissima solis:
    principium capiunt Phoebus et annus idem."
165 post ea mirabar, cur non sine litibus esset
    prima dies. " causam percipe " Ianus ait.

this way and that, whereof one faces the people and the other the house-god; and just as your human porter, seated at the threshold of the house-door, sees who goes out and in, so I, the porter of the heavenly court, behold at once both East and West. Thou seest Hecate's faces turned in three directions that she may guard the crossroads where they branch three several ways; and lest I should lose time by twisting my neck, I am free to look both ways without budging."

¹⁴⁵ Thus spake the god, and by a look confessed that, were I fain to ask him more, he would not grudge reply. I plucked up courage, thanked the god composedly, and with eyes turned to the ground I spoke in few: "Come, say, why doth the new year begin in the cold season? Better had it begun in spring. Then all things flower, then time renews his age, and new from out the teeming vine-shoot swells the bud; in fresh-formed leaves the tree is draped, and from earth's surface sprouts the blade of corn. Birds with their warblings winnow the warm air; the cattle frisk and wanton in the meads. Then suns are sweet, forth comes the stranger swallow and builds her clayey structure under the lofty beam. Then the field submits to tillage and is renewed by the plough. That is the season which rightly should have been called New Year."

¹⁶¹ Thus questioned I at length; he answered prompt and tersely, throwing his words into twain verses, thus: "Midwinter is the beginning of the new sun and the end of the old one. Phoebus and the year take their start from the same point."

¹⁶⁵ Next I wondered why the first day was not exempt from lawsuits. "Hear the cause," quoth

"tempora commisi nascentia rebus agendis,
   totus ab auspicio ne foret annus iners.
quisque suas artes ob idem delibat agendo
170 nec plus quam solitum testificatur opus."
mox ego, "cur, quamvis aliorum numina placem,
   Iane, tibi primum tura merumque fero?"
"ut possis aditum per me, qui limina servo,
   ad quoscumque voles" inquit "habere deos."
175 "at cur laeta tuis dicuntur verba Kalendis,
   et damus alternas accipimusque preces?"
tum deus incumbens baculo, quem dextra gerebat,
   "omina principiis" inquit "inesse solent.
ad primam vocem timidas advertitis aures,
180 et visam primum consulit augur avem.
templa patent auresque deum, nec lingua caducas
   concipit ulla preces, dictaque pondus habent."
desierat Ianus. nec longa silentia feci,
   sed tetigi verbis ultima verba meis:
185 "quid volt palma sibi rugosaque carica" dixi
   "et data sub niveo candida mella cado?"
"omen" ait "causa est, ut res sapor ille sequatur,
   et peragat coeptum dulcis ut annus iter."
"dulcia cur dentur, video. stipis adice causam,
190 pars mihi de festo ne labet ulla tuo."
risit et "o quam te fallunt tua saecula," dixit
   "qui stipe mel sumpta dulcius esse putes!
vix ego Saturno quemquam regnante videbam,
   cuius non animo dulcia lucra forent.
195 tempore crevit amor, qui nunc est summus, habendi:
   vix ultra, quo iam progrediatur, habet.

Janus. " I assigned the birthday of the year to business, lest from the auspice idleness infect the whole. For the same reason every man just handsels his calling, nor does more than but attest his usual work."

171 Next I asked, "Why, Janus, while I propitiate other divinities, do I bring incense and wine first of all to thee?" Quoth he, " It is that through me, who guard the thresholds, you may have access to whatever gods you please." " But why are glad words spoken on thy Calends? and why do we give and receive good wishes?" Then, leaning on the staff he bore in his right hand, the god replied: " Omens are wont," said he, " to wait upon beginnings. At the first word ye prick up anxious ears; from the first bird he sees the augur takes his cue. (On the first day) the temples and ears of the gods are open, the tongue utters no fruitless prayers, and words have weight." So Janus ended. I kept not silence long, but caught up his last words with my own : " What mean the gifts of dates and wrinkled figs," I said, " and honey glistering in snow-white jar?" " It is for the sake of the omen," said he, " that the event may answer to the flavour, and that the whole course of the year may be sweet, like its beginning." " I see," said I, " why sweets are given. But tell me, too, the reason for the gift of cash, that I may be sure of every point in thy festival." The god laughed, and " Oh," quoth he, " how little you know about the age you live in if you fancy that honey is sweeter than cash in hand! Why, even in Saturn's reign I hardly saw a soul who did not in his heart find lucre sweet. As time went on the love of pelf grew, till now it is at its height and scarcely can go

pluris opes nunc sunt, quam prisci temporis annis,
    dum populus pauper, dum nova Roma fuit,
dum casa Martigenam capiebat parva Quirinum,
200   et dabat exiguum fluminis ulva torum.
Iuppiter angusta vix totus stabat in aede,
    inque Iovis dextra fictile fulmen erat.
fro ldibus ornabant quae nunc Capitolia gemmis,
    pascebatque suas ipse senator oves ;
205 nec pudor in stipula placidam cepisse quietem
    et faenum capiti supposuisse fuit.
iura dabat populis posito modo praetor aratro,
    et levis argenti lammina crimen erat.
at postquam fortuna loci caput extulit huius,
210   et tetigit summos vertice Roma deos,
creverunt et opes et opum furiosa cupido,
    et, cum possideant plurima, plura petunt.
quaerere, ut absumant, absumpta requirere certant,
    atque ipsae vitiis sunt alimenta vices.
215 sic quibus intumuit suffusa venter ab unda,
    quo plus sunt potae, plus sitiuntur aquae.
in pretio pretium nunc est : dat census honores,
    census amicitias : pauper ubique iacet.
tu tamen auspicium si sit stipis utile, quaeris,
220   curque iuvent vestras aera vetusta manus ?
aera dabant olim, melius nunc omen in auro est,
    victaque concessit prisca moneta novae.
nos quoque templa iuvant, quamvis antiqua probemus,
    aurea : maiestas convenit ista deo.
225 laudamus veteres, sed nostris utimur annis :
    mos tamen est aeque dignus uterque coli."

---

[a] The *casa Romuli* was preserved on the Palatine Hill.
This was supposed to be the cottage in which Romulus lived.
  [b] He alludes to Cincinnatus, 458 B.C.

farther. Wealth is more valued now than in the years of old, when the people were poor, when Rome was new, when a small hut sufficed to lodge Quirinus,^a son of Mars, and the river sedge supplied a scanty bedding. Jupiter had hardly room to stand upright in his cramped shrine, and in his right hand was a thunderbolt of clay. They decked with leaves the Capitol, which now they deck with gems, and the senator himself fed his own sheep. It was no shame to take one's peaceful rest on straw and to pillow the head on hay. The praetor put aside the plough to judge the people,^b and to own a light piece of silver plate was a crime. But ever since the Fortune of this place has raised her head on high, and Rome with her crest has touched the topmost gods, riches have grown and with them the frantic lust of wealth, and they who have the most possessions still crave for more. They strive to gain that they may waste, and then to repair their wasted fortunes, and thus they feed their vices by ringing the changes on them. So he whose belly swells with dropsy, the more he drinks, the thirstier he grows. Nowadays nothing but money counts : fortune brings honours, friendships ; the poor man everywhere lies low. And still you ask me, What's the use of omens drawn from cash, and why do ancient coppers tickle your palms ! In the olden time the gifts were coppers, but now gold gives a better omen, and the old-fashioned coin has been vanquished and made way for the new. We, too, are tickled by golden temples, though we approve of the ancient ones : such majesty befits a god. We praise the past, but use the present years ; yet are both customs worthy to be kept." He closed his admonitions ;

17

finierat monitus.   placidis ita rursus, ut ante,
   clavigerum verbis adloquor ipse deum :
" multa quidem didici : sed cur navalis in aere
230   altera signata est, altera forma biceps ? "
" noscere me duplici posses sub imagine," dixit
   " ni vetus ipsa dies extenuasset opus.
causa ratis superest : Tuscum rate venit in amnem
   ante pererrato falcifer orbe deus.
235 hac ego Saturnum memini tellure receptum ⟨
   caelitibus regnis a Iove pulsus erat.
inde diu genti mansit Saturnia nomen ;
   dicta quoque est Latium terra, latente deo.
at bona posteritas puppem formavit in aere,
240   hospitis adventum testificata dei.
ipse solum colui, cuius placidissima laevum
   radit harenosi Thybridis unda latus.
hic, ubi nunc Roma est, incaedua silva virebat,
   tantaque res paucis pascua bubus erat.
245 arx mea collis erat, quem volgus nomine nostro
   nuncupat, haec aetas Ianiculumque vocat.
tunc ego regnabam, patiens cum terra deorum
   esset, et humanis numina mixta locis.
nondum Iustitiam facinus mortale fugarat
250   (ultima de superis illa reliquit humum),
proque metu populum sine vi pudor ipse regebat ;
   nullus erat iustis reddere iura labor.
nil mihi cum bello : pacem postesque tuebar
   et " clavem ostendens " haec " ait " arma gero."
255 presserat ora deus.   tunc sic ego nostra resolvi
   voce mea voces eliciente dei :

---

   [a] The ancient *as*. See Smith's *Dict. of Antiq.* i. p. 202,
for a picture.
   [b] Looking down the river ; on the river's left bank was
Rome.

but again in calm speech, as before, I addressed the god who bears the key : " I have learned much indeed ; but why is the figure of a ship stamped on one side of the copper coin,^{a} and a two-headed figure on the other ? " " Under the double image," said he, " you might have recognized myself, if the long lapse of time had not worn the type away. Now for the reason of the ship. In a ship the sickle-bearing god came to the Tuscan river after wandering over the world. I remember how Saturn was received in this land : he had been driven by Jupiter from the celestial realms. From that time the folk long retained the name of Saturnian, and the country, too, was called Latium from the hiding (*latente*) of the god. But a pious posterity inscribed a ship on the copper money to commemorate the coming of the stranger god. Myself inhabited the ground whose left side ^{b} is lapped by sandy Tiber's glassy wave. Here, where now is Rome, green forest stood unfelled, and all this mighty region was but a pasture for a few kine. My castle was the hill which common folk call by my name, and which this present age doth dub Janiculum. I reigned in days when earth could bear with gods, and divinities moved freely in the abodes of men. The sin of mortals had not yet put Justice to flight (she was the last of the celestials to forsake the earth) : honour's self, not fear, ruled the people without appeal to force : toil there was none to expound the right to righteous men. I had naught to do with war : guardian was I of peace and doorways, and these," quoth he, showing the key, " these be the arms I bear." The god now closed his lips. Then I thus opened mine, using my voice to lure the voice

19

" cum tot sint Iani, cur stas sacratus in uno,
    hic ubi iuncta foris templa duobus habes ? "
ille manu mulcens propexam ad pectora barbam
260   protinus Oebalii rettulit arma Tati,
utque levis custos armillis capta Sabinos
    ad summae tacitos duxerit arcis iter.
" inde, velut nunc est, per quem descenditis," inquit
    " arduus in valles et fora clivus erat.
265 et iam contigerant portam, Saturnia cuius
    dempserat oppositas invidiosa seras.
cum tanto veritus committere numine pugnam
    ipse meae movi callidus artis opus,
oraque, qua pollens ope sum, fontana reclusi
270   sumque repentinas eiaculatus aquas;
ante tamen madidis subieci sulphura venis,
    clauderet ut Tatio fervidus humor iter.
cuius ut utilitas pulsis percepta Sabinis,
    quae fuerat, tuto reddita forma loco est.
275 ara mihi posita est parvo coniuncta sacello :
    haec adolet flammis cum strue farra suis."
" at cur pace lates motisque recluderis armis ? "
    nec mora, quaesiti reddita causa mihi est :
" ut populo reditus pateant ad bella profecto,
280   tota patet dempta ianua nostra sera.
pace fores obdo, ne qua discedere possit ;
    Caesareoque diu numine clusus ero."
dixit et attollens oculos diversa videntes
    aspexit toto quicquid in orbe fuit.
285 pax erat et, vestri, Germanice, causa triumphi,

---

    ^a Archways were commonly called *iani* ; but one between
the Forum Romanum and Forum Iulium was a temple, and
had a statue of the god.
    ^b The Sabines claimed descent from the Spartans, and
Oebalus was a king of Sparta.

divine. " Since there are so many archways, why
dost thou stand thus consecrated in one alone, here
where thou hast a temple adjoining two forums *a* ? "
Stroking with his hand the beard that fell upon his
breast, he straightway told the warlike deeds of
Oebalian *b* Tatius, and how the traitress keeper,*c*
bribed by armlets, led the silent Sabines the way
to the summit of the citadel. " From there," quoth
he, " a steep slope, the same by which even now ye
descend, led down into the valleys and the forums.
And now the foe had reached the gate from which
Saturn's envious daughter *d* had removed the opposing
bars. Fearing to engage in fight with so redoubtable
a deity, I slyly had recourse to a device of my own
craft, and by the power I wield I opened the fountains'
mouths and spouted out a sudden gush of water;
but first I threw sulphur into the water channels,
that the boiling liquid might bar the way against
Tatius. This service done, and the Sabines repulsed, the place, now rendered safe, resumed its
former aspect. An altar was set up for me, joined
to a little shrine : in its flames it burns the sacrificial
spelt and cake." " But why hide in time of peace
and open thy gates when men take arms ? " Without delay he rendered me the reason that I sought.
" My gate, unbarred, stands open wide, that when
the people hath gone forth to war, the road for their
return may be open too. I bar the doors in time of
peace, lest peace depart, and under Caesar's star
I shall be long shut up." He spoke, and lifting up
his eyes that saw in opposite directions, he surveyed
all that the whole world held. Peace reigned, and
on the Rhine already, Germanicus, thy triumph had

e Tarpeia.   *d* Juno.

tradiderat famulas iam tibi Rhenus aquas.
Iane, fac aeternos pacem pacisque ministros,
    neve suum, praesta, deserat auctor opus.
quod tamen ex ipsis licuit mihi discere fastis,
290   sacravere patres hac duo templa die.
accepit Phoebo nymphaque Coronide natum
    insula, dividua quam premit amnis aqua.
Iuppiter in parte est ; cepit locus unus utrumque
    iunctaque sunt magno templa nepotis avo.

2. BF   3. CC   4. DC

295 Quis vetat et stellas, ut quaeque oriturque caditque,
    dicere ?   promissi pars fuit ista mei.
felices animae, quibus haec cognoscere primis
    inque domus superas scandere cura fuit !
credibile est illos pariter vitiisque locisque
300   altius humanis exeruisse caput.
non Venus et vinum sublimia pectora fregit
    officiumque fori militiaeve labor ;
nec levis ambitio perfusaque gloria fuco
    magnarumque fames sollicitavit opum.
305 admovere oculis distantia sidera nostris
    aetheraque ingenio supposuere suo.
sic petitur caelum : non ut ferat Ossan Olympus,
    summaque Peliacus sidera tangat apex.
nos quoque sub ducibus caelum metabimur illis
310   ponemusque suos ad vaga signa dies.

---

    [a] The triumph of Germanicus and Tiberius, 26 May A.D. 17.

been won, when the river yielded up her waters to be thy slaves.*ᵃ* O Janus, let the peace and the ministers of peace endure for aye, and grant that its author may never forgo his handiwork.

²⁸⁹ But now for what I have been allowed to learn from the calendar itself. On this day the senate dedicated two temples. The island, which the river hems in with its parted waters, received him whom the nymph Coronis bore to Phoebus.*ᵇ* Jupiter has his share of the site. One place found room for both, and the temples of the mighty grandsire and the grandson are joined together.

²⁹⁵ Who says me nay if I would tell also of the stars, their risings and their settings ? That was part of my promise. Ah happy souls, who first took thought to know these things and scale the heavenly mansions! Well may we believe they lifted up their heads alike above the frailties and the homes of men. Their lofty natures neither love nor wine did break, nor civil business nor the toils of war ; no low ambition tempted them, nor glory's tinsel sheen, nor lust of hoarded pelf. The distant stars they brought within our ken, and heaven itself made subject to their wit. So man may reach the sky : no need that Ossa on Olympus should be piled, and that Pelion's peak should touch the topmost stars. Under these leaders we, too, will plumb the sky and give their own days to the wandering signs.

It had been decreed two years before, so Ovid speaks of it prospectively. The river Rhine, with other rivers and mountains, was actually represented in the procession : see Tacitus, *Ann.* ii. 41.

ᵇ Aesculapius.

Ergo ubi nox aderit venturis tertia Nonis,
 sparsaque caelesti rore madebit humus,
octipedis frustra quaerentur brachia Cancri :
 praeceps occiduas ille subibit aquas.

315 Institerint Nonae, missi tibi nubibus atris
 signa dabunt imbres exoriente Lyra.

5. E NON · F 6. FF 7. GC 8. HC
9. A AGON

Quattuor adde dies ductos ex ordine Nonis,
 Ianus Agonali luce piandus erit.
nominis esse potest succinctus causa minister,
320 hostia caelitibus quo feriente cadit,
qui calido strictos tincturus sanguine cultros
 semper " agone," rogat, nec nisi iussus agit.
pars, quia non veniant pecudes, sed agantur, ab actu
 nomen Agonalem credit habere diem.
325 pars putat hoc festum priscis Agnalia dictum,
 una sit ut proprio littera dempta loco.
an, quia praevisos in aqua timet hostia cultros,
 a pecoris lux est ipsa notata metu ?
fas etiam fieri solitis aetate priorum
330 nomina de ludis Graeca tulisse diem.
et pecus antiquus dicebat agonia sermo ;
 veraque iudicio est ultima causa meo.

---

 [a] Ovid has confused the morning with the evening setting
of the Crab.
 [b] The apparent rising is on November 5, the real rising
still earlier.
 [c] The real meaning of *Agon* in the calendar is not known,
but it may be for *agonium*, a general word for sacrifice.

III. Non. 3rd

311 Therefore when the third night before the Nones has come, and the ground is sprinkled and drenched with heavenly dew, you shall look in vain for the claws of the eight-footed Crab : headlong he'll plunge beneath the western waves [a]

Non. 5th

315 Should the Nones be at hand, showers discharged from sable clouds will be your sign, at the rising of the Lyre.[b]

V. Id. 9th

317 Add four successive days to the Nones, and on the Agonal morn Janus must be appeased.[c] The day may take its name from the attendant who, in garb succinct, fells at a blow the victim of the gods ; for just before he dyes the brandished knife in the warm blood, he always asks "*Agone?*" ("Shall I proceed?"), and not until he is bidden does he proceed. Some believe that the day is named Agonal from the driving of the victims, because the sheep do not come but are driven (*agantur*) to the altar. Others think the ancients called this festival *Agnalia* ("festival of lambs"), dropping a single letter from its proper place. Or perhaps, because the victim fears the knives mirrored in the water before they strike, the day may have been so styled from the brute's agony. It may be also that the day took a Greek name from the games (*agones*) which were wont to be held in the olden time. In the ancient tongue, too, *agonia* meant a sheep, and that last, in my judgement, is the true reason of the name. And though that is not

25

utque ea non certa est, ita rex placare sacrorum
  numina lanigerae coniuge debet ovis.
335 victima, quae dextra cecidit victrice, vocatur;
  hostibus a domitis hostia nomen habet.
ante, deos homini quod conciliare valeret,
  far erat et puri lucida mica salis.
nondum pertulerat lacrimatas cortice murras
340 acta per aequoreas hospita navis aquas,
tura nec Euphrates nec miserat India costum,
  nec fuerant rubri cognita fila croci.
ara dabat fumos herbis contenta Sabinis
  et non exiguo laurus adusta sono.
345 si quis erat, factis prati de flore coronis
  qui posset violas addere, dives erat.
hic, qui nunc aperit percussi viscera tauri,
  in sacris nullum culter habebat opus.
prima Ceres avidae gavisa est sanguine porcae
350 ulta suas merita caede nocentis opes;
nam sata vere novo teneris lactentia sulcis
  eruta saetigerae comperit ore suis.
sus dederat poenas: exemplo territus huius
  palmite debueras abstinuisse, caper.
355 quem spectans aliquis dentes in vite prementem
  talia non tacito dicta dolore dedit:
" rode, caper, vitem! tamen hinc, cum stabis ad aram,
  in tua quod spargi cornua possit, erit."
verba fides sequitur: noxae tibi deditus hostis
360 spargitur adfuso cornua, Bacche, mero.
culpa sui nocuit, nocuit quoque culpa capellae:
  quid bos, quid placidae commeruistis oves?
flebat Aristaeus, quod apes cum stirpe necatas
  viderat inceptos destituisse favos.

certain, still the King of the Sacred Rites is bound to
placate the divinities by sacrificing the mate of a
woolly ewe. The *victim* is so called because it is
felled by a *victorious* right hand ; the *hostia* (sacrificial
victim) takes its name from conquered *hostes* (foes).

³³⁷ Of old the means to win the goodwill of gods for
man were spelt and the sparkling grains of pure salt.
As yet no foreign ship had brought across the ocean
waves the bark-distilled myrrh ; the Euphrates had
sent no incense, India no balm, and the red saffron's
filaments were still unknown. The altar was content
to smoke with savine, and the laurel burned with
crackling loud. To garlands woven of meadow
flowers he who could violets add was rich indeed.
The knife that now lays bare the bowels of the
slaughtered bull had in the sacred rites no work to
do. The first to joy in blood of greedy sow was
Ceres, who avenged her crops by the just slaughter
of the guilty beast ; for she learned that the milky
grain in early spring had been routed up in the
loose furrows by the snout of bristly swine. The
swine was punished : terrified by her example,
billy-goat, you should have spared the vine-shoot.
Watching a he-goat nibbling at a vine somebody
vented his ill-humour in these words : " Pray gnaw
the vine, thou he-goat ; yet when thou standest at
the altar, the vine will yield something that can be
sprinkled on thy horns." The words came true.
Thy foe, Bacchus, is given up to thee for punishment,
and wine out-poured is sprinkled on his horns. The
sow suffered for her crime, and the she-goat suffered,
too, for hers. But the ox and you, ye peaceful sheep,
what was your sin ? Aristaeus wept because he saw
his bees killed, root and branch, and the unfinished

27

365 caerula quem genetrix aegre solata dolentem
    addidit haec dictis ultima verba suis :
  " siste, puer, lacrimas ! Proteus tua damna levabit,
    quoque modo repares quae periere, dabit.
  decipiat ne te versis tamen ille figuris,
370   impediant geminas vincula firma manus."
  pervenit ad vatem iuvenis resolutaque somno
    alligat aequorei brachia capta senis.
  ille sua faciem transformis adulterat arte :
    mox domitus vinclis in sua membra redit,
375 oraque caerulea tollens rorantia barba,
    " qua " dixit " repares arte, requiris, apes ?
  obrue mactati corpus tellure iuvenci :
    quod petis a nobis, obrutus ille dabit."
  iussa facit pastor : fervent examina putri
380   de bove : mille animas una necata dedit.
  poscit ovem fatum : verbenas improba carpsit,
    quas pia dis ruris ferre solebat anus.
  quid tuti superest, animam cum ponat in aris
    lanigerumque pecus ruricolaeque boves ?
385 placat equo Persis radiis Hyperiona cinctum,
    ne detur celeri victima tarda deo.
  quod semel est triplici pro virgine caesa Dianae,
    nunc quoque pro nulla virgine cerva cadit.
  exta canum vidi Triviae libare Sapaeos,
390   et quicumque tuas accolit, Haeme, nives.
  caeditur et rigido custodi ruris asellus ;
    causa pudenda quidem, sed tamen apta deo.
  festa corymbiferi celebrabas, Graecia, Bacchi,

---

    a Cyrene, a water-nymph.
    b Properly an epithet of the sun, " going above."
    c Iphigeneia, at Aulis, according to one version of the tale.

hives abandoned. Scarce could his azure mother[a] soothe his grief, when to her speech she these last words subjoined. "Stay, boy, thy tears! Thy losses Proteus will retrieve and will show thee how to make good all that is gone. But lest he elude thee by shifting his shape, see that strong bonds do shackle both his hands." The stripling made his way to the seer, and bound fast the arms, relaxed in slumber, of the Old Man of the Sea. By his art the wizard changed his real figure for a semblance false; but soon, by the cords mastered, to his true form returned. Then lifting up his dripping face and azure beard, "Dost ask," said he, "in what way thou mayest repair the loss of thy bees? Kill a heifer and bury its carcase in the earth. The buried heifer will give the thing thou seekest of me." The shepherd did his bidding: swarms of bees hive out of the putrid beeve: one life snuffed out brought to the birth a thousand. Death claims the sheep: shameless it cropped the holy herbs which a pious beldame used to offer to the rural gods. What creature is safe, when even the wool-bearing sheep and ploughing oxen lay down their lives upon the altars? Persia propitiates the ray-crowned Hyperion[b] with a horse, for no sluggard victim may be offered to the swift god. Because a hind was once sacrificed to the triple Diana in room of a maiden,[c] a hind is even now felled for her, though not in a maiden's stead. I have seen the entrails of a dog offered to the Goddess of the Triple Roads (*Trivia*) by the Sapaeans and those whose homes border on thy snows, Mount Haemus. A young ass, too, is slain in honour of the stiff guardian of the country-side: the cause is shameful, but beseems the god. A feast of ivy-berried Bacchus, thou

tertia quae solito tempore bruma refert.
395 di quoque cultores in idem venere Lyaei,
    et quicumque iocis non alienus erat,
Panes et in Venerem Satyrorum prona iuventus,
    quaeque colunt amnes solaque rura deae.
venerat et senior pando Silenus asello,
400   quique ruber pavidas inguine terret aves,
dulcia qui dignum nemus in convivia nacti
    gramine vestitis accubuere toris.
vina dabat Liber, tulerat sibi quisque coronam,
    miscendas large rivus agebat aquas.
405 Naïdes effusis aliae sine pectinis usu,
    pars aderant positis arte manuque comis:
illa super suras tunicam collecta ministrat,
    altera dissuto pectus aperta sinu:
exserit haec humerum, vestem trahit illa per herbas,
410   impediunt teneros vincula nulla pedes.
hinc aliae Satyris incendia mitia praebent,
    pars tibi, qui pinu tempora nexa geris.
te quoque, inextinctae Silene libidinis, urunt:
    nequitia est, quae te non sinit esse senem.
415 at ruber, hortorum decus et tutela, Priapus
    omnibus ex illis Lotide captus erat:
hanc cupit, hanc optat, sola suspirat in illa,
    signaque dat nutu, sollicitatque notis.
fastus inest pulchris, sequiturque superbia formam:
420   irrisum voltu despicit illa suo.
nox erat, et vino somnum faciente iacebant
    corpora diversis victa sopore locis.
Lotis in herbosa sub acernis ultima ramis,
    sicut erat lusu fessa, quievit humo.
425 surgit amans animamque tenens vestigia furtim

---

^a That is, a biennial festival, called by the ancient inclusive
mode, triennial (τριετηρίς). See on i. 54, above.

wast wont to hold, O Greece, a feast which the third
winter brought about at the appointed time.[a] Thither
came, too, the gods who wait upon Lyaeus and all
the jocund crew, Pans and young amorous Satyrs,
and goddesses that haunt rivers and lonely wilds.
Thither, too, came old Silenus on an ass with hollow
back, and the Crimson One [b] who by his lewd image
scares the timid birds. They lit upon a dingle
meet for joyous wassails, and there they laid them
down on grassy beds. Liber bestowed the wine :
each had brought his garland : a stream supplied
water in plenty to dilute the wine. Naiads were
there, some with flowing locks uncombed, others with
tresses neatly bound. One waits upon the revellers
with tunic tucked above the knee ; another through
her ripped robe reveals her breast ; another bares
her shoulder ; one trails her skirt along the grass ;
no shoes cumber their dainty feet. So some in
Satyrs kindle amorous fires, and some in thee, whose
brows are wreathed with pine.[c] Thou too, Silenus,
burnest for the nymphs, insatiate lecher ! 'Tis
wantonness alone forbids thee to grow old. But
crimson Priapus, glory and guard of gardens, lost his
heart to Lotis, singled out of the whole bevy. For
her he longs, for her he prays, for her alone he sighs ;
he gives her signs by nodding and woos by making
marks. But the lovely are disdainful, and pride on
beauty waits : she flouted him and cast at him a
scornful look. 'Twas night, and wine makes drowsy,
so here and there they lay overcome with sleep.
Weary with frolic, Lotis, the farthest of them all,
sank to her rest on the grassy ground under the
maple boughs. Up rose her lover, and holding his

[b] Priapus : so ll. 415, 440.   [c] Pan.

suspenso digitis fert taciturna gradu.
ut tetigit niveae secreta cubilia nymphae,
    ipsa sui flatus ne sonet aura, cavet.
et iam finitima corpus librabat in herba :
430   illa tamen multi plena soporis erat.
gaudet et, a pedibus tracto velamine, vota
    ad sua felici coeperat ire via.
ecce rudens rauco Sileni vector asellus
    intempestivos edidit ore sonos.
435 territa consurgit nymphe manibusque Priapum
    reicit et fugiens concitat omne nemus ;
at deus obscena nimium quoque parte paratus
    omnibus ad lunae lumina risus erat.
morte dedit poenas auctor clamoris, et haec est
440   Hellespontiaco victima grata deo.
intactae fueratis aves, solacia ruris,
    adsuetum silvis innocuumque genus,
quae facitis nidos et plumis ova fovetis
    et facili dulces editis ore modos ;
445 sed nil ista iuvant, quia linguae crimen habetis,
    dique putant mentes vos aperire suas.
nec tamen hoc falsum : nam, dis ut proxima quaeque,
    nunc penna veras, nunc datis ore notas.
tuta diu volucrum proles tum denique caesa est,
450   iuveruntque deos indicis exta sui.
ergo saepe suo coniunx abducta marito
    uritur Idaliis alba columba focis ;
nec defensa iuvant Capitolia, quo minus anser
    det iecur in lances, Inachi lauta, tuas ;
455 nocte deae Nocti cristatus caeditur ales,
    quod tepidum vigili provocet ore diem.

---

a *i.e.*, of revealing their secrets to the *augur* and the
auspex, words which are connected with *avis*.

breath stole secretly and silently on tiptoe to the fair. When he reached the lonely pallet of the snow-white nymph, he drew his breath so warily that not a sound escaped. And now upon the sward fast by he balanced on his toes, but still the nymph slept sound. He joyed, and drawing from off her feet the quilt, he set him, happy lover ! to snatch the wished-for hour. But lo, Silenus' saddle-ass, with raucous weasand braying, gave out an ill-timed roar ! The nymph in terror started up, pushed off Priapus, and flying gave the alarm to the whole grove ; but, ready to enter the lists of love, the god in the moonlight was laughed at by all. The author of the hubbub paid for it with his life, and he is now the victim dear to the Hellespontine god.

[441] Ye birds, the solace of the countryside, ye haunters of the woods, ye harmless race, that build your nests and warm your eggs under your plumes, and with glib voices utter descant sweet, ye were inviolate once ; but all that avails not, because ye are accused of chattering,[a] and the gods opine that ye reveal their thoughts. Nor is the charge untrue ; for the nearer ye are to the gods, the truer are the signs ye give, whether by wing or voice. Long time immune, the brood of birds was slaughtered then at last, and the gods gloated on the guts of the talebearing fowls. That is why the white dove, torn from her mate, is often burned upon Idalian hearths ; nor did his saving of the Capitol protect the goose from yielding up his liver on a charger to thee, daughter of Inachus,[b] goddess demure ; by night to Goddess Night the crested fowl is slain, because with wakeful notes he summons up the warm day.

[b] The Egyptian Isis, as identified with Argive Io.

Interea Delphin clarum super aequora sidus
tollitur et patriis exerit ora vadis.

10. B EN

Postera lux hiemem medio discrimine signat,
460   aequaque praeteritae, quae superabit, erit.

11. C CAR · NP 12. DC

Proxima prospiciet Tithono Aurora relicto
    Arcadiae sacrum pontificale deae.
te quoque lux eadem, Turni soror, aede recepit,
    hic ubi Virginea Campus obitur aqua.
465 unde petam causas horum moremque sacrorum ?
    diriget in medio quis mea vela freto ?
ipsa mone, quae nomen habes a carmine ductum,
    propositoque fave, ne tuus erret honor.
orta prior luna (de se si creditur ipsi)
470   a magno tellus Arcade nomen habet.
hic fuit Evander, qui, quamquam clarus utroque,
    nobilior sacrae sanguine matris erat ;
quae simul aetherios animo conceperat ignes,
    ore dabat pleno carmina vera dei.
475 dixerat haec nato motus instare sibique,
    multaque praeterea tempore nacta fidem.

---

    [a] The rising was really on December 31, in Ovid's time.
    [b] The Carmentalia, in honour of Carmenta or Carmentis,
one of the Camenae, mother of Evander.
    [c] The nymph Juturna.
    [d] Aqua Virgo, an aqueduct built by Agrippa in 19 B.C.
which still brings water to Rome, and fills the fountain of
Trevi.

457 Meantime the bright constellation of the Dolphin rises above the sea, and from his native waters puts forth his face.[a]

IV. Id. 10th

459 The morrow marks midwinter ; what remains of winter will be equal to what has gone before.

III. Id. 11th

461 When next Aurora quits Tithonus' couch, she shall behold the rite pontifical of the Arcadian goddess.[b] Thee, too, sister of Turnus,[c] the same morn enshrined at the spot where the Virgin Water[d] circles the Field of Mars. Whence shall I learn the causes and manner of these rites ? Who will pilot my bark in mid ocean ? Thyself, enlighten me, O thou (Carmentis), who dost take thy name from song (carmen), be kind to my emprise, lest I should fail to give thee honour due. The land that rose before the moon (if we may take its word for it) derives its name from the great Arcas.[e] In that land Evander was, who, though illustrious on both sides, yet was the nobler for the blood of his sacred mother (Carmentis), who, soon as her soul conceived the heavenly fire, chanted with swelling voice true strains divine. She had foretold that troubles were at hand for her son and for herself, and much beside she had forecast, which time proved true. Too true, indeed, the

[e] Son of Callisto, ii. 153. " The Arcadians are fabled to have lived before the moon," Apoll. Rhod. iv. 264. See below, p. 79.

nam iuvenis nimium vera cum matre fugatus
  deserit Arcadiam Parrhasiumque larem.
cui genetrix flenti " fortuna viriliter " inquit
480 " (siste, precor, lacrimas) ista ferenda tibi est.
sic erat in fatis ; nec te tua culpa fugavit,
  sed deus ; offenso pulsus es urbe deo.
non meriti poenam pateris, sed numinis iram :
  est aliquid magnis crimen abesse malis.
485 conscia mens ut cuique sua est, ita concipit intra
  pectora pro facto spemque metumque suo.
nec tamen ut primus maere mala talia passus :
  obruit ingentes ista procella viros.
passus idem est, Tyriis qui quondam pulsus ab oris
490 Cadmus in Aonia constitit exul humo :
passus idem Tydeus et idem Pagasaeus Iason,
  et quos praeterea longa referre mora est.
omne solum forti patria est, ut piscibus aequor,
  ut volucri, vacuo quicquid in orbe patet.
495 nec fera tempestas toto tamen horret in anno :
  et tibi (crede mihi) tempora veris erunt."
vocibus Evander firmata mente parentis
  nave secat fluctus Hesperiamque tenet.
iamque ratem doctae monitu Carmentis in amnem
500 egerat et Tuscis obvius ibat aquis :
fluminis illa latus, cui sunt vada iuncta Tarenti,
  aspicit et sparsas per loca sola casas ;
utque erat, immissis puppem stetit ante capillis
  continuitque manum torva regentis iter,
505 et procul in dextram tendens sua bracchia ripam
  pinea non sano ter pede texta ferit ;
neve daret saltum properans insistere terrae,
  vix est Evandri vixque retenta manu.

---

^a The Parrhasii were an Arcadian tribe.
  ^b Boeotia.   ^c A place in the Field of Mars.

mother proved when, banished with her, the youth
forsook Arcadia and the god of his Parrhasian[a] home.
He wept, but she, his mother, said, " Check, prithee,
thy tears ; bear like a man thy fortune. 'Twas
fated so ; no fault of thine has banished thee, the deed
is God's ; an offended god has driven thee from the
city. What thou dost endure is not the punishment
of sin but heaven's ire : in great misfortunes it is
something to be unstained by crime. As each man's
conscience is, so doth it, for his deeds, conceive
within his breast or hope or fear. Nor mourn these
sufferings as if thou wert the first to suffer ; such
storms have whelmed the mighty. Cadmus endured
the same, he, who of old, driven from Tyrian coasts,
halted an exile on Aonian soil.[b] Tydeus endured the
same, and Pagasaean Jason too, and others more
of whom it were long to tell. Every land is to
the brave his country, as to the fish the sea, as to
the bird whatever place stands open in the void
world. Nor does the wild tempest rage the whole
year long ; for thee, too, trust me, there will be spring-
time yet." Cheered by his parent's words, Evander
cleft in his ship the billows and made the Hesperian
land. And now at sage Carmentis' bidding he had
steered his bark into a river and was stemming the
Tuscan stream. Carmentis spied the river bank,
where it is bordered by Tarentum's shallow pool[c] ; she
also spied the huts dotted about these solitudes. And
even as she was, with streaming hair she stood before
the poop and sternly stayed the steersman's hand ;
then stretching out her arms to the right bank, she
thrice stamped wildly on the pinewood deck.
Hardly, yea hardly did Evander hold her back from
leaping in her haste to land. " All hail ! " she cried,

OVID

" di " que " petitorum " dixit " salvete locorum,
510   tuque novos caelo terra datura deos,
fluminaque et fontes, quibus utitur hospita tellus,
    et nemorum nymphae naiadumque chori !
este bonis avibus visi natoque mihique,
    ripaque felici tacta sit ista pede !
515 fallor, an hi fient ingentia moenia colles,
    iuraque ab hac terra cetera terra petet ?
montibus his olim totus promittitur orbis :
    quis tantum fati credat habere locum ?
et iam Dardaniae tangent haec litora pinus :
520   hic quoque causa novi femina Martis erit.
care nepos, Palla, funesta quid induis arma ?
    indue ! non humili vindice caesus eris.
victa tamen vinces eversaque, Troia, resurges :
    obruet hostiles ista ruina domos.
525 urite victrices Neptunia Pergama flammae !
    num minus hic toto est altior orbe cinis ?
iam pius Aeneas sacra et, sacra altera, patrem
    adferet : Iliacos accipe, Vesta, deos !
tempus erit, cum vos orbemque tuebitur idem,
530   et fient ipso sacra colente deo,
et penes Augustos patriae tutela manebit :
    hanc fas imperii frena tenere domum.
inde nepos natusque dei, licet ipse recuset,
    pondera caelesti mente paterna feret ;

ᵃ Lavinia.
ᵇ Pallas, son of Evander, was slain by Turnus ; but was
avenged by Aeneas, who slew Turnus. Ovid has the *Aeneid*
in mind here.
ᶜ The Vestal fire and the Penates of the Roman people
were believed to have been brought by Aeneas from Troy.

38

" Gods of the Promised Land! And hail! thou country that shalt give new gods to heaven! Hail rivers and fountains, which to this hospitable land pertain! Hail nymphs of the groves and bands of Naiads! May the sight of you be of good omen to my son and me! And happy be the foot that touches yonder bank! Am I deceived? or shall yon hills by stately walls be hid, and from this spot of earth shall all the earth take law? The promise runs that the whole world shall one day belong to yonder mountains. Who could believe that the place was big with such a fate? Anon Dardanian barks shall ground upon these shores: here, too, a woman *a* shall be the source of a new war. Pallas, my grandson dear, why don those fatal arms? *b* Ah, put them on! By no mean champion shalt thou be avenged. Howbeit, conquered Troy, thou shalt yet conquer and from thy fall shalt rise again: thy very ruin shall o'erwhelm the dwellings of thy foes. Ye conquering flames, consume Neptunian Pergamum! Shall that prevent its ashes from o'ertopping all the world? Anon pious Aeneas shall hither bring his sacred burden, and, burden no whit less sacred, his own sire; Vesta, admit the gods of Ilium *c*! The time will come when the same hand shall guard you and the world, and when a god shall in his own person hold the sacred rites.*d* In the line of Augustus the guardianship of the fatherland shall abide: it is decreed that his house shall hold the reins of empire. Thereafter the god's son and grandson, despite his own refusal, shall support with heavenly mind the weight his father bore; and even as I myself

d This applies both to Julius and to Augustus, who is the " son " of l. 533 ; the " grandson " is Tiberius.

535 utque ego perpetuis olim sacrabor in aris,
    sic Augusta novum Iulia numen erit."
talibus ut dictis nostros descendit in annos,
    substitit in medios praescia lingua sonos.
puppibus egressus Latia stetit exul in herba,
540   felix, exilium cui locus ille fuit !
nec mora longa fuit : stabant nova tecta, neque alter
    montibus Ausoniis Arcade maior erat.
ecce boves illuc Erytheïdas applicat heros
    emensus longi claviger orbis iter ;
545 dumque huic hospitium domus est Tegeaea, vagantur
    incustoditae lata per arva boves.
mane erat : excussus somno Tirynthius actor
    de numero tauros sentit abesse duos.
nulla videt quaerens taciti vestigia furti :
550   traxerat aversos Cacus in antra ferox,
Cacus, Aventinae timor atque infamia silvae,
    non leve finitimis hospitibusque malum.
dira viro facies, vires pro corpore, corpus
    grande : pater monstri Mulciber huius erat :
555 proque domo longis spelunca recessibus ingens,
    abdita, vix ipsis invenienda feris.
ora super postes adfixaque brachia pendent,
    squalidaque humanis ossibus albet humus.
servata male parte boum Iove natus abibat :
560   mugitum rauco furta dedere sono.
" accipio revocamen " ait, vocemque secutus

---

[a] By the will of Augustus, Livia was adopted into the Julian family and became Julia Augusta: Ovid anticipates her deification by her grandson Claudius (Suetonius, *Claud.* 11).

[b] Evander landed at the foot of the Palatine hill, here called after him " Arcadian."

[c] Hercules came from Spain with the herds of Geryon, which he had taken there, to visit Evander ; Erythea is in

shall one day be sanctified at eternal altars, so shall Julia Augusta[a] be a new divinity." When in these words she had brought her story down to our own time, her prophetic tongue stopped short at the middle of her discourse. Landing from his ships, Evander stood an exile on the Latian sward, fortunate indeed to have that ground for place of exile ! But little time elapsed until new dwellings rose, and of all the Ausonian mounts not one surpassed the Arcadian.[b]

[543] Lo ! the club-bearer[c] hither drives the Erythean kine ; a long road he had travelled across the world ; and while he is kindly entertained in the Tegean house, the kine unguarded stray about the spacious fields. When morning broke, roused from his sleep the Tirynthian drover perceived that of the tale two bulls were missing. He sought but found no tracks of the noiselessly stolen beasts. Fierce Cacus had dragged the bulls backwards into his cave, Cacus the terror and the shame of the Aventine wood, to neighbours and to strangers no small curse. Grim was his aspect, huge his frame, his strength to match ; the monster's sire was Mulciber. For house he had a cavern vast with long recesses, hidden so that hardly could the wild beasts themselves discover it. Above the doorway skulls and arms of men were fastened pendent, while the ground bristled and bleached with human bones. The son of Jove was going off with the loss of part of the herd, when the stolen cattle lowed hoarsely. " I accept the recall," quoth he, and following the sound he came, intent on vengeance,

S.W. Spain. This capture was one of his Labours. He was son of Alcmena, princess of Tiryns. Evander's house is called Tegean, for Arcadian.

    impia per silvas ultor ad antra venit.
  ille aditum fracti praestruxerat obice montis ;
    vix iuga movissent quinque bis illud opus.
565 nititur hic humeris (caelum quoque sederat illis)
    et vastum motu conlabefactat onus.
  quod simul eversum est, fragor aethera terruit ipsum,
    ictaque subsedit pondere molis humus.
  prima movet Cacus collata proelia dextra
570   remque ferox saxis stipitibusque gerit.
  quis ubi nil agitur, patrias male fortis ad artes
    confugit et flammas ore sonante vomit ;
  quas quotiens proflat, spirare Typhoëa credas
    et rapidum Aetnaeo fulgur ab igne iaci.
575 occupat Alcides, adductaque clava trinodis
    ter quater adverso sedit in ore viri.
  ille cadit mixtosque vomit cum sanguine fumos
    et lato moriens pectore plangit humum.
  immolat ex illis taurum tibi, Iuppiter, unum
580   victor et Evandrum ruricolasque vocat,
  constituitque sibi, quae Maxima dicitur, aram,
    hic ubi pars urbis de bove nomen habet.
  nec tacet Evandri mater prope tempus adesse,
    Hercule quo tellus sit satis usa suo.
585 at felix vates, ut dis gratissima vixit,
    possidet hunc Iani sic dea mense diem.

    13. E EID · N͏P   14. F EN DIES · VITIOS · EX · S · C

Idibus in magni castus Iovis aede sacerdos
  semimaris flammis viscera libat ovis ;

---

    a See iv. 491.
    b The Flamen Dialis, who was subject to many ceremonial rules.

through the woods to the unholy cave. But the robber
had blocked the entrance with a barricade of crag;
scarcely could twice five yoke of oxen have stirred that
mass. Hercules shoved it with his shoulders—the
shoulders on which the sky itself had once rested—
and by the shock he loosened the vast bulk. Its overthrow was followed by a crash that startled even the
upper air, and the battered ground sank under the
ponderous weight. At first Cacus fought hand to
hand, and waged battle fierce with rocks and logs.
But when these naught availed him, worsted he had
recourse to his sire's tricks, and belched flames from
his roaring mouth; at every blast you might deem
that Typhoeus blew, and that a sudden blaze shot
out from Etna's fires.ᵃ But Alcides was too quick
for him; up he heaved the triple-knotted club, and
brought it thrice, yea four times down full on the
foeman's face. He fell, vomiting smoke mixed with
blood, and dying beat the ground with his broad breast.
Of the bulls the victor sacrificed one to thee, Jupiter,
and invited Evander and the swains to the feast; and
for himself he set up the altar which is called the
Greatest at the spot where a part of the city takes its
name from an ox. Nor did Evander's mother hide
the truth that the time was at hand when earth
would have done with its hero Hercules. But the
happy prophetess, even as she lived in highest favour
with the gods, so now herself a goddess hath she
this day in Janus' month all to herself.

Idus. 13th

⁵⁸⁷ On the Ides the chaste priest ᵇ offers in the
flames the bowels of a gelded ram in the temple of

redditaque est omnis populo provincia nostro,
590   et tuus Augusto nomine dictus avus.
perlege dispositas generosa per atria ceras :
   contigerunt nulli nomina tanta viro.
Africa victorem de se vocat, alter Isauras
   aut Cretum domitas testificatur opes ;
595 hunc Numidae faciunt, illum Messana superbum,
   ille Numantina traxit ab urbe notam,
et mortem et nomen Druso Germania fecit—
   me miserum, virtus quam brevis illa fuit !
si petat a victis, tot sumat nomina Caesar,
600   quot numero gentes maximus orbis habet.
ex uno quidam celebres aut torquis adempti
   aut corvi titulos auxiliaris habent.
Magne, tuum nomen rerum est mensura tuarum :
   sed qui te vicit, nomine maior erat.
605 nec gradus est supra Fabios cognominis ullus :
   illa domus meritis Maxima dicta suis.
sed tamen humanis celebrantur honoribus omnes :
   hic socium summo cum Iove nomen habet.
sancta vocant augusta patres, augusta vocantur
610   templa sacerdotum rite dicata manu ;
huius et augurium dependet origine verbi,
   et quodcumque sua Iuppiter auget ope.
augeat imperium nostri ducis, augeat annos,
   protegat et vestras querna corona fores,

---

    a Son of Livia by her first husband, Tiberius Claudius
Nero, and brother of the Emperor Tiberius.   He died 9 B.C.,
of a fall from his horse, aged 31.
    b T. Manlius Torquatus, 361 B.C. ;   M. Valerius Corvus
or Corvinus, 349 B.C.
    c The title came from Q. Fabius Maximus, 304 B.C.
    d It was voted to Augustus *in perpetuum*, in token of his
44

great Jove. On that day, too, every province was restored to our people, and thy grandsire received the title of Augustus. Peruse the legends graved on waxen images ranged round noble halls; titles so lofty never were bestowed on man before. Africa named her conqueror after herself; another by his style attests Isaurian or Cretan power subdued: one gloried in Numidians laid low, another in Messana, while from the city of Numantia yet a third drew his renown. To Germany did Drusus *a* owe his title and his death: woe's me! that all that goodness should be so short-lived! Did Caesar take his titles from the vanquished, then must he assume as many names as there are tribes in the whole world. Some have earned fame from single enemies, taking their names either from a necklace won or from a raven confederate in the fight.*b* Pompey, thy name of Great is the measure of thy deeds, but he who conquered thee was greater still in name. No surname can rank above that which the Fabii bear: for their services their family was called the Greatest.*c* But yet the honours bestowed on all of these are human: Augustus alone bears a name that ranks with Jove supreme. Holy things are by the fathers called august: the epithet august is applied to temples that have been duly dedicated by priestly hands: from the same root come augury and all such augmentation as Jupiter grants by his power. May he augment our prince's empire and augment his years, and may an oaken crown *d* protect your doors. Under the auspices of the gods may the

care for his people; and hung up in his palace: " For saving the life of citizens," see *Monumentum Ancyranum*, vi. 3 n., in Velleius Paterculus (Loeb Classical Library), p. 399.

OVID

615 auspicibusque deis tanti cognominis heres
   omine suscipiat, quo pater, orbis onus!

15. G CAR

Respiciet Titan actas ubi tertius Idus,
   fient Parrhasiae sacra relata deae.
Nam prius Ausonias matres carpenta vehebant
620   (haec quoque ab Evandri dicta parente reor);
mox honor eripitur, matronaque destinat omnis
   ingratos nulla prole novare viros,
neve daret partus, ictu temeraria caeco
   visceribus crescens excutiebat onus.
625 corripuisse patres ausas immitia nuptas,
   ius tamen ereptum restituisse ferunt;
binaque nunc pariter Tegeaeae sacra parenti
   pro pueris fieri virginibusque iubent.
scortea non illi fas est inferre sacello,
630   ne violent puros exanimata focos.
siquis amas veteres ritus, adsiste precanti:
   nomina percipies non tibi nota prius.
Porrima placatur Postvertaque, sive sorores
   sive fugae comites, Maenali diva, tuae:
635 altera, quod porro fuerat, cecinisse putatur,
   altera, venturum postmodo quicquid erat.

16. HC

Candida, te niveo posuit lux proxima templo,
   qua fert sublimes alta Moneta gradus:

---

      a See notes on ll. 470, 478.
   b Carmenta; Maenalus was a mountain in Arcadia.

same omens, which attended the sire, wait upon
the heir of so great a surname, when he takes upon
himself the burden of the world.

XVIII. KAL. FEB. 15th

⁶¹⁷ When the third sun shall look back on the past
Ides, the sacred rites will be repeated in honour
of the Parrhasian goddess.ᵃ For of old Ausonian
matrons drove in carriages (*carpenta*), which I ween
were also called after Evander's parent (*Carmentis*).
Afterwards the honour was taken from them, and
every matron vowed not to propagate the line of
her ungrateful spouse by giving birth to offspring;
and lest she should bear children, she rashly by a
secret thrust discharged the growing burden from
her womb. They say the senate reprimanded the
wives for their daring cruelty, but restored the right of
which they had been mulcted; and they ordained
that now two festivals be held alike in honour of
the Tegean mother to promote the birth of boys
and girls. It is not lawful to bring leather into her
shrine, lest her pure hearths should be defiled by
skins of slaughtered beasts. If thou hast any love
of ancient rites, attend the prayers offered to her:
you shall hear names you never knew before.
Porrima and Postverta are placated, whether they
be thy sisters, Maenalian goddess,ᵇ or companions of
thine exile: the one is thought to have sung of
what was long ago (*porro*), the other of what should
come to pass hereafter (*venturum postmodo*).

XVII. KAL. 16th

⁶³⁷ Fair goddess, thee the next morning set in thy
snow-white fane, where high Moneta lifts her steps

47

nunc bene prospicies Latiam, Concordia, turbam,
640　　nunc te sacratae constituere manus.
　　Furius antiquam populi superator Etrusci
　　　　voverat et voti solverat ille fidem.
　　causa, quod a patribus sumptis secesserat armis
　　　　volgus, et ipsa suas Roma timebat opes.
645 causa recens melior : passos Germania crines
　　　　porrigit auspiciis, dux venerande, tuis ;
　　inde triumphatae libasti munera gentis
　　　　templaque fecisti, quam colis ipse, deae.
　　hanc tua constituit genetrix et rebus et ara,
650　　sola toro magni digna reperta Iovis.

17. AC　18. BC　19. CC　20. DC
21. EC　22. FC　23. GC

Haec ubi transierint, Capricorno, Phoebe, relicto
　　per iuvenis curres signa gerentis aquam.

Septimus hinc oriens cum se demiserit undis,
　　fulgebit toto iam Lyra nulla polo.

655 Sidere ab hoc ignis venienti nocte, Leonis
　　qui micat in medio pectore, mersus erit.

24. HC　25. AC　26. BC

Ter quater evolvi signantes tempora fastos,
　　nec Sementiva est ulla reperta dies :

---

　　a The new temple of Juno Moneta was on the Capitol, and
a flight of steps led up from the Forum, near which was the old
temple of Concord.
　　b M. Furius Camillus, 367 B.C. The temple was rebuilt
by Tiberius out of the spoils of Germany, A.D. 10.
　　c Livia.　See vi. 637 below.
　　d The apparent setting then was on January 28, the
true setting on February 9.

sublime:[a] now, Concord, shalt thou well o'erlook the Latin throng, now consecrated hands have stablished thee. Furius, the vanquisher of the Etruscan folk, had vowed the ancient temple, and he kept his vow.[b] The cause was that the common folk had taken up arms and seceded from the nobles, and Rome dreaded her own puissance. The recent cause was better: Germany presented her dishevelled locks at thy command, leader revered; hence didst thou offer the spoil of the vanquished people, and didst build a temple to that goddess whom thou thyself dost worship. That goddess thy mother[c] did stablish both by her life and by an altar, she who alone was found worthy to share the bed of mighty Jupiter.

XVI. Kal. 17th

651 When that is over, thou wilt quit Capricorn, O Phoebus, and wilt take thy course through the sign of the youth who carries water (Aquarius).

X. Kal. 23rd

653 When the seventh sun, reckoned from that day, shall have set in the sea, the Lyre will shine no longer anywhere in the sky.[d]

IX. Kal. 24th

655 After the setting of that constellation (the Lyre), the fire that glitters in the middle of the Lion's breast will be sunk below the horizon at nightfall.[e]

657 Three or four times I searched the record of the calendar, but nowhere did I find the Day of Sowing.

* This is the date of the true morning setting.

49

cum mihi (sensit enim) " lux haec indicitur," inquit
660　Musa, " quid a fastis non stata sacra petis ?
utque dies incerta sacro, sic tempora certa :
　　seminibus iactis est ubi fetus ager."
state coronati plenum ad praesaepe iuvenci :
　　cum tepido vestrum vere redibit opus.
665 rusticus emeritum palo suspendat aratrum :
　　omne reformidat frigida volnus humus.
vilice, da requiem terrae semente peracta ;
　　da requiem, terram qui coluere, viris.
pagus agat festum : pagum lustrate, coloni,
670　et date paganis annua liba focis.
placentur frugum matres, Tellusque Ceresque,
　　farre suo gravidae visceribusque suis.
officium commune Ceres et Terra tuentur :
　　haec praebet causam frugibus, illa locum.
675 " consortes operis, per quas correcta vetustas
　　quernaque glans victa est utiliore cibo,
frugibus immensis avidos satiate colonos,
　　ut capiant cultus praemia digna sui.
vos date perpetuos teneris sementibus auctus,
680　nec nova per gelidas herba sit usta nives.
cum serimus, caelum ventis aperite serenis ;
　　cum latet, aetheria spargite semen aqua.
neve graves cultis Cerialia rura, cavete,
　　agmine laesuro depopulentur aves.
685 vos quoque, formicae, subiectis parcite granis :
　　post messem praedae copia maior erit.
interea crescat scabrae robiginis expers,
　　nec vitio caeli palleat aegra seges,
et neque deficiat macie neque pinguior aequo

Seeing me puzzled, the Muse observed, " That day
is appointed by the priests. Why look for movable
feasts in the calendar ? And while the day of the
feast may shift, the season is fixed : it is when the
seed has been sown and the field fertilized." Ye
steers, take your stand with garlands on your heads
at the full crib : with the warm spring your toil will
return. Let the swain hang up on the post the plough
that has earned its rest : the cold ground shrinks
from every wound inflicted by the share. Thou bailiff,
when the sowing is done, let the land rest, and let
the men who tilled the land rest also. Let the
parish keep festival ; purify the parish, ye husbandmen, and offer the yearly cakes on the parish hearths.
Propitiate Earth and Ceres, the mothers of the corn,
with their own spelt and flesh of teeming sow.
Ceres and Earth discharge a common function :
the one lends to the corn its vital force, the other
lends it room. " Partners in labour, ye who re-
formed the days of old and replaced the acorns of
the oak by food more profitable, O satisfy the eager
husbandmen with boundless crops, that they may reap
the due reward of their tillage. O grant unto the
tender seeds unbroken increase ; let not the sprouting shoot be nipped by chilly snows. When we sow,
let the sky be cloudless and winds blow fair ; but
when the seed is buried, then sprinkle it with water
from the sky. Forbid the birds—pests of the tilled
land—to devastate the fields of corn with their
destructive flocks. You too, ye ants, O spare the
sown grain ; so shall ye have a more abundant booty
after the harvest. Meantime may no scurfy mildew
blight the growing crop nor foul weather blanch it
to a sickly hue ; may it neither shrivel up nor swell

51

690 divitiis pereat luxuriosa suis.
et careant loliis oculos vitiantibus agri,
nec sterilis culto surgat avena solo.
triticeos fetus passuraque farra bis ignem
hordeaque ingenti fenore reddat ager ! "
695 haec ego pro vobis, haec vos optate coloni,
efficiatque ratas utraque diva preces.
bella diu tenuere viros : erat aptior ensis
vomere, cedebat taurus arator equo ;
sarcula cessabant, versique in pila ligones,
700 factaque de rastri pondere cassis erat.
gratia dis domuique tuae ; religata catenis
iampridem vestro sub pede bella iacent.
sub iuga bos veniat, sub terras semen aratas !
pax Cererem nutrit, pacis alumna Ceres.

27. CC   28. DC   29. EC

705 At quae venturas praecedit sexta Kalendas,
hac sunt Ledaeis templa dicata deis :
fratribus illa deis fratres de gente deorum
circa Iuturnae composuere lacus.

30. FNP   31. GC

Ipsum nos carmen deduxit Pacis ad aram.
710 haec erit a mensis fine secunda dies.
frondibus Actiacis comptos redimita capillos,
Pax, ades et toto mitis in orbe mane.

---

^a It was supposed to damage the sight if eaten ; Plautus, *Mil. Gl.* 323 "mirum lolio victitare te," *i.e.* "you cannot see what is before your face."
^b Spelt was toasted before it was baked. See ii. 520.
^c Castor and Pollux. The temple had been dedicated

unduly and be choked by its own rank luxuriance.
May the fields be free from darnel, that spoils the
eyes,[a] and may no barren wild oats spring from the
tilled ground. May the farm yield, with manifold
interest, crops of wheat, of barley, and of spelt, which
twice shall bear the fire."[b] These petitions I offer for
you, ye husbandmen, and do ye offer them yourselves,
and may the two goddesses grant our prayers. Long
time did wars engage mankind; the sword was
handier than the share; the plough ox was ousted by
the charger; hoes were idle, mattocks were turned
into javelins, and a helmet was made out of a heavy
rake. Thanks be to the gods and to thy house!
Under your foot long time War has been laid in
chains. Yoke the ox, commit the seed to the
ploughed earth. Peace is the nurse of Ceres, and
Ceres is the foster-child of Peace.

VI. Kal. 27th

[705] On the sixth day before the coming Calends
a temple was dedicated to Leda's divine sons[c]:
brothers of the race of the gods founded that temple
for the brother gods beside Juturna's[d] pools.

III. Kal. 30th

[709] The course of my song hath led me to the altar
of Peace. The day will be the second from the end
of the month. Come, Peace, thy dainty tresses
wreathed with Actian[e] laurels, and let thy gentle

anew in A.D. 6 by Tiberius, who added the name of his dead
brother Drusus to the dedication.
  [d] See above, l. 463.
  [e] Referring to the victory of Actium, 31 B.C.

dum desint hostes, desit quoque causa triumphi :
    tu ducibus bello gloria maior eris.
715 sola gerat miles, quibus arma coerceat, arma,
    canteturque fera nil nisi pompa tuba.
horreat Aeneadas et primus et ultimus orbis :
    si qua parum Romam terra timebat, amet.
tura, sacerdotes, pacalibus addite flammis,
720   albaque percussa victima fronte cadat,
utque domus, quae praestat eam, cum pace perennet
    ad pia propensos vota rogate deos.
sed iam prima mei pars est exacta laboris,
    cumque suo finem mense libellus habet.

presence abide in the whole world. So but there be nor foes nor food for triumphs, thou shalt be unto our chiefs a glory greater than war. May the soldier bear arms only to check the armed aggressor, and may the fierce trumpet blare for naught but solemn pomp! May the world near and far dread the sons of Aeneas, and if there be any land that feared not Rome, may it love Rome instead! Add incense, ye priests, to the flames that burn on the altar of Peace, let a white victim fall with cloven brow, and ask of the gods, who lend a favouring ear to pious prayers, that the house, which is the warranty of peace, with peace may last for ever.

723 But now the first part of my labour is done, and with the month of which it treats the book doth end.

LIBER SECUNDUS

Ianus habet finem. cum carmine crescit et annus :
    alter ut hic mensis, sic liber alter eat.
nunc primum velis, elegi, maioribus itis :
    exiguum, memini, nuper eratis opus.
5 ipse ego vos habui faciles in amore ministros,
    cum lusit numeris prima iuventa suis.
idem sacra cano signataque tempora fastis :
    ecquis ad haec illinc crederet esse viam ?
haec mea militia est : ferimus quae possumus arma,
10   dextraque non omni munere nostra vacat.
si mihi non valido torquentur pila lacerto,
    nec bellatoris terga premuntur equi,
nec galea tegimur nec acuto cingimur ense,
    (his habilis teliε quilibet esse potest),
15 at tua prosequimur studioso pectore, Caesar,
    nomina, per titulos ingredimurque tuos.
ergo ades et placido paulum mea munera voltu
    respice, pacando si quid ab hoste vacas.

februa Romani dixere piamina patres :
20   nunc quoque dant verbo plurima signa fidem.
pontifices ab rege petunt et flamine lanas,
    quis veterum lingua februa nomen erat,

    ᵃ Augustus. This passage is probably the original dedi-
cation of the *Fasti*.   ᵇ The *Rex Sacrorum*.
56

BOOK II

JANUARY is over. The year progresses with my song : even as this second month, so may my second book proceed.

³ My elegiacs, now for the first time ye do sail with ampler canvas spread : as I remember, up till now your theme was slender. Myself I found you pliant ministers of love, when in the morn of youth I toyed with verse. Myself now sing of sacred rites and of the seasons marked in the calendar : who could think that this could come of that ? Herein is all my soldiership : I bear the only arms I can : my right hand is not all unserviceable. If I can neither hurl the javelin with brawny arm, nor bestride the back of war horse ; if there is no helmet on my head, no sharp sword at my belt—at such weapons any man may be a master of fence—still do I rehearse with hearty zeal thy titles, Caesar,ᵃ and pursue thy march of glory. Come, then, and if the conquest of the foe leaves thee a vacant hour, O cast a kindly glance upon my gift.

¹⁹ Our Roman fathers gave the name of *februa* to instruments of purification : even to this day there are many proofs that such was the meaning of the word. The pontiffs ask the King ᵇ and the Flamen for woollen cloths, which in the tongue of the ancients had the

quaeque capit lictor domibus purgamina versis
    torrida cum mica farra, vocantur idem;
25 nomen idem ramo, qui caesus ab arbore pura
    casta sacerdotum tempora fronde tegit.
ipse ego flaminicam poscentem februa vidi;
    februa poscenti pinea virga data est.
denique quodcumque est, quo corpora nostra piantur
30   hoc apud intonsos nomen habebat avos.
mensis ab his dictus, secta quia pelle Luperci
    omne solum lustrant idque piamen habent,
aut quia placatis sunt tempora pura sepulcris,
    tunc cum ferales praeteriere dies.
35 omne nefas omnemque mali purgamina causam
    credebant nostri tollere posse senes.
Graecia principium moris dedit: illa nocentis
    impia lustratos ponere facta putat.
Actoriden Peleus, ipsum quoque Pelea Phoci
40   caede per Haemonias solvit Acastus aquas:
vectam frenatis per inane draconibus Aegeus
    credulus inmerita Phasida fovit ope:
Amphiareïades Naupactoo Acheloo
    " solve nefas " dixit, solvit et ille nefas.
45 a ! nimium faciles, qui tristia crimina caedis
    fluminea tolli posse putatis aqua !
sed tamen (antiqui ne nescius ordinis erres)
    primus, ut est, Iani mensis et ante fuit;

---

^a Uncertain: perhaps the pine (28).
^b See below, l. 267.
^c See below, l. 533.
^d Patroclus, grandson of Actor.
^e Medea, named from Phasis, a river of Colchis. She
went to Athens from Corinth in a flying chariot drawn by
dragons.
^f Alcmaeon, who had slain his mother Eriphyle, for

58

name of *februa*. When houses are swept out, the
toasted spelt and salt which the officer gets as means
of cleansing are called by the same name. The same
name is given to the bough, which, cut from a pure
tree,[a] wreaths with its leaves the holy brows of priests.
I myself have seen the Flamen's wife (*Flaminica*)
begging for *februa*; at her request for *februa* a twig
of pine was given her. In short, anything used to
cleanse our bodies went by that name in the time of
our unshorn forefathers. The month is called after
these things, because the Luperci[b] purify the whole
ground with strips of hide, which are their instruments of cleansing, or because the season is pure
after that peace-offerings have been made at the
graves and the days devoted to the dead are past.[c]
Our sires believed that every sin and every cause
of ill could be wiped out by rites of purgation.
Greece set the example: she deems that the
guilty can rid themselves of their crimes by being
purified. Peleus cleansed Actorides,[d] and Acastus
cleansed Peleus himself from the blood of Phocus
by the Haemonian waters. Wafted through the
void by bridled dragons, the Phasian witch[e] received
a welcome, which she little deserved, at the hands of
trusting Aegeus. The son of Amphiaraus[f] said to
Naupactian[g] Achelous, "O rid me of my sin," and
the other did rid him of his sin. Fond fools alack!
to fancy murder's gruesome stain by river water
could be washed away! But yet, lest you should
err through ignorance of the ancient order, know
that the month of Janus was of old the first, even as

accepting the bribe of a necklace to persuade him to attack
Thebes. He was purified by water from the Achelous.
  [g] A mistake: Naupactus was far from the Achelous.

qui sequitur Ianum, veteris fuit ultimus anni :
50   tu quoque sacrorum, Termine, finis eras.
primus enim Iani mensis, quia ianua prima est :
    qui sacer est imis manibus, imus erat.
postmodo creduntur spatio distantia longo
    tempora bis quini continuasse viri.

1. H · K · FEB · N

55 Principio mensis Phrygiae contermina Matri
    Sospita delubris dicitur aucta novis.
nunc ubi sint illis, quaeris, sacrata Kalendis
    templa deae ? longa procubuere die.
cetera ne simili caderent labefacta ruina,
60   cavit sacrati provida cura ducis,
sub quo delubris sentitur nulla senectus ;
    nec satis est homines, obligat ille deos.
templorum positor, templorum sancte repostor,
    sit superis, opto, mutua cura tui !
65 dent tibi caelestes, quos tu caelestibus, annos,
    proque tua maneant in statione domo !
tunc quoque vicini lucus celebratur Helerni,[1]
    qua petit aequoreas advena Thybris aquas.
ad penetrale Numae Capitolinumque Tonantem
70   inque Iovis summa caeditur arce bidens.
saepe graves pluvias adopertus nubibus auster
    concitat, aut posita sub nive terra latet.

[1] Helerni *Heinsius*: averni *AX²Mm²*: asyli *UDm¹*: asili *X¹*.

   [a] Ovid seems to have supposed that in the old Roman year
January was the first month and February the last, so that
they were separated by the " long interval " of ten months ;
but the Decemvirs brought them together by making February
to follow January immediately within the same year instead
of immediately preceding it in the last year.
   [b] Near the mouth of the Tiber.
   [c] The temple of Vesta.

now it is; the month that follows January was the
last of the old year.[a] Thy worship too, O Terminus,
formed the close of all the sacred rites. For the
month of Janus came first because the door (*janua*)
comes first; that month was nethermost which to
the nether shades was consecrated. Afterwards
the Decemvirs are believed to have joined together
times which had been parted by a long interval.

KAL. FEB. 1st

⁵⁵ At the beginning of the month Saviour (*Sospita*)
Juno, the neighbour of the Phrygian Mother Goddess,
is said to have been honoured with new shrines.
If you ask, where are now the temples which on those
Calends were dedicated to the goddess? tumbled
down they are with the long lapse of time. All the
rest had in like sort gone to wrack and ruin, had it
not been for the far-seeing care of our sacred chief,
under whom the shrines feel not the touch of eld;
and not content with doing favours to mankind he
does them to the gods. O saintly soul, who dost
build and rebuild the temples, I pray the powers
above may take such care of thee as thou of them!
May the celestials grant thee the length of years
which thou bestowest on them, and may they stand
on guard before thy house!

⁶⁷ Then, too, the grove of Helernus[b] is thronged with
worshippers, fast by the spot where Tiber, coming
from afar, makes for the ocean waves. At Numa's
sanctuary,[c] at the Thunderer's fane upon the Capitol,
and on the summit of Jove's citadel a sheep is slain.
Often, muffled in clouds, the South Wind brings up
heavy rains, or under fallen snow the earth is hid.

OVID

2. AN   3. BN

Proximus Hesperias Titan abiturus in undas
    gemmea purpureis cum iuga demet equis,
75 illa nocte aliquis tollens ad sidera voltum
    dicet " ubi est hodie quae Lyra fulsit heri ? "
dumque Lyram quaeret, medii quoque terga Leonis
    in liquidas subito mersa notabit aquas.

4. CN

Quem modo caelatum stellis Delphina videbas,
80   is fugiet visus nocte sequente tuos :
seu fuit occultis felix in amoribus index,
    Lesbida cum domino seu tulit ille lyram.
quod mare non novit, quae nescit Ariona tellus ?
    carmine currentes ille tenebat aquas.
85 saepe sequens agnam lupus est a voce retentus,
    saepe avidum fugiens restitit agna lupum ;
saepe canes leporesque umbra iacuere sub una,
    et stetit in saxo proxima cerva leae,
et sine lite loquax cum Palladis alite cornix
90   sedit, et accipitri iuncta columba fuit.
Cynthia saepe tuis fertur, vocalis Arion,
    tamquam fraternis obstipuisse modis.
nomen Arionium Siculas impleverat urbes,
    captaque erat lyricis Ausonis ora sonis ;
95 inde domum repetens puppem conscendit Arion,
    atque ita quaesitas arte ferebat opes.
forsitan, infelix, ventos undasque timebas,
    at tibi nave tua tutius aequor erat.

---

[a] See i. 653 note.
[b] The story is told by Herodotus, i. 24.
[c] The owl.   [d] Diana.

IV. Non. 2nd

⁷³ When the next sun, before he sinks into the
western waves, shall from his purple steeds undo
the jewelled yoke, someone that night, looking up
at the stars, shall say, " Where is to-day the Lyre ᵃ
which yesterday shone bright ? " And while he
seeks the Lyre, he will mark that the back of the
Lion also has of a sudden plunged into the watery
waste.

III. Non. 3rd

⁷⁹ The Dolphin, which of late thou didst see
fretted with stars, will on the next night escape thy
gaze. (He was raised to heaven) either because he
was a lucky go-between in love's intrigues, or because
he carried the Lesbian lyre and the lyre's master.
What sea, what land knows not Arion ? ᵇ By his song
he used to stay the running waters. Often at his
voice the wolf in pursuit of the lamb stood still, often
the lamb halted in fleeing from the ravening wolf;
often hounds and hares have couched in the same
covert, and the hind upon the rock has stood beside
the lioness : at peace the chattering crow has sat
with Pallas' bird,ᶜ and the dove has been neighbour
to the hawk. 'Tis said that Cynthia ᵈ oft hath stood
entranced, tuneful Arion, at thy notes, as if the notes
had been struck by her brother's hand. Arion's
fame had filled Sicilian cities, and by the music of
his lyre he had charmed the Ausonian land. Thence
wending homewards, he took ship and carried
with him the wealth his art had won. Perhaps,
poor wretch, thou didst dread the winds and
waves, but in sooth the sea was safer for thee than

OVID

namque gubernator destricto constitit ense
100 ceteraque armata conscia turba manu.
quid tibi cum gladio? dubiam rege, navita, puppem:
non haec sunt digitis arma tenenda tuis.
ille, metu pavidus, " mortem non deprecor " inquit,
" sed liceat sumpta pauca referre lyra."
105 dant veniam ridentque moram. capit ille coronam,
quae possit crines, Phoebe, decere tuos;
induerat Tyrio bis tinctam murice pallam:
reddidit icta suos pollice chorda sonos,
flebilibus numeris veluti canentia dura
110 traiectus penna tempora cantat olor.
protinus in medias ornatus desilit undas:
spargitur impulsa caerula puppis aqua.
inde (fide maius) tergo delphina recurvo
se memorant oneri supposuisse novo;
115 ille sedens citharamque tenet pretiumque vehendi
cantat et aequoreas carmine mulcet aquas.
di pia facta vident: astris delphina recepit
Iuppiter et stellas iussit habere novem.

5. D NON

Nunc mihi mille sonos, quoque est memoratus Achilles,
120 vellem, Maeonide, pectus inesse tuum,
dum canimus sacras alterno pectine Nonas:
maximus hic fastis accumulatur honos.
deficit ingenium, maioraque viribus urgent:
haec mihi praecipuo est ore canenda dies.
125 quid volui demens elegis imponere tantum
ponderis? heroi res erat ista pedis.
sancte pater patriae, tibi plebs, tibi curia nomen

---

^a Homer: an epithet applied to him as, according to some
writers, he was born in Maeonia, the ancient name for a
portion of Lydia. ^b Augustus.

64

thy ship. For the helmsman took his stand with a drawn sword, and the rest of the conspiring gang had weapons in their hands. What wouldst thou with a sword? Steer the crazy bark, thou mariner; these weapons ill befit thy hands. Quaking with fear the bard, " I deprecate not death," said he, " but let me take my lyre and play a little." They gave him leave and laughed at the delay. He took the crown that might well, Phoebus, become thy locks; he donned his robe twice dipped in Tyrian purple: touched by his thumb, the strings gave back a music all their own, such notes as the swan chants in mournful numbers when the cruel shaft has pierced his snowy brow. Straightway, with all his finery on, he leaped plump down into the waves: the refluent water splashed the azure poop. Thereupon they say (it sounds past credence) a dolphin did submit his arched back to the unusual weight; seated there Arion grasped his lyre and paid his fare in song, and with his chant he charmed the ocean waves. The gods see pious deeds: Jupiter received the dolphin among the constellations, and bade him have nine stars.

Non. 5th

129 Now could I wish for a thousand tongues and for that soul of thine, Maeonides,[a] which glorified Achilles, while I sing in distiches the sacred Nones. This is the greatest honour that is heaped upon the calendar. My genius faints; the burden is beyond my strength: this day above all others is to be sung by me. Fool that I was, how durst I lay so great a weight on elegiac verse? the theme was one for the heroic stanza. Holy Father of thy Country,[b] this

D

hoc dedit, hoc dedimus nos tibi nomen, eques.
res tamen ante dedit.   sero quoque vera tulisti
130   nomina, iam pridem tu pater orbis eras.
hoc tu per terras, quod in aethere Iuppiter alto,
   nomen habes : hominum tu pater, ille deum.
Romule, concedes : facit hic tua magna tuendo
   moenia, tu dederas transilienda Remo.
135 te Tatius parvique Cures Caeninaque sensit :
   hoc duce Romanum est solis utrumque latus.
tu breve nescio quid victae telluris habebas :
   quodcumque est alto sub Iove, Caesar habet.
tu rapis, hic castas duce se iubet esse maritas :
140   tu recipis luco, reppulit ille nefas.
vis tibi grata fuit, florent sub Caesare leges.
   tu domini nomen, principis ille tenet.
te Remus incusat, veniam dedit hostibus ille.
   caelestem fecit te pater, ille patrem.
145 iam puer Idaeus media tenus eminet alvo
   et liquidas mixto nectare fundit aquas.
en etiam, siquis Borean horrere solebat,
   gaudeat : a Zephyris mollior aura venit.

6. EN   7. FN   8. GN   9. HN   10. AN

Quintus ab aequoreis nitidum iubar extulit undis
150   Lucifer, et primi tempora veris erunt.

---

[a] See *Monumentum Ancyranum*, vi. 35, in L.C.L. Velleius
Paterculus, p. 401.
[b] Tatius was king and Cures capital of the Sabines :
Caenina, a city of Latium associated with them.
[c] Augustus encouraged marriage by legislation.
[d] Augustus rejected the title *dominus*, " master of slaves,"
see Suetonius, *Aug.* 53. 1, preferring that of *princeps*,
"foremost " or " chief."   There is no proof that Romulus
was ever called *dominus*.
[e] Ganymede, popularly identified with Aquarius.   The

title hath been conferred on thee by the people, by the senate, and by us, the knights.[a] But history had already conferred it ; yet didst thou also receive, though late, thy title true ; long time hadst thou been the Father of the World. Thou bearest on earth the name which Jupiter bears in high heaven : of men thou art the father, he of the gods. Romulus, thou must yield pride of place. Caesar by his guardian care makes great thy city walls ; the walls thou gavest to the city were such as Remus could o'erleap. Thy power was felt by Tatius,[b] the little Cures, and Caenina ; under Caesar's leadership whate'er the sun beholds on either side is Roman. Thou didst own a little stretch of conquered land : all that exists beneath the canopy of Jove is Caesar's own. Thou didst rape wives : Caesar bade them under his rule be chaste.[c] Thou didst admit the guilty to thy grove : he hath repelled the wrong. Thine was a rule of force : under Caesar it is the laws that reign. Thou didst the name of master bear[d] : he bears the name of prince. Thou hast an accuser in thy brother Remus : Caesar pardoned foemen. To heaven thy father raised thee : to heaven Caesar raised his sire.

[145] Already the Idaean boy[e] shows himself down to the waist, and pours a stream of water mixed with nectar. Now joy too, ye who shrink from the north wind ; from out the west a softer gale doth blow.

V. Id. 9th

[149] When five days later the Morning Star has lifted up its radiance bright from out the ocean waves, then is the time that spring begins. But yet be true morning rising was then on January 22, the apparent rising on February 22.

ne fallare tamen, restant tibi frigora, restant,
   magnaque discedens signa reliquit hiems.

11. BN   12. CN

Tertia nox veniat : Custodem protinus Ursae
   aspicies geminos exeruisse pedes.
155 inter Hamadryadas iaculatricemque Dianam
   Callisto sacri pars fuit una chori.
illa deae tangens arcus " quos tangimus arcus,
   este meae testes virginitatis " ait.
Cynthia laudavit, " promissa " que " foedera serva,
160   et comitum princeps tu mihi " dixit " eris."
foedera servasset, si non formosa fuisset :
   cavit mortales, de Iove crimen habet.
mille feras Phoebe silvis venata redibat
   aut plus aut medium sole tenente diem.
165 ut tetigit lucum (densa niger ilice lucus,
   in medio gelidae fons erat altus aquae),
" hic " ait " in silva, virgo Tegeaea, lavemur ! "
   erubuit falso virginis illa sono.
dixerat et nymphis : nymphae velamina ponunt,
170   hanc pudet et tardae dat mala signa morae.
exuerat tunicas ; uteri manifesta tumore
   proditur indicio ponderis ipsa suo.
cui dea " virgineos, periura Lycaoni, coetus
   desere nec castas pollue " dixit " aquas."

---

   [a] Arctophylax, also called Boötes.
   [b] Called also here Cynthia and Phoebe, in Ovid's allusive
way.
   [c] See *Metam.* ii. 409-507.

not deceived, cold days are still in store for thee,
indeed they are : departing winter leaves behind
great tokens of himself.

III. Id. 11th

[153] Come the third night, thou shalt straightway
remark that the Bear-Ward [a] has thrust forth both
his feet. Among the Hamadryads in the train
of the archeress Diana [b] one of the sacred band
was Callisto.[c] Laying her hand on the bow of the
goddess, " Thou bow," quoth she, " which thus I
touch, bear witness to my virginity." Cynthia
approved the vow, and said, " Keep but thy
plighted troth and thou shalt be the foremost of my
company." Her troth she would have kept if she
had not been fair. With mortals she was on her
guard ; it was with Jove she sinned. Of wild beasts
in the forest Phoebe had chased full many a score,
and home she was returning at noon or after noon.
No sooner had she reached the grove—the grove
where the thick holm-oaks cast a gloom and in the
midst a deep fountain of cool water rose—than the
goddess spake : " Here in the wood," quoth she,
" let's bathe, thou maid of Arcady." At the false
name of maid the other blushed. The goddess
spoke to the nymphs as well, and they put off
their robes. Callisto was ashamed and bashfully
delayed. But when she doffed her tunic, too plainly,
self-convicted, her big belly betrayed the weight
she bore. To whom the goddess spake : " Daughter
of Lycaon forsworn, forsake the company of maids and
defile not the pure waters." Ten times the horned

175 luna novum decies implerat cornibus orbem :
    quae fuerat virgo credita, mater erat.
laesa furit Iuno, formam mutatque puellae.
    quid facis ? invito est pectore passa Iovem.
utque ferae vidit turpes in paelice voltus,
180   " huius in amplexus Iuppiter " inquit " eat ! "
ursa per incultos errabat squalida montes,
    quae fuerat summo nuper amata Iovi.
iam tria lustra puer furto conceptus agebat,
    cum mater nato est obvia facto suo.
185 illa quidem, tamquam cognosceret, adstitit amens
    et gemuit : gemitus verba parentis erant.
hanc puer ignarus iaculo fixisset acuto,
    ni foret in superas raptus uterque domos.
signa propinqua micant : prior est, quam dicimus
        Arcton,
190   Arctophylax formam terga sequentis habet.
saevit adhuc canamque rogat Saturnia Tethyn,
    Maenaliam tactis ne lavet Arcton aquis.

13. D EID · N͞P

Idibus agrestis fumant altaria Fauni
    hic, ubi discretas insula rumpit aquas.
195 haec fuit illa dies, in qua Veientibus armis
    ter centum Fabii ter cecidere duo.
una domus vires et onus susceperat urbis :
    sumunt gentiles arma professa manus.
egreditur castris miles generosus ab isdem,
200   e quis dux fieri quilibet aptus erat.

---

    a In northern latitudes the Bear never sets.
    b The island of the Tiber.
    c The family of the Fabii offered to carry on the war against
Veii alone. Three hundred and six went forth through the

moon had filled her orb afresh, when she who had
been thought a maid was proved a mother. The
injured Juno raged and changed the damsel's shape.
Why so ? Against her will Jove ravished her. And
when in the leman she beheld the ugly features of
the brute, quoth Juno, " Let Jupiter now court her
embraces." But she, who of late had been beloved
by highest Jove, now roamed, a shaggy she-bear,
the mountains wild. The child she had conceived in
sin was now in his third lustre when his mother met
him. She indeed, as if she knew him, stood distraught
and growled ; a growl was all the mother's speech.
Her the stripling with his sharp javelin would have
pierced, but that they both were caught up into the
mansions on high. As constellations they sparkle
beside each other. First comes what we call the
Bear ; the Bear-Ward seems to follow at her back.
Still Saturn's daughter frets and begs grey Tethys
never to touch and wash with her waters the Bear
of Maenalus.[a]

Idus. 13th

[193] On the Ides the altars of rustic Faunus smoke,
there where the island[b] breaks the parted waters.
This was the day on which thrice a hundred and thrice
two Fabii fell by Veientine arms.[c] A single house
had undertaken the defence and burden of the city :
the right hands of a single clan proffered and drew
their swords. From the same camp a noble soldiery
marched forth, of whom any one was fit to be a

Carmental gate, and built a fort by the Cremera, which they
held for two years. But in 477 b.c. they were all destroyed
by an ambush. See Livy ii. 48-50.

Carmentis portae dextro[1] est via proxima Iano :
    ire per hanc noli, quisquis es ; omen habet.
illa fama refert Fabios exisse trecentos :
    porta vacat culpa, sed tamen omen habet.
205 ut celeri passu Cremeram tetigere rapacem
    (turbidus hibernis ille fluebat aquis),
castra loco ponunt : destrictis ensibus ipsi
    Tyrrhenum valido Marte per agmen eunt,
non aliter quam cum Libyca de gente leones
210   invadunt sparsos lata per arva greges.
diffugiunt hostes inhonestaque volnera tergo
    accipiunt : Tusco sanguine terra rubet.
sic iterum, sic saepe cadunt. ubi vincere aperte
    non datur, insidias armaque tecta parant.
215 campus erat, campi claudebant ultima colles
    silvaque montanas occulere apta feras.
in medio paucos armentaque rara relinquunt,
    cetera virgultis abdita turba latet.
ecce velut torrens undis pluvialibus auctus
220   aut nive, quae Zephyro victa tepente fluit,
per sata perque vias fertur nec, ut ante solebat,
    riparum clausas margine finit aquas :
sic Fabii vallem latis discursibus implent,
    quodque vident, sternunt, nec metus alter inest.
225 quo ruitis, generosa domus ? male creditis hosti :
    simplex nobilitas, perfida tela cave !
fraude perit virtus : in apertos undique campos
    prosiliunt hostes et latus omne tenent.
quid faciant pauci contra tot milia fortes ?
230   quidve, quod in misero tempore restet, habent ?

---

[1] dextro X^1m^1: dextra $A(corrected) U Mm^2$.

---

^a The right-hand arch of the Porta Carmentalis, next to
the temple of Janus, was unlucky.

leader. The nearest way is by the right-hand arch of Carmentis' gate : [a] go not that way, whoe'er thou art: 'tis ominous. By it, the rumour runs, the three hundred Fabii went forth. No blame attaches to the gate, but still 'tis ominous. When at quick pace they reached the rushing Cremera [b] (it flowed turbid with winter rain) they pitched their camp on the spot, and with drawn swords broke through the Tyrrhenian array right valiantly, even as lions of the Libyan breed attack herds scattered through spacious fields. The foemen flee dispersed, stabbed in the back with wounds dishonourable : with Tuscan blood the earth is red. So yet again, so oft they fall. When open victory was denied them, they set an ambush of armed men in wait. A plain there was, bounded by hills and forest, where the mountain beasts could find commodious lair. In the midst the foe left a few of their number and some scattered herds : the rest of the host lurked hidden in the thickets. Lo, as a torrent, swollen by rain or snow which the warm West Wind has melted, sweeps across the cornfields, across the roads, nor keeps its waters pent within the wonted limit of its banks, so the Fabii rushed here and there broadcast about the vale ; all that they saw they felled ; no other fear they knew. Whither away, ye scions of an illustrious house ? 'Tis ill to trust the foe. O noble hearts and simple, beware of treacherous blades ! By fraud is valour vanquished : from every hand the foe leaps forth into the open plain, and every side they hold. What can a handful of the brave do against so many thousands ? Or where can they look for help in such extremity ? As a

[b] A stream near Veii.

sicut aper longe silvis Laurentibus actus
    fulmineo celeres dissipat ore canes,
mox tamen ipse perit, sic non moriuntur inulti
    volneraque alterna dantque feruntque manu.
235 una dies Fabios ad bellum miserat omnes :
    ad bellum missos perdidit una dies.
ut tamen Herculeae superessent semina gentis,
    credibile est ipsos consuluisse deos ;
nam puer impubes et adhuc non utilis armis
240   unus de Fabia gente relictus erat,
scilicet ut posses olim tu, Maxime, nasci,
    cui res cunctando restituenda foret.

14. EN

Continuata loco tria sidera, Corvus et Anguis
    et medius Crater inter utrumque iacet.
245 Idibus illa latent, oriuntur nocte sequenti.
    quae tibi cur tria sint tam sociata, canam.
forte Iovi Phoebus festum sollemne parabat
    (non faciet longas fabula nostra moras) :
' i, mea " dixit " avis, ne quid pia sacra moretur,
250   et tenuem vivis fontibus adfer aquam."
corvus inauratum pedibus cratera recurvis
    tollit et aërium pervolat altus iter.
stabat adhuc duris ficus densissima pomis :
    temptat eam rostro ; non erat apta legi.
255 inmemor imperii sedisse sub arbore fertur,
    dum fierent tarda dulcia poma mora.
iamque satur nigris longum rapit unguibus hydrum
    ad dominumque redit fictaque verba refert :

---

^a The Fabii claimed descent from Hercules and Evander.
^b Q. Fabius Maximus Cunctator.
^c The astronomical lore is incorrect.

boar, hunted afar from the Laurentine woods, scatters the swift hounds with thunderous snout, but soon himself is slain, so do they die not unavenged, giving and taking wounds alternately. One day sent forth to war the Fabii all: one day undid all that were sent to war. Yet may we believe that the gods themselves took thought to save the seed of the Herculean^a house; for a boy under age, too young to bear arms, was left alone of all the Fabian clan, to the end, no doubt, that thou, Maximus,^b mightest one day be born to save the commonwealth by biding time.

XVI. KAL. MART. 14th

²⁴³ Three constellations are grouped together—the Raven, the Snake, and the Bowl, which lies midway between the other two. On the Ides they are invisible: they rise the following night.^c Why the three are so closely linked together, I will tell to thee in verse. It chanced that Phoebus was preparing a solemn feast for Jupiter : my tale shall not waste time. "Go, my bird," said Phoebus, " that naught may delay the pious rites, and bring a little water from running springs." The raven caught up a gilded bowl in his hooked claws and flew aloft on his airy journey. A fig-tree stood loaded with fruit still unripe : the raven tried it with his beak, but it was not fit to gather. Unmindful of his orders he perched, 'tis said, under the tree to wait till the fruit should sweeten lingeringly. And when at last he ate his fill, he snatched a long watersnake in his black talons, and returning to his master brought back a lying tale : " This snake

75

" hic mihi causa morae, vivarum obsessor aquarum :
260   hic tenuit fontes officiumque meum."
" addis " ait " culpae mendacia," Phoebus " et audes
    fatidicum verbis fallere velle deum ?
at tibi, dum lactens haerebit in arbore ficus,
    de nullo gelidae fonte bibentur aquae."
265 dixit, et antiqui monumenta perennia facti,
    Anguis, Avis, Crater sidera iuncta micant.

15. F LVPER · NP

Tertia post Idus nudos aurora Lupercos
    aspicit, et Fauni sacra bicornis eunt.
dicite, Pierides, sacrorum quae sit origo,
270   attigerint Latias unde petita domos.
Pana deum pecoris veteres coluisse feruntur
    Arcades : Arcadiis plurimus ille iugis.
testis erit Pholoë, testes Stymphalides undae,
    quique citis Ladon in mare currit aquis,
275 cinctaque pinetis nemoris iuga Nonacrini,
    altaque Cyllene[1] Parrhasiaeque nives.
Pan erat armenti, Pan illic numen equarum ;
    munus ob incolumes ille ferebat oves.
transtulit Evander silvestria numina secum ;
280   hic, ubi nunc urbs est, tum locus urbis erat.
inde deum colimus, devectaque sacra Pelasgis

---

[1] cyllene m^1 : cillene X^1 : troezenae $A U m^2$: troezene X^2 :
troezeniae D : troezeniae M^1 : traicene M^2 : Tricrene *Merkel*[1]
(*conjecture*).

---

        [a] Here identified with Faunus.
    [b] A mountain in Arcadia, source of the river Ladon.
        [c] A lake in Arcadia.
      [d] Nonacris, a town of Arcadia.
       [e] A mountain in Arcadia.

was the cause of my delay : he blocked the living water : he kept the spring from flowing and me from doing my duty." "You aggravate your fault," quoth Phoebus, "by your lies, and dare attempt to cheat the god of prophecy by fibs ? But as for you, you shall drink cool water from no spring until the figs upon the tree grow juicy." He spake, and for a perpetual memorial of this ancient incident the constellations of the Snake, the Bird, and the Bowl now sparkle side by side.

XV. Kal. 15th

²⁶⁷ The third morn after the Ides beholds the naked Luperci, and then, too, come the rites of two-horned Faunus. Declare, Pierian Muses, the origin of the rites, and from what quarter they were fetched and reached our Latin homes. The Arcadians of old are said to have worshipped Pan,ᵃ the god of cattle, him who haunts the Arcadian ridges. Witness Mount Pholoe,ᵇ witness the Stymphalian waters,ᶜ and the Ladon that seaward runs with rapid current : witness the ridges of the Nonacrineᵈ grove begirt with pinewoods : witness high Cylleneᵉ and the Parrhasian snows. There Pan was the deity of herds, and there, too, of mares; he received gifts for keeping safe the sheep. Evander brought with him across the sea his woodland deities ; where now the city stands, there was then naught but the city's site. Hence we worship the god, and the Flamen Dialis still performs in the olden way the ritesᶠ

ᶠ The Lupercalia. See Appendix, p. 389.

77

OVID

flamen adhuc prisco more Dialis obit.[1]
cur igitur currant, et cur (sic currere mos est)
  nuda ferant posita corpora veste, rogas ?
285 ipse deus velox discurrere gaudet in altis
  montibus et subitas concipit ipse fugas;
ipse deus nudus nudos iubet ire ministros,
  nec satis ad cursus commoda vestis erat.
ante Iovem genitum terras habuisse feruntur
290   Arcades, et luna gens prior illa fuit.
vita feris similis, nullos agitata per usus :
  artis adhuc expers et rude volgus erat.
pro domibus frondes norant, pro frugibus herbas,
  nectar erat palmis hausta duabus aqua.
295 nullus anhelabat sub adunco vomere taurus,
  nulla sub imperio terra colentis erat :
nullus adhuc erat usus equi, se quisque ferebat :
  ibat ovis lana corpus amicta sua.
sub Iove durabant et corpora nuda gerebant
300   docta graves imbres et tolerare Notos.
nunc quoque detecti referunt monumenta vetusti
  moris et antiquas testificantur opes.
sed cur praecipue fugiat velamina Faunus,
  traditur antiqui fabula plena ioci.
305 forte comes dominae iuvenis Tirynthius ibat :
  vidit ab excelso Faunus utrumque iugo.
vidit et incaluit, " montana " que " numina," dixit
  " nil mihi vobiscum est : hic meus ardor erit."

  [1] adhuc *three* ऽ : ad haec $AUDX^1M^1m^2$: ab hoc M^2m^1ऽ.
obit *Bentley, Madvig* (Adversaria ii. 106, *reading* adhuc *for*
ad haec): erit A(corrected)DM^2: erat UXM^1m: eat *or*
adit *Heinsius* : agit *Burman. The usual reading* ad haec
. . . erat (*or* erit) *yields no adequate sense.* OBIT *for* ERIT
is an easy and probable correction.

brought hither by the Pelasgians.[a] You ask,
Why then do the Luperci run ? and why do they
strip themselves and bear their bodies naked, for so
it is their wont to run ? The god himself loves to
scamper, fleet of foot, about the high mountains,
and he himself takes suddenly to flight. The god
himself is nude and bids his ministers go nude :
besides, raiment sorted not well with running. The
Arcadians are said to have possessed their land before
the birth of Jove, and that folk is older than the
moon.[b] Their life was like that of beasts, unprofit-
ably spent ; artless as yet and raw was the common
herd. Leaves did they use for houses, herbs for
corn : water scooped up in two hollows of the hands
to them was nectar. No bull panted under the
weight of the bent ploughshare : no land was under
the dominion of the husbandman : there was as yet
no use for horses, every man carried his own weight :
the sheep went clothed in its own wool. Under the
open sky they lived and went about naked, inured
to heavy showers and rainy winds. Even to this
day the unclad ministers recall the memory of the
olden custom and attest what comforts the ancients
knew.

[303] But to explain why Faunus should particularly
eschew the use of drapery a merry tale is handed
down from days of old. As chance would have it,
the Tirynthian youth was walking in the company of
his mistress[c] ; Faunus saw them both from a high ridge.
He saw and burned. " Ye mountain elves," quoth
he, " I'm done with you. Yon shall be my true flame."

---

[a] Evander, as an Arcadian, for the Arcadians were said to
be Pelasgians.   [b] They were called προσέληνοι.
[c] Hercules and Omphale, a princess of Lydia (Maeonia).

OVID

ibat odoratis humeros perfusa capillis
310   Maeonis aurato conspicienda sinu :
aurea pellebant tepidos umbracula soles,
  quae tamen Herculeae sustinuere manus.
iam Bacchi nemus et Tmoli vineta tenebat,
  Hesperos et fusco roscidus ibat equo.
315 antra subit tofis laqueata et pumice vivo ;
  garrulus in primo limine rivus erat.
dumque parant epulas potandaque vina ministri,
  cultibus Alciden instruit illa suis.
dat tenuis tunicas Gaetulo murice tinctas,
320   dat teretem zonam, qua modo cincta fuit.
ventre minor zona est ; tunicarum vincla relaxat,
  ut posset magnas exeruisse manus.
fregerat armillas non illa ad brachia factas,
  scindebant magni vincula parva pedes.
325 ipsa capit clavamque gravem spoliumque leonis
  conditaque in pharetra tela minora sua.
sic epulis functi sic dant sua corpora somno,
  et positis iuxta secubuere toris ;
causa, repertori vitis quia sacra parabant,
330   quae facerent pure, cum foret orta dies.
noctis erat medium.   quid non amor improbus audet ?
  roscida per tenebras Faunus ad antra venit,
utque videt comites somno vinoque solutos,
  spem capit in dominis esse soporis idem.
335 intrat, et huc illuc temerarius errat adulter
  et praefert cautas subsequiturque manus.
venerat ad strati captata cubilia lecti

---

a A mountain in Lydia.
b Made of the *murex* dye, for which the north African
coast was famous.

As the Maeonian damsel tripped along, her scented locks streamed down her shoulders; her bosom shone resplendent with golden braid. A golden parasol kept off the sun's warm beams; and yet it was the hands of Hercules that bore it up. Now had she reached the grove of Bacchus and the vineyards of Tmolus,[a] and dewy Hesperus rode on his dusky steed. She passed within a cave, whereof the fretted roof was all of tufa and of living rock, and at the mouth there ran a babbling brook. While the attendants were making ready the viands and the wine for the wassail, she arrayed Alcides in her own garb. She gave him gauzy tunics in Gaetulian purple[b] dipped; she gave him the dainty girdle, which but now had girt her waist. For his belly the girdle was too small; he undid the clasps of the tunics to thrust out his big hands. The bracelets he had broken, not made to fit those arms; his big feet split the little shoes. She herself took the heavy club, the lion's skin, and the lesser weapons stored in their quiver. In such array they feasted, in such array they resigned themselves to slumber, and lay down apart on beds set side by side; the reason was that they were preparing to celebrate in all purity, when day should dawn, a festival in honour of the discoverer of the vine. 'Twas midnight. What durst not wanton love essay? Through the gloom came Faunus to the dewy cave, and when he saw the attendants in drunken slumber sunk, he conceived a hope that their masters might be as sound asleep. He entered and, rash lecher, he wandered to and fro; with hands outstretched before him he felt his cautious way. At last he reached by groping the beds, where they were spread, and at

et felix prima sorte futurus erat.
ut tetigit fulvi saetis hirsuta leonis
340 vellera, pertimuit sustinuitque manum
attonitusque metu rediit, ut saepe viator
turbatus viso rettulit angue pedem.
inde tori, qui iunctus erat, velamina tangit
mollia, mendaci decipiturque nota.
345 ascendit spondaque sibi propiore recumbit,
et tumidum cornu durius inguen erat.
interea tunicas ora subducit ab ima :
horrebant densis aspera crura pilis.
cetera temptantem subito Tirynthius heros
350 reppulit : e summo decidit ille toro.
fit sonus, inclamat comites et lumina poscit
Maeonis : inlatis ignibus acta patent.
ille gemit lecto graviter deiectus ab alto,
membraque de dura vix sua tollit humo.
355 ridet et Alcides et qui videre iacentem,
ridet amatorem Lyda puella suum.
veste deus lusus fallentes lumina vestes
non amat et nudos ad sua sacra vocat.
adde peregrinis causas, mea Musa, Latinas,
360 inque suo noster pulvere currat equus.
cornipedi Fauno caesa de more capella
venit ad exiguas turba vocata dapes.
dumque sacerdotes veribus transuta salignis
exta parant, medias sole tenente vias,
365 Romulus et frater pastoralisque iuventus
solibus et campo corpora nuda dabant ;
caestibus et iaculis et misso pondere saxi
brachia per lusus experienda dabant :
pastor ab excelso " per devia rura iuvencos,
370 Romule, praedones, et Reme," dixit " agunt."

---

^a Hercules and Lydian Omphale.   See ll. 305, 310.

his first venture fortune smiled on him. When he touched the skin, all shagged with bristles, of the tawny lion, he was terrified, and stayed his hand, and thunderstruck recoiled, as oft at sight of a snake a wayfarer starts back dismayed. Next he touched the soft drapery of the neighbouring couch, and its deceptive touch beguiled him. He mounted and laid him down on the nearer side. . . . There he encountered legs that bristled with thick rough hair. When he would have proceeded further, the Tirynthian [a] hero thrust him away of a sudden, and down he fell from the top of the bed. There was a crash. The Maeonian damsel called for her attendants and demanded a light : torches were brought in, and the murder was out. After his heavy fall from the high couch Faunus groaned and scarce could lift his limbs from the hard ground. Alcides laughed, and so did all who saw him lying ; the Lydian wench laughed also at her lover. Thus betrayed by vesture, the god loves not garments which deceive the eye, and he bids his worshippers come naked to his rites.

359 To foreign reasons add, my Muse, some Latin ones, and let my steed career in his own dusty course. A she-goat had been sacrificed as usual to hoof-footed Faunus, and a crowd had come by invitation to partake of the scanty repast. While the priests were dressing the inwards, stuck on willow spits, the sun then riding in mid heaven, Romulus and his brother and the shepherd youth were exercising their naked bodies in the sunshine on the plain ; they tried in sport the strength of their arms by the gloves and javelins and by hurling ponderous stones. Cried a shepherd from a height, " O Romulus and Remus, robbers are driving off the bullocks across the

longum erat armari : diversis exit uterque
   partibus ; occursu praeda recepta Remi.
ut rediit, veribus stridentia detrahit exta
   atque ait " haec certe non nisi victor edet."
375 dicta facit Fabiique simul.   venit inritus illuc
   Romulus et mensas ossaque nuda videt ;
risit et indoluit Fabios potuisse Remumque
   vincere, Quintilios non potuisse suos.
fama manet facti : posito velamine currunt,
380   et memorem famam, quod bene cessit, habet.
forsitan et quaeras, cur sit locus ille Lupercal,
   quaeve diem tali nomine causa notet.
Silvia Vestalis caelestia semina partu
   ediderat patruo regna tenente suo.
385 is iubet auferri parvos et in amne necari :
   quid facis ?   ex istis Romulus alter erit.
iussa recusantes peragunt lacrimosa ministri,
   flent tamen et geminos in loca iussa ferunt.
Albula, quem Tiberim mersus Tiberinus in undis
390   reddidit, hibernis forte tumebat aquis :
hic, ubi nunc fora sunt, lintres errare videres,
   quaque iacent valles, Maxime Circe, tuae.
huc ubi venerunt (neque enim procedere possunt
   longius), ex illis unus et alter ait :
395 " at quam sunt similes ! at quam formosus uterque !
   plus tamen ex illis iste vigoris habet.
si genus arguitur voltu, nisi fallit imago,
   nescio quem in vobis suspicor esse deum—

---

   [a] Ovid is endeavouring to explain the foundations of the
two colleges of Luperci, the Fabii or Fabiani, and the Quintilii
or Quintiliales.
   [b] A cave on the E. of the Palatine, said to have been the
she-wolf's den.   [c] See iv. 47.

pathless lands." To arm would have been tedious ;
out went the brothers both in opposite directions ;
but 'twas Remus who fell in with the freebooters
and brought the booty back. On his return he drew
the hissing inwards from the spits and said, " None
but the victor surely shall eat these." He did as he
had said, he and the Fabii together. Thither came
Romulus foiled, and saw the empty tables and bare
bones. He laughed, and grieved that Remus and the
Fabii could have conquered when his own Quintilii
could not. The fame of the deed endures : they run
stripped, and the success of that day enjoys a lasting
fame.[a]

381 Perhaps you may also ask why that place [b] is called
the Lupercal, and what is the reason for denoting
the day by such a name. Silvia, a Vestal, had given
birth to heavenly babes, what time her uncle sat
upon the throne. He ordered the infant boys to
be carried away and drowned in the river. Rash
man ! one of those babes will yet be Romulus.
Reluctantly his servants carry out the mournful
orders. Yet they weep as they bear the twins to the
place appointed. It chanced that the Albula, which
took the name of Tiber from Tiberinus,[c] drowned
in its waves, was swollen with winter rain : where
now the forums [d] are, and where the valley of the
Circus Maximus lies, you might see boats floating
about. Hither when they were come, for farther
they could not go, one or other of them said : " But
how like they are ! how beautiful is each ! Yet of
the two this one has more vigour. If lineage may
be inferred from features, unless appearances deceive
me, I fancy that some god is in you—but if some god

[d] Forum Romanum and Forum Boarium.

at si quis vestrae deus esset originis auctor,
400   in tam praecipiti tempore ferret opem ;
    ferret opem certe, si non ope mater egeret,
      quae facta est uno mater et orba die.
    nata simul, moritura simul, simul ite sub undas
      corpora ! " desierat deposuitque sinu.
405 vagierunt ambo pariter : sensisse putares.
      hi redeunt udis in sua tecta genis.
    sustinet impositos summa cavus alveus unda :
      heu quantum fati parva tabella tulit !
    alveus in limo silvis adpulsus opacis
410   paulatim fluvio deficiente sedet.
    arbor erat : remanent vestigia, quaeque vocatur
      Rumina nunc ficus, Romula ficus erat.
    venit ad expositos (mirum !) lupa feta gemellos :
      quis credat pueris non nocuisse feram ?
415 non nocuisse parum est, prodest quoque : quos lupa
      nutrit,
      perdere cognatae sustinuere manus.
    constitit et cauda teneris blanditur alumnis
      et fingit lingua corpora bina sua.
    Marte satos scires : timor afuit, ubera ducunt
420   nec sibi promissi lactis aluntur ope.
    illa loco nomen fecit, locus ipse Lupercis.
      magna dati nutrix praemia lactis habet.
    quid vetat Arcadio dictos a monte Lupercos ?
      Faunus in Arcadia templa Lycaeus habet.
425 nupta, quid expectas ? non tu pollentibus herbis

---

    a Rumina or Ruminalis, from *ruma* or *rumis*, a " dug."
    b He now suggests a Greek derivation, on the supposition
that the Lupercalia had been brought from Arcadia. The
mountain is Mt. Lycaeus, where was a sanctuary of Pan,
whom he identifies with Faunus.

were indeed the author of your being, he would come
to your rescue in so perilous an hour ; surely he
would come to the rescue, unless the mother needed
his help, she who has borne and lost her children in
a single day. Ye bodies, born together to die
together, together pass beneath the waves ! " He
ended, and from his bosom he laid down the twins.
Both squalled alike : you would fancy they understood. With wet cheeks the bearers wended their
homeward way. The hollow ark in which the babes
were laid supported them on the surface of the
water : ah me ! how big a fate the little plank
upbore ! The ark drifted towards a shady wood,
and, as the water gradually shoaled, it grounded
on the mud. There was a tree (traces of it still
remain), which is now called the Rumina[a] fig-tree,
but was once the Romulan fig-tree. A she-wolf
which had cast her whelps came, wondrous to tell,
to the abandoned twins : who could believe that
the brute would not harm the boys ? Far from
harming, she helped them ; and they whom ruth-
less kinsfolk would have killed with their own hands
were suckled by a wolf ! She halted and fawned
on the tender babes with her tail, and licked into
shape their two bodies with her tongue. You
might know they were scions of Mars : fearless,
they sucked her dugs and were fed on a supply of
milk that was never meant for them. The she-wolf
(*lupa*) gave her name to the place, and the place gave
their name to the Luperci. Great is the reward the
nurse has got for the milk she gave. Why should
not the Luperci have been named after the Arcadian
mountain? Lycaean Faunus has temples in Arcadia.[b]

425 Thou bride, why tarry ? Neither potent herbs,

OVID

nec prece nec magico carmine mater eris;
excipe fecundae patienter verbera dextrae,
   iam socer optatum nomen habebit avi.
nam fuit illa dies, dura cum sorte maritae
430   reddebant uteri pignora rara sui.
" quid mihi " clamabat " prodest rapuisse Sabinas
   Romulus (hoc illo sceptra tenente fuit)
" si mea non vires, sed bellum iniuria fecit ?
   utilius fuerat non habuisse nurus."
435 monte sub Esquilio multis incaeduus annis
   Iunonis magnae nomine lucus erat.
huc ubi venerunt, pariter nuptaeque virique
   suppliciter posito procubuere genu,
cum subito motae tremuere cacumina silvae
440   et dea per lucos mira locuta suos :
" Italidas matres " inquit " sacer hircus inito."
   obstipuit dubio territa turba sono.
augur erat (nomen longis intercidit annis,
   nuper ab Etrusca venerat exul humo),
445 ille caprum mactat, iussae sua terga puellae
   pellibus exsectis percutienda dabant.
luna resumebat decimo nova cornua motu,
   virque pater subito nuptaque mater erat.
gratia Lucinae !   dedit haec tibi nomina lucus,
450   aut quia principium tu, dea, lucis habes.
parce, precor, gravidis, facilis Lucina, puellis
   maturumque utero molliter aufer onus.

orta dies fuerit, tu desine credere ventis :

---

nor prayer, nor magic spells shall make of thee a
mother; submit with patience to the blows dealt
by a fruitful hand, soon will your husband's sire
enjoy the wished-for name of grandsire. For there
was a day when a hard lot ordained that wives but
seldom gave their mates the pledges of the womb.
Cried Romulus (for this befell when he was on
the throne), "What boots it me to have ravished
the Sabine women, if the wrong I did has brought
me not strength but only war? Better it were
our sons had never wed." Under the Esquiline
Mount a sacred grove, untouched by woodman's
axe for many a year, went by the name of the great
Juno.[a] Hither when they had come, husbands and
wives alike in supplication bowed the knee, when of
a sudden the tops of the trees shook and trembled,
and wondrous words the goddess spake in her own
holy grove: "Let the sacred he-goat," said she, "go
in to Italian matrons." At the ambiguous words the
crowd stood struck with terror. There was a certain
augur (his name has dropped out with the long
years, but he had lately come an exile from the
Etruscan land): he slew a he-goat, and at his bidding
the damsels offered their backs to be beaten with
thongs cut from the hide. When in her tenth circuit
the moon was renewing her horns, the husband was
suddenly made a father and the wife a mother.
Thanks to Lucina! this name, goddess, thou didst
take from the sacred grove (*lucus*), or because with
thee is the fount of light (*lucis*). Gracious Lucina,
spare, I pray, women with child, and gently lift the
ripe burden from the womb.

453 When that day has dawned, then trust no more

perdidit illius temporis aura fidem; `
455 flamina non constant, et sex reserata diebus
    carceris Aeolii ianua lata patet.
iam levis obliqua subsedit Aquarius urna :
    proximus aetherios excipe, Piscis, equos.
te memorant fratremque tuum (nam iuncta micatis
460   signa) duos tergo sustinuisse deos.
terribilem quondam fugiens Typhona Dione,
    tunc cum pro caelo Iuppiter arma tulit,
venit ad Euphraten comitata Cupidine parvo
    inque Palaestinae margine sedit aquae.
465 populus et cannae riparum summa tenebant,.
    spemque dabant salices hos quoque posse tegi.
dum latet, insonuit vento nemus ; illa timore
    pallet et hostiles credit adesse manus,
utque sinu tenuit natum, " succurrite, nymphae,
470   et dis auxilium ferte duobus ! " ait.
nec mora, prosiluit.   pisces subiere gemelli :
    pro quo nunc dignum sidera munus habent.
inde nefas ducunt genus hoc imponere mensis
    nec violant timidi piscibus ora Syri.

16. G EN 17. H QVIR · NP

475 Proxima lux vacua est, at tertia dicta Quirino :
    qui tenet hoc nomen, Romulus ante fuit,
sive quod hasta curis priscis est dicta Sabinis
    (bellicus a telo venit in astra deus),
sive suum regi nomen posuere Quirites,
480   seu quia Romanis iunxerat ille Cures.

---

    [a] Aeolus, king of the winds, kept them in his house (Homer,
Od. x. 1-27, Virg. *Aen.* i. 52).
    [b] Mother of Venus, here for Venus herself.
    [c] See l. 135 n.

the winds : at that season the breezes keep not
faith ; fickle are the blasts, and for six days the
door of the Aeolian *a* gaol unbarred stands open wide.
Now the light Water-Carrier (Aquarius) sets with
his tilted urn : next in turn do thou, O Fish, receive
the heavenly steeds. They say that thou and thy
brother (for ye are constellations that sparkle side
by side) did support twain gods upon your backs.
Once on a time Dione,*b* fleeing from the dreadful
Typhon, when Jupiter bore arms in defence of
heaven, came to the Euphrates, accompanied by
the little Cupid, and sat down by the brink of the
Palestinian water. Poplars and reeds crowned the
top of the banks, and willows offered hope that the
fugitives also could find covert there. While she
lay hid, the grove rustled in the wind. She turned
pale with fear, and thought that bands of foes were
near. Holding her child in her lap, " To the rescue,
nymphs ! " she said, " and to two deities bring
help ! " Without delay she sprang forward. Twin
fish received her on their backs, wherefore they now
possess the stars, a guerdon meet. Hence scrupulous
Syrians count it sin to serve up such fry upon the
table, and will not defile their mouths with fish.

XIII. KAL. 17th

475 Next day is vacant, but the third is dedicated
to Quirinus. He who owns this name was Romulus
before, whether because the ancient Sabines called a
spear *curis*, and by his weapon the warlike god won
his place among the stars ; or because the Quirites
gave their own name to their king ; or because
he united Cures *c* to Rome. For when the father,

91

nam pater armipotens, postquam nova moenia vidit
    multaque Romulea bella peracta manu,
" Iuppiter," inquit, " habet Romana potentia vires :
    sanguinis officio non eget illa mei.
485 redde patri natum.   quamvis intercidit alter,
    pro se proque Remo, qui mihi restat, erit.
' unus erit, quem tu tolles in caerula caeli '
    tu mihi dixisti : sint rata dicta Iovis."
Iuppiter adnuerat.   nutu tremefactus uterque
490   est polus, et caeli pondera movit Atlas.
est locus, antiqui Capreae dixere paludem :
    forte tuis illic, Romule, iura dabas.
sol fugit, et removent subeuntia nubila caelum,
    et gravis effusis decidit imber aquis.
495 hinc tonat, hinc missis abrumpitur ignibus aether :
    fit fuga, rex patriis astra petebat equis.
luctus erat, falsaeque patres in crimine caedis,
    haesissetque animis forsitan illa fides ;
sed Proculus Longa veniebat Iulius Alba,
500   lunaque fulgebat, nec facis usus erat,
cum subito motu saepes tremuere sinistrae :
    rettulit ille gradus, horrueruntque comae.
pulcher et humano maior trabeaque decorus
    Romulus in media visus adesse via
505 et dixisse simul " prohibe lugere Quirites,
    nec violent lacrimis numina nostra suis ;
tura ferant placentque novum pia turba Quirinum
    et patrias artes militiamque colant."
iussit et in tenues oculis evanuit auras ;

---

   [a] Line 487 is borrowed from Ennius.
   [b] This story is told by Cicero, *De rep.* ii. 10. 20, and Livy i,
16. 5.

lord of arms, saw the new walls and the many wars
waged by the hand of Romulus, "O Jupiter,"
he said, "the Roman power hath strength: it
needs not the services of my offspring. To the
sire give back the son. Though one of the two has
perished, the one who is left to me will suffice both
for himself and for Remus. Thou thyself hast said
to me that there will be one whom thou wilt exalt to
the blue welkin.[a] Let the word of Jupiter be kept."
Jupiter nodded assent. At his nod both the poles
shook, and Atlas shifted the burden of the sky.
There is a place which the ancients call the She-
goat's Marsh. It chanced that there, Romulus,
thou wast judging thy people. The sun vanished
and rising clouds obscured the heaven, and there
fell a heavy shower of rain in torrents. Then it
thundered, then the sky was riven by shooting flames.
The people fled, and the king upon his father's
steeds soared to the stars. There was mourning,
and the senators were falsely charged with murder,
and haply that suspicion might have stuck in the
popular mind. But Julius Proculus[b] was coming from
Alba Longa; the moon was shining, and there was
no need of a torch, when of a sudden the hedges on
his left shook and trembled. He recoiled and his hair
bristled up. It seemed to him that Romulus, fair of
aspect, in stature more than human, and clad in a
goodly robe, stood there in the middle of the road
and said, "Forbid the Quirites to mourn, let them
not profane my divinity by their tears. Bid the
pious throng bring incense and propitiate the new
Quirinus, and bid them cultivate the arts their fathers
cultivated, the art of war." So he ordered, and from
the other's eyes he vanished into thin air. Proculus

93

OVID

510   convocat hic populos iussaque verba refert.
    templa deo fiunt, collis quoque dictus ab illo est,
      et referunt certi sacra paterna dies.
    lux quoque cur eadem Stultorum festa vocetur,
      accipe.   parva quidem causa, sed apta subest.
515 non habuit doctos tellus antiqua colonos :
      lassabant agiles aspera bella viros.
    plus erat in gladio quam curvo laudis aratro :
      neglectus domino pauca ferebat ager.
    farra tamen veteres iaciebant, farra metebant,
520   primitias Cereri farra resecta dabant.
    usibus admoniti flammis torrenda dederunt
      multaque peccato damna tulere suo.
    nam modo verrebant nigras pro farre favillas,
      nunc ipsas ignes corripuere casas ;
525 facta dea est Fornax : laeti Fornace coloni
      orant, ut fruges temperet illa suas.
    curio legitimis nunc Fornacalia verbis
      maximus indicit nec stata sacra facit,
    inque foro, multa circum pendente tabella,
530   signatur certa curia quaeque nota ;
    stultaque pars populi, quae sit sua curia, nescit,
      sed facit extrema sacra relata die.

18. AC   19. BC   20. CC   21. D FERAL · F

Est honor et tumulis.   Animas placate paternas
    parvaque in extinctas munera ferte pyras.

---

    a See i. 693.
    b Each tribe was subdivided into ten *curiae,* each with its
curio or warden. These priests formed a college presided
over by one of their number, the *Curio Maximus.*

called the peoples together and reported the words
as he had been bid. Temples were built to the god,
and the hill also was named after him, and the rites
observed by our fathers come round on fixed days.

512 Learn also why the same day is called the Feast
of Fools. The reason for the name is trifling but
apt. The earth of old was tilled by men unlearned :
war's hardships wearied their active frames. More
glory was to be won by the sword than by the curved
plough ; the neglected farm yielded its master but
a small return. Yet spelt *a* the ancients sowed, and
spelt they reaped ; of the cut spelt they offered the
first-fruits to Ceres. Taught by experience they
toasted the spelt on the fire, and many losses they
incurred through their own fault. For at one time
they would sweep up black ashes instead of spelt,
and at another time the fire caught the huts themselves. So they made the oven into a goddess of
that name (*Fornax*) ; delighted with her, the farmers
prayed that she would temper the heat to the corn
committed to her charge. At the present day the
Prime Warden (*Curio Maximus*) *b* proclaims in a set
form of words the time for holding the Feast of Ovens
(*Fornacalia*), and he celebrates the rites at no fixed
date ; and round about the Forum hang many tablets,
on which every ward has its own particular mark.
The foolish part of the people know not which is
their own ward, but hold the feast on the last day to
which it can be postponed.

XII.-IX. Kal. 18th-21st

533 Honour is paid, also, to the tombs. Appease
the souls of your fathers and bring small gifts to the

535 parva petunt manes, pietas pro divite grata est
    munere : non avidos Styx habet ima deos.
tegula porrectis satis est velata coronis
    et sparsae fruges parcaque mica salis
inque mero mollita Ceres violaeque solutae :
540   haec habeat media testa relicta via.
nec maiora veto, sed et his placabilis umbra est :
    adde preces positis et sua verba focis.
hunc morem Aeneas, pietatis idoneus auctor,
    attulit in terras, iuste Latine, tuas ;
545 ille patris Genio sollemnia dona ferebat :
    hinc populi ritus edidicere pios.
at quondam, dum longa gerunt pugnacibus armis
    bella, Parentales deseruere dies.
non impune fuit ; nam dicitur omine ab isto
550   Roma suburbanis incaluisse rogis.
vix equidem credo : bustis exisse feruntur
    et tacitae questi tempore noctis avi,
perque vias urbis latosque ululasse per agros
    deformes animas, volgus inane, ferunt.
555 post ea praeteriti tumulis redduntur honores,
    prodigiisque venit funeribusque modus.
dum tamen haec fiunt, viduae cessate puellae :
    expectet puros pinea taeda dies,
nec tibi, quae cupidae matura videbere matri,
560   comat virgineas hasta recurva comas.
conde tuas, Hymenaee, faces et ab ignibus atris
    aufer ! habent alias maesta sepulchra faces.

---

   a At the *Feralia*, or feasts in memory of the dead, offerings
were made to them.   The chief day was Feb. 21.   *Parentalia*
is also a name of the festival.

extinguished pyres.[a] The ghosts ask but little:
they value piety more than a costly gift : no greedy
gods are they who in the world below do haunt the
banks of Styx. A tile wreathed with votive garlands,
a sprinkling of corn, a few grains of salt, bread soaked
in wine, and some loose violets, these are offerings
enough : set these on a potsherd and leave it in the
middle of the road. Not that I forbid larger offerings,
but even these suffice to appease the shades : add
prayers and the appropriate words at the hearths set
up for the purpose. This custom was introduced
into thy lands, righteous Latinus, by Aeneas, fit
patron of piety. He to his father's spirit solemn
offerings brought ; from him the peoples learned the
pious rites. But once upon a time, waging long wars
with martial arms, they did neglect the All Souls'
Days. The negligence was not unpunished ; for
'tis said that from that ominous day Rome grew hot
with the funeral fires that burned without the city.
They say, though I can hardly think it, that the
ancestral souls did issue from the tombs and make
their moan in the hours of stilly night ; and hideous
ghosts, a shadowy throng, they say, did howl about
the city streets and the wide fields. Afterwards the
honours which had been omitted were again paid to
the tombs, and so a limit was put to prodigies and
funerals. But while these rites are being performed,
ye ladies change not your widowed state ; let the
nuptial torch of pine wait till the days are pure. And
O, thou damsel, who to thine eager mother shalt
appear all ripe for marriage, let not the bent-back
spear comb down thy maiden hair ! O God of
Marriage, hide thy torches, and from these sombre
fires bear them away ! Far other are the torches

di quoque templorum foribus celentur opertis,
 ture vacent arae stentque sine igne foci.
565 nunc animae tenues et corpora functa sepulcris
 errant, nunc posito pascitur umbra cibo.
nec tamen haec ultra, quam tot de mense supersint
 Luciferi, quot habent carmina nostra pedes.
hanc, quia iusta ferunt, dixere Feralia lucem;
570 ultima placandis manibus illa dies.
ecce anus in mediis residens annosa puellis
 sacra facit Tacitae (nec tamen ipsa tacet),
et digitis tria tura tribus sub limine ponit,
 qua brevis occultum mus sibi fecit iter;
575 tunc cantata ligat cum fusco licia plumbo
 et septem nigras versat in ore fabas,
quodque pice adstrinxit, quod acu traiecit aëna,
 obsutum maenae torret in igne caput;
vina quoque instillat: vini quodcumque relictum est,
580 aut ipsa aut comites, plus tamen ipsa, bibit.
" hostiles linguas inimicaque vinximus ora "
 dicit discedens ebriaque exit anus.
protinus a nobis, quae sit dea Muta, requires:
 disce, per antiquos quae mihi nota senes.
585 Iuppiter immodico Iuturnae victus amore
 multa tulit tanto non patienda deo:
illa modo in silvis inter coryleta latebat,
 nunc in cognatas desiliebat aquas.
convocat hic nymphas, Latium quaecumque tenebant,
590 et iacit in medio talia verba choro:

---

 a Eleven, as Ovid reckoned (*Am.* i. 1. 27-30).
 b Or *dea Muta* (l. 583), whom Ovid identifies with the
mother of the public Lares (l. 615). She averted evil words.

that light up the rueful grave. Screen, too, the
gods by shutting up the temple doors; let no incense
burn upon the altars, no fire upon the hearths.
Now do the unsubstantial souls and buried dead
wander about, now doth the ghost batten upon his
dole. But this only lasts until there remain as many
days of the month as there are feet in my verses.[a]
That day they name the Feralia, because they carry
(*ferunt*) to the dead their dues: it is the last day
for propitiating the ghosts.

⁵⁷¹ Lo, an old hag, seated among girls, performs
rites in honour of Tacita[b] ("the Silent Goddess"),
but herself is not silent. With three fingers she
puts three lumps of incense under the threshold,
where the little mouse has made for herself a secret
path. Then she binds enchanted threads together
with dark lead, and mumbles seven black beans in
her mouth; and she roasts in the fire the head of a
small fish which she has sewed up, made fast with
pitch, and pierced through and through with a bronze
needle. She also drops wine on it, and the wine
that is left over she or her companions drink, but she
gets the larger share. Then as she goes off she says,
" We have bound fast hostile tongues and unfriendly
mouths." So exit the old woman drunk.

⁵⁸³ At once you will ask of me, " Who is the goddess
Muta ('the Mute')?" Hear what I learned from
old men gone in years. Conquered by exceeding
love of Juturna, Jupiter submitted to many things
which so great a god ought not to bear. For now
she would hide in the woods among the hazel-
thickets, now she would leap down into her sister
waters. The god called together all the nymphs
who dwell in Latium, and thus in the midst of the

99

" invidet ipsa sibi vitatque, quod expedit illi,
   vestra soror summo concubuisse deo.
consulite ambobus ; nam quae mea magna voluptas,
   utilitas vestrae magna sororis erit.
595 vos illi in prima fugienti obsistite ripa,
   ne sua fluminea corpora mergat aqua."
dixerat : adnuerant nymphae Tiberinides omnes,
   quaeque colunt thalamos, Ilia diva, tuos.
forte fuit nais, Lara nomine, prima sed illi
600   dicta bis antiquum syllaba nomen erat,
ex vitio positum.   saepe illi dixerat Almo
   " nata, tene linguam," nec tamen illa tenet.
quae simul ac tetigit Iuturnae stagna sororis,
   " effuge " ait " ripas " ; dicta refertque Iovis.
605 illa etiam Iunonem adiit, miserataque nuptas
   " naida Iuturnam vir tuus " inquit " amat."
Iuppiter intumuit, quaque est non usa modeste,
   eripit huic linguam Mercuriumque vocat :
" duc hanc ad manes ; locus ille silentibus aptus.
610   nympha, sed infernae nympha paludis erit."
iussa Iovis fiunt. accepit lucus euntes :
   dicitur illa duci tunc placuisse deo.
vim parat hic, voltu pro verbis illa precatur,
   et frustra muto nititur ore loqui.
615 fitque gravis geminosque parit, qui compita servant
   et vigilant nostra semper in urbe, Lares.

---

^a Mother of Romulus.

^b Lala, as if from λαλεῖν, " to prattle."

^c God of the river, a tributary of the Tiber, and father of Lara.

^d The Lares Compitales or Praestites were the public guardians of the city. They were generally enshrined in

100

troop he spake aloud: "Your sister is her own enemy, and shuns that union with the supreme god which is all for her good. Pray look to her interests and to mine, for what is a great pleasure to me will be a great boon to your sister. When she flees, stop her on the edge of the bank, lest she plunge into the water of the river." He spake. Assent was given by all the nymphs of Tiber and by those who haunt, Ilia divine,[a] thy wedding bowers. It chanced there was a Naiad nymph, Lara by name ; but her old name was the first syllable repeated twice, and that was given her to mark her failing.[b] Many a time Almo[c] had said to her, "My daughter, hold thy tongue," but hold it she did not. No sooner did she reach the pools of her sister Juturna than, "Fly the banks," said she, and reported the words of Jupiter. She even visited Juno and, after expressing her pity for married dames, "Your husband," quoth she, "is in love with the Naiad Juturna." Jupiter fumed and wrenched from her the tongue she had used so indiscreetly. He also called for Mercury. "Take her to deadland," said he, "that's the place for mutes. A nymph she is, but a nymph of the infernal marsh she'll be." The orders of Jupiter were obeyed. On their way they came to a grove ; then it was, they say, that she won the heart of her divine conductor. He would have used force ; for want of words she pleaded with a look, and all in vain she strove to speak with her dumb lips. She went with child, and bore twins, who guard the cross-roads and ever keep watch in our city : they are the Lares.[d]

pairs. They were specially worshipped at cross-roads, or *compita*. There was a yearly festival, the *Compitalia*.

101

OVID

22. EC

Proxima cognati dixere Caristia cari,
    et venit ad socios turba propinqua deos.
scilicet a tumulis et, qui periere, propinquis
620   protinus ad vivos ora referre iuvat
postque tot amissos, quicquid de sanguine restat,
    aspicere et generis dinumerare gradus.
innocui veniant: procul hinc, procul impius esto
    frater et in partus mater acerba suos,
625 cui pater est vivax, qui matris digerit annos,
    quae premit invisam socrus iniqua nurum.
Tantalidae fratres absint et Iasonis uxor
    et quae ruricolis semina tosta dedit,
et soror et Procne Tereusque duabus iniquus
630   et quicumque suas per scelus auget opes.
dis generis date tura boni (Concordia fertur
    illa praecipue mitis adesse die)
et libate dapes, ut, grati pignus honoris,
    nutriat incinctos missa patella Lares.
635 iamque ubi suadebit placidos nox humida somnos,
    larga precaturi sumite vina manu,
et "bene vos, bene te, patriae pater, optime Caesar!"
    dicite suffuso per sacra verba mero.

---

    a Atreus and Thyestes.
    b Medea.   *c* Ino ; see iii. 853.
    d Procne and Philomela were daughters of King Pandion.
Procne married Tereus, and had a son Itys. Tereus seduced
Philomela, and cut out her tongue. Procne killed Itys, and
served him up for his father to eat. In the end, Procne

VIII. KAL. 22nd

617 The next day received its name of Caristia
from dear (*cari*) kinsfolk. A crowd of near relations
comes to meet the family gods. Sweet it is, no doubt,
to recall our thoughts to the living soon as they
have dwelt upon the grave and on the dear ones
dead and gone ; sweet, too, after so many lost, to
look upon those of our blood who are left, and to
count kin with them. Come none but the innocent !
Far, far from here be the unnatural brother, and the
mother who is harsh to her own offspring, he whose
father lives too long, he who reckons up his mother's
years, and the unkind mother-in-law who hates and
maltreats her daughter-in-law. Here is no place for
the brothers, scions of Tantalus,[a] for Jason's wife,[b]
for her who gave to husbandmen the toasted seeds,[c]
for Procne and her sister,[d] for Tereus, cruel to them
both, and for him, whoe'er he be, who amasses
wealth by crime. Give incense to the family gods,
ye virtuous ones (on that day above all others Concord
is said to lend her gentle presence) ; and offer food,
that the Lares, in their girt-up robes, may feed at
the platter presented to them as a pledge of the
homage that they love. And now, when dank night
invites to slumber calm, fill high the wine-cup for
the prayer and say, " Hail to you ! hail to thee,
Father of thy Country, Caesar the Good ! " and at
these sacred words pour out the wine.

became a nightingale, Philomela a swallow, and Tereus a
hoopoe. In Latin authors, Philomela is the nightingale,
Procne the swallow.

OVID

23. F TER · NP

Nox ubi transierit, solito celebretur honore
640   separat indicio qui deus arva suo.
Termine, sive lapis, sive es defossus in agro
   stipes, ab antiquis tu quoque numen habes.
te duo diversa domini de parte coronant
   binaque serta tibi binaque liba ferunt.
645 ara fit : huc ignem curto fert rustica testu
   sumptum de tepidis ipsa colona focis.
ligna senex minuit concisaque construit arte
   et solida ramos figere pugnat humo :
tum sicco primas inritat cortice flammas,
650   stat puer et manibus lata canistra tenet.
inde ubi ter fruges medios immisit in ignis,
   porrigit incisos filia parva favos.
vina tenent alii ; libantur singula flammis ;
   spectant, et linguis candida turba favet.
655 spargitur et caeso communis Terminus agno
   nec queritur, lactans cum sibi porca datur.
conveniunt celebrantque dapes vicinia simplex
   et cantant laudes, Termine sancte, tuas :
tu populos urbesque et regna ingentia finis :
660   omnis erit sine te litigiosus ager.
nulla tibi ambitio est, nullo corrumperis auro,
   legitima servas credita rura fide.
si tu signasses olim Thyreatida terram,
   corpora non leto missa trecenta forent,
665 nec foret Othryades congestis lectus in armis.
   o quantum patriae sanguinis ille dedit !
quid, nova cum fierent Capitolia ? nempe deorum

---

a Between Sparta and Argos : three hundred champions
on each side fought for it, and Othryades was the only
survivor of the Spartans.

VII. Kal. 23rd

⁶³⁹ When the night has passed, see to it that the god who marks the boundaries of the tilled lands receives his wonted honour. O Terminus, whether thou art a stone or a stump buried in the field, thou too hast been deified from days of yore. Thou art crowned by two owners on opposite sides; they bring thee two garlands and two cakes. An altar is built. Hither the husbandman's rustic wife brings with her own hands on a potsherd the fire which she has taken from the warm hearth. The old man chops wood, and deftly piles up the billets, and strives to fix the branches in the solid earth: then he nurses the kindling flames with dry bark, the boy stands by and holds the broad basket in his hands. When from the basket he has thrice thrown corn into the midst of the fire, the little daughter presents the cut honeycombs. Others hold vessels of wine. A portion of each is cast into the flames. The company dressed in white look on and hold their peace. Terminus himself, at the meeting of the bounds, is sprinkled with the blood of a slaughtered lamb, and grumbles not when a sucking pig is given him. The simple neighbours meet and hold a feast, and sing thy praises, holy Terminus: thou dost set bounds to peoples and cities and vast kingdoms; without thee every field would be a root of wrangling. Thou courtest no favour, thou art bribed by no gold: the lands entrusted to thee thou dost guard in loyal good faith. If thou of old hadst marked the bounds of the Thyrean land,^a three hundred men had not been done to death, nor had the name of Othryades been read on the piled arms. O how he made his fatherland to bleed! What happened when the new

cuncta Iovi cessit turba locumque dedit:
Terminus, ut veteres memorant, inventus in aede
670   restitit et magno cum Iove templa tenet.
nunc quoque, se supra ne quid nisi sidera cernat,
  exiguum templi tecta foramen habent.
Termine, post illud levitas tibi libera non est:
  qua positus fueris in statione, mane,
675 nec tu vicino quicquam concede roganti,
  ne videare hominem praeposuisse Iovi;
et seu vomeribus seu tu pulsabere rastris,
  clamato " tuus est hic ager, ille suus ! "
est via, quae populum Laurentes ducit in agros,
680   quondam Dardanio regna petita duci:
illa lanigeri pecoris tibi, Termine, fibris
  sacra videt fieri sextus ab urbe lapis.
gentibus est aliis tellus data limite certo:
  Romanae spatium est urbis et orbis idem.

24. G REGIF · N

685 Nunc mihi dicenda est regis fuga: traxit ab illa
  sextus ab extremo nomina mense dies.
ultima Tarquinius Romanae gentis habebat
  regna, vir iniustus, fortis ad arma tamen.
ceperat hic alias, alias everterat urbes
690   et Gabios turpi fecerat arte suos.
namque trium minimus, proles manifesta Superbi,
  in medios hostes nocte silente venit.

---

[a] This was taken as a sign that wherever a boundary-stone was once planted, it was to be sacred and immovable.
[b] Apparently ritual demanded that the stone (or altar) which represented Terminus should stand under the open sky.
[c] The Laurentine way ran towards the sea. The Dardanian chief, Aeneas, landed in the Laurentine territory.

Capitol was being built? Why, the whole company of gods withdrew before Jupiter and made room for him; but Terminus, as the ancients relate, remained where he was found in the shrine, and shares the temple with great Jupiter.[a] Even to this day there is a small hole in the roof of the temple, that he may see naught above him but the stars.[b] From that time, Terminus, thou hast not been free to flit: abide in that station in which thou hast been placed. Yield not an inch to a neighbour, though he ask thee, lest thou shouldst seem to value man above Jupiter. And whether they beat thee with ploughshares or with rakes, cry out, " This is thy land, and that is his." There is a way that leads folk to the Laurentine fields,[c] the kingdom once sought by the Dardanian chief: on that way the sixth milestone from the city witnesses the sacrifice of a woolly sheep's guts to thee, Terminus. The land of other nations has a fixed boundary: the circuit of Rome is the circuit of the world.

VI. KAL. 24th

[685] Now have I to tell of the Flight of the King[d]: from it the sixth day from the end of the month has taken its name. The last to reign over the Roman people was Tarquin, a man unjust, yet puissant in arms. He had taken some cities and overturned others, and had made Gabii his own by foul play.[e] For of the king's three sons the youngest, true scion of his proud sire, came in the silent night into the midst of the foes. They drew

---

[d] Called *Regifugium*. See Appendix, p. 394.

[e] Sextus Tarquin took Gabii by a trick. The story is also in Livy i. 53.

107

OVID

nudarant gladios : " occidite " dixit " inermem !
    hoc cupiant fratres Tarquiniusque pater,
695 qui mea crudeli laceravit verbere terga."
    dicere ut hoc posset, verbera passus erat.
luna fuit : spectant iuvenem gladiosque recondunt
    tergaque deducta veste notata vident.
flent quoque et, ut secum tueatur bella, precantur :
700   callidus ignaris adnuit ille viris.
iamque potens misso genitorem appellat amico,
    perdendi Gabios quod sibi monstret iter.
hortus odoratis suberat cultissimus herbis
    sectus humum rivo lene sonantis aquae :
705 illic Tarquinius mandata latentia nati
    accipit et virga lilia summa metit.
nuntius ut rediit decussaque lilia dixit,
    filius " agnosco iussa parentis " ait.
nec mora, principibus caesis ex urbe Gabina
710   traduntur ducibus moenia nuda suis.
ecce, nefas visu, mediis altaribus anguis
    exit et extinctis ignibus exta rapit.
consulitur Phoebus : sors est ita reddita : " matri
    qui dederit princeps oscula, victor erit."
715 oscula quisque suae matri properata tulerunt,
    non intellecto credula turba deo.
Brutus erat stulti sapiens imitator, ut esset
    tutus ab insidiis, dire Superbe, tuis ;
ille iacens pronus matri dedit oscula Terrae,
720   creditus offenso procubuisse pede.
cingitur interea Romanis Ardea signis

---

    a Another anecdote, brought in abruptly, to introduce
Brutus, author of the *Regifugium*. See Livy, i. 56. 4.

their swords. " Slay an unarmed man ! " said he.
" 'Tis what my brothers would desire, aye and
Tarquin, my sire, who gashed my back with cruel
scourge." In order that he might urge this plea, he
had submitted to a scourging. The moon shone.
They beheld the youth and sheathed their swords,
for they saw the scars on his back, where he drew
down his robe. They even wept and begged that
he would side with them in war. The cunning knave
assented to their unwary suit. No sooner was he
installed in power than he sent a friend to ask
his father to show him the way of destroying Gabii.
Below the palace lay a garden trim of odoriferous
plants, whereof the ground was cleft by a brook of
purling water : there Tarquin received the secret
message of his son, and with his staff he mowed the
tallest lilies. When the messenger returned and
told of the cropped lilies, " I take," quoth the son,
" my father's bidding." Without delay, he put
to the sword the chief men of the city of Gabii
and surrendered the walls, now bereft of their native
leaders.

711 Behold, O horrid sight ! from between the
altars a snake came forth and snatched the sacrificial
meat from the dead fires. Phoebus was consulted.[a]
An oracle was delivered in these terms : " He who
shall first have kissed his mother will be victorious."
Each one of the credulous company, not understand-
ing the god, hasted to kiss his mother. The prudent
Brutus feigned to be a fool, in order that from thy
snares, Tarquin the Proud, dread king, he might be
safe ; lying prone he kissed his mother Earth, but
they thought he had stumbled and fallen. Meantime the Roman legions had compassed Ardea, and

et patitur longas obsidione moras.
dum vacat et metuunt hostes committere pugnam,
    luditur in castris, otia miles agit.
725 Tarquinius iuvenis socios dapibusque meroque
    accipit; ex illis rege creatus ait:
" dum nos sollicitos pigro tenet Ardea bello
    nec sinit ad patrios arma referre deos,
ecquid in officio torus est socialis? et ecquid
730   coniugibus nostris mutua cura sumus?"
quisque suam laudat: studiis certamina crescunt,
    et fervet multo linguaque corque mero.
surgit, cui dederat clarum Collatia nomen:
    " non opus est verbis, credite rebus!" ait.
735 " nox superest: tollamur equis urbemque petamus!"
    dicta placent, frenis impediuntur equi,
pertulerant dominos. regalia protinus illi
    tecta petunt: custos in fore nullus erat.
ecce nurus regis fusis per colla coronis
740   inveniunt posito pervigilare mero.
inde cito passu petitur Lucretia: nebat,
    ante torum calathi lanaque mollis erat.
lumen ad exiguum famulae data pensa trahebant,
    inter quas tenui sic ait illa sono:
745 " mittenda est domino (nunc, nunc properate,
    puellae!)
    quam primum nostra facta lacerna manu.
quid tamen auditis? nam plura audire potestis:
    quantum de bello dicitur esse super?
postmodo victa cades: melioribus, Ardea, restas,
750   improba, quae nostros cogis abesse viros.
sint tantum reduces! sed enim temerarius ille

***

^a A third anecdote: the siege of Ardea, and the rape of
Lucretia by Sextus Tarquin; Livy i. 57. 4.
110

the city suffered a long and lingering siege. While
there was naught to do, and the foe feared to join
battle, they made merry in the camp ; the soldiers
took their ease. Young Tarquin [a] entertained his comrades with feast and wine : among them the king's
son spake : " While Ardea keeps us here on tenter-
hooks with sluggish war, and suffers us not to carry
back our arms to the gods of our fathers, what
of the loyalty of the marriage-bed ? and are we as
dear to our wives as they to us ? " Each praised his
wife : in their eagerness dispute ran high, and every
tongue and heart grew hot with the deep draughts of
wine. Then up and spake the man who from Collatia
took his famous name [b] : " No need of words ! Trust
deeds ! There's night enough. To horse ! and ride
we to the city." The saying pleased them ; the
steeds are bridled and bear their masters to the
journey's end. The royal palace first they seek :
no sentinel was at the door. Lo, they find the king's
daughters-in-law, their necks draped with garlands,
keeping their vigils over the wine. Thence they
galloped to Lucretia : she was spinning : before her
bed were baskets of soft wool. By a dim light the
handmaids were spinning their allotted stints of
yarn. Amongst them the lady spoke in accents soft :
" Haste ye now, haste, my girls ! The cloak our
hands have wrought must to your master be instantly dispatched. But what news have ye ? For
more news comes your way. How much do they say
of the war is yet to come ? Hereafter thou shalt
be vanquished and fall : Ardea, thou dost resist thy
betters, thou jade, that keepest perforce our husbands
far away ! If only they came back ! But mine is

[b] Tarquinius Collatinus.

est meus et stricto qualibet ense ruit.
mens abit, et morior, quotiens pugnantis imago
    me subit, et gelidum pectora frigus habet."
755 desinit in lacrimas intentaque fila remittit,
    in gremio voltum deposuitque suum.
hoc ipsum decuit : lacrimae decuere pudicae,
    et facies animo dignaque parque fuit.
" pone metum, veni ! " coniunx ait.   illa revixit
760   deque viri collo dulce pependit onus.
interea iuvenis furiales regius ignis
    concipit et caeco raptus amore furit.
forma placet niveusque color flavique capilli,
    quique aderat nulla factus ab arte decor ;
765 verba placent et vox, et quod corrumpere non est,
    quoque minor spes est, hoc magis ille cupit.
iam dederat cantus lucis praenuntius ales,
    cum referunt iuvenes in sua castra pedem.
carpitur adtonitos absentis imagine sensus
770   ille.   recordanti plura magisque placent :
" sic sedit, sic culta fuit, sic stamina nevit,
    neglectae collo sic iacuere comae,
hos habuit voltus, haec illi verba fuerunt,
    hic color, haec facies, hic decor oris erat."
775 ut solet a magno fluctus languescere flatu,
    sed tamen a vento, qui fuit, unda tumet,
sic, quamvis aberat placitae praesentia formae,
    quem dederat praesens forma, manebat amor.
ardet et iniusti stimulis agitatus amoris
780   comparat indigno vimque dolumque toro.
" exitus in dubio est : audebimus ultima ! " dixit,
    " viderit ! audentes forsque deusque iuvat.
cepimus audendo Gabios quoque."   talia fatus

112

rash, and with drawn sword he rushes anywhere. I faint, I die, oft as the image of my soldier spouse steals on my mind and strikes a chill into my breast." She ended weeping, dropped the stretched yarn, and buried her face in her lap. The gesture was becoming; becoming, too, her modest tears; her face was worthy of its peer, her soul. "Fear not, I've come," her husband said. She revived and on her spouse's neck she hung, a burden sweet.

761 Meantime the royal youth caught fire and fury, and transported by blind love he raved. Her figure pleased him, and that snowy hue, that yellow hair, and artless grace; pleasing, too, her words and voice and virtue incorruptible; and the less hope he had, the hotter his desire. Now had the bird, the herald of the dawn, uttered his chant, when the young men retraced their steps to camp. Meantime the image of his absent love preyed on his senses crazed. In memory's light more fair and fair she grew. "'Twas thus she sat, 'twas thus she dressed, 'twas thus she spun the yarn, 'twas thus her tresses careless lay upon her neck; that was her look, these were her words, that was her colour, that her form, and that her lovely face." As after a great gale the surge subsides, and yet the billow heaves, lashed by the wind now fallen, so, though absent now that winsome form and far away, the love which by its presence it had struck into his heart remained. He burned, and, goaded by the pricks of an unrighteous love, he plotted violence and guile against an innocent bed. "The issue is in doubt. We'll dare the utmost," said he. "Let her look to it! God and fortune help the daring. By daring we captured Gabii too."

113

ense latus cinxit tergaque pressit equi.
785 accipit aerata iuvenem Collatia porta
condere iam voltus sole parante suos.
hostis ut hospes init penetralia Collatini :
comiter excipitur ; sanguine iunctus erat.
quantum animis erroris inest ! parat inscia rerum
790   infelix epulas hostibus illa suis.
functus erat dapibus : poscunt sua tempora somnum ;
nox erat et tota lumina nulla domo :
surgit et aurata vagina liberat ensem
et venit in thalamos, nupta pudica, tuos.
795 utque torum pressit, " ferrum, Lucretia, mecum est.
natus " ait " regis Tarquiniusque loquor ! "
illa nihil : neque enim vocem viresque loquendi
aut aliquid toto pectore mentis habet,
sed tremit, ut quondam stabulis deprensa relictis
800   parva sub infesto cum iacet agna lupo.
quid faciat ? pugnet ? vincetur femina pugnans.
clamet ? at in dextra, qui vetet, ensis erat.
effugiat ? positis urgentur pectora palmis,
tunc primum externa pectora tacta manu.
805 instat amans hostis precibus pretioque minisque :
nec prece nec pretio nec movet ille minis.
" nil agis : eripiam " dixit " per crimina vitam :
falsus adulterii testis adulter ero :
interimam famulum, cum quo deprensa fereris."
810   succubuit famae victa puella metu.
quid, victor, gaudes ? haec te victoria perdet.
heu quanto regnis nox stetit una tuis !

114

⁷⁸⁴ So saying he girt his sword at his side and bestrode his horse's back. The bronze-bound gate of Collatia opened for him just as the sun was making ready to hide his face. In the guise of a guest the foe found his way into the home of Collatinus. He was welcomed kindly, for he came of kindred blood. How was her heart deceived! All unaware she, hapless dame, prepared a meal for her own foes. His repast over, the hour of slumber came. 'Twas night, and not a taper shone in the whole house. He rose, and from the gilded scabbard he drew his sword, and came into thy chamber, virtuous spouse. And when he touched the bed, "The steel is in my hand, Lucretia," said he, "I that speak am the king's son and Tarquin." She answered never a word. Voice and power of speech and thought itself fled from her breast. But she trembled, as trembles a little lamb that, caught straying from the fold, lies low under a ravening wolf. What could she do? Should she struggle? In a struggle a woman will always be worsted. Should she cry out? But in his clutch was a sword to silence her. Should she fly? His hands pressed heavy on her breast, the breast that till then had never known the touch of stranger hand. Her lover foe is urgent with prayers, with bribes, with threats; but still he cannot move her by prayers, by bribes, by threats. "Resistance is vain," said he, "I'll rob thee of honour and of life. I, the adulterer, will bear false witness to thine adultery. I'll kill a slave, and rumour will have it that thou wert caught with him." Overcome by fear of infamy, the dame gave way. Why, victor, dost thou joy? This victory will ruin thee. Alack, how dear a single night did cost thy kingdom!

iamque erat orta dies : passis sedet illa capillis,
    ut solet ad nati mater itura rogum,
815 grandaevumque patrem fido cum coniuge castris
    evocat, et posita venit uterque mora.
utque vident habitum, quae luctus causa, requirunt,
    cui paret exequias, quove sit icta malo ?
illa diu reticet pudibundaque celat amictu
820   ora : fluunt lacrimae more perennis aquae.
hinc pater, hinc coniunx lacrimas solantur et orant,
    indicet, et caeco flentque paventque metu.
ter conata loqui ter destitit, ausaque quarto
    non oculos ideo sustulit illa suos.
825 " hoc quoque Tarquinio debebimus ? eloquar," inquit,
    " eloquar infelix dedecus ipsa meum ? "
quaeque potest, narrat. restabant ultima : flevit,
    et matronales erubuere genae.
dant veniam facto genitor coniunxque coacto :
830   " quam " dixit " veniam vos datis, ipsa nego."
nec mora, celato fixit sua pectora ferro
    et cadit in patrios sanguinulenta pedes.
tunc quoque iam moriens ne non procumbat honeste,
    respicit ; haec etiam cura cadentis erat.
835 ecce super corpus communia damna gementes
    obliti decoris virque paterque iacent.
Brutus adest tandemque animo sua nomina fallit
    fixaque semianimi corpore tela rapit
stillantemque tenens generoso sanguine cultrum
840   edidit impavidos ore minante sonos :
" per tibi ego hunc iuro fortem castumque cruorem
    perque tuos manes, qui mihi numen erunt,

And now the day had dawned. She sat with
hair dishevelled, like a mother who must attend the
funeral pyre of her son. Her aged sire and faithful
spouse she summoned from the camp, and both
came without delay. When they saw her plight,
they asked why she mourned, whose obsequies she
was preparing, or what ill had befallen her. She
was long silent, and for shame hid her face in her
robe: her tears flowed like a running stream. On
this side and on that her father and her spouse did
soothe her grief and pray her to tell, and in blind
fear they wept and quaked. Thrice she essayed to
speak, and thrice gave o'er, and when the fourth
time she summoned up courage she did not for that
lift up her eyes. " Must I owe this too to Tarquin?
Must I utter," quoth she, " must I utter, woe's me,
with my own lips my own disgrace ? " And what
she can she tells. The end she left unsaid, but wept
and a blush o'erspread her matron cheeks. Her
husband and her sire pardoned the deed enforced.
She said, " The pardon that you give, I do refuse
myself." Without delay, she stabbed her breast
with the steel she had hidden, and weltering in
her blood fell at her father's feet. Even then in
dying she took care to sink down decently : that
was her thought even as she fell. Lo, heedless of
appearances, the husband and father fling themselves on her body, moaning their common loss.
Brutus came, and then at last belied his name ; for
from the half-dead body he snatched the weapon
stuck in it, and holding the knife, that dripped with
noble blood, he fearless spake these words of menace :
" By this brave blood and chaste, and by thy ghost,
who shall be god to me, I swear to be avenged on

117

Tarquinium profuga poenas cum stirpe daturum.
    iam satis est virtus dissimulata diu."
845 illa iacens ad verba oculos sine lumine movit
    visaque concussa dicta probare coma.
fertur in exequias animi matrona virilis
    et secum lacrimas invidiamque trahit.
volnus inane patet.   Brutus clamore Quirites
850   concitat et regis facta nefanda refert.
Tarquinius cum prole fugit, capit annua consul
    iura : dies regnis illa suprema fuit.

25. HC   26. A EN

Fallimur, an veris praenuntia venit hirundo
    nec metuit, ne qua versa recurrat hiems?
855 saepe tamen, Procne, nimium properasse quereris,
    virque tuo Tereus frigore laetus erit.

27. B EQ · NP   28. CC

Iamque duae restant noctes de mense secundo,
    Marsque citos iunctis curribus urget equos :
ex vero positum permansit Equirria nomen,
860   quae deus in Campo prospicit ipse suo.
iure venis, Gradive : locum tua tempora poscunt,
    signatusque tuo nomine mensis adest.
venimus in portum libro cum mense peracto :
    naviget hinc alia iam mihi linter aqua.

Tarquin and on his banished brood. Too long have
I dissembled my manly worth." At these words,
even as she lay, she moved her lightless eyes and
seemed by the stirring of her hair to ratify the speech.
They bore her to burial, that matron of manly
courage ; and tears and indignation followed in her
train. The gaping wound was exposed for all to see.
With a cry Brutus assembled the Quirites and
rehearsed the king's foul deeds. Tarquin and his
brood were banished. A consul undertook the
government for a year. That day was the last of
kingly rule.

V. Kal. 25th IV. Kal. 26th

853 Do I err ? or has the swallow come, the harbinger of spring, and does she not fear lest winter
should turn and come again ? Yet often, Procne,
wilt thou complain that thou hast made too much
haste, and thy husband Tereus will be glad at the
cold thou feelest.

III. Kal. 27th

856 And now two nights of the second month are
left, and Mars urges on the swift steeds yoked to
his chariot. The day has kept the appropriate name
of Equirria (" horse-races "), derived from the races
which the god himself beholds in his own plain.
Thou Marching God (*Gradivus*), in thine own right
thou comest. Thy season demands a place in my
song, and the month marked by the name is at
hand. We have come to port, for the book ends
with the month. From this point may my bark now
sail in other waters.

119

LIBER TERTIUS

Bellice, depositis clipeo paulisper et hasta,
    Mars, ades et nitidas casside solve comas.
forsitan ipse roges, quid sit cum Marte poetae :
    a te, qui canitur, nomina mensis habet.
5 ipse vides manibus peragi fera bella Minervae :
    num minus ingenuis artibus illa vacat ?
Palladis exemplo ponendae tempora sume
    cuspidis : invenies et quod inermis agas.
tunc quoque inermis eras, cum te Romana sacerdos
10   cepit, ut huic urbi semina magna dares.
Silvia Vestalis (quid enim vetat inde moveri ?)
    sacra lavaturas mane petebat aquas.
ventum erat ad molli declivem tramite ripam :
    ponitur e summa fictilis urna coma.
15 fessa resedit humo ventosque accepit aperto
    pectore, turbatas restituitque comas.
dum sedet, umbrosae salices volucresque canorae
    fecerunt somnos et leve murmur aquae.
blanda quies furtim victis obrepsit ocellis,
20   et cadit a mento languida facta manus.
Mars videt hanc visamque cupit potiturque cupita
    et sua divina furta fefellit ope.

---

[a] See Appendix, p. 397.   [b] Silvia. See also ii. 383.

BOOK III

COME, warlike Mars[a]; lay down thy shield and spear for a brief space, and from thy helmet loose thy glistering locks. Haply thou mayest ask, What has a poet to do with Mars? From thee the month which now I sing doth take its name. Thyself dost see that fierce wars are waged by Minerva's hands. Is she for that the less at leisure for the liberal arts? After the pattern of Pallas take a time to put aside the lance. Thou shalt find something to do unarmed. Then, too, wast thou unarmed when the Roman priestess[b] captivated thee, that thou mightest bestow upon this city a great seed.

[11] Silvia the Vestal (for why not start from her?) went in the morning to fetch water to wash the holy things. When she had come to where the path ran gently down the sloping bank, she set down her earthenware pitcher from her head. Weary, she sat her on the ground and opened her bosom to catch the breezes, and composed her ruffled hair. While she sat, the shady willows and the tuneful birds and the soft murmur of the water induced to sleep. Sweet slumber overpowered and crept stealthily over her eyes, and her languid hand dropped from her chin. Mars saw her; the sight inspired him with desire, and his desire was followed by possession, but by his power divine he hid his

somnus abit, iacet ipsa gravis : iam scilicet intra
    viscera Romanae conditor urbis erat.
25 languida consurgit nec scit, cur languida surgat,
    et peragit talis arbore nixa sonos :
  " utile sit faustumque, precor, quod imagine somni
    vidimus.   an somno clarius illud erat ?
ignibus Iliacis aderam, cum lapsa capillis
30   decidit ante sacros lanea vitta focos.
inde duae pariter, visu mirabile, palmae
    surgunt : ex illis altera maior erat,
et gravibus ramis totum protexerat orbem
    contigeratque sua sidera summa coma.
35 ecce meus ferrum patruus molitur in illas :
    terreor admonitu, corque timore micat.
Martia picus avis gemino pro stipite pugnant
    et lupa : tuta per hos utraque palma fuit."
dixerat et plenam non firmis viribus urnam
40   sustulit ; implerat, dum sua visa refert.
interea crescente Remo, crescente Quirino,
    caelesti tumidus pondere venter erat.
quo minus emeritis exiret cursibus annus,
    restabant nitido iam duo signa deo :
45 Silvia fit mater.   Vestae simulacra feruntur
    virgineas oculis opposuisse manus ;
ara deae certe tremuit pariente ministra,
    et subiit cineres territa flamma suos.
hoc ubi cognovit contemptor Amulius aequi
50   (nam raptas fratri victor habebat opes),
amne iubet mergi geminos.   scelus unda refugit ;

---

        a Amulius, king of Alba.

stolen joys. Sleep left her ; she lay big, for already within her womb there was Rome's founder. Languid she rose, nor knew why she rose languid, and leaning on a tree she spake these words : " Useful and fortunate, I pray, may that turn out which I saw in a vision of sleep. Or was the vision too clear for sleep ? Methought I was by the fire of Ilium, when the woollen fillet slipped from my hair and fell before the sacred hearth. From the fillet there sprang— a wondrous sight—two palm-trees side by side. Of them one was the taller and by its heavy boughs spread a canopy over the whole world, and with its foliage touched the topmost stars. Lo, mine uncle [a] wielded an axe against the trees ; the warning terrified me and my heart did throb with fear. A woodpecker—the bird of Mars—and a she-wolf fought in defence of the twin trunks, and by their help both of the palms were saved." She finished speaking, and by a feeble effort lifted the full pitcher ; she had filled it while she was telling her vision. Meantime her belly swelled with a heavenly burden, for Remus was growing, and growing, too, was Quirinus.

[43] When now two heavenly signs remained for the bright god to traverse, before the year could complete its course and run out, Silvia became a mother. The images of Vesta are said to have covered their eyes with their virgin hands ; certainly the altar of the goddess trembled, when her priestess was brought to bed, and the terrified flame sank under its own ashes. When Amulius learned of this, scorner of justice that he was (for he had vanquished his brother and robbed him of power), he ordered the twins to be sunk in the river.

OVID

in sicca pueri destituuntur humo.
lacte quis infantes nescit crevisse ferino,
  et picum expositis saepe tulisse cibos ?
55 non ego te, tantae nutrix Larentia gentis,
  nec taceam vestras, Faustule pauper, opes.
vester honos veniet, cum Larentalia dicam :
  acceptus geniis illa December habet.
Martia ter senos proles adoleverat annos,
60   et suberat flavae iam nova barba comae :
omnibus agricolis armentorumque magistris
  Iliadae fratres iura petita dabant.
saepe domum veniunt praedonum sanguine laeti
  et redigunt actos in sua rura boves.
65 ut genus audierunt, animos pater editus auget,
  et pudet in paucis nomen habere casis,
Romuleoque cadit traiectus Amulius ense,
  regnaque longaevo restituuntur avo.
moenia conduntur, quae quamvis parva fuerunt,
70   non tamen expediit transsiluisse Remo.
iam, modo quae fuerant silvae pecorumque recessus,
  urbs erat, aeternae cum pater urbis ait :
" arbiter armorum, de cuius sanguine natus
  credor (et, ut credar, pignora multa dabo),
75 a te principium Romano dicimus anno :
  primus de patrio nomine mensis erit."
vox rata fit, patrioque vocat de nomine mensem.
  dicitur haec pietas grata fuisse deo.
et tamen ante omnes Martem coluere priores :

ᵃ Romulus and Remus, sons of Ilia (Silvia), or descendants of Ilus (founder of Troy).
ᵇ Mars was worshipped by the Latin and other Italian peoples before the foundation of Rome. He was peculiarly the god of Rome, as Athena was of Athens, Dictynna or Britomartis of Crete, Hephaestus of Lemnos, Hera of Sparta, and Pan of Arcadia.

124

The water shrank from such a crime, and the boys
were left on dry land. Who knows not that the
infants throve on the milk of a wild beast, and that
a woodpecker often brought food to the abandoned
babes? Nor would I pass thee by in silence, Larentia,
nurse of so great a nation, nor the help that thou
didst give, poor Faustulus. Your honour will find
its place when I come to tell of the Larentalia;
that festival falls in December, the month dear to
the mirthful spirits. Thrice six years old was the
progeny of Mars, and already under their yellow
hair sprouted a fresh young beard: to all the husbandmen and masters of herds the brothers, sons of
Ilia,ᵃ gave judgement by request. Often they came
home glad at blood of robbers spilt, and to their
own domain drove back the raided kine. When they
heard the secret of their birth, their spirits rose with
the revelation of their sire, and they thought shame
to have a name in a few huts. Amulius fell, pierced
by the sword of Romulus, and the kingdom was
restored to their aged grandfather. Walls were
built, which, small though they were, it had been
better for Remus not to have overleaped. And
now what of late had been woods and pastoral
solitudes was a city, when thus the father of the
eternal city spake: " Umpire of war, from whose
blood I am believed to have sprung (and to confirm
that belief I will give many proofs), we name the
beginning of the Roman year after thee; the first
month shall be called by my father's name." The
promise was kept; he did call the month by his
father's name: this pious deed is said to have been
well pleasing to the god. And yet the earlier ages
had worshipped Mars above all the gods;ᵇ therein

80   hoc dederat studiis bellica turba suis.
    Pallada Cecropidae, Minoïa Creta Dianam,
       Volcanum tellus Hypsipylea colit,
    Iunonem Sparte Pelopeïadesque Mycenae,
       pinigerum Fauni Maenalis ora caput:
85 Mars Latio venerandus erat, quia praesidet armis:
       arma ferae genti remque decusque dabant.
    quod si forte vacas, peregrinos inspice fastos:
       mensis in his etiam nomine Martis erit.
    tertius Albanis, quintus fuit ille Faliscis,
90   sextus apud populos, Hernica terra, tuos.
    inter Aricinos Albanaque tempora constat
       factaque Telegoni moenia celsa manu.
    quintum Laurentes, bis quintum Aequiculus acer,
       a tribus hunc primum turba Curensis habet;
95 et tibi cum proavis, miles Peligne, Sabinis
       convenit: huic genti quartus utrique deus.
    Romulus hos omnes ut vinceret ordine saltem,
       sanguinis auctori tempora prima dedit.
    nec totidem veteres, quot nunc, habuere Kalendas:
100   ille minor geminis mensibus annus erat.
    nondum tradiderat victas victoribus artes
       Graecia, facundum sed male forte genus.
    qui bene pugnabat, Romanam noverat artem:
       mittere qui poterat pila, disertus erat.
105 quis tunc aut Hyadas aut Pleiadas Atlanteas
       senserat, aut geminos esse sub axe polos?

---

[a] Lemnos, after its queen Hypsipyle.
[b] Arcadia.   [c] Tusculum.
[d] These are local Italian calendars.

a warlike folk followed their bent. Pallas is worshipped by the sons of Cecrops, Diana by Minoan
Crete, Vulcan by the Hypsipylean land,[a] Juno by
Sparta and Pelopid Mycenae, while the Maenalian
country[b] worships Faunus, whose head is crowned
with pine. Mars was the god to be revered by
Latium, for that he is the patron of the sword;
'twas the sword that won for a fierce race empire
and glory.

[87] If you are at leisure, look into the foreign
calendars, and you shall find in them also a month
named after Mars. It was the third month in the
Alban calendar, the fifth in the Faliscan, the sixth
among thy peoples, land of the Hernicans. The
Arician calendar is in agreement with the Alban
and with that of the city[c] whose lofty walls were
built by the hand of Telegonus. It is the fifth
month in the calendar of the Laurentes, the tenth in
the calendar of the hardy Aequians, the fourth in
the calendar of the folk of Cures, and the soldierly
Pelignians agree with their Sabine forefathers; both
peoples reckon Mars the god of the fourth month.[d]
In order that he might take precedence of all these,
Romulus assigned the beginning of the year to the
author of his being.

[99] Nor had the ancients as many Calends as
we have now: their year was short by two
months. Conquered Greece had not yet trans-
mitted her arts to the victors; her people were
eloquent but hardly brave. The doughty warrior
understood the art of Rome, and he who could
throw javelins was eloquent. Who then had noticed
the Hyades or the Pleiades, daughters of Atlas, or
that there were two poles in the firmament? and

esse duas Arctos, quarum Cynosura petatur
  Sidoniis, Helicen Graia carina notet ?
signaque quae longo frater percenseat anno,
110 ire per haec uno mense sororis equos ?
libera currebant et inobservata per annum
  sidera ; constabat sed tamen esse deos.
non illi caelo labentia signa tenebant,
  sed sua, quae magnum perdere crimen erat.
115 illa quidem foeno ; sed erat reverentia foeno,
  quantam nunc aquilas cernis habere tuas.
pertica suspensos portabat longa maniplos,
  unde maniplaris nomina miles habet.
ergo animi indociles et adhuc ratione carentes
120 mensibus egerunt lustra minora decem.
annus erat, decimum cum luna receperat orbem :
  hic numerus magno tunc in honore fuit ;
seu quia tot digiti, per quos numerare solemus,
  seu quia bis quinto femina mense parit,
125 seu quod adusque decem numero crescente venitur,
  principium spatiis sumitur inde novis.
inde patres centum denos secrevit in orbes
  Romulus, hastatos instituitque decem ;
et totidem princeps, totidem pilanus habebat
130 corpora, legitimo quique merebat equo.
quin etiam partes totidem Titiensibus ille,
  quosque vocant Ramnes, Luceribusque dedit.
adsuetos igitur numeros servavit in anno.
  hoc luget spatio femina maesta virum.

---

    [a] Little Bear, κυνὸς οὐρά, the dog's tail.
    [b] Great Bear, ἑλική, the twister.
    [c] Apollo and Diana, the sun and moon, and the signs of
the Zodiac.

that there are two Bears, of which the Sidonians
steer by Cynosura,^a while the Grecian mariner keeps
his eye on Helice^b? and that the signs which the
brother travels through in a long year the horses of
the sister traverse in a single month^c? The stars
ran their courses free and unmarked throughout
the year; yet everybody agreed that they were
gods. Heaven's gliding ensigns were beyond their
reach, not so their own, to lose which was a great
crime. Their ensigns were of hay, but as deep
reverence was paid to hay as now you see paid to
the eagles. A long pole carried the hanging bundles
(*maniplos*); from them the private (*maniplaris*) soldier
takes his name. Hence through ignorance and lack
of science they reckoned lustres, each of which was
too short by ten months. A year was counted when
the moon had returned to the full for the tenth time:
that number was then in great honour, whether
because that is the number of the fingers by which we
are wont to count, or because a woman brings forth in
twice five months, or because the numerals increase
up to ten, and from that we start a fresh round.
Hence Romulus divided the hundred senators into
ten groups, and instituted ten companies of spear-
men (*hastati*); and just so many companies there
were of first-line men (*principes*), and also of
javelin-men (*pilani*); and so too with the men who
served on horses furnished by the state. Nay,
Romulus assigned just the same number of divisions
to the tribes, the Titienses, the Ramnes, as they are
called, and the Luceres. Therefore in his arrange-
ment of the year he kept the familiar number.
That is the period for which a sad wife mourns
for her husband.

135 neu dubites, primae fuerint quin ante Kalendae
    Martis, ad haec animum signa referre potes.
laurea, flaminibus quae toto perstitit anno,
    tollitur, et frondes sunt in honore novae.
ianua tunc regis posita viret arbore Phoebi :
140   ante tuas fit idem, curia prisca, fores.
Vesta quoque ut folio niteat velata recenti,
    cedit ab Iliacis laurea cana focis.
adde, quod arcana fieri novus ignis in aede
    dicitur, et vires flamma refecta capit.
145 nec mihi parva fides, annos hinc isse priores,
    Anna quod hoc coepta est mense Perenna coli.
hinc etiam veteres initi memorantur honores
    ad spatium belli, perfide Poene, tui.
denique quintus ab hoc fuerat Quintilis, et inde
150   incipit, a numero nomina quisquis habet.
primus oliviferis Romam deductus ab arvis
    Pompilius menses sensit abesse duos,
sive hoc a Samio doctus, qui posse renasci
    nos putat, Egeria sive monente sua.
155 sed tamen errabant etiam nunc tempora, donec
    Caesaris in multis haec quoque cura fuit.
non haec ille deus tantaeque propaginis auctor
    credidit officiis esse minora suis,
promissumque sibi voluit praenoscere caelum

---

    a See ii. 527 note.   *b* Vestal.
    c See below, l. 523.
    d If Hannibal is meant here, Ovid refers to the Second Punic
War, which began in 218 B.C., but the practice really varied
until it was finally fixed in 153 B.C. for January 1.
    e Pythagoras.   *f* In 46 B.C.

¹³⁵ If you would convince yourself that the Calends
of March were really the beginning of the year,
you may refer to the following proofs : the laurel
branch of the flamens, after remaining in its place
the whole year, is removed (on that day), and
fresh leaves are put in the place of honour ;
then the king's door is green with the tree of
Phoebus, which is set at it ; and at thy portal,
Old Chapel of the Wards, the same thing is done ; ᵃ
the withered laurel is withdrawn from the Ilian ᵇ
hearth, that Vesta also may make a brave show,
dressed in fresh leaves. Besides 'tis said that
a new fire is lighted in her secret shrine, and the
rekindled flame gains strength. And to my thinking
no small proof that the years of old began with
March is furnished by the observation that Anna
Perenna ᶜ begins to be worshipped in this month.
With March, too, the magistrates are recorded to
have entered on office, down to the time when,
faithless Carthaginian, thou didst wage thy war.ᵈ
Lastly, the month of Quintilis is the fifth (*quintus*)
month, reckoned from March, and with it begin the
months which take their names from numbers.
(Numa) Pompilius, who was escorted to Rome from
the lands where olives grow, was the first to perceive
that two months were lacking to the year, whether
he learned that from the Samian sage ᵉ who thought
that we could be born again, or whether it was his
Egeria who taught him. Nevertheless the calendar
was still erratic down to the time when Caesar took
it, like so much else, in charge.ᶠ That god, the
founder of a mighty line, did not deem the matter
beneath his attention. Fain was he to foreknow that
heaven which was his promised home ; he would not

160   nec deus ignotas hospes inire domos.
    ille moras solis, quibus in sua signa rediret,
      traditur exactis disposuisse notis.
    is decies senos tercentum et quinque diebus
      iunxit et e pleno tempora quinta die.
165 hic anni modus est : in lustrum accedere debet,
      quae consummatur partibus, una dies.

1. D · K · MAR · N℈

" Si licet occultos monitus audire deorum
    vatibus, ut certe fama licere putat,
cum sis officiis, Gradive, virilibus aptus,
170   dic mihi, matronae cur tua festa colant."
sic ego. sic posita dixit mihi casside Mavors,
    sed tamen in dextra missilis hasta fuit :
" nunc primum studiis pacis, deus utilis armis,
    advocor et gressus in nova castra fero,
175 nec piget incepti ; iuvat hac quoque parte morari,
    hoc solam ne se posse Minerva putet.
disce, Latinorum vates operose dierum,
    quod petis, et memori pectore dicta nota.
parva fuit, si prima velis elementa referre,
180   Roma, sed in parva spes tamen huius erat.
moenia iam stabant, populus angusta futuris,
    credita sed turbae tunc nimis ampla suae.
quae fuerit nostri, si quaeris, regia nati,
    aspice de canna straminibusque domum.
185 in stipula placidi capiebat munera somni,
    et tamen ex illo venit in astra toro.

---

    [a] Really a fourth. Ovid seems to have thought that the intercalary day was added in each period of five years.
    [b] The Casa Romuli on the Palatine; see i. 199.

enter as a stranger god mansions unknown. He is
said to have drawn up an exact table of the periods
within which the sun returns to his proper signs.
To three hundred and five days he added ten times
six days and a fifth *a* part of a whole day. That is
the measure of the year. The single day compounded
of the (five) parts is to be added to the lustre.

KAL. MART. 1st

[167] " If bards may list to secret promptings of the
gods, as surely rumour thinks they may, tell me,
thou Marching God (*Gradivus*), why matrons keep
thy feast, whereas thou art apter to receive service
from men." Thus I inquired, and thus did Mars
answer me, laying aside his helmet, though in his
right hand he kept his throwing spear : " Now for
the first time in the year am I, a god of war, invoked
to promote the pursuits of peace, and I march into
new camps, nor does it irk me so to do ; upon
this function also do I love to dwell, lest Minerva
should fancy that such power is hers alone. Thy
answer take, laborious singer of the Latin days, and
write my words on memory's tablets. If you would
trace it back to its beginning, Rome was but little,
nevertheless in that little town was hope of this
great city. The walls were already standing,
boundaries too cramped for future peoples, but
then deemed too large for their inhabitants. If you
ask what my son's palace was, behold yon house of
reeds and straw.*b* There on the litter did he take
the boon of peaceful sleep, and yet from that same
bed he passed among the stars. Already the

iamque loco maius nomen Romanus habebat,
    nec coniunx illi nec socer ullus erat.
spernebant generos inopes vicinia dives,
190   et male credebar sanguinis auctor ego.
in stabulis habitasse et oves pavisse nocebat
    iugeraque inculti pauca tenere soli.
cum pare quaeque suo coeunt volucresque feraeque,
    atque aliquam, de qua procreet, anguis habet ;
195 extremis dantur connubia gentibus : at quae
    Romano vellet nubere, nulla fuit.
indolui ' patriamque dedi tibi, Romule, mentem :
    tolle preces,' dixi ' quod petis arma dabunt.'
festa parat Conso.   Consus tibi cetera dicet
200   illo facta die, dum sua sacra canes.
intumuere Cures et quos dolor attigit idem :
    tum primum generis intulit arma socer.
iamque fere raptae matrum quoque nomen habebant,
    tractaque erant longa bella propinqua mora :
205 conveniunt nuptae dictam Iunonis in aedem,
    quas inter mea sic est nurus ausa loqui :
' o pariter raptae (quoniam hoc commune tenemus)
    non ultra lente possumus esse piae.
stant acies, sed utra di sint pro parte rogandi,
210   eligite : hinc coniunx, hinc pater arma tenet.
quaerendum est, viduae fieri malitis an orbae :
    consilium vobis forte piumque dabo.'
consilium dederat : parent crinesque resolvunt

---

    [a] There were two festivals of Consus (*Consualia*), on
August 21 and December 15.   When he comes to these the
poet will tell of the Rape of the Sabines.   In the last battle,
the wives threw themselves between the combatants, and
persuaded them to make peace.   Livy i. 13.
    [b] A covert allusion to the Civil Wars : Pompey's wife
Julia was Caesar's daughter.
    [c] Romulus, for Mars is speaking.

Roman had a name that reached beyond his city,
but neither wife nor wife's father had he. Wealthy
neighbours scorned to take poor men for their
sons-in-law ; hardly did they believe that I myself
was the author of the breed. It told against the
Romans that they dwelt in cattle-stalls, and fed
sheep, and owned a few acres of waste land. Birds
and beasts mate each with its kind, and a snake has
some female of which to breed. The right of inter-
marriage is granted to peoples far away ; yet was
there no people that would wed with Romans. I
chafed and said, ' Thy father's temper, Romulus, I
have bestowed on thee. A truce to prayers ! What
thou seekest, arms will give.' Romulus prepared a
feast for Consus.[a] The rest that happened on that
day Consus will tell thee, when thou shalt come to
sing of his rites. Cures and all who suffered the
same wrong were furious : then for the first time
did a father wage war upon his daughters' husbands.[b]
And now the ravished brides could claim the style
of mothers also, and yet the war between the
kindred folks kept lingering on, when the wives
assembled by appointment in the temple of Juno.
Among them my son's[c] wife thus made bold to
speak : ' O wives ravished alike—for that is a
trait we have in common—no longer may we dawdle
in our duties to our kin. The battle is set in array,
but choose for which side ye will pray the gods to
intervene : on one side stand your husbands in arms
and on the other side your sires : the question is
whether ye prefer to be widows or orphans. I will
give you a piece of advice both bold and dutiful.'
She gave the advice : they obeyed, and unbound

135

maestaque funerea corpora veste tegunt.
215 iam steterant acies ferro mortique paratae,
    iam lituus pugnae signa daturus erat:
cum raptae veniunt inter patresque virosque,
    inque sinu natos, pignora cara, tenent.
ut medium campi passis tetigere capillis,
220   in terram posito procubuere genu,
et, quasi sentirent, blando clamore nepotes
    tendebant ad avos bracchia parva suos:
qui poterat clamabat avum tum denique visum,
    et qui vix poterat posse coactus erat.
225 tela viris animique cadunt, gladiisque remotis
    dant soceri generis accipiuntque manus,
laudatasque tenent natas, scutoque nepotem
    fert avus: hic scuti dulcior usus erat.
inde diem, quae prima, meas celebrare Kalendas
230   Oebaliae matres non leve munus habent,
aut quia committi strictis mucronibus ausae
    finierant lacrimis Martia bella suis;
vel quod erat de me feliciter Ilia mater,
    rite colunt matres sacra diemque meum.
235 quid, quod hiems adoperta gelu tunc denique cedit,
    et pereunt lapsae sole tepente nives,
arboribus redeunt detonsae frigore frondes,
    uvidaque in tenero palmite gemma tumet,
quaeque diu latuit, nunc se qua tollat in auras,
240   fertilis occultas invenit herba vias?
nunc fecundus ager, pecoris nunc hora creandi,
    nunc avis in ramo tecta laremque parat:
tempora iure colunt Latiae fecunda parentes,

---

[a] Sabine. See i. 260 note.

their hair, and clad their bodies in the sad weeds of
mourners. Already the armies were drawn up in
array, alert for carnage ; already the bugle was about
to give the signal for battle, when the ravished wives
interposed between their fathers and husbands,
bearing at their bosoms the dear pledges of love,
their babes. When with their streaming hair they
reached the middle of the plain, they knelt down on
the ground, and the grandchildren stretched out
their little arms to their grandfathers with winsome
cries, as if they understood. Such as could cried
' Grandfather ! ' to him whom then they saw for
the first time ; such as could hardly do it were forced
to try. The weapons and the passions of the warriors
fall, and laying their swords aside fathers-in-law and
sons-in-law grasp each other's hands. They praise
and embrace their daughters, and the grandsire
carries his grandchild on his shield ; that was a
sweeter use to which to put the shield. Hence the
duty, no light one, of celebrating the first day, my
Calends, is incumbent on Oebalian *a* mothers, either
because, boldly thrusting themselves on the bare
blades, they by their tears did end these martial
wars ; or else mothers duly observe the rites on
my day, because Ilia was happily made a mother
by me. Moreover, frosty winter then at last retires,
and the snows perish, melted by the warm sun ;
the leaves, shorn by the cold, return to the trees, and
moist within the tender shoot the bud doth swell ;
now too the rank grass, long hidden, discovers secret
paths whereby to lift its head in air. Now is the
field fruitful, now is the hour for breeding cattle,
now doth the bird upon the bough construct a nest
and home ; 'tis right that Latin mothers should

137

quarum militiam votaque partus habet.
245 adde quod, excubias ubi rex Romanus agebat,
    qui nunc Esquilias nomina collis habet,
illic a nuribus Iunoni templa Latinis
    hac sunt, si memini, publica facta die.
quid moror et variis onero tua pectora causis ?
250   eminet ante oculos, quod petis, ecce tuos.
mater amat nuptas : matrum me turba frequentat :
    haec nos praecipue tam pia causa decet.''
ferte deae flores : gaudet florentibus herbis
    haec dea : de tenero cingite flore caput :
255 dicite " tu nobis lucem, Lucina, dedisti " :
    dicite " tu voto parturientis ades."
si qua tamen gravida est, resoluto crine precetur,
    ut solvat partus molliter illa suos.

Quis mihi nunc dicet, quare caelestia Martis
260   arma ferant Salii Mamuriumque canant ?
nympha, mone, nemori stagnoque operata Dianae ;
    nympha, Numae coniunx, ad tua facta veni.
vallis Aricinae silva praecinctus opaca
    est lacus, antiqua religione sacer.
265 hic latet Hippolytus loris direptus equorum,
    unde nemus nullis illud aditur equis.
licia dependent longas velantia saepes,
    et posita est meritae multa tabella deae.

---

^a He derives the name from *excubiae*. It may come from
aesculus, " beech." Romulus had a post here set to watch
Titus Tatius on the neighbouring hill.
   ^b The *Matronalia*, in honour of Juno Lucina.
   ^c Dancing priests. They carried a spear and one of the
ancilia or sacred shields. See 377 note, below, and
Appendix, p. 399.
   ^d Lacus Nemorensis, now Nemi. See Appendix, p. 403.
   ^e Hippolytus, after being torn to pieces by his horses near

observe the fruitful season, for in their travail they
both fight and pray. Add to this that where
the Roman king kept watch, on the hill which
now bears the name of Esquiline,ᵃ a temple was
founded, if I remember aright, on this very day by
the Latin matrons in honour of Juno. But why
should I spin out the time and burden your memory
with various reasons ? The answer that you seek
stands out plainly before your eyes. My mother
loves brides ; a crowd of mothers throngs my
temple ; so pious a reason is above all becoming to
her and me." ᵇ Bring ye flowers to the goddess ;
this goddess delights in flowering plants ; with fresh
flowers wreathe your heads. Say ye, " Thou, Lucina,
hast bestowed on us the light (*lucem*) of life " ; say
ye, " Thou dost hear the prayer of women in travail."
But let her who is with child unbind her hair before
she prays, in order that the goddess may gently
unbind her teeming womb.

²⁵⁹ Who will now tell me why the Salii ᶜ bear the
heavenly weapons of Mars and sing of Mamurius ?
Inform me, thou nymph who on Diana's grove and
lake dost wait ; thou nymph, wife of Numa, come
tell of thine own deeds. In the Arician vale there
is a lake begirt by shady woods and hallowed by
religion from of old.ᵈ Here Hippolytus ᵉ lies hid,
who by the reins of his steeds was rent in pieces :
hence no horses enter that grove. The long fence
is draped with hanging threads, and many a tablet
there attests the merit of the goddess. Often doth

Troezen, was restored to life by Aesculapius and transported
by Diana to the woods of Aricia, where he took the name of
Virbius.

saepe potens voti, frontem redimita coronis,
270   femina lucentes portat ab urbe faces.
regna tenent fortes manibus pedibusque fugaces,
   et perit exemplo postmodo quisque suo.
defluit incerto lapidosus murmure rivus :
   saepe, sed exiguis haustibus, inde bibi.
275 Egeria est, quae praebet aquas, dea grata Camenis :
   illa Numae coniunx consiliumque fuit.
principio nimium promptos ad bella Quirites
   molliri placuit iure deumque metu ;
inde datae leges, ne firmior omnia posset,
280   coeptaque sunt pure tradita sacra coli.
exuitur feritas, armisque potentius aequum est,
   et cum cive pudet conseruisse manus ;
atque aliquis, modo trux, visa iam vertitur ara
   vinaque dat tepidis farraque salsa focis.
285 ecce deum genitor rutilas per nubila flammas
   spargit et effusis aethera siccat aquis ;
non alias missi cecidere frequentius ignes :
   rex pavet et volgi pectora terror habet.
cui dea " ne nimium terrere ! piabile fulmen
290   est," ait " et saevi flectitur ira Iovis.
sed poterunt ritum Picus Faunusque piandi
   tradere, Romani numen utrumque soli.
nec sine vi tradent : adhibe tu vincula captis."
   atque ita qua possint edidit arte capi.

---

   a A runaway slave reigns there as Rex Nemorensis, until a
stronger runaway slave dispossesses him. This is the theme
of the *Golden Bough.* See Appendix, p. 403.
   b Egeria was one of the Camenae, water-nymphs whose
spring flowed in a sacred grove outside the Porta Capena ;
but these came to be identified with the Muses.

a woman, whose prayer has been answered, carry from the city burning torches, while garlands wreathe her brows. The strong of hand and fleet of foot do there reign kings,[a] and each is slain thereafter even as himself had slain. A pebbly brook flows down with fitful murmur ; oft have I drunk of it, but in little sips. Egeria it is who doth supply the water, goddess dear to the Camenae [b] ; she was wife and councillor to Numa. At first the Quirites were too prone to fly to arms ; Numa resolved to soften their fierce temper by force of law and fear of gods. Hence laws were made, that the stronger might not in all things have his way, and rites, handed down from the fathers, began to be piously observed. Men put off savagery, justice was more puissant than arms, citizen thought shame to fight with citizen, and he who but now had shown himself truculent would at the sight of an altar be transformed and offer wine and salted spelt on the warm hearths.

[285] Lo, through the clouds the father of the gods scatters red lightnings, then clears the sky after the torrent rain : never before or since did hurtling fires fall thicker. The king quaked, and terror filled the hearts of common folk. To the king the goddess spake : " Fear not over much. It is possible to expiate the thunderbolt, and the wrath of angry Jove can be averted. But Picus and Faunus, each of them a deity native to Roman soil, will be able to teach the ritual of expiation.[c] They will teach it only upon compulsion. Catch them and clap them in bonds." And she revealed the ruse by which they could be caught. Under the Aventine there

[c] Faunus, or Faunus Fatuus, son of Picus, the woodpecker. The Greeks told a like story of Silenus.

141

295 lucus Aventino suberat niger ilicis umbra,
    quo posses viso dicere " numen inest."
  in medio gramen, muscoque adoperta virenti
    manabat saxo vena perennis aquae :
  inde fere soli Faunus Picusque bibebant.
300   huc venit et fonti rex Numa mactat ovem,
    plenaque odorati disponit pocula Bacchi,
    cumque suis antro conditus ipse latet.
  ad solitos veniunt silvestria numina fontes
    et relevant multo pectora sicca mero.
305 vina quies sequitur ; gelido Numa prodit ab antro
    vinclaque sopitas addit in arta manus.
  somnus ut abscessit, pugnando vincula temptant
    rumpere : pugnantes fortius illa tenent.
  tunc Numa : " di nemorum, factis ignoscite nostris,
310   si scelus ingenio scitis abesse meo ;
  quoque modo possit fulmen, monstrate, piari."
    sic Numa ; sic quatiens cornua Faunus ait :
  " magna petis nec quae monitu tibi discere nostro
    fas sit : habent finis numina nostra suos.
315 di sumus agrestes et qui dominemur in altis
    montibus : arbitrium est in sua tela Iovi.
  hunc tu non poteris per te deducere caelo,
    at poteris nostra forsitan usus ope."
  dixerat haec Faunus ; par est sententia Pici :
320   " deme " tamen " nobis vincula," Picus ait :
  " Iuppiter huc veniet, valida perductus ab arte.
    nubila promissi Styx mihi testis erit."
  emissi laqueis quid agant, quae carmina dicant,
    quaque trahant superis sedibus arte Iovem,

lay a grove black with the shade of holm-oaks ; at
sight of it you could say, " There is a spirit here."
A sward was in the midst, and, veiled by green moss,
there trickled from a rock a rill of never-failing
water. At it Faunus and Picus were wont to drink
alone. Hither King Numa came, and sacrificed a
sheep to the spring, and set out bowls full of fragrant
wine. Then with his folk he hid him close within
a cave. To their accustomed springs the woodland
spirits came, and slaked their thirst with copious
draughts of wine. Sleep followed the debauch ;
from the chill cave Numa came forth and thrust the
sleepers' hands into tight shackles. When slumber
left them, they tried and strained to burst the
shackles, but the more they strained the stronger
held the shackles. Then Numa spake : " Gods of
the groves, forgive my deed, if that ye know my
mind harbours no ill intent, and show me in what way
a thunderbolt can be expiated." Thus Numa spake,
and thus, shaking his horns, Faunus replied : " Thou
askest great things, such as it is not lawful for thee
to learn by our disclosure : divinities like ours have
their appointed bounds. Rustic deities are we, who
have dominion in the mountains high : Jove has
the mastery over his own weapons. Him thou
couldst never of thyself draw down from heaven,
but haply thou mayest yet be able, if only thou wilt
make use of our help." So Faunus said. Picus was
of the like opinion : " But take our shackles off,"
quoth he ; " Jupiter will come hither, drawn by
powerful art. Witness my promise, cloudy Styx."
What they did when they were let out of the trap,
what spells they spoke, and by what art they dragged
Jupiter from his home above, 'twere sin for man to

325 scire nefas homini : nobis concessa canentur
  quaeque pio dici vatis ab ore licet.
 eliciunt caelo te, Iuppiter, unde minores
  nunc quoque te celebrant Eliciumque vocant.
 constat Aventinae tremuisse cacumina silvae,
330 terraque subsedit pondere pressa Iovis.
 corda micant regis, totoque e corpore sanguis
  fugit, et hirsutae deriguere comae.
 ut rediit animus, " da certa piamina " dixit
  " fulminis, altorum rexque paterque deum,
335 si tua contigimus manibus donaria puris,
  hoc quoque, quod petitur, si pia lingua rogat."
 adnuit oranti, sed verum ambage remota
  abdidit et dubio terruit ore virum.
 " caede caput " dixit : cui rex " parebimus," inquit
340 " caedenda est hortis eruta caepa meis."
 addidit hic " hominis " : " sumes " ait ille " capillos."
  postulat hic animam, cui Numa " piscis " ait.
 risit et " his " inquit " facito mea tela procures,
  o vir conloquio non abigende deum.
345 sed tibi, protulerit cum totum crastinus orbem
  Cynthius, imperii pignora certa dabo."
 dixit et ingenti tonitru super aethera motum
  fertur, adorantem destituitque Numam.
 ille redit laetus memoratque Quiritibus acta :
350 tarda venit dictis difficilisque fides.
 " at certe credemur," ait " si verba sequetur
  exitus : en audi crastina, quisquis ades.
 protulerit terris cum totum Cynthius orbem,
  Iuppiter imperii pignora certa dabit."

---

a The onion, human hair, and fish, are prescribed as
expiation for a thunderstroke. No one knows why, but
Ovid suggests that they are a substitute for human sacrifice.

know. My song shall deal with lawful things, such
as the lips of pious bard may speak. They drew
(*eliciunt*) thee from the sky, O Jupiter, whence later
generations to this day celebrate thee by the name
of Elicius. Sure it is the tops of the Aventine trees
did quiver, and the earth sank down under the
weight of Jupiter. The king's heart throbbed, the
blood shrank from his whole body, and his bristling
hair stood stiff. When he came to himself, " King and
father of the high gods," he said, " vouchsafe expia-
tions sure for thunderbolts, if with pure hands we have
touched thine offerings, and if for that which now we
ask a pious tongue doth pray." The god granted his
prayer, but hid the truth in sayings dark and tortuous,
and alarmed the man by an ambiguous utterance.
" Cut off the head," said he.[a] The king answered
him, " We will obey. We'll cut an onion, dug up in
my garden." The god added, " A man's." " Thou
shalt get," said the other, " his hair." The god
demanded a life, and Numa answered him, " A fish's
life." The god laughed and said, " See to it that by
these things thou dost expiate my bolts, O man whom
none may keep from converse with the gods ! But
when to-morrow's sun shall have put forth his full
orb, I will give thee sure pledges of empire." He
spake, and in a loud peal of thunder was wafted above
the riven sky, leaving Numa worshipping. The king
returned joyful and told the Quirites of what had
passed. They were slow and loth to believe his
saying. " But surely," said he, " we shall be believed
if the event follow my words. Behold, all ye here
present, hearken to what to-morrow shall bring forth.
When the sun shall have lifted his full orb above the
earth, Jupiter will give sure pledges of empire."

355 discedunt dubii, promissaque tarda videntur,
    dependetque fides a veniente die.
  mollis erat tellus rorata mane pruina:
    ante sui populus limina regis adest.
  prodit et in solio medius consedit acerno.
360   innumeri circa stantque silentque viri.
  ortus erat summo tantummodo margine Phoebus:
    sollicitae mentes speque metuque pavent.
  constitit atque caput niveo velatus amictu
    iam bene dis notas sustulit ille manus,
365 atque ita " tempus adest promissi muneris," inquit
    " pollicitam dictis, Iuppiter, adde fidem."
  dum loquitur, totum iam sol emoverat orbem,
    et gravis aetherio venit ab axe fragor.
  ter tonuit sine nube deus, tria fulmina misit.
370   credite dicenti: mira, sed acta, loquor.
  a media caelum regione dehiscere coepit;
    summisere oculos cum duce turba suo.
  ecce levi scutum versatum leniter aura
    decidit.   a populo clamor ad astra venit.
375 tollit humo munus caesa prius ille iuvenca,
    quae dederat nulli colla premenda iugo,
  idque ancile vocat, quod ab omni parte recisum est,
    quemque notes oculis, angulus omnis abest.
  tum, memor imperii sortem consistere in illo,
380   consilium multae calliditatis init.
  plura iubet fieri simili caelata figura,
    error ut ante oculos insidiantis eat.

ᵃ As though from *ancisus* (in Varro *ambecisus*).

They separated full of doubt, and thought it long to
await the promised sign; their belief hung on the
coming day. Soft was the earth with hoar frost
spread like dew at morn, when the people gathered
at the threshold of their king. Forth he came
and sat him down in their midst upon a throne
of maple wood; unnumbered men stood round him
silent.

361 Scarcely had Phoebus shown a rim above the
horizon : their anxious minds with hope and fear did
quake. The king took his stand, and, his head veiled
in a snow-white hood, lifted up his hands, hands which
the gods already knew so well. And thus he spoke :
" The time has come to receive the promised boon ;
fulfil thy promise, Jupiter." Even while he spoke,
the sun had already lifted his full orb above the
horizon, and a loud crash rang out from heaven's
vault. Thrice did the god thunder from a cloudless
sky, thrice did he hurl his bolts. Take my word
for it : what I say is wonderful but true. At the
zenith the sky began to yawn ; the multitude and
their leader lifted up their eyes. Lo, swaying gently
in the light breeze, a shield fell down. The people
sent up a shout that reached the stars. The king
lifted from the ground the gift, but not till he had
sacrificed a heifer, which had never submitted her
neck to the burden of the yoke, and he called the
shield *ancile*,[a] because it was cut away (*recisum*) on all
sides, and there was no angle that you could mark.
Then, remembering that the fate of empire was
bound up with it, he formed a very shrewd design.
He ordered that many shields should be made,
wrought after the same pattern, in order to deceive a traitor's eyes. The work was finished by

147

Mamurius (morum fabraene exactior artis,
    difficile est ulli dicere) clausit opus.
385 cui Numa munificus " facti pete praemia," dixit ;
    " si mea nota fides, inrita nulla petes."
iam dederat Saliis a saltu nomina dicta
    armaque et ad certos verba canenda modos.
tum sic Mamurius : " merces mihi gloria detur,
390   nominaque extremo carmine nostra sonent."
inde sacerdotes operi promissa vetusto
    praemia persolvunt Mamuriumque vocant.
nubere siqua voles, quamvis properabitis ambo,
    differ ; habent parvae commoda magna morae.
395 arma movent pugnas, pugna est aliena maritis ;
    condita cum fuerint, aptius omen erit.
his etiam coniunx apicati sancta Dialis
    lucibus inpexas debet habere comas.

2. EF   3. FC   4. GC

Tertia nox de mense suos ubi moverit ignes,
400   conditus e geminis Piscibus alter erit.
nam duo sunt : austris hic est, aquilonibus ille
    proximus ; a vento nomen uterque tenet.

5. HC

Cum croceis rorare genis Tithonia coniunx
    coeperit et quintae tempora lucis aget.

---

      a Probably an Oscan name of Mars.
   b He wore a cap with an *apex*, a point or peak.
     c One was called Νότιος, one Βόρειος.
        d Aurora.

Mamurius; whether he was more perfect in character or in smithcraft, it would be hard for any man to say. Bountiful Numa said to him, " Ask a reward for your service. If I have a reputation for honesty, you shall not ask in vain." He had already named the Salii from their dancing (*saltus*), and had given them arms and a song to be sung to a certain tune. Then Mamurius made answer thus : " Give me glory for my reward, and let my name be chanted at the end of the song." Hence the priests pay the reward that was promised for the work of old, and they invoke Mamurius.[a]

393 If, damsel, thou wouldst wed, put off the wedding, however great the haste ye both may be in; short delay hath great advantage. Weapons excite to battle, and battle ill assorts with married folk; when the weapons shall have been stored away, the omens will be more favourable. On these days, too, the holy wife of the Flamen Dialis in his peaked cap [b] must keep her hair uncombed.

V. Non. 3rd

399 When the third night of the month has shifted her starry fires, one of the two Fishes will have disappeared. For there are two : one of them is next neighbour to the South Winds, the other to the North Winds ; each of them takes its name from the wind.[c]

III. Non. 5th

403 When from her saffron cheeks Tithonus' spouse [d] shall have begun to shed the dew at the time of the fifth morn, the constellation, whether it be the Bear-

OVID

405 sive est Arctophylax, sive est piger ille Bootes,
    mergetur visus effugietque tuos.
  at non effugiet Vindemitor : hoc quoque causam
    unde trahat sidus, parva docere mora est.
  Ampelon intonsum satyro nymphaque creatum
410   fertur in Ismariis Bacchus amasse iugis :
  tradidit huic vitem pendentem e frondibus ulmi,
    quae nunc de pueri nomine nomen habet.
  dum legit in ramo pictas temerarius uvas,
    decidit : amissum Liber in astra tulit.

6. AN͟P HOC · DIE · CAESAR · PONTIF · MAXIM · FACT · EST

415 Sextus ubi oceano clivosum scandit Olympum
    Phoebus et alatis aethera carpit equis,
  quisquis ades castaeque colis penetralia Vestae,
    gratare, Iliacis turaque pone focis.
  Caesaris innumeris (quem maluit ille mereri ?)
420   accessit titulis pontificalis honor.
  ignibus aeternis aeterni numina praesunt
    Caesaris : imperii pignora iuncta vides.
  di veteris Troiae, dignissima praeda ferenti,
    qua gravis Aeneas tutus ab hoste fuit,
425 ortus ab Aenea tangit cognata sacerdos
    numina : cognatum, Vesta, tuere caput !
  quos sancta fovet ille manu, bene vivitis ignes :
    vivite inextincti, flammaque duxque, precor.

---

  [a] The Greek ἄμπελος, " vine."
  [b] Augustus accepted the title Pontifex Maximus on
March 6, 12 B.C. As such, he should preside over the Vestal
Virgins. He claimed descent from Aeneas, through his

ward or the sluggard Bootes, will have sunk and will escape thy sight. But not so will the Grape-gatherer escape thee. The origin of that constellation also can be briefly told. 'Tis said that the unshorn Ampelus,[a] son of a nymph and satyr, was loved by Bacchus on the Ismarian hills. Upon him the god bestowed a vine that trailed from an elm's leafy boughs, and still the vine takes from the boy its name. While he rashly culled the gaudy grapes upon a branch, he tumbled down; Liber bore the lost youth to the stars.

PR. NON. 6th

415 When the sixth sun climbs up Olympus' steep from ocean, and through the ether takes his way on his winged steeds, all ye, whoe'er ye are, who worship at the shrine of the chaste Vesta, wish the goddess joy and offer incense on the Ilian hearth. To Caesar's countless titles (which would he rather have earned?) was added the honour of the pontificate.[b] Over the eternal fire the divinity of Caesar, no less eternal, doth preside: the pledges of empire thou seest side by side. Ye gods of ancient Troy, ye worthiest prize to him who bore ye, ye whose weight did save Aeneas from the foe, a priest of the line of Aeneas handles your kindred divinities; Vesta, do thou guard his kindred head![c] Nursed by his sacred hand, ye fires live well. O live undying, flame and leader both, I pray.

adoption by Julius Caesar, and so from Venus, Jupiter, and Saturn, brother of Vesta. [c] Cf. iv. 949.

OVID

7. B NON · F [a]

Una nota est Marti Nonis, sacrata quod illis
430   templa putant lucos Vediovis ante duos. [b]
Romulus ut saxo lucum circumdedit alto,
        " quilibet huc " dixit " confuge, tutus eris."
O quam de tenui Romanus origine crevit !
        turba vetus quam non invidiosa fuit !
435 ne tamen ignaro novitas tibi nominis obstet,
        disce, quis iste deus, curque vocetur ita.
Iuppiter est iuvenis : iuvenalis aspice voltus ;
        aspice deinde manum, fulmina nulla tenet.
fulmina post ausos caelum adfectare Gigantes
440   sumpta Iovi ; primo tempore inermis erat.
ignibus Ossa novis et Pelion altius Ossa
        arsit et in solida fixus Olympus humo.
stat quoque capra simul : nymphae pavisse feruntur
        Cretides ; infanti lac dedit illa Iovi.
445 nunc vocor ad nomen. vegrandia farra colonae
        quae male creverunt, vescaque parva vocant.
vis ea si verbi est, cur non ego Vediovis aedem
        aedem non magni suspicer esse Iovis ?
iamque, ubi caeruleum variabunt sidera caelum,
450   suspice : Gorgonei colla videbis equi. [d]
creditur hic caesa gravidae cervice Medusae
        sanguine respersis prosiluisse iubis.

---

   [a] F, for Fastus. That is, there is no meeting of the
Comitia or the Senate.
   [b] The space between the two peaks of the Capitol, on each
of which were trees originally. Here Romulus enclosed his
lucus, the *asylum* for fugitives.
   [c] The meaning of *ve-* in *Vedjovis* is uncertain. In other
words it does imply " without " in some form.
   [d] Pegasus, which sprang from the severed neck of the
Gorgon Medusa.

Non. 7th

[429] The Nones of March have only one mark[a] in the calendar, because they think that on that day the temple of Vedjovis was consecrated in front of the two groves.[b] When Romulus surrounded the grove with a high stone wall, " Take refuge here," said he, " whoe'er thou art ; thou shalt be safe." O from how small a beginning the Roman took his rise ! How little to be envied was that multitude of old ! But that the strangeness of the name may not prove a stumbling-block to you in your ignorance, learn who that god is, and why he is so called. He is the Young Jupiter : look on his youthful face ; look then on his hand, it holds no thunderbolts. Jupiter assumed the thunderbolts after the giants dared attempt to win the sky ; at first he was unarmed. Ossa blazed with the new fires (of his thunderbolts) ; Pelion, too, higher than Ossa, and Olympus, fixed in the solid ground. A she-goat also stands (beside the image of Vedjovis) ; the Cretan nymphs are said to have fed the god ; it was the she-goat that gave her milk to the infant Jove. Now I am called on to explain the name. Farmers' wives call stunted spelt *vegrandia*, and what is little they call *vesca*. If that is the meaning of the word, may I not suspect that the shrine of Vedjovis is the shrine of the little Jupiter ?[c]

[449] And now when the stars shall spangle the blue sky, look up : you will see the neck of the Gorgonian steed.[d] He is said to have leaped forth from the severed neck of the teeming Medusa, his mane bespattered with blood. As he glided above the

huic supra nubes et subter sidera lapso
 caelum pro terra, pro pede penna fuit,
455 iamque indignanti nova frena receperat ore,
 cum levis Aonias ungula fodit aquas.
nunc fruitur caelo, quod pennis ante petebat,
 et nitidus stellis quinque decemque micat.

Protinus aspicies venienti nocte Coronam
460 Gnosida : Theseo crimine facta dea est.
iam bene periuro mutarat coniuge Bacchum,
 quae dedit ingrato fila legenda viro ;
sorte tori gaudens " quid flebam rustica ? " dixit
 " utiliter nobis perfidus ille fuit."
465 interea Liber depexos crinibus Indos
 vicit et Eoo dives ab orbe redit ;
inter captivas facie praestante puellas
 grata nimis Baccho filia regis erat.
flebat amans coniunx spatiataque litore curvo
470 edidit incultis talia verba comis :
" en iterum, fluctus, similis audite querellas !
 en iterum lacrimas accipe, harena, meas !
dicebam, memini, ' periure et perfide Theseu ! '
 ille abiit ; eadem crimina Bacchus habet.
475 nunc quoque ' nulla viro ' clamabo ' femina credat ! '
 nomine mutato causa relata mea est.
o utinam mea sors, qua primum coeperat, isset,
 iamque ego praesenti tempore nulla forem !

---

^a Hippocrene, the "Horse's Fountain" on Helicon.
^b Ariadne, daughter of Minos, king of Cnossos in Crete,
had a golden crown set with gems ; which at her death was
set in the sky, and the gems became stars.
^c She gave Theseus a clue of thread to guide him out of
the Labyrinth ; Theseus deserted her, and Bacchus found
and wedded her.   Bacchus is said to have conquered India.

clouds and beneath the stars, the sky served him as solid ground, and his wing served him for a foot. Soon indignantly he champed the unwonted bit, when his light hoof struck out the Aonian spring.[a] Now he enjoys the sky, to which aforetime he soared on wings, and he sparkles bright with fifteen stars.

VIII. ID. 8th

[459] Straightway at the fall of night shalt thou see the Cnossian Crown.[b] It was through the fault of Theseus that Ariadne was made a goddess. Already had she happily exchanged a perjured spouse for Bacchus, she who gave to a thankless man a clue to gather up.[c] Joying in her lot of love, " Why like a rustic maiden did I weep ? " quoth she ; " his faithlessness has been my gain." Meantime Liber had conquered the straight-haired Indians and returned, loaded with treasure, from the eastern world. Amongst the fair captive girls there was one, the daughter of a king, who pleased Bacchus all too well. His loving spouse wept, and pacing the winding shore with dishevelled locks she uttered these words : " Lo, yet again, ye billows, list to my like complaint ! Lo, yet again, ye sands, receive my tears ! I used to say, I remember, ' Forsworn and faithless Theseus ! ' He deserted me : now Bacchus does me the same wrong. Now again I will cry, ' Let no woman trust a man ! ' My case has been repeated, only the name is changed. Would that my lot had ended where it first began ! So at this moment had I been no more. Why, Liber, didst

q uid me desertis morituram, Liber, harenis
480   servabas ? potui dedoluisse semel.
Bacche levis leviorque tuis, quae tempora cingunt,
   frondibus, in lacrimas cognite Bacche meas,
ausus es ante oculos adducta paelice nostros
   tam bene compositum sollicitare torum ?
485 heu ubi pacta fides ? ubi, quae iurare solebas ?
   me miseram, quotiens haec ego verba loquar ?
Thesea culpabas fallacemque ipse vocabas :
   iudicio peccas turpius ipse tuo.
ne sciat hoc quisquam, tacitisque doloribus urar,
490   ne totiens falli digna fuisse puter !
praecipue cupiam celari Thesea, ne te
   consortem culpae gaudeat esse suae.
ut puto, praeposita est fuscae mihi candida paelex :
   eveniat nostris hostibus ille color !
495 quid tamen hoc refert ? vitio tibi gratior ipso est.
   quid facis ? amplexus inquinat illa tuos.
Bacche, fidem praesta nec praefer amoribus ullam
   coniugis. adsuevi semper amare virum.
ceperunt matrem formosi cornua tauri,
500   me tua : me laudant, ille pudendus amor.
ne noceat, quod amo ; neque enim tibi, Bacche,
     nocebat,
   quod flammas nobis fassus es ipse tuas.
nec, quod nos uris, mirum facis : ortus in igne
   diceris et patria raptus ab igne manu.
505 illa ego sum, cui tu solitus promittere caelum.
   ei mihi, pro caelo qualia dona fero ! "
dixerat : audibat iamdudum verba querentis
   Liber, ut a tergo forte secutus erat.

---

    a Pasiphaë, who was enamoured of a bull, and brought
forth the Minotaur.
    b See l. 715 note.

thou save me to die on desert sands ? I might have
ended my griefs once and for all. Bacchus, thou light
o' love ! lighter than the leaves that wreathe thy
brows ! Bacchus, whom I have known only that I
should weep ! Hast thou dared to trouble our so
harmonious loves by bringing a leman before mine
eyes ? Ah, where is plighted troth ? Where are the
oaths that thou wast wont to swear ? Woe's me,
how often must I speak these self-same words !
Thou wast wont to blame Theseus ; thou wast wont
thyself to dub him deceiver ; judged by thyself, thine
is the fouler sin. Let no man know of this, and let
me burn with pangs unuttered, lest they should think
that I deserve to be deceived so oft. Above all I
would desire the thing were kept from Theseus, that
he may not joy to know thee a partner in his guilt.
But I suppose a leman fair has been preferred to
dusky me :—may that hue fall to my foes ! But
what does that matter ? She is dearer to thee for
the very blemish. What art thou about ? She
defiles thee by her embrace. Bacchus, keep faith,
nor prefer any woman to a wife's love. I have
learned to love my love for ever. The horns of a
handsome bull won my mother's heart,[a] thine won
mine. They laud me for my passion : hers was a
shameful love. Let me not suffer for my love ; thou
thyself, Bacchus, didst not suffer for avowing thy
flame to me. No wonder that thou dost make me
burn ; they say thou wert born in the fire and wert
snatched from the fire by thy father's hand.[b] I am
she to whom thou wert wont to promise heaven. Ah
me ! what guerdon do I reap instead of heaven !" She
finished speaking. Long time had Liber heard her
plaint, for as it chanced he followed close behind.

157

occupat amplexu lacrimasque per oscula siccat
510   et " pariter caeli summa petamus ! " ait :
" tu mihi iuncta toro mihi iuncta vocabula sumes,
   nam tibi mutatae Libera nomen erit ;
sintque tuae tecum faciam monumenta coronae,
   Volcanus Veneri quam dedit, illa tibi."
515 dicta facit gemmasque novem transformat in ignes :
   aurea per stellas nunc micat illa novem.

      8. CF   9. DC   10. EC   11. FC
   12. GC   13. H EN   14. A EQ · NP

Sex ubi sustulerit, totidem demerserit orbes,
   purpureum rapido qui vehit axe diem,
altera gramineo spectabis Equirria Campo,
520   quem Tiberis curvis in latus urget aquis.
qui tamen eiecta si forte tenebitur unda,
   Caelius accipiet pulverulentus equos.

       15. B EID · NP

Idibus est Annae festum geniale Perennae
   non procul a ripis, advena Thybri, tuis.
525 plebs venit ac virides passim disiecta per herbas
   potat, et accumbit cum pare quisque sua.
sub Iove pars durat, pauci tentoria ponunt,
   sunt quibus e ramis frondea facta casa est,
pars, ubi pro rigidis calamos statuere columnis,
530   desuper extentas imposuere togas.
sole tamen vinoque calent annosque precantur,
   quot sumant cyathos, ad numerumque bibunt.

---

^a See above, l. 146, and Appendix, p. 405.

He put his arms about her, with kisses dried her tears, and " Let us fare together," quoth he, " to heaven's height. As thou hast shared my bed, so shalt thou share my name, for in thy changed state thy name shall be Libera ; and I will see to it that with thee there shall be a memorial of thy crown, that crown which Vulcan gave to Venus, and she to thee." He did as he had said and changed the nine jewels of her crown into fires. Now the golden crown doth sparkle with nine stars.

Pr. Id.   14th

517 When he who bears the purple day on his swift car shall six times have lifted up his disc and as often sunk it low, thou shalt a second time behold horse races (*Equirria*) on that grassy plain whose side is hugged by Tiber's winding waters. But if perchance the wave has overflowed and floods the plain, the dusty Caelian hill shall receive the horses.

Idus.   15th

523 On the Ides is held the jovial feast of Anna Perenna *a* not far from thy banks, O Tiber, who comest from afar. The common folk come, and scattered here and there over the green grass they drink, every lad reclining beside his lass. Some camp under the open sky ; a few pitch tents ; some make a leafy hut of boughs. Others set up reeds in place of rigid pillars, and stretching out their robes place them upon the reeds. But they grow warm with sun and wine, and they pray for as many years as they take cups, and they count the cups they drink. There

159

invenies illic, qui Nestoris ebibat annos,
  quae sit per calices facta Sibylla suos.
535 illic et cantant, quicquid didicere theatris,
  et iactant faciles ad sua verba manus
et ducunt posito duras cratere choreas,
  cultaque diffusis saltat amica comis.
cum redeunt, titubant et sunt spectacula volgi,
540   et fortunatos obvia turba vocat.
occurrit nuper (visa est mihi digna relatu)
  pompa : senem potum pota trahebat anus.
quae tamen haec dea sit, quoniam rumoribus errat,
  fabula proposito nulla tegenda meo.
545 arserat Aeneae Dido miserabilis igne,
  arserat exstructis in sua fata rogis ;
compositusque cinis, tumulique in marmore carmen
  hoc breve, quod moriens ipsa reliquit, erat :
PRAEBUIT AENEAS ET CAUSAM MORTIS ET ENSEM.
550   IPSA SUA DIDO CONCIDIT USA MANU.
protinus invadunt Numidae sine vindice regnum,
  et potitur capta Maurus Iarba domo,
seque memor spretum, " Thalamis tamen " inquit
  " Elissae
en ego, quem totiens reppulit illa, fruor."
555 diffugiunt Tyrii, quo quemque agit error, ut olim
  amisso dubiae rege vagantur apes.
tertia nudandas acceperat area messes,
  inque cavos ierant tertia musta lacus :
pellitur Anna domo lacrimansque sororia linquit

---

^a Iarbas was a suitor for Dido (Virgil, *Aen.* iv. 36, 196) :
Elissa was Dido's name.
  ^b The Carthaginians came from Tyre.
  ^c Dido's sister.

shall you find a man who drains as many goblets as
Nestor numbered years, and a woman who would
live to the Sibyl's age if cups could work the charm.
There they sing the ditties they picked up in the
theatres, beating time to the words with nimble
hands ; they set the bowl down, and trip in dances
lubberly, while the spruce sweetheart skips about
with streaming hair. On the way home they reel,
a spectacle for vulgar eyes, and the crowd that meets
them calls them " blest." I met the procession
lately ; I thought it notable ; a drunk old woman
lugged a drunk old man.

⁵⁴³ But since erroneous rumours are rife as to who
this goddess is, I am resolved to throw no cloak about
her tale. Poor Dido had burned with the fire of
love for Aeneas ; she had burned, too, on a pyre
built for her doom. Her ashes were collected, and
on the marble of her tomb was this short stanza,
which she herself dying had left :

> Aeneas caused her death and lent the blade :
> Dido by her own hand in dust was laid.

⁵⁵¹ Straightway the Numidians invaded the de-
fenceless realm, and Iarba the Moor ^a captured and
took possession of the palace ; and remembering how
she had spurned his suit, " Lo, now," quoth he, " I
enjoy Elissa's bridal bower, I whom she so oft
repelled." The Tyrians ^b fled hither and thither, as
each one chanced to stray, even as bees oft wander
doubtingly when they have lost their king. For the
third time the reaped corn had been carried to the
threshing-floor to be stripped of the husk, and for the
third time the new wine had poured into the hollow
vats, when Anna ^c was driven from home, and weeping

560 moenia : germanae iusta dat ante suae.
mixta bibunt molles lacrimis unguenta favillae,
vertice libatas accipiuntque comas ;
terque " vale ! " dixit, cineres ter ad ora relatos
pressit, et est illis visa subesse soror.
565 nancta ratem comitesque fugae pede labitur aequo
moenia respiciens, dulce sororis opus.
fertilis est Melite[a] sterili vicina Cosyrae[b]
insula, quam Libyci verberat unda freti.
hanc petit hospitio regis confisa vetusto :
570 hospes opum dives rex ibi Battus erat.
qui postquam didicit casus utriusque sororis,
" haec " inquit " tellus quantulacumque tua est."
et tamen hospitii servasset ad ultima munus,
sed timuit magnas Pygmalionis[c] opes.
575 signa recensuerat bis sol sua, tertius ibat
annus, et exilio terra paranda nova est.
frater adest belloque petit. rex arma perosus
" nos sumus inbelles, tu fuge sospes ! " ait.
iussa fugit ventoque ratem committit et undis :
580 asperior quovis aequore frater erat.
est prope piscosos lapidosi Crathidis amnes
parvus ager : Cameren[d] incola turba vocat.
illuc cursus erat, nec longius afuit inde,
quam quantum novies mittere funda potest :
585 vela cadunt primo et dubia librantur ab aura.
" findite remigio " navita dixit " aquas ! "

---

[a] Malta.
[b] Now Pantellaria, about 60 miles from Malta.
[c] Brother of Dido and Anna, and their enemy.
[d] Unknown.

162

left her sister's walls; but first she paid the honours due to her dead sister. The soft ashes drank unguents mixed with tears, and they received an offering of hair clipped from her head. And thrice she said, "Farewell!" thrice she took the ashes up and pressed them to her lips, and under them she thought she saw her sister. Having found a ship and comrades to share her flight, she glided before the wind, looking back at the city walls, her sister's darling work.

⁵⁶⁷ There is a fertile island Melite,ᵃ lashed by the waves of the Libyan sea and neighbour to the barren Cosyra.ᵇ Anna steered for it, trusting to the king's hospitality, which she had known of old; for Battus there was king, a wealthy host. When he learned the misfortunes of the two sisters, "This land," said he, "small though it be, is thine," and he would have observed the duties of hospitality to the end, but that he feared Pygmalion'sᶜ mighty power. Twice had the sun traversed the signs of the zodiac, and a third year was passing, when Anna was compelled to seek a new land of exile. Her brother came and demanded her surrender with threat of war. The king loathed arms and said to Anna, "We are unwarlike. Do thou seek safety in flight." At his bidding she fled and committed her bark to the wind and the waves. Her brother was more cruel than any sea. Near the fishy streams of stony Crathis there is a champain small; the natives call it Camere.ᵈ Thither she bent her course, and was no farther off than nine shots of a sling, when the sails at first dropped and flapped in the puffs of wind. "Cleave the water with the oars," the seaman said.

dumque parant torto subducere carbasa lino,
    percutitur rapido puppis adunca noto
inque patens aequor frustra pugnante magistro
590   fertur, et ex oculis visa refugit humus.
adsiliunt fluctus, imoque a gurgite pontus
    vertitur, et canas alveus haurit aquas.
vincitur ars vento, nec iam moderator habenis
    utitur ; a votis is quoque poscit opem.
595 iactatur tumidas exul Phoenissa per undas
    humidaque opposita lumina veste tegit :
tunc primum Dido felix est dicta sorori
    et quaecumque aliquam corpore pressit humum.
figitur ad Laurens ingenti flamine litus
600   puppis et expositis omnibus hausta perit.
iam pius Aeneas regno nataque Latini
    auctus erat, populos miscueratque duos.
litore dotali solo comitatus Achate
    secretum nudo dum pede carpit iter,
605 aspicit errantem nec credere sustinet Annam
    esse : " quid in Latios illa veniret agros ? "
dum secum Aeneas, " Anna est ! " exclamat Achates :
    ad nomen voltus sustulit illa suos.
heu ! fugiat ? quid agat ? quos terrae quaerat
    hiatus ?
610   ante oculos miserae fata sororis erant.
sensit et adloquitur trepidam Cythereïus heros
    (flet tamen admonitu motus, Elissa, tui) :
" Anna, per hanc iuro, quam quondam audire solebas
    tellurem fato prosperiore dari,
615 perque deos comites, hac nuper sede locatos,

---

    [a] Aeneas was son of Venus, called Cytherea from her sacred
island Cythera.

And while they made ready to furl the sails with the ropes, the swift south wind struck the curved poop and swept the ship, despite the captain's efforts, into the open sea; the land receded from their sight. The surge assails them, and from its lowest depths the ocean is upheaved: the hull gulps down the foaming waters. Seamanship is powerless against the wind, and the steersman no longer handles the helm; he, too, resorts to prayers for help. The Phoenician exile is tossed on the swelling waves and hides her wet eyes in her robe: then for the first time did she call her sister Dido happy, and happy any woman who anywhere did tread dry land. A mighty blast drove the ship on the Laurentine shore; she went down and perished, but all on board got safe to land.

601 By this time Aeneas had gained the kingdom and the daughter of Latinus and had blended the two peoples. While, accompanied by Achates alone, he paced barefoot a lonely path on the shore with which his wife had dowered him, he spied Anna wandering, nor could bring himself to think that it was she. Why should she come into the Latin land? thought he to himself. Meantime, "'Tis Anna!" cried Achates. At the sound of the name she looked up. Alas! should she flee? what should she do? where should she look for the earth to yawn for her? Her hapless sister's fate rose up before her eyes. The Cytherean *a* hero perceived her distress and accosted her; yet did he weep, touched by memory of thee, Elissa. "Anna, by this land which in days gone by thou usedst to hear a happier fate had granted me; and by the gods who followed me and here of late have found a home,

165

saepe meas illos increpuisse moras.
    nec timui de morte tamen, metus abfuit iste.
    ei mihi ! credibili fortior illa fuit.
    ne refer : aspexi non illo corpore digna
620   volnera Tartareas ausus adire domos.
    at tu, seu ratio te nostris appulit oris
    sive deus, regni commoda carpe mei.
    multa tibi memores, nil non debemus Elissae :
    nomine grata tuo, grata sororis, eris."
625 talia dicenti (neque enim spes altera restat)
    credidit, errores exposuitque suos.
    utque domum intravit Tyrios induta paratus,
    incipit Aeneas (cetera turba silet) :
    " hanc tibi cur tradam, pia causa, Lavinia coniunx,
630   est mihi : consumpsi naufragus huius opes.
    orta Tyro est, regnum Libyca possedit in ora ;
    quam precor ut carae more sororis ames."
    omnia promittit falsumque Lavinia volnus
    mente premit tacita dissimulatque fremens ;
635 donaque cum videat praeter sua lumina ferri
    multa palam, mitti clam quoque multa putat.
    non habet exactum, quid agat ; furialiter odit
    et parat insidias et cupit ulta mori.
    nox erat : ante torum visa est adstare sororis
640   squalenti Dido sanguinulenta coma
    et "fuge, ne dubita, maestum fuge " dicere
        " tectum ! "
    sub verbum querulas impulit aura fores.
    exilit et velox humili super arva fenestra
    se iacit : audacem fecerat ipse timor.

I swear that they did often chide my loiterings.
Nor yet did I dread her death; far from me was
that fear. Woe's me! her courage surpassed belief.
Tell not the tale. I saw the unseemly wounds upon
her body what time I dared to visit the house of
Tartarus. But thou, whether thine own resolve or
some god has brought thee to our shores, do thou
enjoy my kingdom's comforts. Much our gratitude
doth owe to thee, and something, too, to Elissa.
Welcome shalt thou be for thine own sake and
welcome for thy sister's." She believed his words,
for no other hope was left her, and she told her
wanderings. And when she entered the palace,
clad in Tyrian finery, Aeneas opened his lips, while
the rest of the assembly kept silence: " My wife
Lavinia, I have a dutiful reason for entrusting this
lady to thy care; when I was shipwrecked I consumed her substance. She is of Tyrian descent;
she owns a kingdom on the Libyan coast; I pray
thee, love her as a dear sister." Lavinia promised
everything, but in the silence of her heart she
hid her fancied wrong and dissembled her rage;
and when she saw many presents carried openly
before her eyes, she thought that many were also
sent secretly. She had not decided what to do.
She hated like a fury, and hatched a plot, and
longed to die avenged. 'Twas night: before her
sister's bed it seemed that Dido stood, her unkempt
hair dabbled in blood. " Fly, fly this dismal
house," she seemed to say, " O falter not!" At
the word a blast did slam the creaking door.
Up she leaped, and quick she threw herself out
of the low window upon the ground: her very
fear had made her bold. And where her terror

167

645 quaque metu rapitur, tunica velata recincta
    currit, ut auditis territa damma lupis.
corniger hanc tumidis rapuisse Numicius undis
    creditur et stagnis occuluisse suis.
Sidonis interea magno clamore per agros
650   quaeritur : apparent signa notaeque pedum :
ventum erat ad ripas : inerant vestigia ripis.
    sustinuit tacitas conscius amnis aquas.
ipsa loqui visa est " placidi sum nympha Numici :
    amne perenne latens Anna Perenna vocor."
655 protinus erratis laeti vescuntur in agris
    et celebrant largo seque diemque mero.

sunt quibus haec Luna est, quia mensibus impleat
    annum ;
    pars Themin, Inachiam pars putat esse bovem.
invenies, qui te nymphen Atlantida dicant
660   teque Iovi primos, Anna, dedisse cibos.
haec quoque, quam referam, nostras pervenit ad
    aures
    fama nec a veri dissidet illa fide.
plebs vetus et nullis etiam nunc tuta tribunis
    fugit et in Sacri vertice montis erat ;
665 iam quoque, quem secum tulerant, defecerat illos
    victus et humanis usibus apta Ceres.
orta suburbanis quaedam fuit Anna Bovillis,
    pauper, sed multae sedulitatis anus.
illa levi mitra canos incincta capillos
670   fingebat tremula rustica liba manu,

---

    a A river in Latium ; rivers are called horned, being
personified as bulls.
    b He probably means Isis, who was identified with Io.
    c This refers to the Secession of the Plebs in 494 B.C.

carried her, she ran, clad in her ungirt tunic,
as runs a frightened doe that hears the wolves.
'Tis thought the horned Numicius *a* swept her away
in his swollen stream and hid her in his pools.
Meantime with clamour loud they sought the lost
Sidonian lady through the fields : traces and foot-
prints met their eyes : on coming to the banks
they found her tracks upon the banks. The conscious river checked and hushed his stream. Herself appeared to speak : " I am a nymph of the
calm Numicius. In a perennial river I hide, and
Anna Perenna is my name." Straightway they
feast joyfully in the fields over which they had
roamed, and toast themselves and the day in deep
draughts of wine.

657 Some think that this goddess is the moon, because
the moon fills up the measure of the year (*annus*) by
her months ; others deem that she is Themis ; others
suppose that she is the Inachian cow.*b* You shall find
some to say that thou, Anna, art a nymph, daughter of
Atlas, and that thou didst give Jupiter his first food.
Yet another report, which I will relate, has come to
my ears, and it is not far from what we may take as
true. The common folk of old, not yet protected by
tribunes, had fled, and abode upon the top of the
Sacred Mount *c* ; now, too, the provisions which they
had brought with them and the bread fit for human
use had failed them. There was a certain Anna,
born at suburban Bovillae, a poor old woman, but
very industrious.*d* She, with her grey hair bound up
in a light cap, used to mould country cakes with
tremulous hand, and it was her wont at morn to

d This story seems told to account for the worship of Anna
Perenna at Bovillae.

atque ita per populum fumantia mane solebat
    dividere : haec populo copia grata fuit.
pace domi facta signum posuere Perennae,
    quod sibi defectis illa ferebat opem.

675 nunc mihi cur cantent superest obscena puellae
    dicere ; nam coeunt certaque probra canunt.
nuper erat dea facta : venit Gradivus ad Annam
    et cum seducta talia verba facit :
" mense meo coleris, iunxi mea tempora tecum :
680   pendet ab officio spes mihi magna tuo.
armifer armiferae correptus amore Minervae
    uror et hoc longo tempore volnus alo.
effice, di studio similes coeamus in unum :
    conveniunt partes hae tibi, comis anus."
685 dixerat.   illa deum promisso ludit inani
    et stultam dubia spem trahit usque mora.
saepius instanti " mandata peregimus," inquit
    " evicta est, precibus vix dedit illa manus."
credit amans thalamosque parat.   deducitur illuc
690   Anna tegens voltus, ut nova nupta, suos.
oscula sumpturus subito Mars aspicit Annam :
    nunc pudor elusum, nunc subit ira deum.
ridet amatorem carae nova diva Minervae,
    nec res hac Veneri gratior ulla fuit.
695 inde ioci veteres obscenaque dicta canuntur,
    et iuvat hanc magno verba dedisse deo.

praeteriturus eram gladios in principe fixos,
    cum sic a castis Vesta locuta focis :

---

^a Minerva in this story has probably taken the place of
Nerio, an old goddess, the wife of Mars. See Appendix,
p. 407.
^b The murder of Julius Caesar, 44 B.C., on the Ides of
March.

distribute them piping hot among the people: the supply was welcome to the people. When peace was made at home, they set up a statue to Perenna, because she had supplied them in their time of need.

675 Now it remains for me to tell why girls chant ribald songs ; for they assemble and sing certain scurrilous verses. When Anna had been but lately made a goddess, the Marching God (*Gradivus*) came to her, and taking her aside spoke as follows : " Thou art worshipped in my month, I have joined my season to thine : I have great hope in the service that thou canst render me. An armed god myself, I have fallen in love with the armed goddess Minerva [a] ; I burn and for a long time have nursed this wound. She and I are deities alike in our pursuits ; contrive to unite us. That office well befits thee, kind old dame." So he spoke. She duped the god by a false promise, and kept him dangling on in foolish hope by dubious delays. When he often pressed her, " I have done thy bidding," said she, " she is conquered and has yielded at last to thine entreaties." The lover believed her and made ready the bridal chamber. Thither they escorted Anna, like a bride, with a veil upon her face. When he would have kissed her, Mars suddenly perceived Anna ; now shame, now anger moved the god befooled. The new goddess laughed at dear Minerva's lover. Never did anything please Venus more than that. So old jokes are cracked and ribald songs are sung, and people love to remember how Anna choused the great god.

697 I was about to pass by in silence the swords that stabbed the prince,[b] when Vesta spoke thus from

171

OVID

" ne dubita meminisse : meus fuit ille sacerdos,
700   sacrilegae telis me petiere manus.
ipsa virum rapui simulacraque nuda reliqui :
    quae cecidit ferro, Caesaris umbra fuit."
ille quidem caelo positus Iovis atria vidit
et tenet in magno templa dicata foro.
705 at quicumque nefas ausi, prohibente deorum
    numine, polluerant pontificale caput,
morte iacent merita.   testes estote Philippi,
et quorum sparsis ossibus albet humus.
hoc opus, haec pietas, haec prima elementa fuerunt
710   Caesaris, ulcisci iusta per arma patrem.

16. C F

Postera cum teneras aurora refecerit herbas,
    Scorpios a prima parte videndus erit.

17. D LIB · NP

Tertia post Idus lux est celeberrima Baccho :
Bacche, fave vati, dum tua festa cano.
715 nec referam Semelen, ad quam nisi fulmina secum
    Iuppiter adferret, parvus inermis eras ;
nec, puer ut posses maturo tempore nasci,
    expletum patrio corpore matris opus.
Sithonas et Scythicos longum narrare triumphos
720   et domitas gentes, turifer Inde, tuas.

---

a Pontifex Maximus.
    b Semele, mother of Bacchus, requested Jupiter to show
himself in full majesty.   His lightning blasted her, and
Jupiter caught up her unborn child, and sewed him into his
own thigh, until the proper time for birth.
172

her chaste hearth : " Doubt not to recall them : he was my priest,[a] it was at me these sacrilegious hands struck with the steel. I myself carried the man away, and left naught but his wraith behind ; what fell by the sword was Caesar's shade." Transported to the sky he saw the halls of Jupiter, and in the great Forum he owns a temple dedicated to him. But all the daring sinners who, in defiance of the gods' will, profaned the pontiff's head, lie low in death, the death they merited. Witness Philippi and they whose scattered bones whiten the ground. This, this was Caesar's work, his duty, his first task by righteous arms to avenge his father.

XVII. KAL. APR. 16th

711 When the next dawn shall have refreshed the tender grass, the Scorpion will be visible in his first part.

XVI. KAL. 17th

713 The third day after the Ides is a very popular celebration of Bacchus. O Bacchus, be gracious to thy bard while he sings of thy festival. But I shall not tell of Semele [b] ; if Jupiter had not brought his thunderbolts with him to her, thou hadst been a puny unarmed wight. Nor shall I tell how, in order that thou mightest be born as a boy in due time, the function of a mother was completed in thy father's body. It were long to relate the triumphs won by the god over the Sithonians and the Scythians, and how he subdued the peoples of India, that incense-bearing land. I will say naught of him who

173

tu quoque Thebanae mala praeda tacebere matris,
    inque tuum furiis acte, Lycurge, genu.
ecce libet subitos pisces Tyrrhenaque monstra
    dicere, sed non est carminis huius opus ;
725 carminis huius opus causas exponere, quare
    vilis anus populos ad sua liba vocet.
ante tuos ortus arae sine honore fuerunt,
    Liber, et in gelidis herba reperta focis.
te memorant Gange totoque Oriente subacto
730   primitias magno seposuisse Iovi.
cinnama tu primus captivaque tura dedisti
    deque triumphato viscera tosta bove.
nomine ab auctoris ducunt libamina nomen
    libaque, quod sanctis pars datur inde focis.
735 liba deo fiunt, sucis quia dulcibus idem
    gaudet, et a Baccho mella reperta ferunt.
ibat harenoso satyris comitatus ab Hebro
    (non habet ingratos fabula nostra iocos),
iamque erat ad Rhodopen Pangaeaque florida
    ventum :
740   aeriferae comitum concrepuere manus.
ecce novae coeunt volucres tinnitibus actae,
    quosque movent sonitus aera, sequuntur apes.
colligit errantes et in arbore claudit inani
    Liber et inventi praemia mellis habet.
745 ut satyri levisque senex tetigere saporem,
    quaerebant flavos per nemus omne favos.
audit in exesa stridorem examinis ulmo,
    aspicit et ceras dissimulatque senex ;

---

[a] When Bacchus brought his rites to Thebes, the king,
Pentheus, disbelieved in him ; and he was torn to pieces by
his mother Agave and the bacchant women. Lycurgus,
king of the Edonians, expelled Bacchus ; he was driven mad,
and killed his own son with an axe, in mistake for a vine :
then lopped off his own extremities.

fell a mournful prey to his own Theban mother,[a] nor
of Lycurgus, whom frenzy drove to hack at his own
knee. Lo now, fain would I speak of the Tyrrhenian
monsters, men suddenly transformed into fish,[b] but
that is not the business of this song; the business
of this song is to set forth the reasons why a vulgar
old woman hawks cakes to the people. Before thy
birth, Liber, the altars were without offerings, and
grass grew on the cold hearths. They tell how, after
subjugating the Ganges and the whole East, thou
didst set apart first-fruits for great Jupiter. Thou
wert the first to offer cinnamon and incense from the
conquered lands, and the roast flesh of oxen led in
triumph. Libations (*libamina*) derive their name from
their author, and so do cakes (*liba*), because part of
them is offered on the hallowed hearths. Cakes are
made for the god, because he delights in sweet juices,
and they say that honey was discovered by Bacchus.
Attended by the satyrs he was going from sandy
Hebrus (my tale includes a pleasant jest), and had
come to Rhodope and flowery Pangaeus, when the
cymbals in the hands of his companions clashed.
Lo, drawn by the tinkle, winged things, as yet unknown, assemble, and the bees follow the sounding
brass. Liber collected the stragglers and shut them
up in a hollow tree; and he was rewarded by the discovery of honey. Once the satyrs and the bald-pated
ancient [c] had tasted it, they sought for the yellow
combs in every grove. In a hollow elm the old fellow
heard the humming of a swarm; he spied the combs

[b] Bacchus was captured at sea by pirates; but he drove
them mad, they leaped overboard, and became dolphins.
[c] Silenus, the merry companion of the satyrs.

utque piger pandi tergo residebat aselli,
750   applicat hunc ulmo corticibusque cavis.
constitit ipse super ramoso stipite nixus
    atque avide trunco condita mella petit.
milia crabronum coeunt et vertice nudo
    spicula defigunt oraque sima notant.
755 ille cadit praeceps et calce feritur aselli
    inclamatque suos auxiliumque rogat.
concurrunt satyri turgentiaque ora parentis
    rident : percusso claudicat ille genu.
ridet et ipse deus limumque inducere monstrat ;
760   hic paret monitis et linit ora luto.
melle pater fruitur, liboque infusa calenti
    iure repertori candida mella damus.
femina cur presset, non est rationis opertae :
    femineos thyrso concitat ille choros.
765 cur anus hoc faciat, quaeris ?   vinosior aetas
    haec est et gravidae munera vitis amat.
cur hedera cincta est ? hedera est gratissima Baccho :
    hoc quoque cur ita sit, dicere nulla mora est.
Nysiadas nymphas puerum quaerente noverca
770   hanc frondem cunis opposuisse ferunt.
restat, ut inveniam, quare toga libera detur
    Lucifero pueris, candide Bacche, tuo :
sive quod ipse puer semper iuvenisque videris,
    et media est aetas inter utrumque tibi :
775 seu, quia tu pater es, patres sua pignora, natos,
    commendant curae numinibusque tuis :
sive, quod es Liber, vestis quoque libera per te

---

and kept his counsel. And sitting lazily on the back
of an ass, that bent beneath his weight, he rode
the beast up to the elm, where the bark was hollow.
Then he stood on the ass, and leaning upon a branch-
ing stump he greedily reached at the honey stored
in the bole. Thousands of hornets gathered, and
thrust their stings into his bald pate, and left their
mark on his snub-nosed face. Headlong he fell,
and the ass kicked him, while he called to his
comrades and implored their help. The satyrs ran
to the spot and laughed at their parent's swollen
face : he limped on his hurt knee. Bacchus himself laughed and taught him to smear mud on his
wounds; Silenus took the hint and smudged his
face with mire. The father god[a] enjoys honey,
and it is right that we should give to its discoverer
clear honey infused in hot cakes. The reason why
a woman should knead the cakes is plain enough :
Bacchus rouses bands of women by his thyrsus.
You ask why it is an old woman who does it. That
age is more addicted to wine, and loves the bounty
of the teeming vine. Why is she wreathed with
ivy ? Ivy is most dear to Bacchus. Why that is
so can also soon be told. They say that when the
stepmother[b] was searching for the boy, the nymphs
of Nysa screened the cradle in ivy leaves.

[771] It remains for me to discover why the gown of
liberty[c] is given to boys, fair Bacchus, on thy day,
whether it be because thou seemest ever to be a
boy and a youth, and thy age is midway between
the two ; or it may be that, because thou art a father,
fathers commend to thy care and divine keeping the
pledges that they love, their sons ; or it may be that
because thou art Liber, the gown of liberty is assumed

177

sumitur et vitae liberioris iter :
an quia, cum colerent prisci studiosius agros,
780   et faceret patrio rure senator opus,
et caperet fasces a curvo consul aratro,
nec crimen duras esset habere manus,
rusticus ad ludos populus veniebat in urbem
(sed dis, non studiis ille dabatur honor :
785 luce sua ludos uvae commentor habebat,
quos cum taedifera nunc habet ille dea) :
ergo ut tironem celebrare frequentia posset,
visa dies dandae non aliena togae ?
mite caput, pater, huc placataque cornua vertas
790   et des ingenio vela secunda meo.

Itur ad Argeos (qui sint, sua pagina dicet)
hac, si commemini, praeteritaque die.
stella Lycaoniam vergit declivis ad Arcton
Miluus : haec illa nocte videnda venit.
795 quid dederit volucri, si vis cognoscere, caelum :
Saturnus regnis a Iove pulsus erat ;
concitat iratus validos Titanas in arma,
quaeque fuit fatis debita, temptat opem.
matre satus Terra, monstrum mirabile, taurus
800   parte sui serpens posteriore fuit :
hunc triplici muro lucis incluserat atris
Parcarum monitu Styx violenta trium.
viscera qui tauri flammis adolenda dedisset,
sors erat aeternos vincere posse deos.
805 immolat hunc Briareus facta ex adamante securi,

---

a Bacchus.
b Ceres (Demeter). The games are the Cerealia, April 19.
c See v. 621, and App. p. 425.
d The star is unknown; but the coming of the bird was a sign of spring. The Bear was supposed to be Callisto, daughter of Lycaon.
178

and a freer (*liberior*) life is entered upon under thine
auspices. Or was it because, in the days when the
ancients tilled the fields more diligently, and
a senator laboured on his ancestral land, when a
consul exchanged the bent plough for the rods and
axes of office, and it was no crime to have horny hands,
the country folk used to come to the city for the
games (but that was an honour paid to the gods,
not a concession to popular tastes, the discoverer of
the grape *a* held on his own day those games which
now he shares with the torch-bearing goddess *b*); and
the day therefore seemed not unsuitable for conferring the gown, in order that a crowd might gather
round the novice ? Thou Father God, hither turn thy
horned head, mild and propitious, and to the favouring breezes spread the sails of my poetic art !

⁷⁹² On this day, if I remember aright, and on the
preceding day, there is a procession to the Argei.
What the Argei are, will be told in the proper
place. *c* The star of the Kite *d* slopes downwards
towards the Lycaonian Bear: on that night it
becomes visible. If you would know what raised
the bird to heaven, Saturn had been dethroned by
Jupiter. In his wrath he stirred up the strong
Titans to take arms and sought the help the Fates
allowed him. There was a bull born of its mother
Earth, a wondrous monster, the hinder part whereof
was a serpent: him, at the warning of the three
Fates, grim Styx had shut up in gloomy woods
enclosed by a triple wall. There was an oracle
that he who should burn the inwards of the bull in
the flames would be able to conquer the eternal
gods. Briareus sacrificed him with an axe made

179

OVID

et iam iam flammis exta daturus erat :
Iuppiter alitibus rapere imperat ; attulit illi
miluus et meritis venit in astra suis.

18. EC   19. F QVIN·N   20. GC   21. HC   22. AN

Una dies media est, et fiunt sacra Minervae,
810   nomina quae iunctis quinque diebus habent.
sanguine prima vacat, nec fas concurrere ferro :
causa, quod est illa nata Minerva die.
altera tresque super strata celebrantur harena :
ensibus exertis bellica laeta dea est.
815 Pallada nunc pueri teneraeque orate puellae :
qui bene placarit Pallada, doctus erit.
Pallade placata lanam mollire puellae
discant et plenas exonerare colos.
illa etiam stantis radio percurrere telas
820   erudit et rarum pectine denset opus.
hanc cole, qui maculas laesis de vestibus aufers,
hanc cole, velleribus quisquis aëna paras ;
nec quisquam invita faciet bene vincula plantae
Pallade, sit Tychio doctior ille licet ;
825 et licet antiquo manibus conlatus Epeo
sit prior, irata Pallade mancus erit.
vos quoque, Phoebea morbos qui pellitis arte,
munera de vestris pauca referte deae :
nec vos, turba fere censu fraudata,[1] magistri,

[1] fraudata *Um*[2] : fraudate *AXm* : fraudante *DMm*[2]ς.

---

[a] *Quinquatrus*, Qᴠɪɴ in the calendar, properly the name
of one day, the fifth after the Ides ; but it was commonly
taken to mean a period of five days.

[b] For gladiatorial shows.

[c] Tychius is said to have invented shoe-making. Homer
calls him the best of leather-cutters, *Il.* vii. 219-223.

of adamant, and was just about to put the entrails on the fire : Jupiter commanded the birds to snatch them away ; the kite brought them to him and was promoted to the stars for his services.

XIV. KAL. 19th

809 After an interval of one day rites are performed in honour of Minerva, which get their name from a group of five days.*a* The first day is bloodless, and it is unlawful to combat with the sword, because Minerva was born on that day. The second day and three besides are celebrated by the spreading of sand *b* : the warlike goddess delights in drawn swords. Ye boys and tender girls, pray now to Pallas ; he who shall have won the favour of Pallas will be learned. When once they have won the favour of Pallas, let girls learn to card the wool and to unload the full distaffs. She also teaches how to traverse the upright warp with the shuttle, and she drives home the loose threads with the comb. Worship her, thou who dost remove stains from damaged garments ; worship her, thou who dost make ready the brazen caldrons for the fleeces. If Pallas frown, no man shall make shoes well, though he were more skilful than Tychius *c* ; and though he were more adroit with his hands than Epeus *d* of old, yet shall he be helpless, if Pallas be angry with him. Ye too, who banish sicknesses by Phoebus' art, bring from your earnings a few gifts to the goddess.*e* And spurn her not, ye schoolmasters,

d Who made the Wooden Horse.
e Minerva Medica.

830   spernite ; discipulos attrahit illa novos :
     quique moves caelum, tabulamque coloribus uris,
       quique facis docta mollia saxa manu.
     mille dea est operum : certe dea carminis illa est;
       si mereor, studiis adsit amica meis.

835 Caelius ex alto qua mons descendit in aequum,
     hic, ubi non plana est, sed prope plana via,
     parva licet videas Captae delubra Minervae,
       quae dea natali coepit habere suo.
     nominis in dubio causa est.   capitale vocamus
840   ingenium sollers : ingeniosa dea est.
     an quia de capitis fertur sine matre paterni
       vertice cum clipeo prosiluisse suo ?
     an quia perdomitis ad nos captiva Faliscis
       venit ?   et hoc ipsum littera prisca docet.
845 an quod habet legem, capitis quae pendere poenas
     ex illo iubeat furta reperta loco ?
     a quacumque trahis ratione vocabula, Pallas,
       pro ducibus nostris aegida semper habe.

23. B TVBIL · NP

     Summa dies e quinque tubas lustrare canoras
850   admonet et forti sacrificare deae.
     nunc potes ad solem sublato dicere voltu
       " hic here Phrixeae vellera pressit ovis."

---

   a The *Quinquatrus* was a holiday: the master on that day
collected pennies from his boys, which it appears he had
to hand over to Minerva. Ovid suggests that the boys
might defraud their schoolmasters (or, reading *fraudante*,
exhorts the masters not to cheat the goddess of her little
earnings).

   b He suggests that *capta* comes from *caput*, and adds that
Minerva is *capitalis*, " tiptop."

ye tribe too often cheated of your income,[a] she attracts new pupils ; and thou who dost ply the graving tool and paint pictures in encaustic colours, and thou who dost mould the stone with deft hand (spurn not the goddess). She is the goddess of a thousand works : certainly she is the goddess of song ; may she be friendly to my pursuits, if I deserve it.

[835] Where the Caelian Mount descends from the height into the plain, at the point where the street is not level but nearly level, you may see the small shrine of Minerva Capta, which the goddess owned for the first time upon her birthday. The origin of the name Capta is doubtful. We call ingenuity " capital " ; the goddess herself is ingenious.[b] Did she get the name of Capta because she is said to have leaped forth motherless with her shield from the crown of her father's head (*caput*) ? Or because she came to us as a captive at the conquest of Falerii[c] ? This very fact is attested by an ancient inscription. Or was it because she has a law which ordains capital punishment for thefts proved to have been committed in that place ? From whatsoever source thou dost derive the title, O Pallas, do thou hold thine aegis ever before our leaders.

X. KAL. 23rd

[849] The last day of the five reminds us to purify the melodious trumpets[d] and to sacrifice to the strong goddess.[e]

[851] Now you can look up to the sun and say, " Yesterday he set foot on the fleece of the Phrixean

---

[c] This is probably the right reason.
[d] *Tubilustrium.*   [e] Minerva.

OVID

seminibus tostis sceleratae fraude novercae
    sustulerat nullas, ut solet, herba comas.
855 mittitur ad tripodas, certa qui sorte reportet,
    quam sterili terrae Delphicus edat opem.
hic quoque corruptus cum semine nuntiat Helles
    et iuvenis Phrixi funera sorte peti ;
utque recusantem cives et tempus et Ino
860   compulerunt regem iussa nefanda pati,
et soror et Phrixus, velati tempora vittis,
    stant simul ante aras iunctaque fata gemunt.
aspicit hos, ut forte pependerat aethere, mater
    et ferit attonita pectora nuda manu,
865 inque draconigenam nimbis comitantibus urbem
    desilit et natos eripit inde suos ;
utque fugam capiant, aries nitidissimus auro
    traditur : ille vehit per freta longa duos.
dicitur infirma cornu tenuisse sinistra
870   femina, cum de se nomina fecit aquae.
paene simul periit, dum volt succurrere lapsae
    frater, et extentas porrigit usque manus.
flebat, ut amissa gemini consorte pericli,
    caeruleo iunctam nescius esse deo.
875 litoribus tactis aries fit sidus, at huius
    pervenit in Colchas aurea lana domos.

24. C Q · REX · C · F   25. DC   26. EC

Tres ubi Luciferos veniens praemiserit Eos,
    tempora nocturnis aequa diurna feres.

---

   [a] That is, entered the sign of the Ram. Athamas, king of
Boeotia, had a son Phrixus and a daughter Helle. Their
mother, Nephele, died, and he married Ino. She plotted
their death as described here.
   [b] Ino.   [c] Thebes.   [d] Hellespont.
184

sheep."[a] By the guile of a wicked stepmother[b] the seeds had been roasted, so that no corn sprouted in the wonted way. A messenger was sent to the tripods to report, by a sure oracle, what remedy the Delphic god would prescribe for the dearth. But he, corrupted like the seed, brought word that the oracle demanded the death of Helle and the stripling Phrixus; and when the citizens, the season, and Ino compelled the reluctant king to submit to the wicked command, Phrixus and his sister, their brows veiled with fillets, stood together before the altars and bewailed the fate they shared. Their mother spied them, as by chance she hovered in the air, and thunder-struck she beat her naked breast with her hand: then, accompanied by clouds, she leaped down into the dragon-begotten city[c] and snatched from it her children, and that they might take to flight, a ram all glistering with gold was delivered to them. The ram bore the two over wide seas. It is said that the sister relaxed the hold of her left hand on the ram's horn, when she gave her own name to the water.[d] Her brother almost perished with her in attempting to succour her as she fell, and in holding out his hands at the utmost stretch. He wept at losing her who had shared his double peril, wotting not that she was wedded to the blue god. On reaching the shore the ram was made a constellation, but his golden fleece was carried to Colchian homes.

VII. Kal. 26th

[877] When thrice the Morning Star shall have heralded the coming Dawn, you shall reckon the time of day equal to the time of night.

OVID

F N̶P̶ HOC · DIE CAESAR · ALEXAND · RECEPIT
28. GC   29. HC   30. AC (N̶P̶)

Inde quater pastor saturos ubi clauserit haedos,
880   canuerint herbae rore recente quater,
Ianus adorandus cumque hoc Concordia mitis
et Romana Salus araque Pacis erit.

31. CC

Luna regit mensis : huius quoque tempora mensis
finit Aventino Luna colenda iugo.

III. KAL. 30th

879 When four times from that day the shepherd shall have folded the cloyed kids, and four times the grass shall have whitened under the fresh dew, it will be time to adore Janus, and gentle Concord with him, and Roman Safety, and the altar of Peace.

PR. KAL. 31st

883 The moon rules the months : the period of this month also ends with the worship of the Moon on the Aventine Hill.

LIBER QUARTUS

" Alma, fave," dixi " geminorum mater Amorum ! "
    ad vatem voltus rettulit illa suos :
" quid tibi " ait " mecum ?   certe maiora canebas.
    num vetus in molli pectore volnus habes ? "
5 " scis, dea," respondi " de volnere."   risit, et aether
    protinus ex illa parte serenus erat.
" saucius an sanus numquid tua signa reliqui ?
    tu mihi propositum, tu mihi semper opus.
quae decuit, primis sine crimine lusimus annis,
10   nunc teritur nostris area maior equis :
tempora cum causis annalibus eruta priscis
    lapsaque sub terras ortaque signa cano.
venimus ad quartum, quo tu celeberrima mense :
    et vatem et mensem scis, Venus, esse tuos."
15 mota Cytheriaca leviter mea tempora myrto
    contigit et " coeptum perfice " dixit " opus."
sensimus, et causae subito patuere dierum :
    dum licet et spirant flamina, navis eat.

Si qua tamen pars te de fastis tangere debet,
20   Caesar, in Aprili, quo tenearis, habes.

---

^a Eros and Anteros.
^b Augustus, adopted by Julius Caesar, who traced his descent from Venus, through Aeneas.

188

BOOK IV

" O GRACIOUS Mother of the Twin Loves,[a] " said
I, " grant me thy favour." The goddess looked back
at the poet. "What wouldst thou with me ? " she
said, " surely thou wast wont to sing of loftier
themes. Hast thou an old wound rankling in thy
tender breast ? " " Goddess," I answered, " thou
wottest of my wound." She laughed, and straightway the sky was serene in that quarter. " Hurt
or whole, did I desert thy standards ? Thou,
thou hast ever been the task I set myself. In
my young years I toyed with themes to match, and
gave offence to none ; now my steeds tread a larger
field. I sing the seasons, and their causes, and
the starry signs that set beneath the earth and
rise again, drawing my lore from annals old. We
have come to the fourth month in which thou art
honoured above all others, and thou knowest, Venus,
that both the poet and the month are thine." The
goddess was moved, and touching my brows lightly
with myrtle of Cythera, " Complete," said she, " the
work thou hast begun." I felt her inspiration, and
suddenly my eyes were opened to the causes of the
days : proceed, my bark, while still thou mayest
and the breezes blow.

[19] Yet if any part of the calendar should interest
thee, Caesar,[b] thou hast in April matter of concern.

189

hic ad te magna descendit imagine mensis
et fit adoptiva nobilitate tuus.
hoc pater Iliades, cum longum scriberet annum,
vidit et auctores rettulit ipse suos :
25 utque fero Marti primam dedit ordine sortem,
quod sibi nascenti proxima causa fuit,
sic Venerem gradibus multis in gente repertam
alterius voluit mensis habere locum ;
principiumque sui generis revolutaque quaerens
30 saecula cognatos venit adusque deos.
Dardanon Electra nesciret Atlantide natum
scilicet, Electram concubuisse Iovi ?
huius Erichthonius : Tros est generatus ab illo :
Assaracon creat hic, Assaracusque Capyn.
35 proximus Anchises, cum quo commune parentis
non dedignata est nomen habere Venus.
hinc satus Aeneas, pietas spectata, per ignes
sacra patremque humeris, altera sacra, tulit.
venimus ad felix aliquando nomen Iuli,
40 unde domus Teucros Iulia tangit avos.
Postumus hinc, qui quod silvis fuit ortus in altis,
Silvius in Latia gente vocatus erat.
isque, Latine, tibi pater est.   subit Alba Latinum :
proximus est titulis Epytus, Alba, tuis.
45 ille dedit Capyi recidiva vocabula Troiae
et tuus est idem, Calpete, factus avus.
cumque patris regnum post hunc Tiberinus haberet,
dicitur in Tuscae gurgite mersus aquae.

---

[a] Romulus, as descended from Aeneas and so from Ilus,
founder of Ilium.
190

This month thou hast inherited by a great pedigree,
and it has been made thine by virtue of thine adoption
into a noble house. When the Ilian sire^a was
putting the long year on record, he saw the relation-
ship and commemorated the authors of his race:
and as he gave the first lot in the order of the
months to fierce Mars, because he was the immediate
cause of his own birth, so he willed that the place
of the second month should belong to Venus, because
he ascertained his descent from her through many
generations. In seeking the origin of his race, he
turned over the roll of the centuries and came at last
to the gods whose blood he shared. How, prithee,
should he not know that Dardanus was born of Electra,
daughter of Atlas, and that Electra had lain with
Jupiter ? Dardanus had a son Erichthonius, who
begat Tros ; and Tros begat Assaracus, and Assaracus
begat Capys. Next came Anchises, with whom
Venus did not disdain to share the name of parent.
Of them was born Aeneas, whose piety was proved
when on his shoulders through the fire he bore the
holy things and his own sire, a charge as holy.
Now at last have we come to the lucky name of
Julus, through whom the Julian house reaches back
to Teucrian ancestors. He had a son Postumus,
who, because he was born in the deep woods, was
called Silvius among the Latin folk. He was thy
father, Latinus ; Latinus was succeeded by Alba,
and next to Alba on the list was Epytus. He gave
to his son Capys a Trojan name, revived for the
purpose, and he was also the grandfather of Calpetus.
And when Tiberinus possessed his father's kingdom
after the death of Calpetus, he was drowned, it is
said, in a deep pool of the Tuscan river. Yet before

iam tamen Agrippan natum Remulumque nepotem
50   viderat : in Remulum fulmina missa ferunt.
venit Aventinus post hos, locus unde vocatur,
    mons quoque.   post illum tradita regna Procae.
quem sequitur duri Numitor germanus Amuli.
    Ilia cum Lauso de Numitore sati.
55 ense cadit patruo Lausus : placet Ilia Marti
    teque parit, gemino iuncte Quirine Remo.
ille suos semper Venerem Martemque parentes
    dixit et emeruit vocis habere fidem ;
neve secuturi possent nescire nepotes,
60   tempora dis generis continuata dedit.
sed Veneris mensem Graio sermone notatum
    auguror : a spumis est dea dicta maris.
nec tibi sit mirum Graeco rem nomine dici ;
    Itala nam tellus Graecia maior erat.
65 venerat Evander plena cum classe suorum :
    venerat Alcides, Graius uterque genus
(hospes Aventinis armentum pavit in herbis
    claviger, et tanto est Albula pota deo) :
dux quoque Neritius ; testes Laestrygones extant
70   et quod adhuc Circes nomina litus habet.
et iam Telegoni, iam moenia Tiburis udi
    stabant, Argolicae quod posuere manus.
venerat Atridae fatis agitatus Halesus,
    a quo se dictam terra Falisca putat.
75 adice Troianae suasorem Antenora pacis
    et generum Oeniden, Apule Daune, tuum.

---

[a] Aphrodite, from ἀφρός, " foam."
[b] Ulysses, after the hill Neriton in Ithaca. Lamus, king of the Laestrygones, was thought to have founded Formiae. Ulysses visited the Laestrygonians, as described in Hom. *Od.* x. 81.
[c] The promontory *Circeium.*   [d] Tusculum.

that he had seen the birth of a son Agrippa and of a grandson Remulus; but Remulus, they say, was struck by levin-bolts. After them came Aventinus, from whom the place and also the hill took their name. After him the kingdom passed to Proca, who was succeeded by Numitor, brother of hard-hearted Amulius. Ilia and Lausus were born to Numitor. Lausus fell by his uncle's sword: Ilia found favour in the eyes of Mars and gave birth to thee, Quirinus, and thy twin brother Remus. He always averred that his parents were Venus and Mars, and he deserved to be believed when he said so; and that his descendants after him might know the truth, he assigned successive periods to the gods of his race. But I surmise that the month of Venus took its name from the Greek language: the goddess was called after the foam of the sea.*ᵃ* Nor need you wonder that a thing was called by a Greek name, for the Italian land was Greater Greece. Evander had come to Italy with a fleet full of his people; Alcides also had come; both of them were Greeks by race. As a guest, the club-bearing hero fed his herd on the Aventine grass, and the great god drank of the Albula. The Neritian chief also came *ᵇ*: witness the Laestrygones and the shore which still bears the name of Circe.*ᶜ* Already the walls of Telegonus *ᵈ* were standing, and the walls of moist Tibur, built by Argive hands. Driven from home by the tragic doom of Atrides, Halesus had come, after whom the Faliscan land deems that it takes its name. Add to these Antenor,*ᵉ* who advised the Trojans to make peace, and (Diomedes) the Oenid, son-in-law to Apulian Daunus. Aeneas

* Said to have founded Patavium.

serus ab Iliacis et post Antenora flammis
    attulit Aeneas in loca nostra deos.
huius erat Solymus Phrygia comes unus ab Ida,
80   a quo Sulmonis moenia nomen habent,
Sulmonis gelidi, patriae, Germanice, nostrae.
    me miserum, Scythico quam procul illa solo est!
ergo ego tam longe—sed subprime, Musa, querellas!
    non tibi sunt maesta sacra canenda lyra.
85 quo non livor adit? sunt qui tibi mensis honorem
    eripuisse velint invideantque, Venus.
nam quia ver aperit tunc omnia, densaque cedit
    frigoris asperitas, fetaque terra patet,
Aprilem memorant ab aperto tempore dictum,
90   quem Venus iniecta vindicat alma manu.
illa quidem totum dignissima temperat orbem;
    illa tenet nullo regna minora deo,
iuraque dat caelo, terrae, natalibus undis,
    perque suos initus continet omne genus.
95 illa deos omnes (longum est numerare) creavit:
    illa satis causas arboribusque dedit:
illa rudes animos hominum contraxit in unum
    et docuit iungi cum pare quemque sua.
quid genus omne creat volucrum, nisi blanda
    voluptas?
100   nec coeant pecudes, si levis absit amor.
cum mare trux aries cornu decertat; at idem
    frontem dilectae laedere parcit ovis.
deposita sequitur taurus feritate iuvencam,
    quem toti saltus, quem nemus omne tremit.
105 vis eadem, lato quodcumque sub aequore vivit,
    servat et innumeris piscibus implet aquas.

---

^a See Introduction, p. viii.

from the flames of Ilium brought his gods into our
land, arriving late and after Antenor. He had a
comrade Solymus, who came from Phrygian Ida;
from him the walls of Sulmo take their name—cool
Sulmo, my native town, Germanicus. Woe's me,
how far is Sulmo from the Scythian land! Therefore shall I so far away—but check, my Muse, thy
plaints; 'tis not for thee to warble sacred themes
on mournful strings.ᵃ

⁸⁵ Where doth not sallow envy find a way? Some
there are who grudge thee the honour of the month,
and would snatch it from thee, Venus. For they
say that April was named from the open (*apertum*)
season, because spring then opens (*aperit*) all things,
and the sharp frost-bound cold departs, and earth
unlocks her teeming soil, though kindly Venus
claims the month and lays her hand on it. She
indeed sways, and well deserves to sway, the world
entire; she owns a kingdom second to that of
no god; she gives laws to heaven and earth and
to her native sea, and by her inspiration she keeps
every species in being. She created all the gods—
'twere long to number them; she bestowed on
seeds and trees their origins. She drew rude-
minded men together and taught them to pair each
with his mate. What but bland pleasure brings
into being the whole brood of birds? Cattle, too,
would not come together, were loose love wanting.
The savage ram butts at the wether, but would not
hurt the forehead of the ewe he loves. The bull,
whom all the woodland pastures, all the groves do
dread, puts off his fierceness and follows the heifer.
The same force preserves all living things under
the broad bosom of the deep, and fills the waters

prima feros habitus homini detraxit : ab illa
  venerunt cultus mundaque cura sui.
primus amans carmen vigilatum nocte negata
110 dicitur ad clausas concinuisse fores,
eloquiumque fuit duram exorare puellam,
  proque sua causa quisque disertus erat.
mille per hanc artes motae ; studioque placendi
  quae latuere prius, multa reperta ferunt.
115 hanc quisquam titulo mensis spoliare secundi
  audeat ? a nobis sit furor iste procul.
quid, quod ubique potens templisque frequentibus
    aucta,
  urbe tamen nostra ius dea maius habet ?
pro Troia, Romane, tua Venus arma ferebat,
120 cum gemuit teneram cuspide laesa manum :
caelestesque duas Troiano iudice vicit
  (a ! nolim victas hoc meminisse deas !),
Assaracique nurus dicta est, ut scilicet olim
  magnus Iuleos Caesar haberet avos.
125 nec Veneri tempus quam ver erat aptius ullum :
  vere nitent terrae, vere remissus ager,
nunc herbae rupta tellure cacumina tollunt,
  nunc tumido gemmas cortice palmes agit.
et formosa Venus formoso tempore digna est,
130 utque solet, Marti continuata suo est :
vere monet curvas materna per aequora puppes
  ire nec hibernas iam timuisse minas.

---

  a Wounded by Diomede, *Iliad*, v. 335.
  b Paris, the Trojan, adjudged to her the apple, the prize of
beauty ; and her rivals, Juno (Hera) and Athena, bore a
grudge for their defeat.
  c Anchises, grandson of Assaracus. The Julian line
claimed descent from Iulus, son of Aeneas.

with unnumbered fish. That force first stripped
man of his savage garb ; from it he learned decent
attire and personal cleanliness. A lover was the
first, they say, to serenade by night the mistress
who denied him entrance, while he sang at her
barred door, and to win the heart of a coy maid
was eloquence indeed ; every man then pleaded his
own cause. This goddess has been the mother of
a thousand arts ; the wish to please has given birth
to many inventions that were unknown before.
And shall any man dare rob this goddess of the
honour of giving her name to the second month ?
Far from me be such a frenzy. Besides, while
everywhere the goddess is powerful and her temples
are thronged with worshippers, she possesses yet
more authority in our city. Venus, O Roman, bore
arms for thy Troy, what time she groaned at the
spear wound in her dainty hand [a]; and by a Trojan's
verdict she defeated two heavenly goddesses.[b] Ah
would that they had not remembered their defeat !
And she was called the bride of Assaracus' son,[c]
in order, to be sure, that in time to come great
Caesar might count the Julian line among his
sires. And no season was more fitting for Venus
than spring. In spring the landscape glistens ; soft
is the soil in spring ; now the corn pushes its
blades through the cleft ground ; now the vine-
shoot protrudes its buds in the swelling bark.
Lovely Venus deserves the lovely season and is
attached, as usual, to her dear Mars : in spring
she bids the curved ships fare across her natal seas
and fear no more the threats of winter.

OVID

1. CK · A[PRIL · N[^P]

Rite deam colitis Latiae matresque nurusque
  et vos, quis vittae longaque vestis abest.[^a]
135 aurea marmoreo redimicula demite collo,
  demite divitias : tota lavanda dea est.
aurea siccato redimicula reddite collo :
  nunc alii flores, nunc nova danda rosa est.
vos quoque sub viridi myrto iubet ipsa lavari :
140   causaque, cur iubeat (discite !), certa subest
litore siccabat rorantes nuda capillos :
  viderunt satyri, turba proterva, deam.
sensit et opposita texit sua corpora myrto :
  tuta fuit facto vosque referre iubet.
145 discite nunc, quare Fortunae tura Virili
  detis eo, calida qui locus umet aqua.
accipit ille locus posito velamine cunctas
  et vitium nudi corporis omne videt;
ut tegat hoc celetque viros, Fortuna Virilis
150   praestat et hoc parvo ture rogata facit.
nec pigeat tritum niveo cum lacte papaver
  sumere et expressis mella liquata favis ;
cum primum cupido Venus est deducta marito,
  hoc bibit : ex illo tempore nupta fuit.
155 supplicibus verbis illam placate : sub illa
  et forma et mores et bona fama manet.
Roma pudicitia proavorum tempore lapsa est :
  Cymaeam, veteres, consuluistis anum.[^c]
templa iubet fieri Veneri, quibus ordine factis
160   inde Venus verso nomina corde tenet.

[^a]: Courtesans, who were forbidden to wear the garb of matrons.
[^b]: Venus, to whom the month of April belonged. Her statue was washed. On April 1, women of the lower sort bathed in the men's public baths, and worshipped Fortuna Virilis.
[^c]: The Sibyl.

KAL. APR. 1st

¹³³ Duly do ye worship the goddess, ye Latin mothers and brides, and ye, too, who wear not the fillets and long robe.^a Take off the golden necklaces from the marble neck of the goddess ^b; take off her gauds; the goddess must be washed from top to toe. Then dry her neck and restore to it her golden necklaces; now give her other flowers, now give her the fresh-blown rose. Ye, too, she herself bids bathe under the green myrtle, and there is a certain reason for her command; learn what it is. Naked, she was drying on the shore her oozy locks, when the satyrs, a wanton crew, espied the goddess. She perceived it, and screened her body by myrtle interposed: that done, she was safe, and she bids you do the same. Learn now why ye give incense to Virile Fortune in the place which reeks of warm water. All women strip when they enter that place, and every blemish on the naked body is plain to see; Virile Fortune undertakes to conceal the blemish and to hide it from the men, and this she does for the consideration of a little incense. Nor grudge to take poppy pounded with snowy milk and liquid honey squeezed from the comb; when Venus was first escorted to her eager spouse, she drank that draught: from that time she was a bride. Propitiate her with supplications; beauty and virtue and good fame are in her keeping. In the time of our forefathers Rome had fallen from a state of chastity, and the ancients consulted the old woman of Cumae.^c She ordered a temple to be built to Venus, and when that was duly done, Venus took the name of Changer of the Heart

semper ad Aeneadas placido, pulcherrima, voltu
   respice totque tuas, diva, tuere nurus.
dum loquor, elatae metuendus acumine caudae
   Scorpios in viridis praecipitatur aquas.

2. D [F]

165 Nox ubi transierit, caelumque rubescere primo
     coeperit, et tactae rore querentur aves,
  semiustamque facem vigilata nocte viator
     ponet, et ad solitum rusticus ibit opus,
  Pleiades incipient humeros relevare paternos,
170   quae septem dici, sex tamen esse solent:
seu quod in amplexum sex hinc venere deorum,
     (nam Steropen Marti concubuisse ferunt,
Neptuno Alcyonen et te, formosa Celaeno,
     Maian et Electram Taygetemque Iovi),
175 septima mortali Merope tibi, Sisyphe, nupsit;
     paenitet, et facti sola pudore latet:
sive quod Electra Troiae spectare ruinas
     non tulit, ante oculos opposuitque manum.

3. EC   4. FC LVDI · MATR · MAG

Ter sine perpetuo caelum versetur in axe,
180   ter iungat Titan terque resolvat equos,
protinus inflexo Berecyntia tibia cornu
   flabit, et Idaeae festa parentis erunt.

---

    ^a Real setting April 26.   Apparent setting May 13.
   ^b Atlas.   ^c Phrygian (from Mount Berecyntus).

(*Verticordia*) from the event. Fairest of goddesses, ever behold the sons of Aeneas with look benign, and guard thine offspring's numerous wives.

163 While I speak, the Scorpion, the tip of whose swinged tail strikes fear, plunges into the green waters.*a*

IV. Non. 2nd

165 When the night has passed, and the sky has just begun to blush, and dew-besprinkled birds are twittering plaintively, and the wayfarer, who all night long has waked, lays down his half-burnt torch. and the swain goes forth to his accustomed toil, the Pleiades will commence to lighten the burden that rests on their father's *b* shoulders; seven are they usually called, but six they usually are; whether it be that six of the sisters were embraced by gods (for they say that Sterope lay with Mars, Alcyone and fair Celaeno with Neptune, and Maia, Electra, and Taygete with Jupiter); the seventh, Merope, was married to a mortal man, to Sisyphus, and she repents of it, and from shame at the deed she alone of the sisters hides herself; or whether it be that Electra could not brook to behold the fall of Troy, and so covered her eyes with her hand.

Pr. Non. 4th

179 Let the sky revolve thrice on its never-resting axis; let Titan thrice yoke and thrice unyoke his steeds, straightway the Berecyntian *c* flute will blow a blast on its bent horn, and the festival of the

OVID

ibunt semimares et inania tympana tundent,
    aeraque tinnitus aere repulsa dabunt :
185 ipsa sedens molli comitum cervice feretur
    urbis per medias exululata vias.
scaena sonat, ludique vocant. spectate, Quirites,
    et fora Marte suo litigiosa vacent.
quaerere multa libet, sed me sonus aeris acuti
190   terret et horrendo lotos adunca sono.
  " da, dea, quem sciter." doctas Cybeleïa neptes
    vidit et has curae iussit adesse meae.
  " pandite, mandati memores, Heliconis alumnae,
    gaudeat assiduo cur dea Magna sono."
195 sic ego. sic Erato (mensis Cythereïus illi
    cessit, quod teneri nomen amoris habet) :
  " reddita Saturno sors haec erat, ' optime regum,
    a nato sceptris excutiere tuis.'
ille suam metuens, ut quaeque erat edita, prolem
200   devorat, immersam visceribusque tenet.
saepe Rhea questa est, totiens fecunda nec umquam
    mater, et indoluit fertilitate sua.
Iuppiter ortus erat (pro magno teste vetustas
    creditur ; acceptam parce movere fidem) :
205 veste latens saxum caelesti gutture sedit :
    sic genitor fatis decipiendus erat.
ardua iamdudum resonat tinnitibus Ide,
    tutus ut infanti vagiat ore puer.
pars clipeos rudibus, galeas pars tundit inanes :
210   hoc Curetes habent, hoc Corybantes opus.

---

    a Cybele, the Asiatic goddess. The feast was called the
Megalensian (Megale, great goddess). Her attendants, the
Galli, were eunuchs.
    b The Muses, whose father Jupiter was son of Cybele.
    c Eros, Love.   *d* Cybele.   *e* Of Saturn (Cronos).

Idaean Mother will have come.[a] Eunuchs will march
and thump their hollow drums, and cymbals clashed
on cymbals will give out their tinkling notes : seated
on the unmanly necks of her attendants, the goddess
herself will be borne with howls through the streets in
the city's midst. The stage is clattering, the games
are calling. To your places, Quirites ! and in the
empty law-courts let the war of suitors cease ! I
would put many questions, but I am daunted by
the shrill cymbal's clash and the bent flute's thrilling
drone. " Grant me, goddess, someone whom I may
question." The Cybelean goddess spied her learned
granddaughters [b] and bade them attend to my inquiry.
" Mindful of her command, ye nurslings of Helicon,
disclose the reason why the Great Goddess delights
in a perpetual din." So did I speak, and Erato [c]
did thus reply (it fell to her to speak of Venus'
month, because her own name is derived from
tender love) : " Saturn was given this oracle : ' Thou
best of kings, thou shalt be ousted of thy sceptre
by thy son.' In fear, the god devoured his offspring
as fast as they were born, and he kept them sunk in
his bowels. Many a time did Rhea [d] grumble, to
be so often big with child, yet never be a mother ;
she repined at her own fruitfulness. Then Jove
was born. The testimony of antiquity passes for
good ; pray do not shake the general faith. A
stone concealed in a garment went down the
heavenly throat [e] ; so had fate decreed that the sire
should be beguiled. Now rang steep Ida loud and
long with clangorous music, that the boy might
pule in safety with his infant mouth. Some beat
their shields, others their empty helmets with staves ;
that was the task of the Curetes and that, too, of the

res latuit, priscique manent imitamina facti ;
    aera deae comites raucaque terga movent.
cymbala pro galeis, pro scutis tympana pulsant ;
    tibia dat Phrygios, ut dedit ante, modos."
215 desierat.   coepi : " cur huic genus acre leonum
    praebent insolitas ad iuga curva iubas ? "
desieram.   coepit : " feritas mollita per illam
    creditur ; id curru testificata suo est."
" at cur turrifera caput est onerata corona ?
220   an primis turres urbibus illa dedit ? "
annuit. " unde venit " dixi " sua membra secandi
    impetus ? " ut tacui, Pieris orsa loqui :
" Phryx puer in silvis, facie spectabilis, Attis
    turrigeram casto vinxit amore deam.
225 hunc sibi servari voluit, sua templa tueri,
    et dixit ' semper fac puer esse velis.'
ille fidem iussis dedit et ' si mentiar,' inquit
    ' ultima, qua fallam, sit Venus illa mihi.'
fallit et in nympha Sagaritide desinit esse
230   quod fuit : hinc poenas exigit ira deae.
Naida volneribus succidit in arbore factis,
    illa perit : fatum Naidos arbor erat.
hic furit et credens thalami procumbere tectum
    effugit et cursu Dindyma summa petit
235 et modo ' tolle faces ! ' ' remove ' modo ' verbera ! '
    clamat ;

---

   [a] No doubt named from the river Sangarius or Sagaris, in
Phrygia. She appears to have been nymph of a neighbouring tree. The jealous goddess punished Attis by driving him
mad.

Corybantes. The secret was kept, and the ancient deed is still acted in mimicry; the attendants of the goddess thump the brass and the rumbling leather; cymbals they strike instead of helmets, and drums instead of shields; the flute plays, as of yore, the Phrygian airs."

²¹⁵ The goddess ended. I began: "Why for her sake doth the fierce breed of lions yield their unwonted manes to the curved yoke?" I ended. She began: " 'Tis thought, the wildness of the brute was tamed by her: that she testifies by her (lion-drawn) car." "But why is her head weighted with a turreted crown? Is it because she gave towers to the first cities?" The goddess nodded assent. "Whence came," said I, "the impulse to cut their members?" When I was silent, the Pierian goddess began to speak: "In the woods a Phrygian boy of handsome face, Attis by name, had attached the tower-bearing goddess to himself by a chaste passion. She wished that he should be kept for herself and should guard her temple, and she said, "Resolve to be a boy for ever." He promised obedience, and, "If I lie," quoth he, "may the love for which I break faith be my last love of all." He broke faith; for, meeting the nymph Sagaritis,ᵃ he ceased to be what he had been before. For that the angry goddess wreaked vengeance. By wounds inflicted on the tree she cut down the Naiad, who perished thus; for the fate of the Naiad was bound up with the tree. Attis went mad, and, imagining that the roof of the chamber was falling in, he fled and ran for the top of Mount Dindymus. And he kept crying, at one moment, 'Take away the torches!' at another, 'Remove the whips!' And

205

saepe Palaestinas iurat adesse deas.
ille etiam saxo corpus laniavit acuto,
   longaque in immundo pulvere tracta coma est,
voxque fuit ' merui ! meritas do sanguine poenas.
240   a ! pereant partes, quae nocuere mihi !
a ! pereant ' dicebat adhuc, onus inguinis aufert,
   nullaque sunt subito signa relicta viri.
venit in exemplum furor hic, mollesque ministri
   caedunt iactatis vilia membra comis."
245 talibus Aoniae facunda voce Camenae
   reddita quaesiti causa furoris erat.
" hoc quoque, dux operis, moneas, precor, unde petita
   venerit. an nostra semper in urbe fuit ? "
" Dindymon et Cybelen et amoenam fontibus Iden
250   semper et Iliacas Mater amavit opes :
cum Troiam Aeneas Italos portaret in agros,
   est dea sacriferas paene secuta rates,
sed nondum fatis Latio sua numina posci
   senserat, adsuetis substiteratque locis.
255 post, ut Roma potens opibus iam saecula quinque
   vidit et edomito sustulit orbe caput,
carminis Euboici fatalia verba sacerdos
   inspicit ; inspectum tale fuisse ferunt :
' mater abest : matrem iubeo, Romane, requiras.
260   cum veniet, casta est accipienda manu.'
obscurae sortis patres ambagibus errant,
   quaeve parens absit, quove petenda loco.

---

^a The Furies : why so called is unknown.
^b In 204 B.C., year of Rome 549, the Sibylline books were

oft he swore that the Palaestinian goddesses*a* were
on him. He mangled, too, his body with a sharp
stone, and trailed his long hair in the filthy dust;
and his cry was, 'I have deserved it! With my
blood I pay the penalty that is my due. Ah, perish
the parts that were my ruin! Ah, let them perish,'
still he said. He retrenched the burden of his groin,
and of a sudden was bereft of every sign of
manhood. His madness set an example, and still
his unmanly ministers cut their vile members while
they toss their hair." In such words the Aonian
Muse eloquently answered my question as to the
cause of the madness of the votaries.

247 "Instruct me, too, I pray, my guide, whence was
she fetched, whence came? Was she always in our
city?" "The Mother Goddess ever loved Dindymus,
and Cybele, and Ida, with its delightful springs,
and the realm of Ilium. When Aeneas carried
Troy to the Italian fields, the goddess almost
followed the ships that bore the sacred things; but
she felt that fate did not yet call for the intervention
of her divinity in Latium, and she remained behind
in her accustomed place. Afterwards, when mighty
Rome had already seen five centuries,*b* and had lifted
up her head above the conquered world, the priest
consulted the fateful words of the Euboean song.
They say that what he found ran thus: 'The
Mother is absent; thou Roman, I bid thee seek
the Mother. When she shall come, she must be
received by chaste hands.' The ambiguity of
the dark oracle puzzled the senators to know who
the Parent was, and where she was to be sought.

consulted. The Sibyl lived at Cumae, a colony of Euboea.
See Livy xxix. 10, 11, 14.

consulitur Paean, ' divum ' que ' arcessite Matrem,'
    inquit ' in Idaeo est invenienda iugo.'
265 mittuntur proceres.   Phrygiae tunc sceptra tenebat
    Attalus : Ausoniis rem negat ille viris.
mira canam.   longo tremuit cum murmure tellus,
    et sic est adytis diva locuta suis :
' ipsa peti volui, nec sit mora, mitte volentem.
270   dignus Roma locus, quo deus omnis eat.'
ille soni terrore pavens ' proficiscere,' dixit
    ' nostra eris : in Phrygios Roma refertur avos.'
protinus innumerae caedunt pineta secures
    illa, quibus fugiens Phryx pius usus erat :
275 mille manus coeunt, et picta coloribus ustis
    caelestum Matrem concava puppis habet.
illa sui per aquas fertur tutissima nati
    longaque Phrixeae stagna sororis adit
Rhoeteumque rapax Sigeaque litora transit
280   et Tenedum et veteres Eetionis opes.
Cyclades excipiunt, Lesbo post terga relicta,
    quaeque Carysteis frangitur unda vadis.
transit et Icarium, lapsas ubi perdidit alas
    Icarus et vastae nomina fecit aquae.
285 tum laeva Creten, dextra Pelopeïdas undas
    deserit et Veneris sacra Cythera petit.
hinc mare Trinacrium, candens ubi tinguere ferrum
    Brontes et Steropes Acmonidesque solent,

---

^a Delphic Apollo.   The envoys sent from Rome, M.
Valerius Laevinus, M. Caecilius Metellus, Ser. Sulpicius
Gallus, consulted the oracle at Delphi on their way and
received a favourable answer.
    ^b This is not borne out by Livy.
    ^c Aeneas.
    ^d Helles-pontus.   See above, iii. 851 note.
    ^e Eëtion was father of Andromache, and king of Thebe
in the Troad.

Paean [a] was consulted and said, ' Fetch the Mother of the Gods ; she is to be found on Mount Ida.' Nobles were sent. The sceptre of Phrygia was then held by Attalus ; he refused the favour to the Ausonian lords.[b] Wonders to tell, the earth trembled and rumbled long, and in her shrine thus did the goddess speak : ' 'Twas my own will that they should send for me. Tarry not : let me go, it is my wish. Rome is a place meet to be the resort of every god.' Quaking with terror at the words Attalus said, Go forth. Thou wilt still be ours. Rome traces its origin to Phrygian ancestors.' Straightway unnumbered axes fell those pinewoods which had supplied the pious Phrygian [c] with timber in his flight : a thousand hands assemble, and the Mother of the Gods is lodged in a hollow ship painted in encaustic colours. She is borne in perfect safety across the waters of her son and comes to the long strait named after the sister of Phrixus [d] ; she passes Rhoeteum, where the tide runs fast, and the Sigean shores, and Tenedos, and Eetion's ancient realm.[e] Leaving Lesbos behind, she came next to the Cyclades and to the wave that breaks on the Carystian shoals.[f] She passed the Icarian Sea also, where Icarus lost his wings that slipped, and where he gave his name to a great water. Then she left Crete on the larboard and the Pelopian billows on the starboard, and steered for Cythera, the sacred isle of Venus. Thence she passed to the Trinacrian [g] Sea, where Brontes and Steropes and Acmonides [h] are wont to dip the white-hot iron.

[f] South of Euboea.   [g] Sicilian.
[h] Usually called Pyracmon. These are the three Cyclopes who forged Jupiter's thunderbolts under Mount Etna.

    aequoraque Afra legit Sardoaque regna sinistris
290   respicit a remis Ausoniamque tenet.
    Ostia contigerat, qua se Tiberinus in altum
        dividit et campo liberiore natat :
    omnis eques mixtaque gravis cum plebe senatus
        obvius ad Tusci fluminis ora venit.
295 procedunt pariter matres nataeque nurusque
        quaeque colunt sanctos virginitate focos.
    sedula fune viri contento brachia lassant :
        vix subit adversas hospita navis aquas.
    sicca diu fuerat tellus, sitis usserat herbas :
300   sedit limoso pressa carina vado.
    quisquis adest operi, plus quam pro parte laborat,
        adiuvat et fortis voce sonante manus.
    illa velut medio stabilis sedet insula ponto :
        attoniti monstro stantque paventque viri.
305 Claudia Quinta genus Clauso referebat ab alto,
        nec facies impar nobilitate fuit :
    casta quidem, sed non et credita : rumor iniquus
        laeserat, et falsi criminis acta rea est ;
    cultus et ornatis varie prodisse capillis
310   obfuit, ad rigidos promptaque lingua senes.
    conscia mens recti famae mendacia risit,
        sed nos in vitium credula turba sumus.
    haec ubi castarum processit ab agmine matrum
        et manibus puram fluminis hausit aquam,
315 ter caput inrorat, ter tollit in aethera palmas
        (quicumque aspiciunt, mente carere putant)
    summissoque genu voltus in imagine divae

---

    [a] A Sabine leader, said to have assisted Aeneas : Virgil,
Aen. vii. 706. Ancestor of the Claudian house.

She skirted the African main, and beheld astern to larboard the Sardinian realms, and made Ausonia.

291 " She had arrived at Ostia, where the Tiber divides to join the sea and flows with ampler sweep. All the knights and the grave senators, mixed up with the common folk, came to meet her at the mouth of the Tuscan river. With them walked mothers and daughters and brides, and the virgins who tended the sacred hearths. The men wearied their arms by tugging lustily at the rope ; hardly did the foreign ship make head against the stream. A drought had long prevailed ; the grass was parched and burnt ; the loaded bark sank in the muddy shallows. Every man who lent a hand toiled beyond his strength and cheered on the workers by his cries. Yet the ship stuck fast, like an island firmly fixed in the middle of the sea. Astonished at the portent, the men did stand and quake. Claudia Quinta traced her descent from Clausus[a] of old, and her beauty matched her nobility. Chaste was she, though not reputed so. Rumour unkind had wronged her, and a false charge had been trumped up against her : it told against her that she dressed sprucely, that she walked abroad with her hair dressed in varied fashion, that she had a ready tongue for gruff old men. Conscious of innocence, she laughed at fame's untruths ; but we of the multitude are prone to think the worst. When she had stepped forth from the procession of the chaste matrons, and taken up the pure water of the river in her hands, she thrice let it drip on her head, and thrice lifted her palms to heaven (all who looked on her thought that she was out of her mind), and bending the knee she fixed her eyes on

figit et hos edit crine iacente sonos :
' supplicis, alma, tuae, genetrix fecunda deorum,
320 accipe sub certa condicione preces.
casta negor. si tu damnas, meruisse fatebor ;
 morte luam poenas iudice victa dea.
sed si crimen abest, tu nostrae pignora vitae
 re dabis et castas casta sequere manus.'
325 dixit et exiguo funem conamine traxit
 (mira, sed et scaena testificata loquar) :
mota dea est sequiturque ducem laudatque sequendo :
 index laetitiae fertur ad astra sonus.
fluminis ad flexum veniunt (Tiberina priores
330 atria dixerunt), unde sinister abit.
nox aderat : querno religant in stipite funem
 dantque levi somno corpora functa cibo.
lux aderat : querno solvunt a stipite funem ;
 ante tamen posito tura dedere foco,
335 ante coronarunt puppem et sine labe iuvencam
 mactarunt operum coniugiique rudem.
est locus, in Tiberim qua lubricus influit Almo
 et nomen magno perdit in amne minor :
illic purpurea canus cum veste sacerdos
340 Almonis dominam sacraque lavit aquis.
exululant comites, furiosaque tibia flatur,
 et feriunt molles taurea terga manus.
Claudia praecedit laeto celeberrima voltu,
 credita vix tandem teste pudica dea ;
345 ipsa sedens plaustro porta est invecta Capena :
 sparguntur iunctae flore recente boves.

---

^a It was probably acted at the Megalensia, the Great
Mother's festival. ^b Left for one ascending the Tiber.

the image of the goddess, and with dishevelled hair
uttered these words : ' Thou fruitful Mother of
the Gods, graciously accept thy suppliant's prayers
on one condition. They say I am not chaste. If
thou dost condemn me, I will confess my guilt ;
convicted by the verdict of a goddess, I will pay
the penalty with my life. But if I am free of crime,
give by thine act a proof of my innocency, and,
chaste as thou art, do thou yield to my chaste
hands.' She spoke, and drew the rope with a slight
effort. My story is a strange one, but it is attested
by the stage.[a] The goddess was moved, and followed
her leader, and by following bore witness in her
favour : a sound of joy was wafted to the stars.
They came to a bend in the river, where the stream
turns away to the left [b] : men of old named it the
Halls of Tiber. Night drew on ; they tied the rope
to an oaken stump, and after a repast disposed themselves to slumber light. At dawn of day they loosed
the rope from the oaken stump ; but first they set
down a brazier and put incense on it, and crowned
the poop, and sacrificed an unblemished heifer that
had known neither the yoke nor the bull. There
is a place where the smooth Almo flows into the
Tiber, and the lesser river loses its name in the
great one. There a hoary-headed priest in purple
robe washed the Mistress and her holy things in the
waters of Almo. The attendants howled, the mad
flute blew, and hands unmanly beat the leathern
drums. Attended by a crowd, Claudia walked in
front with joyful face, her chastity at last vindicated
by the testimony of the goddess. The goddess
herself, seated in a wagon, drove in through the
Capene Gate ; fresh flowers were scattered on the

Nasica accepit. templi non perstitit auctor :
    Augustus nunc est, ante Metellus erat."
substitit hic Erato. mora fit ; sic cetera quaero :
350 " dic," inquam " parva cur stipe quaerat opes."
" contulit aes populus, de quo delubra Metellus
    fecit," ait " dandae mos stipis inde manet."
cur vicibus factis ineant convivia, quaero,
    tunc magis, indictas concelebrentque dapes.
355 " quod bene mutarit sedem Berecyntia," dixit
    " captant mutatis sedibus omen idem."
institeram, quare primi Megalesia ludi
    urbe forent nostra, cum dea (sensit enim)
" illa deos " inquit " peperit. cessere parenti,
360   principiumque dati Mater honoris habet."
" cur igitur Gallos, qui se excidere, vocamus,
    cum tanto a Phrygia Gallica distet humus ? "
" inter " ait " viridem Cybelen altasque Celaenas
    amnis it insana, nomine Gallus, aqua.
365 qui bibit inde, furit : procul hinc discedite, quis est
    cura bonae mentis : qui bibit inde, furit."
" non pudet herbosum " dixi " posuisse moretum
    in dominae mensis. an sua causa subest ? "
" lacte mero veteres usi narrantur et herbis,
370   sponte sua si quas terra ferebat " ait.
" candidus elisae miscetur caseus herbae,
    cognoscat priscos ut dea prisca cibos."

---

    a P. Corn. Scipio Nasica, a young man, was commissioned
to receive the goddess.
    b The temple was dedicated in 191 B.C. It was burnt
down in 111 B.C., when one Metellus restored it (? Q. Caecilius
Metellus) ; and in A.D. 3, when Augustus restored it (*Mon.
Ancyr.* iv. 19, in L.C.L. Velleius Paterculus, p. 376).
    c This feast was a great time for hospitality ; and the
words used for invitations were *mutitare, mutitatio.*

yoked oxen. Nasica received her.[a] The name of the
founder of the temple has not survived ; now it is
Augustus ; formerly it was Metellus." [b]

349 Here Erato stopped. There was a pause. Then
I put the rest of my questions thus. " Why," said I,
" does the goddess collect money in small coins ? "
" The people contributed their coppers, with which
Metellus built her fane," said she ; " hence the custom
of giving a small coin abides." I asked why then more
than at other times people entertain each other to
feasts and hold banquets for which they issue invitations. " Because," said she, " the Berecyntian goddess
luckily changed her home, people try to get the
same good luck by going from house to house." [c]
I was about to ask why the Megalesia are the
first games of the year in our city, when the goddess
took my meaning and said, " She gave birth to the
gods. They gave place to their parent, and the
Mother has the honour of precedence." " Why then
do we give the name of Galli to the men who unman
themselves, when the Gallic land is so far from
Phrygia ? " " Between," said she, " green Cybele
and high Celaenae [d] a river of mad water flows, 'tis
named the Gallus. Who drinks of it goes mad.
Far hence depart, ye who care to be of sound mind.
Who drinks of it goes mad." " They think no
shame," said I, " to set a dish of herbs on the tables
of the Mistress. Is there a good reason at the
bottom of it ? " " People of old," she answered,
" are reported to have subsisted on pure milk and
such herbs as the earth bore of its free will. White
cheese is mixed with pounded herbs, that the
ancient goddess may know the ancient foods."

[d] In Phrygia.

OVID

5. G NON LVDI

Postera cum caelo motis Pallantias astris
    fulserit, et niveos Luna levarit equos,
375 qui dicet " quondam sacrata est colle Quirini
    hac Fortuna die Publica," verus erit.

6. HN̄P LVDI 7. AN LVDI 8. BN LVDI 9. CN LVDI

Tertia lux (memini) ludis erat, ac mihi quidam
    spectanti senior continuusque loco
" haec " ait " illa dies, Libycis qua Caesar in oris
380   perfida magnanimi contudit arma Iubae.
dux mihi Caesar erat, sub quo meruisse tribunus
    glorior : officio praefuit ille meo.
hanc ego militia sedem, tu pace parasti,
    inter bis quinos usus honore viros."
385 plura locuturi subito seducimur imbre :
    pendula caelestis Libra movebat aquas.

Ante tamen, quam summa dies spectacula sistat,
    ensifer Orion aequore mersus erit.

10. DN LVD · IN · CIR

Proxima victricem cum Romam inspexerit Eos,
390   et dederit Phoebo stella fugata locum,

---

^a Pallantias, Aurora. Ovid regards her as daughter of
the giant Pallas.
    ^b Thapsus, 46 B.C.
    ^c The *Decemviri stlitibus iudicandis* had special seats in
front.
    ^d True setting began April 10 (morning) ; apparent setting
May 18.

NON. 5th

373 When the next Dawn *a* shall have shone in the
sky, and the stars have vanished, and the Moon
shall have unyoked her snow-white steeds, he who
shall say, " On this day of old the temple of Public
Fortune was dedicated on the hill of Quirinus " will
tell the truth.

VIII. ID. 6th

377 It was, I remember, the third day of the games,
when a certain elderly man, who sat next to me at
the show, observed to me, " This was the famous
day when on the Libyan shores Caesar crushed
proud Juba's treacherous host.*b* Caesar was my
commander ; under him I am proud to have served
as colonel ; at his hands did I receive my com-
mission. This seat I won in war, and thou didst
win in peace,*c* by reason of thine office in the College
of the Ten." We were about to say more when
a sudden shower of rain parted us ; the Balance
hung in heaven released the heavenly waters.

V. ID. 9th

387 But before the last day shall have put an end
to the shows, sworded Orion will have sunk in the
sea.*d*

IV. ID. 10th

389 When the next Dawn shall have looked on
victorious Rome, and the stars shall have been put
to flight and given place to the sun, the Circus will

OVID

circus erit pompa celeber numeroque deorum,
    primaque ventosis palma petetur equis.

11. EN 12. FN LVDI · CERERI

Hinc Cereris ludi. non est opus indice causae ;
    sponte deae munus promeritumque patet.
395 panis erat primis virides mortalibus herbae,
    quas tellus nullo sollicitante dabat ;
et modo carpebant vivax e cespite gramen,
    nunc epulae tenera fronde cacumen erant.
postmodo glans nata est : bene erat iam glande
    reperta,
400   duraque magnificas quercus habebat opes.
prima Ceres homine ad meliora alimenta vocato
    mutavit glandes utiliore cibo.
illa iugo tauros collum praebere coegit :
    tunc primum soles eruta vidit humus.
405 aes erat in pretio, chalybeïa massa latebat :
    eheu ! perpetuo debuit illa tegi.
pace Ceres laeta est ; et vos orate, coloni,
    perpetuam pacem pacificumque ducem.
farra deae micaeque licet salientis honorem
410   detis et in veteres turea grana focos,
et, si tura aberunt, unctas accendite taedas :
    parva bonae Cereri, sint modo casta, placent.
a bove succincti cultros removete ministri :
    bos aret ; ignavam sacrificate suem.
415 apta iugo cervix non est ferienda securi :
    vivat et in dura saepe laboret humo.

218

be thronged with a procession and an array of the
gods, and the horses, fleet as the wind, will contend
for the first palm.

Pr. Id. 12th

393 Next come the games of Ceres. There is no
need to declare the reason; the bounty and the
services of the goddess are manifest. The bread
of the first mortals consisted of the green herbs
which the earth yielded without solicitation; and
now they plucked the living grass from the turf,
and now the tender leaves of tree-tops furnished
a feast. Afterwards the acorn was produced; it
was well when they had found the acorn, and the
sturdy oak afforded a splendid affluence. Ceres was
the first who invited man to better sustenance
and exchanged acorns for more useful food. She
forced bulls to yield their necks to the yoke; then
for the first time did the upturned soil behold the
sun. Copper was now held in esteem; iron ore
still lay concealed; ah, would that it had been
hidden for ever! Ceres delights in peace; and
you, ye husbandmen, pray for perpetual peace and
for a pacific prince. You may give the goddess
spelt, and the compliment of spurting salt, and
grains of incense on old hearths; and if there is
no incense, kindle resinous torches. Good Ceres
is content with little, if that little be but pure. Ye
attendants, with tucked up robes, take the knives
away from the ox; let the ox plough; sacrifice
the lazy sow. The axe should never smite the neck
that fits the yoke; let him live and often labour in
the hard soil.

OVID

Exigit ipse locus, raptus ut virginis edam :
    plura recognosces, pauca docendus eris.
terra tribus scopulis vastum procurrit in aequor
420   Trinacris, a positu nomen adepta loci,
grata domus Cereri. multas ea possidet urbes,
    in quibus est culto fertilis Henna solo.
frigida caelestum matres Arethusa vocarat :
    venerat ad sacras et dea flava dapes.
425 filia, consuetis ut erat comitata puellis,
    errabat nudo per sua prata pede.
valle sub umbrosa locus est aspergine multa
    uvidus ex alto desilientis aquae.
tot fuerant illic, quot habet natura, colores,
430   pictaque dissimili flore nitebat humus.
quam simul aspexit, " comites, accedite " dixit
    " et mecum plenos flore referte sinus."
praeda puellares animos prolectat inanis,
    et non sentitur sedulitate labor.
435 haec implet lento calathos e vimine nexos,
    haec gremium, laxos degravat illa sinus :
illa legit calthas, huic sunt violaria curae,
    illa papavereas subsecat ungue comas :
has, hyacinthe, tenes ; illas, amarante, moraris :
440   pars thyma, pars rorem, pars meliloton amat.
plurima lecta rosa est, sunt et sine nomine flores ;
    ipsa crocos tenues liliaque alba legit.
carpendi studio paulatim longius itur,
    et dominam casu nulla secuta comes.
445 hanc videt et visam patruus velociter aufert

---

      a Sicily.   *b* In Sicily ; often called Enna.
    c Nymph of the fountain Arethusa, in Syracuse. She had
invited the matrons, so that Persephone, or Proserpine,
daughter of Ceres, was left unguarded.
    a Pluto, or Dis, brother of Jupiter.

417 The subject requires that I should narrate the rape of the Virgin : in my narrative you will read much that you knew before ; a few particulars will be new to you.

420 The Trinacrian land *a* got its name from its natural position : it runs out into the vast ocean in three rocky capes. It is the favourite home of Ceres : she owns many cities, among them fertile Henna *b* with its well-tilled soil. Cool Arethusa *c* had invited the mothers of the gods, and the yellow-haired goddess had also come to the sacred banquet. Attended as usual by her wonted damsels, her daughter roamed bare-foot through the familiar meadows. In a shady vale there is a spot moist with the abundant spray of a high waterfall. All the hues that nature owns were there displayed, and the pied earth was bright with various flowers. As soon as she espied it, "Come hither, comrades," she said, "and with me bring home lapfuls of flowers." The bauble booty lured their girlish minds, and they were too busy to feel fatigue. One filled baskets plaited of supple withes, another loaded her lap, another the loose folds of her robe ; one gathered marigolds, another paid heed to beds of violets ; another nipped off heads of poppies with her nails ; some are attracted by the hyacinth, others lingered over amaranth ; some love thyme, others rosemary, others melilot ; full many a rose was culled, and flowers without a name. Persephone herself plucked dainty crocuses and white lilies. Intent on gathering, she, little by little, strayed far, and it chanced that none of her companions followed their mistress. Her father's brother *d* saw her, and no sooner did he see her than he swiftly

regnaque caeruleis in sua portat equis.
illa quidem clamabat " io, carissima mater,
    auferor ! " ipsa suos abscideratque sinus :
panditur interea Diti via, namque diurnum
450   lumen inadsueti vix patiuntur equi.
at chorus aequalis, cumulatis flore canistris,
    " Persephone," clamant " ad tua dona veni ! "
ut clamata silet, montes ululatibus implent
    et feriunt maesta pectora nuda manu.
455 attonita est plangore Ceres (modo venerat Hennam)
    nec mora, " me miseram ! filia," dixit " ubi es ? "
mentis inops rapitur, quales audire solemus
    Threïcias fusis maenadas ire comis.
ut vitulo mugit sua mater ab ubere rapto
460   et quaerit fetus per nemus omne suos :
sic dea nec retinet gemitus et concita cursu
    fertur et a campis incipit, Henna, tuis.
inde puellaris nacta est vestigia plantae
    et pressam noto pondere vidit humum ;
465 forsitan illa dies erroris summa fuisset,
    si non turbassent signa reperta sues.
iamque Leontinos Amenanaque flumina cursu
    praeterit et ripas, herbifer Aci, tuas ;
praeterit et Cyanen et fontes lenis Anapi
470   et te, verticibus non adeunde Gela.
liquerat Ortygien Megareaque Pantagienque,
    quaque Symaetheas accipit aequor aquas,
antraque Cyclopum positis exusta caminis,
    quique locus curvae nomina falcis habet,

---

a Either Zancle (an ancient name of Messene) or
Drepanum, named after ζάγκλον or δρέπανον, " a sickle."
The other places named are also in Sicily. " Tempe of
Helorus " (l. 477) is the upper gorge of the river-course, re
calling Tempe in Thessaly.

arried her off and bore her on his dusky steeds into
is own realm. She in sooth cried out, "Ho,
dearest mother, they are carrying me away!" and
he rent the bosom of her robe. Meantime a road is
pened up for Dis; for his steeds can hardly brook
the unaccustomed daylight. But her troop of play-
mates, when they had heaped their baskets with
flowers, cried out, "Persephone, come to the gifts
we have for thee!" When she answered not their
all, they filled the mountain with shrieks, and smote
their bare bosoms with their sad hands.

455 Ceres was startled by the loud lament; she had
just come to Henna, and straightway, "Woe's me!
my daughter," said she, "where art thou?" Dis-
raught she hurried along, even as we hear that
Thracian Maenads rush with streaming hair. As
a cow, whose calf has been torn from her udder,
bellows and seeks her offspring through every grove,
so the goddess did not stifle her groans and ran
at speed, starting from the plains of Henna. From
here she lit on prints of the girlish feet and marked
the traces of the familiar figure on the ground.
Perhaps that day had been the last of her wanderings if swine had not foiled the trail she found.
Already in her course she had passed Leontini,
and the river Amenanus, and the grassy banks
of Acis. She had passed Cyane, and the springs of
gently flowing Anapus, and the Gelas with its whirl-
pools not to be approached. She had left behind
Ortygia and Megara and the Pantagias, and the
place where the sea receives the water of the
Symaethus, and the caves of the Cyclopes, burnt
by the forges set up in them, and the place that
takes its name from a curved sickle,[a] and Himera,

475 Himeraque et Didymen Acragantaque Tauromenum
que
sacrarumque Melan pascua laeta boum.
hinc Camerinan adit Thapsonque et Heloria Tempe
quaque iacet Zephyro semper apertus Eryx.
iamque Peloriadem Lilybaeaque, iamque Pachynon
480 lustrarat, terrae cornua trina suae.
quacumque ingreditur, miseris loca cuncta querellis
implet, ut amissum cum gemit ales Ityn,
perque vices modo " Persephone ! " modo " filia !
clamat,
clamat et alternis nomen utrumque ciet.
485 sed neque Persephone Cererem nec filia matrem
audit, et alternis nomen utrumque perit ;
unaque, pastorem vidisset an arva colentem,
vox erat " hac gressus ecqua puella tulit ? "
iam color unus inest rebus, tenebrisque teguntur
490 omnia, iam vigiles conticuere canes :
alta iacet vasti super ora Typhoëos Aetne,
cuius anhelatis ignibus ardet humus ;
illic accendit geminas pro lampade pinus :
hinc Cereris sacris nunc quoque taeda datur.
495 est specus exesi structura pumicis asper,
non homini regio, non adeunda ferae :
quo simul ac venit, frenatos curribus angues
iungit et aequoreas sicca pererrat aquas.
effugit et Syrtes et te, Zanclaea Charybdis,
500 et vos, Nisaei, naufraga monstra, canes,
Hadriacumque patens late bimaremque Corinthum
sic venit ad portus, Attica terra, tuos.

---

* Unknown.
b The nightingale : see ii. 629 note.
* See i. 573. The monster was imprisoned beneath Etna.
224

and Didyme, and Acragas, and Tauromenum, and the Melas,[a] where are the rich pastures of the sacred kine. Next she came to Camerina, and Thapsus, and the Tempe of Helorus, and where Eryx lies for ever open to the western breeze. Already had she traversed Pelorias, and Lilybaeum, and Pachynum, the three horns of her land. And wherever she set her foot she filled every place with her sad plaints, as when the bird doth mourn her Itys lost.[b] In turn she cried, now "Persephone!" now "Daughter!" She cried and shouted either name by turns; but neither did Persephone hear Ceres, nor the daughter hear her mother; both names by turns died away. And whether she spied a shepherd or a husbandman at work, her one question was, "Did a girl pass this way?" Now o'er the landscape stole a sober hue, and darkness hid the world : now the watchful dogs were hushed. Lofty Etna lies over the mouth of huge Typhoeus, whose fiery breath sets the ground aglow.[c] There the goddess kindled two pine-trees to serve her as a light; hence to this day a torch is given out at the rites of Ceres. There is a cave all fretted with the seams of scolloped pumice, a region not to be approached by man or beast. Soon as she came hither, she yoked the bitted serpents to her car and roamed, unwetted, o'er the ocean waves. She shunned the Syrtes, and Zanclaean Charybdis, and you, ye Nisaean hounds,[d] monsters of shipwreck ; she shunned the Adriatic, stretching far and wide, and Corinth of the double seas.

502 Thus she came to thy havens, land of Attica.

---

[d] He confuses the sea-monster Scylla with Scylla daughter of Nisus, as Virgil did, *Ecl.* vi. 74–77.

hic primum sedit gelido maestissima saxo :
    illud Cecropidae nunc quoque triste vocant.
505 sub Iove duravit multis inmota diebus,
    et lunae patiens et pluvialis aquae.
fors sua cuique loco est: quod nunc Cerialis Eleusin
    dicitur, hoc Celei rura fuere senis.
ille domum glandes excussaque mora rubetis
510 portat et arsuris arida ligna focis.
filia parva duas redigebat monte capellas,
    et tener in cunis filius aeger erat.
" mater ! " ait virgo (mota est dea nomine matris)
    " quid facis in solis incomitata locis ? "
515 restitit et senior, quamvis onus urget, et orat,
    tecta suae subeat quantulacumque casae.
illa negat.   simularat anum mitraque capillos
    presserat.   instanti talia dicta refert :
" sospes eas semperque parens ! mihi filia rapta est.
520 heu, melior quanto sors tua sorte mea est ! "
dixit, et ut lacrimae (neque enim lacrimare deorum
    est)
    decidit in tepidos lucida gutta sinus.
flent pariter molles animis virgoque senexque ;
    e quibus haec iusti verba fuere senis :
525 " sic tibi, quam raptam quaeris, sit filia sospes,
    surge nec exiguae despice tecta casae."
cui dea " duc ! " inquit " scisti, qua cogere posses,
    seque levat saxo subsequiturque senem.
dux comiti narrat, quam sit sibi filius aeger
530 nec capiat somnos invigiletque malis.

There for the first time she sat her down most
rueful on a cold stone : that stone even now the
Cecropids ^a call the Sorrowful. For many days she
tarried motionless under the open sky, patiently
enduring the moonlight and the rain. Not a place
but has its own peculiar destiny : what now is
named the Eleusis of Ceres was then the plot of
land of aged Celeus. He carried home acorns and
blackberries, knocked from bramble bushes, and dry
wood to feed the blazing hearth. A little daughter
drove two nanny-goats back from the mountain, and
an infant son was sick in his cradle. " Mother,"
said the maid—the goddess was touched by the
name of mother—" what dost thou all alone in
solitary places ? " The old man, too, halted, despite
the load he bore, and prayed that she would pass
beneath the roof of his poor cottage. She refused.
She had disguised herself as an old dame and covered
her hair with a cap. When he pressed her, she
answered thus : " Be happy ! may a parent's joy
be thine for ever ! My daughter has been taken
from me. Alas ! how much better is thy lot than
mine ! " She spoke, and like a tear (for gods can
never weep) a crystal drop fell on her bosom warm.
They wept with her, those tender hearts, the old
man and the maid ; and these were the words of
the worthy old man : " So may the ravished
daughter, whom thou seekest, be restored safe to
thee, as thou shalt arise, nor scorn the shelter of
my humble hut." The goddess answered him,
" Lead on ; thou hast found the way to force me " ;
and she rose from the stone and followed the old
man. As he led her and she followed, he told her
how his son was sick and sleepless, kept wakeful

illa soporiferum, parvos initura penates,
    colligit agresti lene papaver humo ;
dum legit, oblito fertur gustasse palato
    longamque imprudens exsoluisse famem.
535 quae quia principio posuit ieiunia noctis,
    tempus habent mystae sidera visa cibi.
limen ut intravit, luctus videt omnia plena :
    iam spes in puero nulla salutis erat.
matre salutata (mater Metanira vocatur)
540   iungere dignata est os puerile suo.
pallor abit, subitasque vident in corpore vires :
    tantus caelesti venit ab ore vigor.
tota domus laeta est, hoc est materque paterque
    nataque : tres illi tota fuere domus.
545 mox epulas ponunt, liquefacta coagula lacte
    pomaque et in ceris aurea mella suis.
abstinet alma Ceres somnique papavera causas
    dat tibi cum tepido lacte bibenda, puer.
noctis erat medium placidique silentia somni :
550   Triptolemum gremio sustulit illa suo
terque manu permulsit eum, tria carmina dixit,
    carmina mortali non referenda sono,
inque foco corpus pueri vivente favilla
    obruit, humanum purget ut ignis onus.
555 excutitur somno stulte pia mater et amens
    " quid facis ? " exclamat membraque ab igne rapit.
cui dea " dum non es " dixit " scelerata, fuisti :
    inrita materno sunt mea dona metu.
iste quidem mortalis erit, sed primus arabit
560   et seret et culta praemia tollet humo."

by his ills. As she was about to pass within the lowly dwelling, she plucked a smooth, a slumbrous poppy that grew on the waste ground ; and as she plucked, 'tis said she tasted it forgetfully, and so unwitting stayed her long hunger. Hence, because she broke her fast at nightfall, the initiates time their meal by the appearance of the stars. When she crossed the threshold, she saw the household plunged in grief ; all hope of saving the child was gone. The goddess greeted the mother (her name was Metanira) and deigned to put her lips to the child's lips. His pallor fled, and strength of a sudden was visibly imparted to his frame ; such vigour flowed from lips divine. There was joy in the whole household, that is, in mother, father, and daughter ; for they three were the whole household. Anon they set out a repast—curds liquefied in milk, and apples, and golden honey in the comb. Kind Ceres abstained, and gave the child poppies to drink in warm milk to make him sleep. It was midnight, and there reigned the silence of peaceful sleep ; the goddess took up Triptolemus in her lap, and thrice she stroked him with her hand, and spoke three spells, spells not to be rehearsed by mortal tongue, and on the hearth she buried the boy's body in live embers, that the fire might purge away the burden of humanity. His fond-foolish mother awoke from sleep and distractedly cried out, " What dost thou ? " and she snatched his body from the fire. To her the goddess said : " Meaning no wrong, thou hast done grievous wrong : my bounty has been baffled by a mother's fear. That boy of yours will indeed be mortal, but he will be the first to plough and sow and reap a guerdon from the turned-up soil."

OVID

dixit et egrediens nubem trahit inque dracones
 transit et alifero tollitur axe Ceres.
Sunion expositum Piraeaque tuta recessu
 linquit et in dextrum quae iacet ora latus.
565 hinc init Aegaeum, quo Cycladas aspicit omnes,
 Ioniumque rapax Icariumque legit,
perque urbes Asiae longum petit Hellespontum,
 diversumque locis alta pererrat iter.
nam modo turilegos Arabas, modo despicit Indos,
570 hinc Libys, hinc Meroë siccaque terra subest;
nunc adit Hesperios Rhenum Rhodanumque Padum-
  que
 teque, future parens, Thybri, potentis aquae.
quo feror? inmensum est erratas dicere terras:
 praeteritus Cereri nullus in orbe locus.
575 errat et in caelo liquidique inmunia ponti
 adloquitur gelido proxima signa polo:
" Parrhasides stellae (namque omnia nosse potestis,
 aequoreas numquam cum subeatis aquas),
Persephonen natam miserae monstrate parenti! "
580 dixerat. huic Helice talia verba refert:
" crimine nox vacua est; Solem de virgine rapta
 consule, qui late facta diurna videt."
Sol aditus " quam quaeris," ait " ne vana labores,
 nupta Iovis fratri tertia regna tenet."
585 questa diu secum, sic est adfata Tonantem,
 maximaque in voltu signa dolentis erant:
" si memor es, de quo mihi sit Proserpina nata,
 dimidium curae debet habere tuae.

---

 ^a A headland of Attica.
 ^b She turns from N.E. to S.E. and S.W., passing between
Libya and Ethiopia, thence to Europe.
 ^c The constellation of the Great Bear (also Helice), as
identified with Arcadian Callisto: Parrhasian stands for
Arcadian. See above, ii. 155, iii. 108.

⁵⁶¹ She said, and forth she fared, trailing a cloud behind her, and passed to her dragons, then soared aloft in her winged car. She left behind bold Sunium,ᵃ and the snug harbour of Piraeus, and the coast that lies on the right hand. From there she came to the Aegean, where she beheld all the Cyclades; she skimmed the wild Ionian and the Icarian Sea; and passing through the cities of Asia she made for the long Hellespont, and pursued aloft a roving course, this way and that.ᵇ For now she looked down on the incense-gathering Arabs, and now on the Indians: beneath her lay on one side Libya, on the other side Meroe, and the parched land. Now she visited the western rivers, the Rhine, the Rhone, the Po, and thee, Tiber, future parent of a mighty water. Whither do I stray? 'Twere endless to tell of the lands over which she wandered. No spot in the world did Ceres leave unvisited. She wandered also in the sky, and accosted the constellations that lie next to the cold pole and never dip in the ocean wave. " Ye Parrhasian stars,ᶜ reveal to a wretched mother her daughter Persephone; for ye can know all things, since never do ye plunge under the waters of the sea." So she spoke, and Helice answered her thus : " Night is blameless. Ask of the Sun concerning the ravished maid : far and wide he sees the things that are done by day." Appealed to, the Sun said, " To spare thee vain trouble, she whom thou seekest is wedded to Jove's brother and rules the third realm."

⁵⁸⁵ After long moaning to herself she thus addressed the Thunderer, and in her face there were deep lines of sorrow : " If thou dost remember by whom I got Persephone, she ought to have half of thy care. By

orbe pererrato sola est iniuria facti
590   cognita : commissi praemia raptor habet.
at neque Persephone digna est praedone marito,
    nec gener hoc nobis more parandus erat.
quid gravius victore Gyge captiva tulissem,
    quam nunc te caeli sceptra tenente tuli ?
595 verum impune ferat, nos haec patiemur inultae ;
    reddat et emendet facta priora novis."
Iuppiter hanc lenit factumque excusat amore,
    " nec gener est nobis ille pudendus " ait.
" non ego nobilior : posita est mihi regia caelo,
600   possidet alter aquas, alter inane chaos.
sed si forte tibi non est mutabile pectus,
    statque semel iuncti rumpere vincla tori,
hoc quoque temptemus, siquidem ieiuna remansit ;
    si minus, inferni coniugis uxor erit."
605 Tartara iussus adit sumptis Caducifer alis
    speque redit citius visaque certa refert :
" rapta tribus " dixit " solvit ieiunia granis,
    Punica quae lento cortice poma tegunt."
non secus indoluit, quam si modo rapta fuisset,
610   maesta parens, longa vixque refecta mora est,
atque ita " nec nobis caelum est habitabile " dixit ;
    " Taenaria recipi me quoque valle iube."
et factura fuit, pactus nisi Iuppiter esset,
    bis tribus ut caelo mensibus illa foret.
615 tum demum voltumque Ceres animumque recepit

---

    [a] He confuses the hundred-handed brothers with the giants who tried to storm heaven (see iii. 805).

    [b] She has wedded Pluto or Hades, himself a king like Jupiter and Poseidon. Chaos, the abyss, is used for Hades. See i. 103, note.

    [c] Tartarus, since there was supposed to be a mouth of hell at Taenarum, a promontory in Laconia.

wandering round the world I have learned naught but the knowledge of the wrong: the ravisher enjoys the reward of his crime. But neither did Persephone deserve a robber husband, nor was it meet that in this fashion we should find a son-in-law. What worse wrong could I have suffered if Gyges[a] had been victorious and I his captive, than now I have sustained while thou art sceptered king of heaven? But let him escape unpunished; I'll put up with it nor ask for vengeance; only let him restore her and repair his former deeds by new." Jupiter soothed her, and on the plea of love excused the deed. "He is not a son-in-law," said he, "to put us to shame: I myself am not a whit more noble: my royalty is in the sky, another owns the waters, and another the void of chaos.[b] But if haply thy mind is set immutably, and thou art resolved to break the bonds of wedlock, once contracted, come let us try to do so, if only she has kept her fast; if not, she will be the wife of her infernal spouse." The Herald God received his orders and assumed his wings: he flew to Tartarus and returning sooner than he was looked for brought tidings sure of what he had seen. "The ravished Maid," said he, "did break her fast on three grains enclosed in the tough rind of a pomegranate." Her rueful parent grieved no less than if her daughter had just been reft from her, and it was long before she was herself again, and hardly then. And thus she spoke: "For me, too, heaven is no home; order that I too be admitted to the Taenarian vale.[c]" And she would have done so, if Jupiter had not promised that Persephone should be in heaven for twice three months. Then at last Ceres recovered her

imposuitque suae spicea serta comae ;
largaque provenit cessatis messis in arvis,
   et vix congestas area cepit opes.
alba decent Cererem : vestis Cerialibus albas
620   sumite ; nunc pulli velleris usus abest.

13. G EID · N͞P lvdi

Occupat Aprilis Idus cognomine Victor
   Iuppiter : hac illi sunt data templa die.
hac quoque, ni fallor, populo dignissima nostro
   atria Libertas coepit habere sua.

14. HN lvdi

625 Luce secutura tutos pete, navita, portus :
   ventus ab occasu grandine mixtus erit.
sit licet ut fuerit, tamen hac Mutinensia Caesar
   grandine militia perculit arma sua.

15. A FORD · N͞P lvdi   16. BN lvdi

Tertia post Veneris cum lux surrexerit Idus,
630   pontifices, forda sacra litate bove.
forda ferens bos est fecundaque, dicta ferendo :
   hinc etiam fetus nomen habere putant.
nunc gravidum pecus est, gravidae quoque semine
      terrae :
   Telluri plenae victima plena datur.
635 pars cadit arce Iovis, ter denas curia vaccas
   accipit et largo sparsa cruore madet.

---

   ^a Vowed by Q. Fabius Maximus, 295 b.c.
   ^b Atrium Libertatis, not far from the Forum.
   ^c He relieved the siege of Mutina in 43 b.c., against
Antony.   ^d See ii. 530 note, iii. 140.
234

looks and her spirits, and set wreaths of corn ears
on her hair; and the laggard fields yielded a
plenteous harvest, and the threshing-floor could
hardly hold the high-piled sheaves. White is Ceres'
proper colour; put on white robes at Ceres'
festival; now no one wears dun-coloured wool.

Id. 13th

⁶²¹ The Ides of April belong to Jupiter under the
title of Victor: a temple was dedicated to him on
that day.ᵃ On that day, too, if I mistake not,
Liberty began to own a hall well worthy of our
people.ᵇ

XVIII. Kal. Mai. 14th

⁶²⁵ On the next day steer for safe harbours, thou
mariner: the wind from the west will be mixed
with hail. Yet be that as it may, on that day, a
day of hail, Caesar in battle-array smote hip and
thigh his foes at Modena.ᶜ

XVII. Kal. 15th

⁶²⁹ When the third day shall have dawned after
the Ides of Venus, ye pontiffs, offer in sacrifice a
pregnant (*forda*) cow. *Forda* is a cow with calf
and fruitful, so called from *ferendo* (" bearing "):
they think that *fetus* is derived from the same root.
Now are the cattle big with young; the ground,
too, is big with seed: to teeming Earth is given a
teeming victim. Some are slain in the citadel of
Jupiter; the wards (*Curiae*)ᵈ get thrice ten cows,
and are splashed and drenched with blood in plenty.

ast ubi visceribus vitulos rapuere ministri
    sectaque fumosis exta dedere focis,
igne cremat vitulos quae natu maxima virgo est,
640   luce Palis populos purget ut ille cinis.
rege Numa, fructu non respondente labori,
    inrita decepti vota colentis erant.
nam modo siccus erat gelidis aquilonibus annus,
    nunc ager assidua luxuriabat aqua :
645 saepe Ceres primis dominum fallebat in herbis,
    et levis obsesso stabat avena solo,
et pecus ante diem partus edebat acerbos,
    agnaque nascendo saepe necabat ovem.
silva vetus nullaque diu violata securi
650   stabat, Maenalio sacra relicta deo :
ille dabat tacitis animo responsa quieto
    noctibus.   hic geminas rex Numa mactat oves.
prima cadit Fauno, leni cadit altera Somno :
    sternitur in duro vellus utrumque solo.
655 bis caput intonsum fontana spargitur unda,
    bis sua faginea tempora fronde tegit.
usus abest Veneris, nec fas animalia mensis
    ponere, nec digitis anulus ullus inest.
veste rudi tectus supra nova vellera corpus
660   ponit, adorato per sua verba deo.
interea placidam redimita papavere frontem
    nox venit et secum somnia nigra trahit.
Faunus adest, oviumque premens pede vellera duro
    edidit a dextro talia verba toro :
665 " morte boum tibi, rex, Tellus placanda duarum :

---

        a See below, l. 721.   *b* Pan.

But when the attendants have torn the calves from
the bowels of their dams, and put the cut entrails on
the smoking hearths, the eldest (Vestal) Virgin burns
the calves in the fire, that their ashes may purify
the people on the day of Pales.[a] When Numa was
king, the harvest did not answer to the labour
bestowed on it; the husbandman was deceived,
and his prayers were offered in vain. For at one
time the year was dry, the north winds blowing
cold; at another time the fields were rank with
ceaseless rain; often at its first sprouting the crop
balked its owner, and the light oats overran the
choked soil, and the cattle dropped their unripe
young before the time, and often the ewe perished
in giving birth to her lamb. There was an ancient
wood, long unprofaned by the axe, left sacred to
the god of Maenalus.[b] He to the quiet mind gave
answers in the silence of the night. Here Numa
sacrificed two ewes. The first fell in honour of
Faunus, the second fell in honour of gentle Sleep :
the fleeces of both were spread on the hard ground.
Twice the king's unshorn head was sprinkled with
water from a spring ; twice he veiled his brows with
beechen leaves. He refrained from the pleasures
of love ; no flesh might be served up to him at
table ; he might wear no ring on his fingers.
Covered with a rough garment he laid him down
on the fresh fleeces after worshipping the god in
the appropriate words. Meantime, her calm brow
wreathed with poppies, Night drew on, and in her
train brought darkling dreams. Faunus was come,
and setting his hard hoof on the sheep's fleeces
uttered these words on the right side of the bed :
" O King, thou must appease Earth by the death

det sacris animas una íuvenca duas."
excutitur terrore quies : Numa visa revolvit
   et secum ambages caecaque iussa refert.
expedit errantem nemori gratissima coniunx
670   et dixit " gravidae posceris exta bovis."
exta bovis gravidae dantur, fecundior annus
   provenit, et fructum terra pecusque ferunt.
hanc quondam Cytherea diem properantius ire
   iussit et admissos praecipitavit equos,
675 ut titulum imperij quam primum luce sequenti
   Augusto iuveni prospera bella darent.

17. CN LVDI   18. DN LVDI

Sed iam praeteritas quartus tibi Lucifer Idus
   respicit : hac Hyades Dorida nocte tenent.

19. E CER · N LVD · IN · CIR

Tertia post Hyadas cum lux erit orta remotas
680   carcere partitos Circus habebit equos.
cur igitur missae vinctis ardentia taedis
   terga ferant volpes, causa docenda mihi est.
frigida Carseolis nec olivis apta ferendis
   terra, sed ad segetes ingeniosus ager ;
685 hac ego Pelignos, natalia rura, petebam,
   parva, sed assiduis uvida semper aquis.

---

    [a] Egeria.
    [b] Venus, as the ancestress of the Julian house, is made to
hasten the sun's setting on April 15, that he might rise the
sooner on the 16th, when the title of Imperator was given him
for his relief of Mutina.
    [c] The true evening setting was on April 20.
    [d] Because this loosing of foxes was part of the Games of
Ceres.   [e] Compare Judges xv. 4-6.

of two cows: let one heifer yield two lives in
sacrifice." Fear banished sleep : Numa pondered
the vision, and revolved in his mind the dark sayings
and mysterious commands. His wife,[a] the darling
of the grove, extricated him from his doubts and
said, "What is demanded of thee are the inwards
of a pregnant cow." The inwards of a pregnant
cow were offered ; the year proved more fruitful,
and earth and cattle yielded their increase. This
day once on a time Cytherea commanded to go
faster and hurried the galloping horses down hill,
that on the next day the youthful Augustus might
receive the sooner the title of emperor for his
victories in war.[b]

XV. Kal. 17th

[677] But when you shall have counted the fourth day
after the Ides, the Hyades will set in the sea that
night.[c]

XIII. Kal. 19th

[679] When the third morn shall have risen after
the disappearance of the Hyades, the horses will
be in the Circus, each team in its separate stall. I
must therefore[d] explain the reason why foxes are
let loose with torches tied to their burning backs.[e]
The land of Carseoli[f] is cold and not suited for the
growth of olives, but the soil is well adapted for
corn. By it I journeyed on my way to the Pelignian
land, my native country, a country small but always
moist with never-failing water. There I entered,

[f] A Latin town, on the road to Paelignian Corfinium.

hospitis antiqui solitas intravimus aedes ;
  dempserat emeritis iam iuga Phoebus equis.
is mihi multa quidem, sed et haec narrare solebat,
690   unde meum praesens instrueretur opus :
" hoc " ait " in campo " (campumque ostendit)
    " habebat
rus breve cum duro parca colona viro.
ille suam peragebat humum, sive usus aratri
  seu curvae falcis sive bidentis erat.
695 haec modo verrebat stantem tibicine villam,
  nunc matris plumis ova fovenda dabat,
aut virides malvas aut fungos colligit albos,
  aut humilem grato calfacit igne focum.
et tamen assiduis exercet brachia telis
700   adversusque minas frigoris arma parat,
filius huius erat primo lascivus in aevo
  addideratque annos ad duo lustra duos,
is capit extremi volpem convalle salicti :
  abstulerat multas illa cohortis aves.
705 captivam stipula faenoque involvit et ignes
  admovet : urentes effugit illa manus :
qua fugit, incendit vestitos messibus agros ;
  damnosis vires ignibus aura dabat.
factum abiit, monumenta manent ; nam dicere certa
710   nunc quoque lex volpem Carseolana vetat ;
utque luat poenas gens haec Cerialibus ardet,
  quoque modo segetes perdidit, ipsa perit."

20. FN

Proxima cum veniet terras visura patentes
  Memnonis in roseis lutea mater equis,[a]

---

[a] Aurora.

as usual, the house of an old host; Phoebus had
already unyoked his spent steeds. My host was
wont to tell me many things, and among them
matters which were to be embodied in my present
work. " In yonder plain," said he, and he pointed
it out, " a thrifty countrywoman had a small croft,
she and her sturdy spouse. He tilled his own
land, whether the work called for the plough, or
the curved sickle, or the hoe. She would now sweep
the cottage, supported on props; now she would
set the eggs to be hatched under the plumage of
the brooding hen; or she gathered green mallows
or white mushrooms, or warmed the low hearth
with welcome fire. And yet she diligently employed her hands at the loom, and armed herself
against the threats of winter. She had a son, in
childhood frolicsome, who now had seen twice five
years and two more. He in a valley at the end of
a willow copse caught a vixen fox which had carried
off many farmyard fowls. The captive brute he
wrapped in straw and hay, and set a light to her;
she escaped the hands that would have burned her.
Where she fled, she set fire to the crops that clothed
the fields, and a breeze fanned the devouring flames.
The incident is forgotten, but a memorial of it
survives; for to this day a certain law of Carseoli
forbids to name a fox; and to punish the species a
fox is burned at the festival of Ceres, thus perishing
itself in the way it destroyed the crops."

XII. Kal. 20th

713 When next day Memnon's saffron-robed mother[a]
on her rosy steeds shall come to view the far-spread

241

715 de duce lanigeri pecoris, qui prodidit Hellen,
    sol abit: egresso victima maior adest.
vacca sit an taurus, non est cognoscere promptum:
    pars prior apparet, posteriora latent.
seu tamen est taurus sive est hoc femina signum,
720   Iunone invita munus amoris habet.

21. G PAR · NP

Nox abiit, oriturque Aurora. Parilia[1] poscor:
    non poscor frustra, si favet alma Pales.
alma Pales, faveas pastoria sacra canenti,
    prosequor officio si tua festa meo.
725 certe ego de vitulo cinerem stipulasque fabalis
    saepe tuli plena, februa casta, manu:
certe ego transilui positas ter in ordine flammas,
    udaque roratas laurea misit aquas.
mota dea est operique favet: navalibus exit
730   puppis, habent ventos iam mea vela suos.
i, pete virginea, populus, suffimen ab ara:
    Vesta dabit, Vestae munere purus eris.
sanguis equi suffimen erit vitulique favilla,
    tertia res durae culmen inane fabae.
735 pastor, oves saturas ad prima crepuscula lustra:
    unda prius spargat, virgaque verrat humum,
frondibus et fixis decorentur ovilia ramis,
    et tegat ornatas longa corona fores.

---

[1] parilia *AU*: palilia *DXMm and most MSS.* ("*caeteri*" *Merkel*).

---

[a] See iii. 851-876.
[b] Whether it be Io as a cow, or the bull that carried off Europa, Juno is equally offended at the reminder of her husband's unfaithfulness.
[c] See Appendix, p. 411.   [d] See Appendix, p. 413.

lands, the sun departs from the sign of the leader
of the woolly flock, the ram which betrayed Helle;[a]
and when he has passed out of that sign, a larger
victim meets him. Whether that victim is a cow
or a bull, it is not easy to know; the fore part is
visible, the hinder part is hid. But whether the sign
be a bull or a cow, it enjoys this reward of love
against the will of Juno.[b]

XI. KAL. 21st

[721] The night has gone, and Dawn comes up. I
am called upon to sing of the Parilia,[c] and not in
vain shall be the call, if kindly Pales favours me.
O kindly Pales, favour me when I sing of pastoral
rites, if I pay my respects to thy festival. Sure
it is that I have often brought with full hands the
ashes of the calf and the beanstraws, chaste means
of expiation. Sure it is that I have leaped over the
flames ranged three in a row, and the moist laurel-
bough has sprinkled water on me. The goddess is
moved and favours the work I have in hand. My
bark is launched; now fair winds fill my sails.

[731] Ye people, go fetch materials for fumigation
from the Virgin's altar. Vesta will give them; by
Vesta's gift ye shall be pure. The materials for
fumigation will be the blood of a horse and the
ashes of a calf; the third thing will be the empty
stalks of hard beans.[d] Shepherd, do thou purify
thy well-fed sheep at fall of twilight; first sprinkle
the ground with water and sweep it with a broom.
Deck the sheepfold with leaves and branches
fastened to it; adorn the door and cover it with

243

caerulei fiant puro de sulphure fumi,
740 tactaque fumanti sulphure balet ovis.
ure mares oleas taedamque herbasque Sabinas,
et crepet in mediis laurus adusta focis.
libaque de milio milii fiscella sequatur:
rustica praecipue est hoc dea laeta cibo.
745 adde dapes mulctramque suas, dapibusque resectis
silvicolam tepido lacte precare Palem.
" consule " dic " pecori pariter pecorisque magistris:
effugiat stabulis noxa repulsa meis.
sive sacro pavi sedive sub arbore sacra,
750 pabulaque e bustis inscia carpsit ovis:
si nemus intravi vetitum, nostrisve fugatae
sunt oculis nymphae semicaperque deus:
si mea falx ramo lucum spoliavit opaco,
unde data est aegrae fiscina frondis ovi:
755 da veniam culpae. nec, dum degrandinet, obsit
agresti fano supposuisse pecus,
nec noceat turbasse lacus. ignoscite, nymphae,
mota quod obscuras ungula fecit aquas.
tu, dea, pro nobis fontes fontanaque placa
760 numina, tu sparsos per nemus omne deos.
nec Dryadas nec nos videamus labra Dianae,
nec Faunum, medio cum premit arva die.[a]
pelle procul morbos; valeant hominesque gregesque,
et valeant vigiles, provida turba, canes.
765 neve minus multos redigam, quam mane fuerunt,
neve gemam referens vellera rapta lupo.
absit iniqua fames: herbae frondesque supersint,
quaeque lavent artus quaeque bibantur aquae.

---

[a] It was dangerous to disturb Pan (Faunus) at midday,
or to see satyrs and nymphs at their gambols. He alludes
also to the story of Actaeon and Diana, *Metam.* iii. 161.

a long festoon. Make blue smoke with pure
sulphur, and let the sheep, touched with the smoking
sulphur, bleat. Burn wood of male olives and pine
and savines, and let the singed laurel crackle in
the midst of the hearth. And let a basket of millet
accompany cakes of millet; the rural goddess particularly delights in that food. Add viands and a pail of
milk, such as she loves; and when the viands have
been cut up, pray to sylvan Pales, offering warm milk
to her. Say, " O, take thought alike for the cattle
and the cattle's masters; ward off from my stalls all
harm, O let it flee away! If I have fed my sheep on
holy ground, or sat me down under a sacred tree,
and my sheep unwittingly have browsed on graves; if
I have entered a forbidden grove, or the nymphs
and the half-goat god have been put to flight at
sight of me; if my pruning-knife has robbed a
sacred copse of a shady bough, to fill a basket with
leaves for a sick sheep, pardon my fault. Count
it not against me if I have sheltered my flock
in a rustic shrine till the hail left off, and may I
not suffer for having troubled the pools: forgive
it, nymphs, if the trampling of hoofs has made your
waters turbid. Do thou, goddess, appease for us
the springs and their divinities; appease the gods
dispersed through every grove. May we not see
the Dryads, nor Diana's baths, nor Faunus,[a] when
he lies in the fields at noon. Drive far away
diseases: may men and beasts be hale, and hale
too the sagacious pack of watch-dogs. May I drive
home my flocks as numerous as they were at
morn, nor sigh as I bring back fleeces snatched
from the wolf. Avert dire hunger. Let grass
and leaves abound, and water both to wash and

ubera plena premam, referat mihi caseus aera,
770   dentque viam liquido vimina rara sero.
sitque salax aries, conceptaque semina coniunx
    reddat, et in stabulo multa sit agna meo.
lanaque proveniat nullas laesura puellas,
    mollis et ad teneras quamlibet apta manus.
775 quae precor eveniant, et nos faciemus ad annum
    pastorum dominae grandia liba Pali."
his dea placanda est : haec tu conversus ad ortus
    dic quater et vivo perlue rore manus.
tum licet adposita, veluti cratere, camella
780   lac niveum potes purpureamque sapam ;
moxque per ardentes stipulae crepitantis acervos
    traicias celeri strenua membra pede.
expositus mos est : moris mihi restat origo :
    turba facit dubium coeptaque nostra tenet.
785 omnia purgat edax ignis vitiumque metallis
    excoquit : idcirco cum duce purgat ovis.
an, quia cunctarum contraria semina rerum
    sunt duo discordes, ignis et unda, dei,
iunxerunt elementa patres aptumque putarunt
790   ignibus et sparsa tangere corpus aqua ?
an, quod in his vitae causa est, haec perdidit exul,
    his nova fit coniunx, haec duo magna putant ?
vix equidem credo: sunt qui Phaëthonta referri
    credant et nimias Deucalionis aquas.
795 pars quoque, cum saxis pastores saxa feribant,
    scintillam subito prosiluisse ferunt ;
prima quidem periit, stipulis excepta secunda est :

---

[a] Fire and water were supposed in combination to create
life. The exiled man was debarred from fire and water
("igni atque aqua interdictus"); and these two were presented
to the bride as she entered her new home.

drink. Full udders may I milk; may my cheese
bring me in money; may the sieve of wicker-work
give passage to the liquid whey; lustful be the
ram, and may his mate conceive and bear, and
many a lamb be in my fold. And let the wool
grow so soft that it could not fret the skin of girls
nor chafe the tenderest hands. May my prayer
be granted, and we will year by year make great
cakes for Pales, the shepherds' mistress." With
these things is the goddess to be propitiated;
these words pronounce four times, facing the east,
and wash thy hands in living dew. Then mayest
thou set a wooden bowl to serve as mixer, and mayest
quaff the snow-white milk and purple must; anon
leap with nimble foot and straining thews across
the burning heaps of crackling straw.

783 I have set forth the custom; it remains for
me to tell its origin. The multitude of explanations
creates a doubt and thwarts me at the outset.
Devouring fire purges all things and melts the dross
from out the metals; therefore it purges the shepherd
and the sheep. Or are we to suppose that, because
all things are composed of opposite principles, fire and
water—those two discordant deities—therefore our
fathers did conjoin these elements and thought meet
to touch the body with fire and sprinkled water?
Or did they deem these two important because they
contain the source of life, the exile loses the use
of them, and by them the bride is made a wife?[a]
Some suppose (though I can hardly do so) that
the allusion is to Phaethon and Deucalion's flood.
Some people also say that when shepherds were
knocking stones together, a spark suddenly leaped
forth; the first indeed was lost, but the second

hoc argumentum flamma Parilis habet?
an magis hunc morem pietas Aeneïa fecit,
800 innocuum victo cui dedit ignis iter?
num tamen est vero propius, cum condita Roma est,
transferri iussos in nova tecta Lares
mutantesque domum tectis agrestibus ignem
et cessaturae supposuisse casae,
805 per flammas saluisse pecus, saluisse colonos?
quod fit natali nunc quoque, Roma, tuo.

Ipse locus causas vati facit. urbis origo
venit. ades factis, magne Quirine, tuis!
iam luerat poenas frater Numitoris, et omne
810 pastorum gemino sub duce volgus erat.
contrahere agrestes et moenia ponere utrique
convenit: ambigitur, moenia ponat uter.
" nil opus est " dixit " certamine " Romulus " ullo:
magna fides avium est, experiamur aves."
815 res placet. alter adit nemorosi saxa Palati,
alter Aventinum mane cacumen init.
sex Remus, hic volucres bis sex videt ordine. pacto
statur, et arbitrium Romulus urbis habet.
apta dies legitur, qua moenia signet aratro.
820 sacra Palis suberant: inde movetur opus.
fossa fit ad solidum, fruges iaciuntur in ima
et de vicino terra petita solo.

---

a The Palilia.   *b* Amulius. See iii. 67.
c See *Mundus*, Appendix, p. 417.
248

was caught in straw ; is that the reason of the
flame at the Parilia ? Or is the custom rather
based on the piety of Aeneas, whom, even in the
hour of defeat, the fire allowed to pass unscathed ?
Or is it haply nearer the truth that, when Rome
was founded, orders were given to transfer the
household gods to the new houses, and in changing
homes the husbandmen set fire to their country
houses and to the cottages they were about to
abandon, and that they and their cattle leaped
through the flames ? Which happens even to the
present time on the birthday of Rome.[a]

807 The subject of itself furnishes a theme for the
poet. We have arrived at the foundation of the city
Great Quirinus, help me to sing thy deeds. Already
the brother of Numitor [b] had suffered punishment,
and all the shepherd folk were subject to the twins.
The twins agreed to draw the swains together and
found a city ; the doubt was which of the two
should found it. Romulus said, "There needs no
contest. Great faith is put in birds ; let's try the
birds." The proposal was accepted. One of the
two betook him to the rocks of the wooded Palatine ;
the other hied at morn to the top of the Aventine.
Remus saw six birds ; Romulus saw twice six, one
after the other : they stood by their compact, and
Romulus was accorded the government of the city.
A suitable day was chosen on which he should mark
out the line of the walls with the plough. The festival
of Pales was at hand ; on that day the work began.[c]
A trench was dug down to the solid rock ; fruits
of the earth were thrown into the bottom of it,
and with them earth fetched from the neighbouring

249

fossa repletur humo, plenaeque imponitur ara,
    et novus accenso fungitur igne focus.
825 inde premens stivam designat moenia sulco ;
    alba iugum niveo cum bove vacca tulit.
vox fuit haec regis : " condenti, Iuppiter, urbem
    et genitor Mavors Vestaque mater, ades ;
quosque pium est adhibere deos, advertite cuncti.
830   auspicibus vobis hoc mihi surgat opus.
longa sit huic aetas dominaeque potentia terrae,
    sitque sub hac oriens occiduusque dies."
ille precabatur, tonitru dedit omina laevo
    Iuppiter, et laevo fulmina missa polo.
835 augurio laeti iaciunt fundamina cives,
    et novus exiguo tempore murus erat.
hoc Celer urget opus, quem Romulus ipse vocarat,
    " sint," que " Celer, curae " dixerat " ista tuae,
neve quis aut muros aut factam vomere fossam
840   transeat : audentem talia dede neci."
quod Remus ignorans humiles contemnere muros
    coepit et " his populus " dicere " tutus erit ? "
nec mora, transiluit. rutro Celer occupat ausum ;
    ille premit duram sanguinulentus humum.
845 haec ubi rex didicit, lacrimas introrsus obortas
    devorat et clausum pectore volnus habet.
flere palam non volt exemplaque fortia servat,
    " sic " que " meos muros transeat hostis " ait.
dat tamen exequias nec iam suspendere fletum
850   sustinet, et pietas dissimulata patet ;
osculaque adplicuit posito suprema feretro

soil. The trench was filled up with mould, and on
the top was set an altar, and a fire was duly lit on
a new hearth. Then pressing on the plough-
handle he drew a furrow to mark out the line of the
walls : the yoke was borne by a white cow and
snow-white steer. The king spoke thus : " O
Jupiter, and Father Mavors, and Mother Vesta,
stand by me as I found the city ! O take heed,
all ye gods whom piety bids summon ! Under
your auspices may this my fabric rise ! May this
imperial country long endure and its dominion !
May East and West be subject unto it ! " So he
prayed. Jupiter vouchsafed omens by thunder on
the left and lightnings flashing in the leftward sky.
Glad at the augury, the citizens laid the foundations,
and in a short time the new wall stood. The work
was urged on by Celer, whom Romulus himself had
named and said, " Celer, be this thy care ; let no
man cross the walls nor the trench which the
share hath made : who dares to do so, put him to
death." Ignorant of this, Remus began to mock
the lowly walls and say, " Shall these protect the
people ? " And straightway he leaped across them.
Instantly Celer struck the rash man with a shovel.
Covered with blood, Remus sank on the stony
ground. When the king heard of this, he smothered
the springing tears and kept his grief locked up
within his breast. He would not weep in public ;
he set an example of fortitude, and " So fare,"
quoth he, " the foe who shall cross my walls." Yet
he granted funeral honours, and could no longer
bear to check his tears, and the affection which he
had dissembled was plain to see. When they set
down the bier, he gave it a last kiss, and said,

atque ait " invito frater adempte, vale ! "
arsurosque artus unxit.   fecere, quod ille,
   Faustulus et maestas Acca soluta comas.
855 tum iuvenem nondum facti flevere Quirites ;
   ultima plorato subdita flamma rogo est.
urbs oritur (quis tunc hoc ulli credere posset ?)
   victorem terris impositura pedem.
cuncta regas et sis magno sub Caesare semper,
860   saepe etiam pluris nominis huius habe ;
et quotiens steteris domito sublimis in orbe,
   omnia sint humeris inferiora tuis.

22. HN   23. A VIN · N^P

Dicta Pales nobis, idem Vinalia dicam ;
   una tamen media est inter utramque dies.
865 numina volgares Veneris celebrate puellae :
   multa professarum quaestibus apta Venus.
poscite ture dato formam populique favorem,
   poscite blanditias dignaque verba ioco,
cumque sua dominae date grata sisymbria myrto
870   tectaque composita iuncea vincla rosa.
templa frequentari Collinae proxima portae
   nunc decet, a Siculo nomina colle tenent ;
utque Syracusas Arethusidas abstulit armis
   Claudius et bello te quoque cepit, Eryx,
875 carmine vivacis Venus est translata Sibyllae,
   inque suae stirpis maluit urbe coli.

---

^a M. Claudius Marcellus captured Syracuse, 212 B.C.

" Snatched from thy brother, loath to part, brother,
farewell ! " With that he anointed the body before
committing it to the flames. Faustulus and Acca,
her mournful hair unbound, did the same. Then
the Quirites, though not yet known by that name,
wept for the youth, and last of all a light was put
to the pyre, wet with their tears. A city arose
destined to set its victorious foot upon the neck of
the whole earth ; who at that time could have
believed in such a prophecy ? Rule the universe,
O Rome, and mayest thou ever be subject to great
Caesar, and mayest thou often have several of that
name, and whensoe'er thou standest sublime in a
conquered world, may all else reach not up to thy
shoulders !

IX. Kal. 23rd

863 I have told of Pales, I will now tell of the
festival of the Vinalia ; but there is one day interposed between the two. Ye common wenches,
celebrate the divinity of Venus : Venus favours the
earnings of ladies of a liberal profession. Offer
incense and pray for beauty and popular favour ;
pray to be charming and witty ; give to the Queen
her own myrtle and the mint she loves, and bands
of rushes hid in clustered roses. Now is the time
to throng her temple next the Colline gate ; the
temple takes its name from the Sicilian hill. When
Claudius carried Arethusian Syracuse ^a by force of
arms, and captured thee, too, Eryx, in war, Venus
was transferred to Rome in obedience to an oracle
of the long-lived Sibyl, and chose to be worshipped
in the city of her own offspring. You ask, Why then

cur igitur Veneris festum Vinalia dicant,
    quaeritis, et quare sit Iovis ista dies ?
Turnus an Aeneas Latiae gener esset Amatae,
880   bellum erat : Etruscas Turnus adorat opes.
clarus erat sumptisque ferox Mezentius armis
    et vel equo magnus vel pede maior erat;
quem Rutuli Turnusque suis adsciscere temptat
    partibus. haec contra dux ita Tuscus ait :
885 " stat mihi non parvo virtus mea : volnera testor
    armaque, quae sparsi sanguine saepe meo.
qui petis auxilium, non grandia divide mecum
    praemia, de lacubus proxima musta tuis.
nulla mora est operae : vestrum est dare, vincere
    nostrum.
890   quam velit Aeneas ista negata mihi ! "
adnuerant Rutuli. Mezentius induit arma,
    induit Aeneas alloquiturque Iovem :
" hostica Tyrrheno vota est vindemia regi :
    Iuppiter, e Latio palmite musta feres ! "
895 vota valent meliora. cadit Mezentius ingens
    atque indignanti pectore plangit humum.
venerat Autumnus calcatis sordidus uvis :
    redduntur merito debita vina Iovi.
dicta dies hinc est Vinalia : Iuppiter illam
900   vindicat et festis gaudet inesse suis.

24. BC 25. C ROB · NP

Sex ubi, quae restant, luces Aprilis habebit,
    in medio cursu tempora veris erunt,
et frustra pecudem quaeres Athamantidos Helles,

---

^a Apparent setting was on March 20, true setting on
April 5.

do they call the Vinalia a festival of Venus? And why does that day belong to Jupiter? There was war to decide whether Turnus or Aeneas should be the husband of Latin Amata's daughter: Turnus sued the help of the Etruscans. Mezentius was famous and a haughty man-at-arms; mighty was he on horseback, but mightier still on foot. Turnus and the Rutulians attempted to win him to their side. To these overtures the Tuscan chief thus replied: "My valour costs me dear. Witness my wounds and those weapons which oft I have bedabbled with my blood. You ask my help: divide with me the next new wine from your vats—surely no great reward. Delay there need be none: 'tis yours to give, and mine to conquer. How would Aeneas wish you had refused my suit!" The Rutulians consented. Mezentius donned his arms, Aeneas donned them too, and thus he spoke to Jupiter. "The foe has pledged his vintage to the Tyrrhenian king; Jupiter, thou shalt have the new wine from the Latin vines." The better vows prevailed: huge Mezentius fell, and with his breast indignant smote the ground. Autumn came round, stained with the trodden grapes; the wine that was his due was justly paid to Jupiter. Hence the day is called the Vinalia: Jupiter claims it for his own, and loves to be present at his own feast.

VII. Kal. 25th

901 When April shall have six days left, the season of spring will be in mid course, and in vain will you look for the ram of Helle, daughter of Athamas[a];

signaque dant imbres, exoriturque Canis.
905 hac mihi Nomento Romam cum luce redirem,
    obstitit in media candida turba via.
flamen in antiquae lucum Robiginis ibat,
    exta canis flammis, exta daturus ovis.
protinus accessi, ritus ne nescius essem :
910   edidit haec flamen verba, Quirine, tuus :
" aspera Robigo, parcas Cerialibus herbis,
    et tremat in summa leve cacumen humo.
tu sata sideribus caeli nutrita secundis
    crescere, dum fiant falcibus apta, sinas.
915 vis tua non levis est : quae tu frumenta notasti,
    maestus in amissis illa colonus habet.
nec venti tantum Cereri nocuere nec imbres,
    nec sic marmoreo pallet adusta gelu,
quantum, si culmos Titan incalfacit udos :
920   tunc locus est irae, diva timenda, tuae.
parce, precor, scabrasque manus a messibus aufer
    neve noce cultis : posse nocere sat est.
nec teneras segetes, sed durum amplectere ferrum,
    quodque potest alios perdere, perde prior.
925 utilius gladios et tela nocentia carpes :
    nil opus est illis, otia mundus agit.
sarcula nunc durusque bidens et vomer aduncus,
    ruris opes, niteant ; inquinet arma situs,
conatusque aliquis vagina ducere ferrum
930   adstrictum longa sentiat esse mora.
at tu ne viola Cererem, semperque colonus
    absenti possit solvere vota tibi."
dixerat : a dextra villis mantele solutis

---

     a The Dog-star then rose in the morning of August 2
set in the evening of May 1 ; not in April.
     b See Appendix, p. 420.

the rains will be your sign, and the constellation of the Dog will rise.[a]

905 On that day, as I was returning from Nomentum to Rome, a white-robed crowd blocked the middle of the road. A flamen was on his way to the grove of ancient Mildew (*Robigo*),[b] to throw the entrails of a dog and the entrails of a sheep into the flames. Straightway I went up to him to inform myself of the rite. Thy flamen, O Quirinus, pronounced these words : " Thou scaly Mildew, spare the sprouting corn, and let the smooth top quiver on the surface of the ground. O let the crops, nursed by the heaven's propitious stars, grow till they are ripe for the sickle. No feeble power is thine : the corn on which thou hast set thy mark, the sad husbandman gives up for lost. Nor winds, nor showers, nor glistening frost, that nips the sallow corn, harm it so much as when the sun warms the wet stalks ; then, dread goddess, is the hour to wreak thy wrath. O spare, I pray, and take thy scabby hands from off the harvest ! Harm not the tilth ; 'tis enough that thou hast the power to harm. Grip not the tender crops, but rather grip the hard iron. Forestall the destroyer. Better that thou shouldst gnaw at swords and baneful weapons There is no need of them : the world is at peace. Now let the rustic gear, the rakes, and the hard hoe, and the curved share be burnished bright ; but let rust defile the arms, and when one essays to draw the sword from the scabbard, let him feel it stick from long disuse. But do not thou profane the corn, and ever may the husbandman be able to pay his vows to thee in thine absence." So he spoke. On his right hand hung a napkin

cumque meri patera turis acerra fuit.
935 tura focis vinumque dedit fibrasque bidentis
turpiaque obscenae (vidimus) exta canis.
tum mihi " cur detur sacris nova victima, quaeris ? "
(quaesieram) " causam percipe " flamen ait.
" est Canis, Icarium dicunt, quo sidere moto
940 tosta sitit tellus, praecipiturque seges.
pro cane sidereo canis hic imponitur arae,
et quare pereat, nil nisi nomen habet."

26. DF 27. EC 28. F N͆ LVD · FLOR
29. GC LVDI 30. HC LVDI

Cum Phrygis Assaraci Tithonia fratre relicto
sustulit inmenso ter iubar orbe suum,
945 mille venit variis florum dea nexa coronis :
scaena ioci morem liberioris habet.
exit et in Maias sacrum Florale Kalendas ;
tunc repetam, nunc me grandius urget opus.
aufer Vesta diem ! cognati Vesta recepta est
950 limine : sic iusti constituere patres.
Phoebus habet partem, Vestae pars altera cessit ;
quod superest illis, tertius ipse tenet.
state Palatinae laurus, praetextaque quercu
stet domus : aeternos tres habet una deos.

---

[a] The dog.
[b] Supposed to be the dog Maera, which discovered the body of his master Icarius.
[c] According to Homer, Tithonus was a distant cousin of Assaracus. *Frater* is often used loosely.
[d] When Augustus was made Pontifex Maximus, he should have taken up his residence in the *Regia* near Vesta's temple, but instead he built a chapel of Vesta in his own house on the Palatine, and dedicated it on April 28, which was made a public holiday. The mention of Phoebus refers to the

with a loose nap, and he had a bowl of wine and a casket of incense. The incense, and wine, and sheep's guts, and the foul entrails of a filthy dog, he put upon the hearth—we saw him do it. Then to me he said, "Thou askest why an unwonted victim *a* is assigned to these rites?" Indeed, I had asked the question. "Learn the cause," the flamen said. "There is a Dog (they call it the Icarian dog),*b* and when that constellation rises the earth is parched and dry, and the crop ripens too soon. This dog is put on the altar instead of the starry dog, and the only reason for killing him is his name."

IV. KAL. 28th

943 When the spouse of Tithonus has left the brother of Phrygian Assaracus,*c* and thrice has lifted up her radiant light in the vast firmament, there comes a goddess decked with garlands of a thousand varied flowers, and the stage enjoys a customary licence of mirth. The rites of Flora also extend into the Calends of May. Then I will resume the theme: now a loftier task is laid upon me. O Vesta, take thy day! Vesta has been received in the home of her kinsman: so have the Fathers righteously decreed. Phoebus owns part of the house; another part has been given up to Vesta; what remains is occupied by Caesar himself. Long live the laurels of the Palatine! Long live the house wreathed with the oaken boughs! A single house holds three eternal gods.*d*

temple of Apollo built on the Palatine containing the famous library. Here, as in iii. 425, the poet claims kinship for Augustus with Vesta through Aeneas. For the oaken boughs *cf.* p. 44, note *d*.

LIBER QUINTUS

Quaeritis, unde putem Maio data nomina mensi ?
　　non satis est liquido cognita causa mihi.
ut stat et incertus qua sit sibi nescit eundum,
　　cum videt ex omni parte viator iter :
5 sic, quia posse datur diversas reddere causas,
　　qua ferar, ignoro, copiaque ipsa nocet.
dicite, quae fontes Aganippidos Hippocrenes
　　grata Medusaei signa tenetis equi.
dissensere deae.　quarum Polyhymnia coepit
10　prima ; silent aliae dictaque mente notant.
　" post chaos ut primum data sunt tria corpora mundo,
　　inque novas species omne recessit opus,
pondere terra suo subsedit et aequora traxit,
　　at caelum levitas in loca summa tulit ;
15 sol quoque cum stellis nulla gravitate retentus
　　et vos lunares exiluistis equi.
sed neque Terra diu Caelo, nec cetera Phoebo
　　sidera cedebant ; par erat omnis honos.
saepe aliquis solio, quod tu, Saturne, tenebas,
20　ausus de media plebe sedere deus,

---

a Aganippe and Hippocrene, two springs associated with
the Muses, on Mount Helicon. Hippocrene (not A.) was
supposed to have gushed from the rock where the hoof of
Pegasus struck the ground. Here the two are identified.
For Medusa see iii. 450.

BOOK V

You ask whence I suppose the name of the month of May to be derived. The reason is not quite clearly known to me. As a wayfarer stands in doubt, and knows not which way to go, when he sees roads in all directions, so, because it is possible to assign different reasons, I know not where to turn; the very abundance of choice is an embarrassment. Declare to me, ye who haunt the springs of Aganippian Hippocrene, those dear traces of the Medusaean steed.[a] The goddesses disagreed; of them Polyhymnia began the first; the others were silent, and noted her sayings in their mind. " After chaos, as soon as the three elements were given to the world, and the whole creation resolved itself into new species, the earth subsided by its own weight, and drew the seas after it, but the sky was borne to the highest regions by its own lightness; the sun, too, not checked by gravity, and the stars, and you, ye horses of the moon, ye bounded high. But for a long time neither did Earth yield pride of place to Sky, nor did the other heavenly bodies to Phoebus; their honours were all equal. Often someone of the common sort of gods would dare to sit upon the throne which thou, Saturn, didst own; not one of the upstart deities

OVID

nec latus Oceano quisquam deus advena iunxit,[1]
  et Themis extremo saepe recepta loco est,
donec Honor placidoque decens Reverentia voltu
  corpora legitimis inposuere toris.[2]
25 hinc sata Maiestas, quae mundum temperat omnem,
  quaque die partu est edita, magna fuit.
nec mora, consedit medio sublimis Olympo
  aurea purpureo conspicienda sinu.
consedere simul Pudor et Metus : omne videres
30 numen ad hanc voltus composuisse suos.
protinus intravit mentes suspectus honorum :
  fit pretium dignis, nec sibi quisque placet.
hic status in caelo multos permansit in annos,
  dum senior fatis excidit arce deus.
35 Terra feros partus, immania monstra, Gigantas
  edidit ausuros in Iovis ire domum ;
mille manus illis dedit et pro cruribus angues,
  atque ait ' in magnos arma movete deos.'
extruere hi montes ad sidera summa parabant
40 et magnum bello sollicitare Iovem ;
fulmina de caeli iaculatus Iuppiter arce
  vertit in auctores pondera vasta suos.
his bene Maiestas armis defensa deorum
  restat et ex illo tempore culta manet ;
45 assidet inde Iovi, Iovis est fidissima custos
  et praestat sine vi sceptra tenenda Iovi.
venit et in terras : coluerunt Romulus illam
  et Numa, mox alii, tempore quisque suo.

---

[1] nec latus Oceano quisquam deus advena iunxit. *This is the reading of almost all the* mss., *except that A has* lacus *for* latus, *and that many of them (including UXM) read* et *for* nec.

[2] *The best manuscript (A) ends with this line. Henceforward the principal manuscript is U (codex Ursinianus).*

took the outer side of Ocean,[a] and Themis was often relegated to the lowest place, until Honour and comely Reverence with her calm look united in lawful wedlock. From that union sprang Majesty, who regulates the whole world, and who was great on the very day she was born. Without delay she took her seat high in the midst of Olympus, a golden figure far seen in purple vest. With her sat Modesty and Fear. You might see every divinity modelling his aspect upon hers. Straightway respect for dignities made its way into their minds ; the worthy got their due, and nobody thought much of himself. This state of things in heaven lasted for many a year, till fate banished the elder god from heaven's citadel. Earth brought forth the Giants,[b] a fierce brood, enormous monsters, who durst assault Jove's mansion ; she gave them a thousand hands, and snakes for legs, and said, ' Take arms against the great gods.' They set themselves to pile up the mountains to the topmost stars and to harass great Jupiter in war. From heaven's citadel Jupiter hurled thunderbolts and turned the ponderous weights upon their movers. These weapons of the gods protected Majesty well ; she survived and has been worshipped ever since. Hence she sits beside Jupiter, she is Jupiter's most faithful guardian ; she assures to him his sceptre's peaceful tenure. She came also to earth. Romulus and Numa worshipped her, and others after them, each in his time. She

---

[a] For *latus claudere* or *tegere*, to take the left hand in walking together (*i.e.* to be *exterior*) ; originally to defend the unshielded side, then a mode of honour (*cf.* 68 below). Ocean and Themis were among the primaeval deities.

[b] See iii. 439.

illa patres in honore pio matresque tuetur,
50　illa comes pueris virginibusque venit,
illa datos fasces commendat eburque curule,
　illa coronatis alta triumphat equis."
finierat voces Polyhymnia : dicta probarunt
　Clioque et curvae scita Thalia lyrae.
55 excipit Uranie : fecere silentia cunctae,
　et vox audiri nulla nisi illa potest.
" magna fuit quondam capitis reverentia cani,
　inque suo pretio ruga senilis erat.
Martis opus iuvenes animosaque bella gerebant
60　et pro dis aderant in statione suis :
viribus illa minor nec habendis utilis armis
　consilio patriae saepe ferebat opem.
nec nisi post annos patuit tunc curia seros,
　nomen et aetatis mite senatus erat.
65 iura dabat populo senior, finitaque certis
　legibus est aetas, unde petatur honor ;
et medius iuvenum, non indignantibus ipsis,
　ibat et interior, si comes unus erat.
verba quis auderet coram sene digna rubore
70　dicere ? censuram longa senecta dabat.
Romulus hoc vidit selectaque pectora patres
　dixit : ad hos urbis summa relata novae.
hinc sua maiores tribuisse vocabula Maio
　tangor et aetati consuluisse suae.
75 et Numitor dixisse potest ' da, Romule, mensem
　hunc senibus ' nec avum sustinuisse nepos.
nec leve propositi pignus successor honoris
　Iunius, a iuvenum nomine dictus, habet."

---

　　[a] The first such law was passed in 180 B.C. by L. Villius.
　　[b] *Tangor* seems to be used for " I am influenced," *inducor
ut credam* : compare Tac. *Ann.* iv. 57 " permoveor (ut
quaeram) num . . . verius sit."

keeps fathers and mothers in honour due; she bears boys and maidens company; she enhances the lictor's rods and the ivory chair of office; she rides aloft in triumph on the festooned steeds."

[53] Polyhymnia ended. Clio and Thalia, mistress of the curved lyre, approved her words. Urania took up the tale; all kept silence, and not a voice but hers could be heard. "Great was of old the reverence for the hoary head, and wrinkled eld was valued at its true worth. Martial exploits and doughty wars were work for youths, who in defence of their own gods kept watch and ward. In strength unequal, and for arms unfit, age often stood the country in good stead by its advice. The senate-house was then open only to men of mature years, and the very name of senate signified a ripe old age. The elders legislated for the people, and certain laws defined the age at which office might be sought.[a] An elder man used to walk between younger men, at which they did not repine, and if he had only one companion, the elder walked on the inner side. Who would dare to talk bawdy in the presence of an old man? Old age conferred a right of censorship. This Romulus perceived, and on the men of his choice he bestowed the title of Fathers: on them the government of the new city was conferred. Hence I incline to think[b] that the elders (*maiores*) gave their own name to the month of May, and that in doing so they had their own age in view. And Numitor may have said, 'Romulus, grant this month to the old men,' and the grandson may not have been able to resist his grandsire. No slight proof of the proposed honour is furnished by the next month, the month of June, which is named after young men

tunc sic, neglectos hedera redimita capillos,
80   prima sui coepit Calliopea chori :
    " duxerat Oceanus quondam Titanida Tethyn,
    qui terram liquidis, qua patet, ambit aquis.
    hinc sata Pleïone cum caelifero Atlante
    iungitur, ut fama est, Pleïadasque parit.
85 quarum Maia suas forma superasse sorores
    traditur et summo concubuisse Iovi.
    haec enixa iugo cupressiferae Cyllenes,
    aetherium volucri qui pede carpit iter.
    Arcades hunc Ladonque rapax et Maenalus ingens
90   rite colunt, luna credita terra prior.
    exul ab Arcadia Latios Evander in agros
    venerat, impositos attuleratque deos.
    hic, ubi nunc Roma est, orbis caput, arbor et herbae
    et paucae pecudes et casa rara fuit.
95 quo postquam ventum est, 'consistite!' praescia
      mater
    'nam locus imperii rus erit istud' ait.
    et matri et vati paret Nonacrius heros
    inque peregrina constitit hospes humo,
    sacraque multa quidem sed Fauni prima bicornis
100   has docuit gentes alipedisque dei.
    semicaper, coleris cinctutis, Faune, Lupercis,
    cum lustrant celebres vellera secta vias.
    at tu materno donasti nomine mensem,
    inventor curvae, furibus apte, fidis.
105 nec pietas haec prima tua est : septena putaris,
    Pleïadum numerum, fila dedisse lyrae."

---

         a See iv. 169.   *b* See i. 469.
    c Nonacris, a city of Arcadia.   *d* Mercury (Hermes).
      e See above, ii. 267, and Appendix, p. 390.
266

(*iuvenes*)." Then Calliope, her unkempt hair bound up with ivy, thus began, first of her choir : " Tethys, the Titaness, was wedded of old by Ocean, who encompasses the earth, far as it stretches, with his flowing waters. Their daughter Pleione, as report has it, was united to Atlas, who upholds the sky, and she gave birth to the Pleiades.*a* Of them Maia is said to have surpassed her sisters in beauty and to have lain with sovran Jove. She on the ridge of Mount Cyllene, wooded with cypresses, gave birth to him who speeds through the air on winged foot. Him the Arcadians, and hurrying Ladon, and huge Maenalus—that land accounted older than the moon*b* — worship with honours due. An exile from Arcadia, Evander came to the Latin fields and brought his gods on shipboard. On the spot where now stands Rome, the capital of the world, there were trees, and grass, and a few sheep, and here and there a cottage. When they had come hither, ' Halt ye,' said his prophetic mother, ' for that rural scene will be a place of empire.' The Nonacrian*c* hero obeyed the prophetess his mother, and halted as a stranger in a foreign land. He taught the natives many sacred rites, but first of all the rites of two-horned Faunus and of the wing-footed god.*d* Faunus, thou half-goat god, thou art worshipped by the Luperci in their loin-cloths what time the severed hides purify the crowded streets.*e* But thou didst bestow thy mother's name upon the month, O thou inventor of the curved lyre, patron of thieves.*d* Nor was this the first proof that thou didst give of thine affection : thou art supposed to have given to the lyre seven strings, the number of the Pleiades." Calliopea ended in

267

OVID

haec quoque desierat : laudata est voce sororum.
    quid faciam ?   turbae pars habet omnis idem.
gratia Pieridum nobis aequaliter adsit,
110   nullaque laudetur plusve minusve mihi.

1. [A · K · MAI · N͞P LVDI]   2. [BF LVDI]

Ab Iove surgat opus.   prima mihi nocte videnda
    stella est in cunas officiosa Iovis :
nascitur Oleniae signum pluviale Capellae ;
    illa dati caelum praemia lactis habet.
115 Naïs Amalthea, Cretaea nobilis Ida,
    dicitur in silvis occuluisse Iovem.
huic fuit haedorum mater formosa duorum,
    inter Dictaeos conspicienda greges,
cornibus aeriis atque in sua terga recurvis,
120   ubere, quod nutrix posset habere Iovis.
lac dabat illa deo.   sed fregit in arbore cornu
    truncaque dimidia parte decoris erat.
sustulit hoc nymphe cinxitque recentibus herbis
    et plenum pomis ad Iovis ora tulit.
125 ille ubi res caeli tenuit solioque paterno
    sedit, et invicto nil Iove maius erat,
sidera nutricem, nutricis fertile cornu
    fecit, quod dominae nunc quoque nomen habet.
praestitibus Maiae Laribus videre Kalendae
130   aram constitui parvaque signa deum :
voverat illa quidem Curius : sed multa[1] vetustas

---

[1] voverat *UM²m¹*: struxerat *one ϛ(cited by Heinsius)*:
ara erat *DXM¹m²BC and many ϛ* : vota erat *one ϛ* : arserat
H. Peter (following M. Haupt and H. Jordan): ars erat
Merkel³. curius *Ūm¹*: curibus *DXM¹m²*: laribus *M²ϛ*.
multa *Xm¹C and some ϛ* : longa *UDMm² and most MSS.*

---

[a] Apparent morning rising of Capella was on April 7.

268

her turn and was praised by the voices of her sisters. What am I to do? Each side has the same number of votes. May the favour of all the Muses alike attend me, and let me never praise anyone of them more or less than the rest.

KAL. MAI. 1st

[111] Begin the work with Jupiter. On the first night is visible the star that tended the cradle of Jupiter [a]; the rainy sign of the Olenian [b] She-goat rises. She has her place in the sky as a reward for the milk she gave the babe. The Naiad Amalthea, famous on the Cretan Mount Ida, is said to have hidden Jupiter in the woods. She owned a she-goat, conspicuous among the Dictaean flocks, the fair dam of two kids; her airy horns bent over on her back; her udder was such as the nurse of Jove might have. She suckled the god. But she broke a horn on a tree, and was shorn of half her charm. The nymph picked it up, wrapped it in fresh herbs, and carried it, full of fruit, to the lips of Jove. He, when he had gained the kingdom of heaven and sat on his father's throne, and there was nothing greater than unconquered Jove, made his nurse and her horn of plenty into stars: the horn still keeps its mistress' name.[c]

[129] The Calends of May witnessed the foundation of an altar to the Guardian Lares, together with small images of the gods. Curius indeed had vowed them, but length of time destroys many things,

[b] Perhaps from Olene in Achaea.
[c] The horn of Amalthea, or *cornucopiae*, "Horn of Plenty," which was supposed to produce for its possessor whatever he wished.

destruit, et saxo longa senecta nocet.
causa tamen positi fuerat cognominis illis,
    quod praestant oculis omnia tuta suis.
135 stant quoque pro nobis et praesunt moenibus urbis
    et sunt praesentes auxiliumque ferunt.
at canis ante pedes saxo fabricatus eodem
    stabat : quae standi cum Lare causa fuit ?
servat uterque domum, domino quoque fidus uterque :
140   compita grata deo, compita grata cani.
exagitant et Lar et turba Diania fures :
    pervigilantque Lares pervigilantque canes.
bina gemellorum quaerebam signa deorum
    viribus annosae facta caduca morae :
145 mille Lares Geniumque ducis, qui tradidit illos,
    urbs habet, et vici numina trina colunt.
quo feror ? Augustus mensis mihi carminis huius
    ius habet : interea Diva canenda Bona est.
est moles nativa loco, res nomina fecit :
150   appellant Saxum ; pars bona montis ea est.
huic Remus institerat frustra, quo tempore fratri
    prima Palatinae signa dedistis aves.
templa Patres illic oculos exosa viriles
    leniter acclini constituere iugo.
155 dedicat haec veteris Clausorum nominis heres,
    virgineo nullum corpore passa virum :
Livia restituit, ne non imitata maritum
    esset et ex omni parte secuta suum.

---

a *Praestites*, " guardians," because they " stand before "
and so guard.
  b Lares Compitales.
  c Augustus made 265 *vici* in Rome, and each had a
shrine of the Lares Compitales. The Lares were two ; and
the figure of Augustus was set up with them.
  d The Good Goddess was formerly an Earth-goddess.

and age prolonged wears out a stone. The reason for the epithet[a] applied to them is that they guard all things by their eyes. They also stand for us, and preside over the city walls, and they are present and bring us aid. But a dog, carved out of the same stone, used to stand before their feet. What was the reason for its standing with the Lar? Both guard the house: both are faithful to their master: cross-roads are dear to the god,[b] cross-roads are dear to dogs: the Lar and Diana's pack give chase to thieves; and wakeful are the Lares, and wakeful too are dogs. I sought for the images of the twin gods, but by the force of yearlong time they had decayed. In the city there are a thousand Lares, and the Genius of the chief, who handed them over to the public; the parishes worship the three divinities.[c]

[147] Whither do I stray? The month of August has a rightful claim to that subject of my verse: meantime the Good Goddess[d] must be the theme of my song. There is a natural knoll, which gives its name to the place; they call it the Rock[e]; it forms a good part of the hill. On it Remus took his stand in vain, what time, birds of the Palatine, ye did vouchsafe the first omens to his brother. There, on the gentle slope of the ridge, the Senate founded a temple which abhors the eyes of males. It was dedicated by an heiress of the ancient name of the Clausi, who in her virgin body had never known a man:[f] Livia restored it, that she might imitate her husband and follow him in everything.

Men were not allowed to enter her temple. See Appendix, p. 423.   [e] The peak of the Aventine.
   [f] See iv. 305 note. Livia is the wife of Augustus.

Postera cum roseam pulsis Hyperionis astris
160   in matutinis lampada tollet equis,
    frigidus Argestes summas mulcebit aristas,
        candidaque a Calabris vela dabuntur aquis.
    at simul inducent obscura crepuscula noctem,
        pars Hyadum toto de grege nulla latet.
165 ora micant Tauri septem radiantia flammis,
        navita quas Hyadas Graius ab imbre vocat;
    pars Bacchum nutrisse putat, pars credidit esse
        Tethyos has neptes Oceanique senis.
    nondum stabat Atlas humeros oneratus Olympo,
170   cum satus est forma conspiciendus Hyas;
    hunc stirps Oceani maturis nixibus Aethra
        edidit et nymphas, sed prior ortus Hyas.
    dum nova lanugo est, pavidos formidine cervos
        terret, et est illi praeda benigna lepus.
175 at postquam virtus annis adolevit, in apros
        audet et hirsutas comminus ire leas,
    dumque petit latebras fetae catulosque leaenae,
        ipse fuit Libycae praeda cruenta ferae.
    mater Hyan et Hyan maestae flevere sorores
180   cervicemque polo suppositurus Atlas,
    victus uterque parens tamen est pietate sororum :
        illa dedit caelum, nomina fecit Hyas.

---

[a] He alludes to the derivation from ὗς, whence they were
called *suculae*.

[b] True morning rising was on May 16, apparent June 9;
true evening setting, May 3.

VI. Non.   2nd

¹⁵⁹ When next Hyperion's daughter on the steeds
of morn shall lift her rosy lamp, and the stars are put
to flight, the cold north-west wind will sleek the topmost corn-ears, and white sails will put out from
Calabrian waters. But no sooner shall the dusk of
twilight lead on the night, than no single part of
the whole flock ^a of the Hyades will be invisible.^b The
head of the Bull sparkles radiant with seven flames,
which the Grecian sailor calls the Hyades after the
word for rain (*hyein*). Some think that they nursed
Bacchus ; some believe that they are the granddaughters of Tethys and old Ocean. Not yet did
Atlas stand bearing the burden of Olympus upon
his shoulders when Hyas was born, of loveliness
far-seen ; to him and to the nymphs did Aethra,
of the stock of Ocean, give birth in due time, but
Hyas was the elder. While the down was fresh
upon his cheeks, he was the terror of the bucks that
shied at his snares, and he was glad to bag a hare.
But when with his years his manly spirit grew, he
dared to close with boars and shaggy lionesses, and
while he sought out the lair and the whelps of a
lioness with young, he himself fell a blood-stained
prey to the Libyan brute. For Hyas his mother
wept, and for Hyas his sad sisters, and Atlas, soon
to bow his neck to the burden of the pole, yet
the love of the sisters exceeded that of both parents :
it won for them a place in the sky, but Hyas gave
them their name (of Hyades).

" Mater, ades, florum, ludis celebranda iocosis !
　　distuleram partes mense priore tuas.
185 incipis Aprili, transis in tempora Mai :
　　alter te fugiens, cum venit, alter habet.
　cum tua sint cedantque tibi confinia mensum,
　　convenit in laudes ille vel ille tuas.
　Circus in hunc exit clamataque palma theatris :
190　hoc quoque cum Circi munere carmen eat.
　ipsa doce, quae sis.　hominum sententia fallax :
　　optima tu proprii nominis auctor eris."
　sic ego.　sic nostris respondit diva rogatis
　　(dum loquitur, vernas efflat ab ore rosas):
195 " Chloris eram, quae Flora vocor : corrupta Latino
　　nominis est nostri littera Graeca sono.
　Chloris eram, nymphe campi felicis, ubi audis
　　rem fortunatis ante fuisse viris.
　quae fuerit mihi forma, grave est narrare modestae
200　sed generum matri repperit illa deum.
　ver erat, errabam : Zephyrus conspexit, abibam.
　　insequitur, fugio : fortior ille fuit,
　et dederat fratri Boreas ius omne rapinae
　　ausus Erechthea praemia ferre domo.
205 vim tamen emendat dando mihi nomina nuptae,
　　inque meo non est ulla querella toro.
　vere fruor semper : semper nitidissimus annus,
　　arbor habet frondes, pabula semper humus.
　est mihi fecundus dotalibus hortus in agris :

---

　　　a The Floralia extended over six days, April 28 to May 3.
　　　b Flora is obviously from *flos*, and has nothing to do with
Chloris.
　　　c Boreas carried off Oreithyia, daughter of Erechtheus.

V. Non. 3rd

[183] " Come, Mother of Flowers, that we may
honour thee with merry games ; last month I put
off giving thee thy due. Thou dost begin in April
and passest into the time of May [a] ; the one month
claims thee as it flies, the other as it comes. Since
the borders of the months are thine and appertain
to thee, either of the two is a fitting time to sing
thy praises. The games of the circus and the victor's
palm, acclaimed by the spectators, fall in this
month ; let my song run side by side with the
shows in the circus. Tell me thyself who thou art ;
the opinion of men is fallacious ; thou wilt be the
best voucher of thine own name."

[193] So I spoke, and the goddess answered my
question thus, and while she spoke, her lips breathed
vernal roses : " I who now am called Flora was
formerly Chloris : a Greek letter of my name is
corrupted in the Latin speech.[b] Chloris I was, a
nymph of the happy fields where, as you have heard,
dwelt fortunate men of old. Modesty shrinks from
describing my figure ; but it procured the hand of
a god for my mother's daughter. 'Twas spring,
and I was roaming ; Zephyr caught sight of me ;
I retired ; he pursued and I fled ; but he was the
stronger, and Boreas had given his brother full right
of rape by daring to carry off the prize from the
house of Erechtheus.[c] However, he made amends
for his violence by giving me the name of bride, and
in my marriage-bed I have naught to complain of.
I enjoy perpetual spring ; most buxom is the year
ever ; ever the tree is clothed with leaves, the ground
with pasture. In the fields that are my dower, I

210   aura fovet, liquidae fonte rigatur aquae.
      hunc meus implevit generoso flore maritus
        atque ait ' arbitrium tu, dea, floris habe.'
      saepe ego digestos volui numerare colores
        nec potui : numero copia maior erat.
215 roscida cum primum foliis excussa pruina est,
        et variae radiis intepuere comae,
      conveniunt pictis incinctae vestibus Horae
        inque leves calathos munera nostra legunt.
      protinus accedunt Charites nectuntque coronas
220   sertaque caelestes implicitura comas.
      prima per immensas sparsi nova semina gentes :
        unius tellus ante coloris erat.
      prima Therapnaeo feci de sanguine florem,
        et manet in folio scripta querella suo.
225 tu quoque nomen habes cultos, Narcisse, per hortos,
        infelix, quod non alter et alter eras.
      quid Crocon aut Attin referam Cinyraque creatum,
        de quorum per me volnere surgit honor ?
      Mars quoque, si nescis, per nostras editus artes :
230   Iuppiter hoc, ut adhuc, nesciat usque, precor.
      sancta Iovem Iuno, nata sine matre Minerva,
        officio doluit non eguisse suo.
      ibat, ut Oceano quereretur facta mariti ;
        restitit ad nostras fessa labore fores.
235 quam simul aspexi, ' quid te, Saturnia,' dixi

---

    [a] Purple iris, with marks of AI (αιαî) : said to have sprung from the blood of Hyacinthus, slain by Apollo. Therapnaean = Spartan, as Therapne was a town in Laconia and Hyacinthus was the son of the Spartan King Amyclas. See *Met.* x. 162-219.

    [b] Narcissus, a beautiful youth, died for love of his own image reflected in a pool. See *Met.* iii. 402-510.

have a fruitful garden, fanned by the breeze and
watered by a spring of running water. This garden
my husband filled with noble flowers and said,
'Goddess, be queen of flowers.' Oft did I wish to
count the colours in the beds, but could not ; the
number was past counting. Soon as the dewy rime
is shaken from the leaves, and the varied foliage is
warmed by the sunbeams, the Hours assemble, clad
in dappled weeds, and cull my gifts in light
baskets. Straightway the Graces draw near, and
twine garlands and wreaths to bind their heavenly
hair. I was the first to scatter new seeds among the
countless peoples ; till then the earth had been of
but one colour. I was the first to make a flower out of
Therapnaean blood, and on its petals the lament
remains inscribed.ᵃ Thou, too, Narcissus, hast a
name in the trim gardens, unhappy thou in that thou
hadst not a double of thyself.ᵇ What need to tell
of Crocus,ᶜ and Attis,ᵈ and the son of Cinyras,ᵉ from
whose wounds by my art doth beauty spring ? Mars,
too, was brought to the birth by my contrivance ;
perhaps you do not know it, and I pray that Jupiter,
who thus far knows it not, may never know it. Holy
Juno ᶠ grieved that Jupiter had not needed her
services when Minerva was born without a mother.
She went to complain of her husband's doings to
Ocean ; tired by the journey, she halted at my door.
As soon as I set eyes on her, 'What brings thee here,'

ᶜ Crocus, another fair youth, who was turned into the
flower so named. See *Met*. iv. 283.

ᵈ Violets were thought to have sprung from the blood of
his wound. See iv. 223 for the story.

ᵉ Adonis : the red anemone is said to have sprung from
his blood ; see *Met*. x. 710-739.

ᶠ That is, Juno Lucina ; see above, iii. 841.

'attulit ? ' exponit, quem petat illa locum,
addidit et causam.   verbis solabar amicis :
   ' non ' inquit ' verbis cura levanda mea est.
si pater est factus neglecto coniugis usu
240   Iuppiter et solus nomen utrumque tenet,
cur ego desperem fieri sine coniuge mater
   et parere intacto, dummodo casta, viro ?
omnia temptabo latis medicamina terris
   et freta Tartareos excutiamque sinus.'
245 vox erat in cursu : voltum dubitantis habebam.
   ' nescio quid, nymphe, posse videris ' ait.
ter volui promittere opem, ter lingua retenta est :
   ira Iovis magni causa timoris erat.
' fer, precor, auxilium ! ' dixit ' celabitur auctor
250   et Stygiae numen testificabor aquae.'
' quod petis, Oleniis ' inquam ' mihi missus ab arvis
   flos dabit : est hortis unicus ille meis.
qui dabat, " hoc " dixit " sterilem quoque tange
    iuvencam,
   mater erit."   tetigi, nec mora, mater erat.'
255 protinus haerentem decerpsi pollice florem :
   tangitur et tacto concipit illa sinu.
iamque gravis Thracen et laeva Propontidos intrat
   fitque potens voti, Marsque creatus erat.
qui memor accepti per me natalis ' habeto
260   tu quoque Romulea ' dixit ' in urbe locum.'
forsitan in teneris tantum mea regna coronis
   esse putes ?   tangit numen et arva meum.
si bene floruerint segetes, erit area dives ;

---

[a] The great oath of the gods was taken by this water
" eldest daughter of Oceanus " (Hesiod, *Theog.* 776).

I said, 'daughter of Saturn?' She set forth her journey's goal, adding its reason. I consoled her with friendly words. 'My grief, quoth she, 'is not to be assuaged with words. If Jupiter has become a father without the use of a wife, and unites both titles in his single person, why should I despair of becoming a mother without a husband, and of bringing forth without contact with a man, always supposing that I am chaste? I will try all the drugs in the wide world, and I will explore the seas and the depths of Tartarus.' Her speech would have flowed on, but on my face there was a look of doubt. 'Thou seemest, nymph,' said she, 'to have some power to help me.' Thrice did I wish to promise help, but thrice my tongue was tied: the anger of great Jupiter filled me with fear. 'Help me, I pray,' she said, 'the helper's name will be kept secret, and I will call on the divinity of the Stygian water to be my witness.'[a] 'Thy wish,' quoth I, 'will be accomplished by a flower that was sent me from the fields of Olenus. It is the only flower of the kind in my garden.' He who gave it me said, 'Touch also with this a barren heifer; she will be a mother.' I touched, and without delay she was a mother. Straightway I plucked with my thumb the clinging flower and touched Juno, and she conceived when it touched her bosom. And now being with child, she passed to Thrace and the left shores of the Propontis; her wish was granted, and Mars was born. In memory of the birth he owed to me, he said, 'Do thou also have a place in the city of Romulus.' Perhaps you may think that I am queen only of dainty garlands; but my divinity has to do also with the tilled fields. If the crops have blossomed well, the threshing-floor

si bene floruerit vinea, Bacchus erit ;
265 si bene floruerint oleae, nitidissimus annus,
    pomaque proventum temporis huius habent.
flore semel laeso pereunt viciaeque fabaeque,
    et pereunt lentes, advena Nile, tuae.
vina quoque in magnis operose condita cellis
270   florent, et nebulae dolia summa tegunt.
mella meum munus : volucres ego mella daturas
    ad violam et cytisos et thyma cana voco.
[nos quoque idem facimus tunc, cum iuvenalibus annis
    luxuriant animi, corporaque ipsa vigent.]"
275 talia dicentem tacitus mirabar.   at illa
    " ius tibi discendi, si qua requiris " ait.
" dic, dea," respondi " ludorum quae sit origo."
    vix bene desieram, rettulit illa mihi :
" cetera luxuriae nondum instrumenta vigebant,
280   aut pecus aut latam dives habebat humum ;
hinc etiam locuples, hinc ipsa pecunia dicta est.
    sed iam de vetito quisque parabat opes :
venerat in morem populi depascere saltus,
    idque diu licuit, poenaque nulla fuit.
285 vindice servabat nullo sua publica volgus ;
    iamque in privato pascere inertis erat.
plebis ad aediles perducta licentia talis
    Publicios : animus defuit ante viris.
rem populus recipit, multam subiere nocentes :
290   vindicibus laudi publica cura fuit.
multa data est ex parte mihi, magnoque favore

---

    a locuples, i.e. *loco-ples*, from *locus* and the root of *plenus*,
first in the sense of owning landed property ; *pecunia*, from
pecus. These derivations are correct, for a wonder.
    b L. and Manlius Publicius Malleolus, aediles, 240 B.C.

280

will be piled high ; if the vines have blossomed well,
there will be wine ; if the olive-trees have blossomed
well, most buxom will be the year; and the fruitage will
be according to the time of blossoming. If once the
blossom is nipped, the vetches and beans wither, and
thy lentils, O Nile that comest from afar, do likewise
wither. Wines also bloom, laboriously stored in great
cellars, and a scum covers their surface in the jars.
Honey is my gift. 'Tis I who call the winged
creatures, which yield honey, to the violet, and the
clover, and the grey thyme. 'Tis I, too, who discharge the same function when in youthful years
spirits run riot and bodies are robust."

275 I silently admired her as she spoke thus. But
she said, " Thou art free to learn the answers to
any questions thou mayest put." " Say, goddess,"
I replied, " what is the origin of the games." Scarce
had I ended when she answered me. " The other
instruments of luxury were not yet in vogue : the
rich man owned either cattle or broad lands ; hence
came the name for rich, and hence the name for
money itself.^{a} But already some amassed wealth
from unlawful sources : it had become a custom to
graze the public pastures, the thing was suffered
long, and no penalty was exacted. Common folk
had no champion to protect their share in public
property ; and at last it was deemed the sign
of a poor spirit in a man to graze his cattle on his
own land. Such licence was brought to the notice
of the plebeian aediles, the Publicii ^{b} ; till then
men's hearts had failed them.. The case was tried
before the people : the guilty were fined : the
champions were praised for their public spirit.
Part of the fine was given to me ; and the winners

281

OVID

victores ludos instituere novos.
　parte locant clivum, qui tunc erat ardua rupes :
　　utile nunc iter est, Publiciumque vocant."
295 annua credideram spectacula facta. negavit,
　　addidit et dictis altera verba suis :
　" nos quoque tangit honor: festis gaudemus et aris,
　　turbaque caelestes ambitiosa sumus.
　saepe deos aliquis peccando fecit iniquos,
300 　et pro delictis hostia blanda fuit ;
　saepe Iovem vidi, cum iam sua mittere vellet
　　fulmina, ture dato sustinuisse manum.
　at si neglegimur, magnis iniuria poenis
　　solvitur, et iustum praeterit ira modum.
305 respice Thestiaden : flammis absentibus arsit ;
　　causa est, quod Phoebes ara sine igne fuit.
　respice Tantaliden : eadem dea vela tenebat ;
　　virgo est, et spretos bis tamen ulta focos.
　Hippolyte infelix, velles coluisse Dionen,
310 　cum consternatis diripereris equis.
　longa referre mora est correcta oblivia damnis.
　　me quoque Romani praeteriere patres.
　quid facerem, per quod fierem manifesta doloris ?
　　exigerem nostrae qualia damna notae ?
315 excidit officium tristi mihi. nulla tuebar
　　rura, nec in pretio fertilis hortus erat :
　lilia deciderant, violas arere videres,
　　filaque punicei languida facta croci.

---

　　[a] A road up the Aventine, made by L. and M. Publicii,
as aediles, 240 B.C.
　　[b] Meleager, son of Oeneus, king of Calydon, by Althaea,
daughter of Thestius. Oeneus had neglected Diana (Artemis),
and in revenge she sent a boar to ravage Calydon. In a
dispute, Meleager killed his mother's brothers ; and she in
revenge burnt a fatal brand upon which his life depended.
See *Met.* viii. 270-525.

of the suit instituted new games with great applause. With part of the fine they contracted for making a way up the slope, which then was a steep rock : now it is a serviceable road, and they call it the Publician road." [a] I had thought that the shows were annual ; the goddess denied it and added to her former discourse a second speech. " We, too, are touched by honour ; we delight in festivals and altars ; we heavenly beings are a greedy gang. Often by sinning has a man disposed the gods against him, and a sacrificial victim has been a sop for crimes. Often have I seen Jupiter, when he was just about to launch his thunderbolts, hold his hand on the receipt of incense. But if we are neglected, we avenge the wrong by heavy penalties, and our wrath exceeds just bounds. Remember Thestiades [b] : he was burnt by flames afar ; the reason was that no fire blazed on Phoebe's altar. Remember Tantalides [c] : the same goddess detained the fleet ; she is a virgin, yet she twice avenged her slighted hearths. [d] Unhappy Hippolytus, [e] fain wouldst thou have worshipped Dione [f] when thy scared steeds were rending thee asunder ! 'Twere long to tell of cases of forgetfulness redressed by forfeitures. I myself was once neglected by the Roman senate. What was I to do ? By what could I show my resentment ? What punishment exact for the slight put on me ? In my gloom I relinquished my office. I guarded not the countryside, and the fruitful garden was naught to me. The lilies had dropped ; you might see the violets withering, and the tendrils of the crimson saffron languishing.

[c] Agamemnon, as descended from Tantalus.
[d] In the cases of Oeneus and of Agamemnon.
[e] See iv. 265, vi. 737.   [f] Used for Venus (Aphrodite).

saepe mihi Zephyrus ' dotes corrumpere noli
320   ipsa tuas ' dixit : dos mihi vilis erat.
florebant oleae ; venti nocuere protervi :
    florebant segetes ; grandine laesa seges :
in spe vitis erat ; caelum nigrescit ab Austris,
    et subita frondes decutiuntur aqua.
325 nec volui fieri nec sum crudelis in ira,
    cura repellendi sed mihi nulla fuit.
convenere patres et, si bene floreat annus,
    numinibus nostris annua festa vovent.
annuimus voto.   consul cum consule ludos
330   Postumio Laenas persoluere mihi."
quaerere conabar, quare lascivia maior
    his foret in ludis liberiorque iocus,
sed mihi succurrit numen non esse severum
    aptaque deliciis munera ferre deam.
335 tempora sutilibus cinguntur pota coronis,
    et latet iniecta splendida mensa rosa ;
ebrius incinctis philyra conviva capillis
    saltat et imprudens utitur arte meri ;
ebrius ad durum formosae limen amicae
340   cantat, habent unctae mollia serta comae.
nulla coronata peraguntur seria fronte,
    nec liquidae vinctis flore bibuntur aquae ;
donec eras mixtus nullis, Acheloe, racemis,
    gratia sumendae non erat ulla rosae.
345 Bacchus amat flores : Baccho placuisse coronam
    ex Ariadneo sidere nosse potes.
scaena levis decet hanc : non est, mihi credite, non est
    illa coturnatas inter habenda deas.

---

    a Consuls 173 B.C.
    b Achelous is used for water simply. The meaning is,
that there is a natural connexion between wine-drinking and
chaplets of flowers.   *c* See iii. 459-515.
284

Often Zephyr said to me, ' Spoil not thine own dowry.'
But my dowry was worthless in my sight. The
olive-trees were in blossom ; the wanton winds
blighted them : the crops were in blossom ; the
crop was blasted by the hail : the vines were pro-
mising ; the sky grew black under the south wind,
and the leaves were shaken down by a sudden
shower. I did not will it so, nor am I cruel in my
anger ; but I did not care to ward off these ills.
The senate assembled and voted an annual festival
to my divinity if the year should prove fruitful. I
accepted the vow. The consuls [a] Laenas and Postumius celebrated the games which had been vowed
to me."

[331] I was about to ask why these games are
marked by greater wantonness and broader jests ;
but it occurred to me that the divinity is not strait-
laced, and that the gifts she brings lend themselves to delights. The brows of wassailers are
wreathed with stitched garlands, and the polished
table is buried under a shower of roses. Maudlin
the guest dances, his hair bound with linden bark,
and all unwitting plies the tipsy art. Maudlin the
lover sings at the hard threshold of his lady fair :
soft garlands crown his perfumed locks. No serious
business does he do whose brow is garlanded ; no
water of the running brook is quaffed by such as
twine their hair with flowers : so long as thy stream,
Achelous, was dashed with no juice of grapes, none
cared to pluck the rose.[b] Bacchus loves flowers ;
that he delights in a floral crown, you may know
from Ariadne's clustered stars.[c] A rakish stage fits
Flora well ; she is not, believe me she is not, to
be counted among your buskined goddesses. The

turba quidem cur hos celebret meretricia ludos,
350 non ex difficili causa petita subest.
non est de tetricis, non est de magna professis,
     volt sua plebeio sacra patere choro,
et monet aetatis specie, dum floreat, uti ;
     contemni spinam, cum cecidere rosae.
355 cur tamen, ut dantur vestes Cerialibus albae,
     sic haec est cultu versicolore decens ?
an quia maturis albescit messis aristis,
     et color et species floribus omnis inest ?
annuit, et motis flores cecidere capillis,
360 accidere in mensas ut rosa missa solet.
lumina restabant, quorum me causa latebat,
     cum sic errores abstulit illa meos :
" vel quia purpureis collucent floribus agri,
     lumina sunt nostros visa decere dies ;
365 vel quia nec flos est hebeti nec flamma colore,
     atque oculos in se splendor uterque trahit ;
vel quia deliciis nocturna licentia nostris
     convenit. a vero tertia causa venit."
" est breve praeterea, de quo mihi quaerere restat,
370 si liceat " dixi : dixit et illa " licet."
" cur tibi pro Libycis clauduntur rete leaenis
     imbelles capreae sollicitusque lepus ? "
non sibi, respondit, silvas cessisse, sed hortos
     arvaque pugnaci non adeunda ferae.
375 omnia finierat : tenues secessit in auras,
     mansit odor : posses scire fuisse deam.
floreat ut toto carmen Nasonis in aevo,
     sparge, precor, donis pectora nostra tuis.

ᵃ That is, hunted in the arena at the Floralia.

reason why a crowd of drabs frequents these games is not hard to discover. She is none of your glum, none of your high-flown ones : she wishes her rites to be open to the common herd ; and she warns us to use life's flower, while it still blooms ; for the thorn, she reminds us, is flouted when the roses have fallen away.

355 But why is it that whereas white robes are given out at the festival of Ceres, Flora is neatly clad in attire of many colours ? Is it because the harvest whitens when the ears are ripe, but flowers are of every hue and every shape ? She nodded assent and at the motion of her tresses the flowers dropped down, as falls the rose cast by a hand upon a table.

361 There yet remained the lights, the reason whereof escaped me ; when the goddess thus removed my doubts : " Lights are thought to befit my days either because the fields do glow with purple flowers ; or because neither flowers nor flames are of a dull colour, and the splendour of both attracts the eye ; or because nocturnal licence befits my revels. The third reason comes nearest the truth."

369 " There is yet a small matter about which it remains, with thy leave, to put a question." " Thou hast my leave," said she. " Why, instead of Libyan lionesses, are unwarlike roes and shy hares pent in thy nets *? " She replied that her province was not woods, but gardens and fields, where no fierce beast may come.

375 Her tale was ended, and she vanished into thin air. A fragrance lingered ; you could know a goddess had been there. That Naso's lay may bloom for aye, O strew, I pray thee, goddess, thy boons upon my breast !

287

OVID

3. [CC LVD · IN · CIR]

Nocte minus quarta promet sua sidera Chiron
380   semivir et flavi corpore mixtus equi.
Pelion Haemoniae mons est obversus in Austros :
    summa virent pinu, cetera quercus habet.
Phillyrides tenuit. saxo stant antra vetusto,
    quae iustum memorant incoluisse senem.
385 ille manus olim missuras Hectora leto
    creditur in lyricis detinuisse modis.
venerat Alcides exhausta parte laborum,
    iussaque restabant ultima paene viro.
stare simul casu Troiae duo fata videres :
390   hinc puer Aeacides, hinc Iove natus erat.
excipit hospitio iuvenem Philyreïus heros,
    et causam adventus hic rogat, ille docet.
respicit interea clavam spoliumque leonis,
    " vir " que ait " his armis, armaque digna viro ! "
395 nec se, quin horrens auderent tangere saetis
    vellus, Achilleae continuere manus.
dumque senex tractat squalentia tela venenis,
    excidit et laevo fixa sagitta pede est.
ingemuit Chiron traxitque e corpore ferrum,
400   et gemit Alcides Haemoniusque puer.
ipse tamen lectas Pagasaeis collibus herbas
    temperat et vana volnera mulcet ope :
virus edax superabat opem, penitusque recepta
    ossibus et toto corpore pestis erat.

---

^a The Centaur : true evening rising, May 3 ; apparent,
April 15.   ^b Thessaly.   ^c Chiron.
  ^d The descendant of Aeacus is Achilles. Hercules, " son
of Jupiter," destroyed Troy, because Laomedon had broken
faith with him.
  ^e See 405. Hercules poisoned his arrows with the hydra's
blood.

V. Non. 3rd

379 In less than four nights the semi-human Chiron,
who is compounded with the body of a tawny horse,
will put forth his stars.[a] Pelion is a mountain of
Haemonia[b] which looks southward : its top is green
with pinewoods : the rest is draped with oaks. It
was the home of Philyra's son.[c] There remains an
ancient rocky cave, which they say was inhabited
by the righteous old man. He is believed to have
employed, in strumming the lyre, those hands
which were one day to send Hector to death.
Alcides had come after accomplishing a part of his
labours, and little but the last orders remained for
the hero to obey. You might see standing by chance
together the two masters of the fate of Troy, on the
one side the boyish descendant of Aeacus, on the other
the son of Jupiter.[d] The Philyrean hero received
Hercules hospitably and asked the reason of his
coming, and Hercules informed him. Meantime
Chiron looked askance at the club and lion's skin and
said, " Man worthy of those arms, and arms worthy
the man ! " Nor could Achilles keep his hands from
daring to touch the skin all shaggy with bristles.
And while the old man fingered the shafts clotted
with poison,[e] one of the arrows fell out of the quiver
and stuck in his left foot. Chiron groaned and drew
the steel from his body ; and Alcides groaned, and
so did the Haemonian boy. The centaur himself, however, compounded herbs gathered on the Pagasaean
hills and assuaged the wounds by bootless remedies ;
but the gnawing poison defied all remedies, and
the bane soaked into the bones and the whole body.

L

405 sanguine centauri Lernaeae sanguis echidnae
    mixtus ad auxilium tempora nulla dabat.
stabat, ut ante patrem, lacrimis perfusus Achilles :
    sic flendus Peleus, si moreretur, erat.
saepe manus aegras manibus fingebat amicis
410   (morum, quos fecit, praemia doctor habet),
oscula saepe dedit, dixit quoque saepe iacenti
    " vive, precor, nec me, care, relinque, pater ! "
nona dies aderat, cum tu, iustissime Chiron,
    bis septem stellis corpora cinctus eras.

4. [DC] 5

415 Hunc Lyra curva sequi cuperet, sed idonea nondum
    est via : nox aptum tertia tempus erit.

6. FC

Scorpios in caelo, cum cras lucescere Nonas
    dicimus, a media parte notandus erit.

7. G NON · N   8. HF   9. A LEM · N

Hinc ubi protulerit formosa ter Hesperus ora,
420   ter dederint Phoebo sidera victa locum,
ritus erit veteris, nocturna Lemuria, sacri :
    inferias tacitis manibus illa dabunt.
annus erat brevior, nec adhuc pia februa norant,
    nec tu dux mensum, Iane biformis, eras :
425 iam tamen extincto cineri sua dona ferebant,

---

    a The constellation of Chiron.
    b True evening rising, April 23 ; apparent, April 15.
    c True morning setting, April 26 ; apparent, May 13.
But there were many stars in it.
    d See Appendix, p. 424.

The blood of the Lernaean hydra, mingled with
the centaur's blood, left no time for rescue. Achilles,
bathed in tears, stood before him as before a father;
so would he have wept for Peleus at the point of
death. Often he fondled the feeble hands with
his own loving hands; the teacher reaped the reward
of the character he had moulded. Often Achilles
kissed him, and often said to him as he lay there,
"Live, I pray thee, and do not forsake me, dear
father." The ninth day was come when thou, most
righteous Chiron, didst gird thy body with twice
seven stars.[a]

III. Non. 5th

[415] The curved Lyre [b] would wish to follow the
Centaur, but the road is not yet clear. The third
night will be the proper time.

Pr. Non. 6th

[417] The Scorpion [c] will be visible from its middle
in the sky, when we say that to-morrow the Nones
will dawn.

VII. Id. 9th

[419] When from that day the Evening Star shall
thrice have shown his beauteous face, and thrice
the vanquished stars shall have retreated before
Phoebus, there will be celebrated an olden rite,
the nocturnal Lemuria [d] : it will bring offerings to
the silent ghosts. The year was formerly shorter,
and the pious rites of purification (*februa*) were
unknown, and thou, two-headed Janus, wast not
the leader of the months. Yet even then people
brought gifts to the ashes of the dead, as their

compositique nepos busta piabat avi.
mensis erat Maius, maiorum nomine dictus,
   qui partem prisci nunc quoque moris habet.
nox ubi iam media est somnoque silentia praebet,
430   et canis et variae conticuistis aves,
ille memor veteris ritus timidusque deorum
   surgit (habent gemini vincula nulla pedes)
signaque dat digitis medio cum pollice iunctis,
   occurrat tacito ne levis umbra sibi.
435 cumque manus puras fontana perluit unda,
   vertitur et nigras accipit ante fabas
aversusque iacit ; sed dum iacit, " haec ego mitto,
   his " inquit " redimo meque meosque fabis."
hoc novies dicit nec respicit : umbra putatur
440   colligere et nullo terga vidente sequi.
rursus aquam tangit Temesaeaque concrepat aera
   et rogat, ut tectis exeat umbra suis.
cum dixit novies " Manes exite paterni,"
   respicit et pure sacra peracta putat.
445 dicta sit unde dies, quae nominis extet origo,
   me fugit : ex aliquo est invenienda deo.
Pleiade nate, mone, virga venerande potenti :
   saepe tibi est Stygii regia visa Iovis.
venit adoratus Caducifer. accipe causam
450   nominis : ex ipso est cognita causa deo.
Romulus ut tumulo fraternas condidit umbras,
   et male veloci iusta soluta Remo,

---

   a The charm to avert the evil eye ; it is called in Italian
" the fig," *la fica* or *mano fica.*
   b Copper mines near Temesa in Bruttium.
   c Hermes (Mercury), son of Maia.

due, and the grandson paid his respects to the
tomb of his buried grandsire. It was the month
of May, so named after our forefathers (*maiores*),
and it still retains part of the ancient custom.
When midnight has come and lends silence to sleep,
and dogs and all ye varied fowls are hushed, the
worshipper who bears the olden rite in mind and
fears the gods arises; no knots constrict his feet;
and he makes a sign with his thumb in the middle
of his closed fingers,[a] lest in his silence an unsubstantial shade should meet him. And after washing
his hands clean in spring water, he turns, and first
he receives black beans and throws them away with
face averted; but while he throws them, he says:
" These I cast; with these beans I redeem me and
mine." This he says nine times, without looking
back: the shade is thought to gather the beans,
and to follow unseen behind. Again he touches
water, and clashes Temesan[b] bronze, and asks the
shade to go out of his house. When he has said
nine times, " Ghosts of my fathers, go forth !" he
looks back, and thinks that he has duly performed
the sacred rites.

445 Why the day was called Lemuria, and what
is the origin of the name, escapes me; it is for some
god to discover it. Son of the Pleiad,[c] thou reverend
master of the puissant wand, inform me: oft hast
thou seen the palace of the Stygian Jove. At my
prayer the Bearer of the Herald's Staff (*Caducifer*)
was come. Learn the cause of the name; the god
himself made it known. When Romulus had buried
his brother's ghost in the grave, and the obsequies
had been paid to the too nimble Remus, un-

OVID

Faustulus infelix et passis Acca capillis
  spargebant lacrimis ossa perusta suis.
455 inde domum redeunt sub prima crepuscula maesti,
  utque erat, in duro procubuere toro.
umbra cruenta Remi visa est assistere lecto
  atque haec exiguo murmure verba loqui :
" en ego dimidium vestri parsque altera voti,
460   cernite, sim qualis, qui modo qualis eram !
qui modo, si volucres habuissem regna iubentes,
  in populo potui maximus esse meo,
nunc sum elapsa rogi flammis et inanis imago :
  haec est ex illo forma relicta Remo !
465 heu ubi Mars pater est ? si vos modo vera locuti,
  uberaque expositis ille ferina dedit.
quem lupa servavit, manus hunc temeraria civis
  perdidit. o quanto mitior illa fuit !
saeve Celer, crudelem animam per volnera reddas,
470   utque ego, sub terras sanguinulentus eas.
noluit hoc frater, pietas aequalis in illo est :
  quod potuit, lacrimas manibus ille dedit.
hunc vos per lacrimas, per vestra alimenta rogate,
  ut celebrem nostro signet honore diem."
475 mandantem amplecti cupiunt et bracchia tendunt :
  lubrica prensantes effugit umbra manus.
ut secum fugiens somnos abduxit imago,
  ad regem voces fratris uterque ferunt.
Romulus obsequitur, lucemque Remuria dicit
480   illam, qua positis iusta feruntur avis.
aspera mutata est in lenem tempore longo
  littera, quae toto nomine prima fuit ;

---

  [a] See iii. 55, iv. 854.
  [b] Who killed Remus, according to Ovid ; see iv. 837.

happy Faustulus and Acca,[a] with streaming hair,
sprinkled the burnt bones with their tears. Then at
twilight's fall they sadly took the homeward way,
and flung themselves on their hard couch, just as it
was. The gory ghost of Remus seemed to stand
at the bedside and to speak these words in a faint
murmur : " Look on me, who shared the half,
the full half of your tender care, behold what I am
come to, and what I was of late ! A little while
ago I might have been the foremost of my people, if
but the birds had assigned the throne to me. Now
I am an empty wraith, escaped from the flames of
the pyre ; that is all that remains of the once great
Remus. Alas, where is my father Mars ? If only
you spoke the truth, and it was he who sent the
wild beast's dugs to suckle the abandoned babes.
A citizen's rash hand undid him whom the she-wolf
saved ; O how far more merciful was she ! Ferocious
Celer,[b] mayest thou yield up thy cruel soul through
wounds, and pass like me all bloody underneath the
earth ! My brother willed not this : his love's a
match for mine : he gave to my departed soul—
'twas all he could—his tears. Pray him by your
tears, by your fosterage, that he would celebrate
a day by signal honour done to me." As the ghost
gave this charge, they yearned to embrace him
and stretched forth their arms ; the slippery shade
escaped the clasping hands. When the vision fled
and carried slumber with it, the pair reported to
the king his brother's words. Romulus complied,
and gave the name of Remuria to the day on which
due worship is paid to buried ancestors. In course
of ages the rough letter, which stood at the beginning
of the name, was changed into the smooth ; and soon

mox etiam lemures animas dixere silentum :
　　hic sensus verbi, vis ea vocis erat.
485 fana tamen veteres illis clausere diebus,
　　ut nunc ferali tempore operta vides.
nec viduae taedis eadem nec virginis apta
　　tempora : quae nupsit, non diuturna fuit.
hac quoque de causa, si te proverbia tangunt,
490　mense malum Maio nubere volgus ait.
sed tamen haec tria sunt sub eodem tempore festa
　　inter se nulla continuata die.

10. BC   11. C LEM · N

Quorum si mediis Boeotum Oriona quaeres,
　　falsus eris.　signi causa canenda mihi.
495 Iuppiter et lato qui regnat in aequore frater
　　carpebant socias Mercuriusque vias.
tempus erat, quo versa iugo referuntur aratra,
　　et pronus saturae lac bibit agnus ovis.
forte senex Hyrieus, angusti cultor agelli,
500　hos videt, exiguam stabat ut ante casam ;
atque ita " longa via est, nec tempora longa super-
　　　sunt,"
　　dixit " et hospitibus ianua nostra patet."
addidit et voltum verbis iterumque rogavit :
　　parent promissis dissimulantque deos.
505 tecta senis subeunt nigro deformia fumo ;
　　ignis in hesterno stipite parvus erat.
ipse genu nixus flammas exsuscitat aura
　　et promit quassas comminuitque faces.
stant calices ; minor inde fabas, holus alter habebat,

---

the souls of the silent multitude were also called *Lemures* : that is the meaning of the word, that is the force of the expression. But the ancients shut the temples on these days, as even now you see them closed at the season sacred to the dead. The times are unsuitable for the marriage both of a widow and a maid : she who marries then, will not live long. For the same reason, if you give weight to proverbs, common folk say 'tis ill to wed in May. But these three festivals fall about the same time, though not on three consecutive days.

V. Id. 11th

493 If you look for Boeotian Orion on the middle of these three days, you will be disappointed.ᵃ I must now sing of the cause of the constellation. Jupiter, and his brother who reigns in the deep sea, and Mercury, were journeying together. It was the time when the yoked kine draw home the upturned plough, and the lamb lies down and drinks the milk of the full ewe. An old man Hyrieus, who cultivated a tiny farm, chanced to see them as he stood before his little cottage ; and thus he spoke : " Long is the way, but short the hours of daylight left, and my door is open to strangers." He enforced his words by a look, and again invited them. They accepted the offer and dissembled their divinity. They passed beneath the old man's roof, begrimed with black smoke ; a little fire was glimmering in the log of yesterday. He knelt and blew up the flames with his breath, and drawing forth the stumps of torches he chopped them up. Two pipkins stood on the fire ; the lesser contained beans, the other

510 et spumat testu pressus uterque suo.
dumque mora est, tremula dat vina rubentia dextra :
accipit aequoreus pocula prima deus.
quae simul exhausit, " da nunc bibat ordine " dixit
" Iuppiter." audito palluit ille Iove.
515 ut rediit animus, cultorem pauperis agri
immolat et magno torret in igne bovem ;
quaeque puer quondam primis diffuderat annis,
promit fumoso condita vina cado.
nec mora, flumineam lino celantibus ulvam,
520 sic quoque non altis, incubuere toris.
nunc dape, nunc posito mensae nituere Lyaeo :
terra rubens crater, pocula fagus erant.
verba fuere Iovis : " siquid fert impetus, opta :
omne feres." placidi verba fuere senis :
525 " cara fuit coniunx, primae mihi flore iuventae
cognita. nunc ubi sit, quaeritis ? urna tegit.
huic ego iuratus, vobis in verba vocatis,
' coniugio ' dixi ' sola fruere meo.'
et dixi et servo. sed enim diversa voluntas
530 est mihi ; nec coniunx, sed pater esse volo."
annuerant omnes : omnes ad terga iuvenci
constiterant—pudor est ulteriora loqui—
tum superiniecta texere madentia terra ;
iamque decem menses, et puer ortus erat.
535 hunc Hyrieus, quia sic genitus, vocat Uriona :
perdidit antiquum littera prima sonum.
creverat immensum ; comitem sibi Delia sumpsit,
ille deae custos, ille satelles erat.

ᵃ The absurd derivation of Orion from οὖρον, " urine,"
explains what had been done upon the hide ; thus Orion
should have been created without a mother. Various tales
are told of his death : here he is defender of Latona, the

kitchen herbs ; both boiled, each under the pressure of its lid. While he waited, he served out red wine with shaky hand. The god of the sea received the first cup. When he had drained it, " Now serve the drink," said he, " to Jupiter in order." At the word Jupiter the old man paled. When he recovered himself, he sacrificed the ox that ploughed his poor land, and he roasted it in a great fire ; and the wine which as a boy he had laid up in his early years, he brought forth stored in its smoky jar. And straightway they reclined on mattresses stuffed with river sedge and covered with linen, but lowly still. The table shone, now with the viands, now with the wine set down on it : the bowl was of red earthenware, the cups were beechen wood. Quoth Jupiter : " If thou hast any fancy, choose : all will be thine." The calm old man thus spoke : " I had a dear wife, whose love I won in the flower of early youth. Where is she now ? you ask. The urn her ashes holds. To her I swore, and called you gods to witness, ' Thou shalt be my only spouse.' I gave my word, and I keep it. But a different wish is mine : I would be, not a husband, but a father." All the gods assented ; all took their stand at the bullock's hide — I am ashamed to describe what followed — then they covered the reeking hide by throwing earth on it : when ten months had passed, a boy was born. Him Hyrieus called Urion on account of the mode of his begetting : [a] the first letter of his name has lost its ancient sound. He grew to an enormous size ; the Delian goddess took him to be her companion ; he was her guardian, he

goddess who brought forth her twins, Apollo and Artemis, in Delos.

verba movent iram non circumspecta deorum :
540   "quam nequeam " dixit " vincere, nulla fera est."
scorpion immisit Tellus : fuit impetus illi
   curva gemelliparae spicula ferre deae ;
obstitit Orion. Latona nitentibus astris
   addidit et " meriti praemia " dixit " habe."

12. D NP LVD · MART · IN · CIRC

545 Sed quid et Orion et cetera sidera mundo
   cedere festinant, noxque coartat iter ?
quid solito citius liquido iubar aequore tollit
   candida, Lucifero praeveniente, dies ?
fallor, an arma sonant ? non fallimur, arma sonabant :
550   Mars venit et veniens bellica signa dedit.
Ultor ad ipse suos caelo descendit honores
   templaque in Augusto conspicienda foro.
et deus est ingens et opus : debebat in urbe
   non aliter nati Mars habitare sui.
555 digna Giganteis haec sunt delubra tropaeis :
   hinc fera Gradivum bella movere decet,
seu quis ab Eoo nos impius orbe lacesset,
   seu quis ab occiduo sole domandus erit.
prospicit armipotens operis fastigia summi
560   et probat invictos summa tenere deos.
prospicit in foribus diversae tela figurae
   armaque terrarum milite victa suo.
hinc videt Aenean oneratum pondere caro
   et tot Iuleae nobilitatis avos :

---

[a] See 577. The future Augustus had vowed a temple to
Mars Ultor, if he should avenge the death of Julius Caesar :
this he dedicated in 2 B.C., but on August 1. Augustus had
built another temple to the same god for the standards recovered from the Parthians in 20 B.C., which Ovid may have
confused with this.

her attendant. Heedless words excite the wrath
of gods. "There is no wild beast," said he, "which
I cannot master." Earth egged on a scorpion: its
mission was to attack the Goddess Mother of Twins
with its hooked fangs. Orion threw himself in the
way. Latona set him among the shining stars, and
said, "Take thy well-earned reward."

IV. Id. 12th

545 But why do Orion and the other stars haste to
withdraw from the sky? And why does night shorten
her course? Why does the bright day, heralded
by the Morning Star, raise its radiant light faster
than usual from the watery main? Do I err, or was
there a clash of arms? I err not, there was a clash
of arms. Mars comes, and at his coming he gave
the sign of war. The Avenger descends himself
from heaven to behold his own honours and his
splendid temple in the forum of Augustus.ᵃ The god
is huge, and so is the structure: no otherwise ought
Mars to dwell in his son's city. That shrine is
worthy of trophies won from giants; from it might
the Marching God fitly open his fierce campaigns,
whether an impious foe shall assail us from the
eastern world or whether another will have to be
vanquished where the sun goes down. The god of
arms surveys the pinnacles of the lofty edifice,
and approves that the highest places should be
filled by the unconquered gods. He surveys on the
doors weapons of diverse shapes, and arms of lands
subdued by his soldiery. On this side he sees
Aeneas laden with his dear burden, and many an
ancestor of the noble Julian line. On the other side

565 hinc videt Iliaden humeris ducis arma ferentem,
    claraque dispositis acta subesse viris.
    spectat et Augusto praetextum nomine templum,
    et visum lecto Caesare maius opus.
    voverat hoc iuvenis tunc, cum pia sustulit arma :
570   a tantis Princeps incipiendus erat.
    ille manus tendens, hinc stanti milite iusto,
    hinc coniuratis, talia dicta dedit :
    " si mihi bellandi pater est Vestaeque sacerdos
    auctor, et ulcisci numen utrumque paro :
575 Mars, ades et satia scelerato sanguine ferrum,
    stetque favor causa pro meliore tuus.
    templa feres et, me victore, vocaberis Ultor."
    voverat et fuso laetus ab hoste redit.
    nec satis est meruisse semel cognomina Marti :
580   persequitur Parthi signa retenta manu.
    gens fuit et campis et equis et tuta sagittis
    et circumfusis invia fluminibus.
    addiderant animos Crassorum funera genti,
    cum periit miles signaque duxque simul.
585 signa, decus belli, Parthus Romana tenebat,
    Romanaeque aquilae signifer hostis erat.
    isque pudor mansisset adhuc, nisi fortibus armis
    Caesaris Ausoniae protegerentur opes.
    ille notas veteres et longi dedecus aevi
590   sustulit : agnorunt signa recepta suos.

---

     a The *spolia opima* taken from Acron.
     b To punish Brutus and Cassius.
     c Julius Caesar, Pontifex Maximus ; see iii. 699.
     d M. Licinius Crassus, killed with his son Publius, and his
army destroyed, by the Parthians at Carrhae, 53 B.C.
Augustus recovered the captured standards in 20 B.C.

he sees Romulus carrying on his shoulders the arms of the conquered leader,[a] and their famous deeds inscribed beneath the statues arranged in order. He beholds, too, the name of Augustus on the front of the temple; and the building seems to him still greater, when he reads the name of Caesar. Augustus had vowed it in his youth at the time when he took up arms in duty's cause.[b] Deeds so great were worthy to inaugurate a prince's reign. While the loyal troops stood on the one side, and the conspirators on the other, he stretched forth his hands and spoke these words : " If my father,[c] Vesta's priest, is my warrant for waging war, and I do now prepare to avenge both his divinity and hers, come, Mars, and glut the sword with knavish blood, and grant thy favour to the better cause. Thou shalt receive a temple, and shalt be called Avenger, when victory is mine." So he vowed, and returned rejoicing from the routing of the foe. Nor is he content to have earned once for all the surname of Avenger for Mars : he tracks down the standards detained by the hands of the Parthians. These were a nation whom their plains, their horses, and their arrows rendered safe, and surrounding rivers made inaccessible. The pride of the nation had been fostered by the deaths of Crassus and his son, when soldiers, general, and standards perished together.[d] The Parthians kept the Roman standards, the glory of war, and a foe was the standard-bearer of the Roman eagle. That shame would have endured till now, had not Ausonia's empire been guarded by Caesar's powerful arms. He put an end to the old reproach, to the disgrace of a whole generation : the recovered standards knew their true owners again.

quid tibi nunc solitae mitti post terga sagittae,
　　quid loca, quid rapidi profuit usus equi,
Parthe ? refers aquilas, victos quoque porrigis arcus :
　　pignora iam nostri nulla pudoris habes.
595 rite deo templumque datum nomenque bis ulto,
　　et meritus voti debita solvit honor.
sollemnes ludos Circo celebrate, Quirites !
　　non visa est fortem scaena decere deum.

13. E LEM · N

Pliadas aspicies omnes totumque sororum
600　agmen, ubi ante Idus nox erit una super.
tum mihi non dubiis auctoribus incipit aestas,
　　et tepidi finem tempora veris habent.

14. FC

Idibus ora prior stellantia tollere Taurum
　　indicat.　huic signo fabula nota subest.
605 praebuit, ut taurus, Tyriae sua terga puellae
　　Iuppiter et falsa cornua fronte tulit.
illa iubam dextra, laeva retinebat amictus,
　　et timor ipse novi causa decoris erat.
aura sinus implet, flavos movet aura capillos :
610　Sidoni, sic fueras aspicienda Iovi.
saepe puellares subduxit ab aequore plantas
　　et metuit tactus assilientis aquae :

---

　　a Probably he really referred to the Hyades : their true
morning rising was on May 16 ; apparent, on June 9.
　　b Europa.

What now availed thee, thou Parthian, the arrows thou
art wont to shoot behind thy back ? What availed thy
deserts ? What the use of the fleet steed ? Thou
bringest back the eagles ; thou tenderest, too, thy
conquered bows. Now thou hast no tokens of our
shame. Justly have the temple and the title of
Avenger been given to the god, who has earned that
title twice over ; and the well-deserved honour has
paid the debt incurred by the vow. Quirites, celebrate the solemn games in the Circus : the stage
seems little to befit a valiant god.

III. Id. 13th

[599] You will behold all the Pleiades, even the whole
bevy of sisters, when there shall be one night remaining before the Ides. Then summer begins, as
I learn from sure authorities, and the season of warm
spring comes to an end.

Pr. Id. 14th

[603] The day before the Ides marks the time when
the Bull lifts his starry front.[a] This constellation is
explained by a familiar tale. Jupiter in the shape
of a bull offered his back to the Tyrian maid [b] and
wore horns on his false brow. She held the bull's
mane in her right hand, her drapery in her left ;
and her very fear lent her fresh grace. The breeze
fills the robe on her bosom, it stirs her yellow hair ;
Sidonian damsel, thus indeed it became thee to
meet the gaze of Jove. Oft did she withdraw her
girlish soles from the sea, and feared the contact of

saepe deus prudens tergum demisit in undas,
 haereat ut collo fortius illa suo.
615 litoribus tactis stabat sine cornibus ullis
 Iuppiter inque deum de bove versus erat.
taurus init caelum : te, Sidoni, Iuppiter implet,
 parsque tuum terrae tertia nomen habet.
hoc alii signum Phariam dixere iuvencam,[a]
620 quae bos ex homine est, ex bove facta dea.
tum quoque priscorum virgo simulacra virorum
 mittere roboreo scirpea ponte solet.
625 fama vetus tunc, cum Saturnia terra vocata est,
 talia fatidici dicta fuisse Iovis :
" falcifero libata seni duo corpora, gentes,
 mittite, quae Tuscis excipiantur aquis : "
donec in haec venit Tirynthius arva, quotannis
630 tristia Leucadio[c] sacra peracta modo ;
illum stramineos in aquam misisse Quirites :
 Herculis exemplo corpora falsa iaci.
pars putat, ut ferrent iuvenes suffragia soli,
 pontibus infirmos praecipitasse senes.
623 corpora post decies senos qui credidit annos
624 missa neci, sceleris crimine damnat avos.
635 Thybri, doce verum.   tua ripa vetustior urbe est,
 principium ritus tu bene nosse potes.
Thybris harundiferum medio caput extulit alveo
 raucaque dimovit talibus ora sonis :
" haec loca desertas vidi sine moenibus herbas :

---

  [a] Io, often identified with Egyptian Isis.
  [b] The Vestals.   See Appendix, p. 425, *The Argei*.
  [c] The " lover's leap " at the promontory of Leucas is well known.   A man used to be cast from it every year ; but all possible means were taken to make his fall easy and to save him.

the dashing wave; often the god knowingly plunged his back into the billows, that she might cling the closer to his neck. On reaching the shore, Jupiter stood without any horns, and the bull was turned into the god. The bull passed into the sky: thou, Sidonian damsel, wast got with child by Jupiter, and a third part of the earth doth bear thy name. Others say that this constellation is the Pharian heifer, which from a human being was made a cow, and from a cow was made a goddess.[a]

621 Then, too, the Virgin[b] is wont to throw the rush-made effigies of ancient men from the oaken bridge. There is an old tradition, that when the land was called Saturnia these words were spoken by sooth-saying Jove: "Ye clans, cast into the water of the Tuscan river two bodies as a sacrifice to the Ancient who bears the sickle." The gloomy rite was performed, so runs the tale, in the Leucadian manner[c] every year, until the Tirynthian hero came to these fields; he cast men of straw into the water, and now dummies are thrown after the example set by Hercules. Some think that the young men used to hurl the feeble old men from the bridges,[d] in order that they themselves alone should have the vote. He who believes that after sixty years men were put to death, accuses our forefathers of a wicked crime. "O Tiber, inform me of the truth: thy bank is older than the city: thou canst well know the origin of the rite." The Tiber raised his reed-crowned head from the mid channel, and opened his hoarse mouth to utter these words: "These regions I have seen when they were solitary grass-lands

[d] The *pontes* here are the raised passages, through which voters used to be ushered into the *septa* (i. 53).

640 pascebat sparsas utraque ripa boves,
et quem nunc gentes Tiberim noruntque timentque,
tunc etiam pecori despiciendus eram.
Arcadis Evandri nomen tibi saepe refertur :
ille meas remis advena torsit aquas.
645 venit et Alcides, turba comitatus Achiva
(Albula, si memini, tunc mihi nomen erat):
excipit hospitio iuvenem Pallantius heros,
et tandem Caco debita poena venit.
victor abit secumque boves, Erytheïda praedam,
650 abstrahit. at comites longius ire negant
(magnaque pars horum desertis venerat Argis) :
montibus his ponunt spemque laremque suum.
saepe tamen patriae dulci tanguntur amore,
atque aliquis moriens hoc breve mandat opus :
655 ' mittite me in Tiberim, Tiberinis vectus ut undis
litus ad Inachium pulvis inanis eam.'
displicet heredi mandati cura sepulchri :
mortuus Ausonia conditur hospes humo,
scirpea pro domino Tiberi iactatur imago,
660 ut repetat Graias per freta longa domos.''
hactenus, et subiit vivo rorantia saxo
antra : leves cursum sustinuistis aquae.

15 G EID · NP   16. HF   17. AC
18. BC   19. CC

Clare nepos Atlantis, ades, quem montibus olim
edidit Arcadiis Pleïas una Iovi,

ᵃ See i. 469, iv. 65.   ᵇ See ii. 389.
ᶜ Evander, born at Pallantium in Arcadia.
ᵈ See above, i. 550.
ᵉ Mercury ; he was worshipped by merchants at Rome, as
the patron of gain. See above, l. 104. So the Greek Hermes
of commerce, Ἐμπολαῖος.

without any city walls: scattered kine pastured on either bank; and I, the Tiber, whom the nations now both know and fear, was then a thing to be despised even by cattle. You often hear mention of the name of Arcadian Evander [a]: he came from far and churned my waters with his oars. Alcides also came, attended by a troop of Greeks. At that time, if I remember aright, my name was Albula.[b] The Pallantian hero [c] received him hospitably; and Cacus [d] got at last the punishment he deserved. The victorious Hercules departed and carried off with him the kine, the booty he had taken from Erythea. But his companions refused to go farther: a great part of them had come from Argos, which they abandoned. On these hills they set their hope and their home; yet were they often touched by the sweet love of their native land, and one of them in dying gave this brief charge: ' Throw me into the Tiber, that, borne upon his waves, my empty dust may pass to the Inachian shore.' His heir disliked the charge of sepulture thus laid on him: the dead stranger was buried in Ausonian ground, and an effigy of rushes was thrown into the Tiber instead of him, that it might return to his Greek home across the waters wide." Thus far did Tiber speak, then passed into the dripping cave of living rock: ye nimble waters checked your flow.

Idus. 15th

663 Come, thou famed grandson [e] of Atlas, thou whom of old upon the Arcadian mountains one of the Pleiads bore to Jupiter. Thou arbiter of peace

665 pacis et armorum superis imisque deorum
    arbiter, alato qui pede carpis iter,
laete lyrae pulsu, nitida quoque laete palaestra,
    quo didicit culte lingua docente loqui,
templa tibi posuere patres spectantia Circum
670   Idibus : ex illo est haec tibi festa dies.
te, quicumque suas profitentur vendere merces,
    ture dato, tribuas ut sibi lucra, rogant.
est aqua Mercurii portae vicina Capenae ;
    si iuvat expertis credere, numen habet.
675 huc venit incinctus tunica mercator et urna
    purus suffita, quam ferat, haurit aquam.
uda fit hinc laurus, lauro sparguntur ab uda
    omnia, quae dominos sunt habitura novos ;
spargit et ipse suos lauro rorante capillos
680   et peragit solita fallere voce preces :
" ablue praeteriti periuria temporis," inquit
    " ablue praeteritae perfida verba die.
sive ego te feci testem falsove citavi
    non audituri numina magna Iovis,
685 sive deum prudens alium divamve fefelli,
    abstulerint celeres improba verba Noti,
et pateant veniente die periuria nobis,
    nec curent superi si qua locutus ero.
da modo lucra mihi, da facto gaudia lucro,
690   et fac, ut emptori verba dedisse iuvet."
talia Mercurius poscentem ridet ab alto,
    se memor Ortygias surripuisse boves.

---

[a] 495 B.C.
[b] Belonging to Apollo, who was born in Delos (Ortygia).

and war to gods above and gods below, thou who
dost ply thy way on winged foot; thou who dost
delight in the music of the lyre, and dost delight
too in the wrestling-school, glistening with oil; thou
by whose instruction the tongue learns to discourse
elegantly, the senate founded for thee on the Ides[a]
a temple looking towards the Circus: since then
the day has been thy festival. All who make a
business of selling their wares give thee incense and
beg that thou wouldst grant them gain. There is
a water of Mercury near the Capene Gate: if you
care to take the word of those who have tried it,
there is a divinity in the water. Hither comes the
merchant with his tunic girt up, and, ceremonially
pure, draws water in a fumigated jar to carry it
away. With the water he wets a laurel bough, and
with the wet bough he sprinkles all the goods that
soon are to change owners; he sprinkles, too, his own
hair with the dripping laurel and recites prayers in
a voice accustomed to deceive. "Wash away the
perjuries of past time," says he, "wash away my
glozing words of the past day. Whether I have
called thee to witness, or have falsely invoked the
great divinity of Jupiter, in the expectation that he
would not hear, or whether I have knowingly taken
in vain the name of any other god or goddess, let
the swift south winds carry away the wicked words,
and may to-morrow open the door for me to fresh
perjuries, and may the gods above not care if I shall
utter any! Only grant me profits, grant me the
joy of profit made, and see to it that I enjoy cheating
the buyer!" At such prayers Mercury laughs from
on high, remembering that he himself stole the
Ortygian[b] kine.

OVID

20. DC

At mihi pande, precor, tanto meliora petenti,
    in Geminos ex quo tempore Phoebus eat.
695 " cum totidem de mense dies superesse videbis,
    quot sunt Herculei facta laboris " ait.
" dic " ego respondi " causam mihi sideris huius."
    causam facundo reddidit ore deus :
" abstulerant raptas Phoeben Phoebesque sororem
700   Tyndaridae fratres, hic eques, ille pugil.
bella parant repetuntque suas et frater et Idas,
    Leucippo fieri pactus uterque gener.
his amor, ut repetant, illis, ut reddere nolint,
    suadet ; et ex causa pugnat uterque pari.
705 effugere Oebalidae cursu potuere sequentes,
    sed visum celeri vincere turpe fuga.
liber ab arboribus locus est, apta area pugnae :
    constiterant illic : nomen Aphidna loco.
pectora traiectus Lynceo Castor ab ense
710   non expectato volnere pressit humum.
ultor adest Pollux et Lyncea perforat hasta,
    qua cervix humeros continuata premit.
ibat in hunc Idas vixque est Iovis igne repulsus,
    tela tamen dextrae fulmine rapta negant.
715 iamque tibi, Pollux, caelum sublime patebat,
    cum ' mea ' dixisti ' percipe verba, pater :
quod mihi das uni caelum, partire duobus :

---

a Castor (horseman) and Pollux (boxer), sons of Tyndareus,
carried off Phoebe and Hilaira, daughters of Leucippus.
betrothed to Idas and Lynceus. Oebalus was father of
Tyndareus.

XIII. Kal. Ivn. 20th

693 But I put up a far better prayer. Unfold to
me, I beseech thee, at what time Phoebus passes
into the sign of the Twins. " When thou shalt see,"
he answered, " that as many days of the month
remain over as are the labours of Hercules." " Tell
me," I replied, " the cause of this constellation."
The god in answer explained the cause in eloquent
speech. The brother Tyndarids, the one a horseman,
the other a boxer, had ravished and carried away
Phoebe and Phoebe's sister.[a] Idas and his brother
prepare for war and demand the restitution of
their brides; for both of them had covenanted
with Leucippus to be his sons-in-law. Love
prompts the one pair to demand the restitution,
the other to refuse it; each pair is spurred on to
fight by the like motive. The Oebalids might have
escaped their pursuers by superior speed; but it
seemed base to win by rapid flight. There is a
place free from trees, a suitable ground for a fight:
they took their stand there: the name of the place
is Aphidna. Pierced through the breast by the
sword of Lynceus—a wound he had not looked for
—Castor fell to the ground. Pollux comes up to
avenge him, and runs Lynceus through with his
spear at the point where the neck joins on to and
presses upon the shoulders. Idas attacked him,
and scarcely was repulsed by the fire of Jupiter;
yet they say that his weapon was not wrested from
his right hand by the thunderbolt. And already
the lofty heaven opened its door for thee, Pollux,
when thou saidst, " Hear my words, O Father.
The heaven that thou dost give to me alone, O

313

dimidium toto munere maius erit.'
dixit et alterna fratrem statione redemit.
720   utile sollicitae sidus utrumque rati."

21. E AGON · NP

Ad Ianum redeat, qui quaerit, Agonia quid sint :
quae tamen in fastis hoc quoque tempus habent.

22. FN

Nocte sequente diem canis Erigoneïus exit:
est alio signi reddita causa loco.

23. G TVB · NP

725 Proxima Volcani lux est, Tubilustria dicunt ƚ
lustrantur purae, quas facit ille, tubae.

24. HQ · R · C · F

Quattuor inde notis locus est, quibus ordine lectis
vel mos sacrorum vel fuga regis inest.

---

^a Pollux was born immortal, but Castor mortal ; hence
Pollux can offer his price and share his immortality with
Castor. They were worshipped by sailors, as harbingers of
calm.

^b See i. 317.

^c Sirius : true morning rising was on July 19 ; apparent,
August 2.   ^d See iii. 849.

^e This was to have come later, but the poem was never
finished.

share between us two; one-half the gift will be greater than the whole." He spoke, and redeemed his brother from death by changing places with him alternately. Both stars are helpful to the storm-tossed bark.[a]

XII. KAL.   21st

[721] He who would learn what the Agonia are, may turn back to January, though they have a place in the calendar at this season.[b]

XI. KAL.   22nd

[723] In the night that follows the day the dog of Erigone rises[c]: I have given the explanation of this constellation in another place.[d]

X. KAL.   23rd

[725] The next day belongs to Vulcan; they call it Tubilustria.[e] The trumpets which he makes are then cleansed and purified.

IX. KAL.   24th

[727] The next place is marked by four letters, which, read in order, signify either the custom of the sacred rites or the Flight of the King.[f]

[f] " Quando Rex Comitiavit Fas." The Regifugium was on February 24. The alternative wrongly suggested by Ovid is " Quod Rex Comitio Fugerat." See above, i. 54 note.

OVID

Nec te praetereo, populi Fortuna potentis
730   Publica, cui templum luce sequente datum est.
hanc ubi dives aquis acceperit Amphitrite,
grata Iovi fulvae rostra videbis avis.

Auferet ex oculis veniens aurora Booten,
continuaque die sidus Hyantis erit.

---

^a The Eagle : only one day too late.

VIII. Kal. 25th

729 Nor will I pass thee over, thou Public Fortune of the powerful people, to whom a temple was dedicated next day. When that day shall have sunk into Amphitrite's wealth of waters, thou wilt see the beak of the tawny bird, dear to Jupiter.[a]

VII. Kal. 26th

733 The coming morn will remove Bootes from thy sight, and next day the constellation of Hyas will be visible.

LIBER SEXTUS

Hic quoque mensis habet dubias in nomine causas,
    quae placeant, positis omnibus ipse leges.
facta canam ; sed erunt qui me finxisse loquantur
    nullaque mortali numina visa putent.
5 est deus in nobis ; agitante calescimus illo :
    impetus hic sacrae semina mentis habet.
fas mihi praecipue voltus vidisse deorum,
    vel quia sum vates, vel quia sacra cano.
est nemus arboribus densum, secretus ab omni
10   voce locus, si non obstreperetur aquis.
hic ego quaerebam, coepti quae mensis origo
    esset, et in cura nominis huius eram.
ecce deas vidi, non quas praeceptor arandi
    viderat, Ascraeas cum sequeretur oves,
15 nec quas Priamides in aquosae vallibus Idae
    contulit : ex illis sed tamen una fuit.
ex illis fuit una, sui germana mariti ;
    haec erat (agnovi) quae stat in arce Iovis.
horrueram tacitoque animum pallore fatebar ;
20   tum dea, quos fecit, sustulit ipsa metus.
namque ait " o vates, Romani conditor anni,

---

   a Hesiod of Ascra : *Theogonia* 22.
   b The Judgement of Paris, on " many-fountained Ida,"
Ἴδη πολυπίδαξ. This *una* is Juno, " Iovis et soror et coniux,"
Virg. *Aen.* i. 46. The great temple on the Capitol contained
318

BOOK VI

THE explanations of this month's name also are doubtful. I will state them all, and you shall choose which you please. I'll sing the truth, but some will say I lied, and think that no deities were ever seen by mortal. There is a god within us. It is when he stirs us that our bosom warms; it is his impulse that sows the seeds of inspiration. I have a peculiar right to see the faces of the gods, whether because I am a bard, or because I sing of sacred things. There is a grove where trees grow thick, a spot sequestered from every sound except the purl of water. There I was musing on what might be the origin of the month just begun, and was meditating on its name. Lo, I beheld the goddesses, but not those whom the teacher of ploughing beheld when he followed his Ascraean sheep [a]; nor those whom Priam's son compared in watery Ida's dells; [b] yet one there was of these. Of these there was one, the sister of her husband: she it was, I recognized, who stands within Jove's citadel. I shivered, and, speechless though I was, my pallid hue betrayed my feeling; then the goddess herself removed the fears she had inspired. For she said, " O poet, minstrel of the Roman year,

three shrines, dedicated to Jupiter, Juno, and Minerva. Compare ll. 52, 73, below.

ause per exiguos magna referre modos,
ius tibi fecisti numen caeleste videndi,
   cum placuit numeris condere festa tuis.
25 ne tamen ignores volgique errore traharis,
   Iunius a nostro nomine nomen habet.
est aliquid nupsisse Iovi, Iovis esse sororem :
   fratre magis, dubito, glorier, anne viro.
si genus aspicitur, Saturnum prima parentem
30   feci, Saturni sors ego prima fui.
a patre dicta meo quondam Saturnia Roma est :
   haec illi a caelo proxima terra fuit.
si torus in pretio est, dicor matrona Tonantis,
   iunctaque Tarpeio sunt mea templa Iovi.
35 an potuit Maio paelex dare nomina mensi,
   hic honor in nobis invidiosus erit ?
cur igitur regina vocor principesque dearum ?
   aurea cur dextrae sceptra dedere meae ?
an facient mensem luces, Lucinaque ab illis
40   dicar et a nullo nomina mense traham ?
tum me paeniteat posuisse fideliter iras
   in genus Electrae Dardaniamque domum.
causa duplex irae : rapto Ganymede dolebam,
   forma quoque Idaeo iudice victa mea est.
45 paeniteat, quod non foveo Carthaginis arces,
   cum mea sint illo currus et arma loco :
paeniteat Sparten Argosque measque Mycenas
   et veterem Latio supposuisse Samon :
adde senem Tatium Iunonicolasque Faliscos,
50   quos ego Romanis succubuisse tuli.

---

    a Dardanus, son of Electra, by Zeus.
    b Virgil, *Aen.* i. 12-18 "hic illius arma, hic currus fuit."
    c He alludes to Juno Curitis, Curritis, or Quiritis, whose worship Titus Tatius, Sabine king, is said to have introduced at Rome, setting up a table in her honour in each *curia.*

thou who hast dared to chronicle great things in
slender couplets, thou hast won for thyself the right
to look upon a celestial divinity by undertaking to
celebrate the festivals in thy numbers. But lest
thou should be ignorant and led astray by vulgar
error, know that June takes its name from mine.
It is something to have married Jupiter and to be
Jupiter's sister. I doubt whether I am prouder of
my brother or of my husband. If descent is considered, I was the first to call Saturn by the name
of father : I was the first child whom fate bestowed
on him. Rome was once named Saturnia after
my sire : this land was the next he came to after
heaven. If the marriage-bed counts for much, I
am called the consort of the Thunderer, and my
temple is joined to that of Tarpeian Jupiter. If a
leman could give her name to the month of May,
shall a like honour be grudged to me ? To what
purpose, then, am I called Queen and chief of
goddesses ? Why did they put a golden sceptre
in my right hand ? Shall the days (*luces*) make up
a month and I be called Lucina after them, and
yet shall I take a name from not a single month ?
Then indeed might I repent of having loyally laid
aside my anger at the offspring of Electra and the
Dardanian house.[a] I had a double cause of anger :
I fretted at the rape of Ganymede, and my beauty
was misprized by the Idaean judge. It might repent
me that I cherish not the battlements of Carthage,
since my chariot and arms are there.[b] It might
repent me that I have laid Sparta, and Argos, and
my Mycenae, and ancient Samos, under the heel of
Latium ; add to these old Tatius,[c] and the Faliscans,
who worship Juno, and whom I nevertheless suffered

M

sed neque paeniteat, nec gens mihi carior ulla est :
    hic colar, hic teneam cum Iove templa meo.
ipse mihi Mavors ' commendo moenia ' dixit
    ' haec tibi. tu pollens urbe nepotis eris.'
55 dicta fides sequitur : centum celebramur in aris,
    nec levior quovis est mihi mensis honor.
nec tamen hunc nobis tantummodo praestat honorem
    Roma : suburbani dant mihi munus idem.
inspice, quos habeat nemoralis Aricia fastos
60   et populus Laurens Lanuviumque meum ;
est illic mensis Iunonius.   inspice Tibur
    et Praenestinae moenia sacra deae ;
Iunonale leges tempus.   nec Romulus illas
    condidit : at nostri Roma nepotis erat."
65 finierat Iuno. respeximus : Herculis uxor
    stabat, et in voltu signa vigoris erant.
" non ego, si toto mater me cedere caelo
    iusserit, invita matre morabor " ait.
" nunc quoque non luctor de nomine temporis huius
70   blandior et partes paene rogantis ago
remque mei iuris malim tenuisse precando,
    et faveas causae forsitan ipse meae.
aurea possedit socio Capitolia templo
    mater et, ut debet, cum Iove summa tenet.
75 at decus omne mihi contingit origine mensis :
    unicus est, de quo sollicitamur, honor.
quid grave, si titulum mensis, Romane, dedisti
    Herculis uxori, posteritasque memor ?

ᵃ Called Junonius at Aricia and Praeneste.
ᵇ Hebe, daughter of Zeus and Hera, whom he thinks of
by the Latin name Iuventas.

to succumb to the Romans. Yet let me not repent, for there is no people dearer to me : here may I be worshipped, here may I occupy the temple with my own Jupiter. Mavors himself hath said to me, ' I entrust these walls to thee. Thou shalt be mighty in the city of thy grandson.' His words have been fulfilled : I am celebrated at a hundred altars, and not the least of my honours is that of the month (named after me). Nevertheless it is not Rome alone that does me that honour : the inhabitants of neighbouring towns pay me the same compliment. Look at the calendar of woodland Aricia, and the calendars of the Laurentine folk and of my own Lanuvium ; there, too, there is a month of June.ᵃ Look at Tibur and at the sacred walls of the Praenestine goddess : there shalt thou read of Juno's season. Yet Romulus did not found these towns ; but Rome was the city of my grandson."

⁶⁵ So Juno ended. I looked back. The wife of Hercules stood by, and in her face were signs of vigour.ᵇ " If my mother were to bid me retire from heaven outright," quoth she, " I would not tarry against my mother's will. Now, too, I do not contend about the name of this season. I coax, and I act the part almost of a petitioner, and I should prefer to maintain my right by prayer alone. Thou thyself mayest haply favour my cause. My mother owns the golden Capitol, where she shares the temple, and, as is right, occupies the summit along with Jupiter. But all my glory comes from the naming of the month ; the honour about which they tease me is the only one I enjoy. What harm was it if thou didst, O Roman, bestow the title of a month upon the wife of Hercules, and if posterity

323

haec quoque terra aliquid debet mihi nomine magni
80   coniugis ; huc captas appulit ille boves,
hic male defensus flammis et dote paterna
    Cacus Aventinam sanguine tinxit humum.
ad propiora vocor. populum digessit ab annis
    Romulus, in partes distribuitque duas :
85 haec dare consilium, pugnare paratior illa est ;
    haec aetas bellum suadet, at illa gerit.
sic statuit mensesque nota secrevit eadem :
    Iunius est iuvenum ; qui fuit ante, senum.''
dixit. et in litem studio certaminis issent,
90   atque ira pietas dissimulata foret :
venit Apollinea longas Concordia lauro
    nexa comas, placidi numen opusque ducis.
haec ubi narravit Tatium fortemque Quirinum
    binaque cum populis regna coisse suis
95 et lare communi soceros generosque receptos,
    " his nomen iunctis Iunius " inquit " habet.''
dicta triplex causa est. at vos ignoscite, divae :
    res est arbitrio non dirimenda meo.
ite pares a me. perierunt iudice formae
100   Pergama : plus laedunt, quam iuvat una, duae.

1. [HK · IVN ·]N

Prima dies tibi, Carna, datur. dea cardinis haec est :
    numine clausa aperit, claudit aperta suo.

---

    a See i. 543 ff.   *b* Compare v. 59.
    c See i. 637-650.   *d* See iii. 195-228.
    e Probably the name is derived from *caro, carnis,* " flesh,"
but Ovid has confounded her with *Cardea,* goddess of hinges,
as if from *cardo.*

remembered and ratified the gift? This land also owes me something on account of my great husband. Hither he drove the captured kine *ᵃ* : here Cacus, ill protected by the flames, his father's gift, dyed with his blood the soil of the Aventine. But I am called to nearer themes. Romulus divided and distributed the people into two parts according to their years. The one was readier to give counsel, the other to fight ; the one age advised war, the other waged it. So he decreed, and he distinguished the months by the same token. June is the month of the young (*iuvenes*) ; the preceding is the month of the old." *ᵇ*

⁸⁹ So she spoke, and in the heat of rivalry the goddesses might have engaged in a dispute, wherein anger might have belied natural affection. But Concord came,*ᶜ* at once the deity and the work of the pacific chief, her long tresses twined with Apollo's laurel. When she had told how Tatius and brave Quirinus, and their two kingdoms and peoples, had united in one, and how fathers-in-law and sons-in-law were received in a common home, " The month of June," quoth she, " gets its name from their junction." *ᵈ*

⁹⁷ Thus were three causes pleaded. But pardon me, ye goddesses ; the matter is not one to be decided by my judgement. Depart from me all equal. Pergamum was ruined by him who adjudged the prize of beauty : two goddesses mar more than one can make.

KAL. IVN. 1st

¹⁰¹ The first day is given to thee, Carna.*ᵉ* She is the goddess of the hinge : by her divine power she opens what is closed, and closes what is open.

unde datas habeat vires, obscurior aevo
    fama, sed e nostro carmine certus eris.
105 adiacet antiquus Tiberino lucus Helerni:
    pontifices illuc nunc quoque sacra ferunt.
inda sata est nymphe (Cranen[1] dixere priores)
    nequiquam multis saepe petita procis.
rura sequi iaculisque feras agitare solebat
110   nodosasque cava tendere valle plagas.
non habuit pharetram, Phoebi tamen esse sororem
    credebant; nec erat, Phoebe, pudenda tibi.
huic aliquis iuvenum dixisset amantia verba,
    reddebat tales protinus illa sonos:
115 " haec loca lucis habent nimis et cum luce pudoris:
    si secreta magis ducis in antra, sequor."
credulus ante ut iit, frutices haec nacta resistit
    et latet et nullo est invenienda modo.
viderat hanc Ianus visaeque cupidine captus
120   ad duram verbis mollibus usus erat.
nympha iubet quaeri de more remotius antrum
    utque comes sequitur destituitque ducem.
stulta! videt Ianus, quae post sua terga gerantur:
    nil agis, et latebras respicit ille tuas.
125 nil agis, en! dixi: nam te sub rupe latentem
    occupat amplexu speque potitus ait:
" ius pro concubitu nostro tibi cardinis esto:
    hoc pretium positae virginitatis habe."
sic fatus spinam, qua tristes pellere posset
130   a foribus noxas (haec erat alba), dedit.
sunt avidae volucres, non quae Phineïa mensis

---

[1] cranen U^2: grannen U^1: granen m^2: granem M:
gramen Xm^1: ganien Dm^2: cranaen *Merkel*.

---

[a] See ii. 67.
[b] Branches of whitethorn, or buckthorn, kept out witches,
and protected against wandering ghosts. See below, l. 165.

Time has dimmed the tradition which sets forth how she acquired the powers she owns, but you shall learn it from my song. Near to the Tiber lies an ancient grove of Helernus;[a] the pontiffs still bring sacrifices thither. There a nymph was born (men of old named her Crane), often wooed in vain by many suitors. Her wont it was to scour the countryside and chase the wild beasts with her darts, and in the hollow vale to stretch the knotty nets. No quiver had she, yet they thought that she was Phoebus' sister; and, Phoebus, thou needst not have been ashamed of her. If any youth spoke to her words of love, she straightway made him this answer : " In this place there is too much of light, and with the light too much of shame ; if thou wilt lead to a more retired cave, I'll follow." While he confidingly went in front, she no sooner reached the bushes than she halted, and hid herself, and was nowise to be found. Janus had seen her, and the sight had roused his passion ; to the hard-hearted nymph he used soft words. The nymph as usual bade him seek a more sequestered cave, and she pretended to follow at his heels, but deserted her leader. Fond fool! Janus sees what goes on behind his back ; vain is thine effort ; he sees thy hiding-place behind him. Vain is thine effort, lo ! said I. For he caught thee in his embrace as thou didst lurk beneath a rock, and having worked his will he said : " In return for our dalliance be thine the control of hinges ; take that for the price of thy lost maidenhood." So saying, he gave her a thorn—and white it was—wherewith she could repel all doleful harm from doors.[b] There are greedy birds, not those that cheated Phineus' maw of its

327

guttura fraudabant, sed genus inde trahunt :
grande caput, stantes oculi, rostra apta rapinis,
canities pinnis, unguibus hamus inest.
135 nocte volant puerosque petunt nutricis egentes
et vitiant cunis corpora rapta suis.
carpere dicuntur lactentia viscera rostris
et plenum poto sanguine guttur habent.
est illis strigibus nomen ; sed nominis huius
140   causa, quod horrendum stridere nocte solent.
sive igitur nascuntur aves, seu carmine fiunt
naeniaque in volucres Marsa figurat anus,
in thalamos venere Procae.   Proca natus in illis
praeda recens avium quinque diebus erat,
145 pectoraque exsorbent avidis infantia linguis ;
at puer infelix vagit opemque petit.
territa voce sui nutrix accurrit alumni
et rigido sectas invenit ungue genas.
quid faceret ? color oris erat, qui frondibus olim
150   esse solet seris, quas nova laesit hiems.
pervenit ad Cranen et rem docet.   illa " timorem
pone : tuus sospes " dixit " alumnus erit."
venerat ad cunas : flebant materque paterque :
" sistite vos lacrimas, ipsa medebor " ait.
155 protinus arbutea postes ter in ordine tangit
fronde, ter arbutea limina fronde notat ;
spargit aquis aditus (et aquae medicamen habebant)
extaque de porca cruda bimenstre tenet ;
atque ita " noctis aves, extis puerilibus " inquit
160   " parcite : pro parvo victima parva cadit.

---

^a The Harpies.   See Virg. *Aen.* iii. 225.
^b Marsians were famous for wizardry.
^c King of Alba Longa.

328

repast,ᵃ though from those they are descended. Big is
their head, goggle their eyes, their beaks are formed
for rapine, their wings are blotched with grey, their
claws fitted with hooks. They fly by night and attack
nurseless children, and defile their bodies, snatched
from their cradles. They are said to rend the flesh
of sucklings with their beaks, and their throats are
full of the blood which they have drunk. Screech-
owl is their name, but the reason of the name is that
they are wont to screech horribly by night. Whether,
therefore, they are born birds, or are made such by
enchantment and are nothing but beldames transformed into fowls by a Marsian ᵇ spell, they came into
the chambers of Proca.ᶜ In the chambers Proca, a
child five days old, was a fresh prey for the birds.
They sucked his infant breast with greedy tongues,
and the poor child squalled and craved help. Alarmed
by the cry of her fosterling, the nurse ran to him
and found his cheeks scored by their rigid claws.
What was she to do? The colour of the child's
face was like the common hue of late leaves
nipped by an early frost. She went to Crane and
told what had befallen. Crane said, "Lay fear
aside; thy nursling will be safe." She went to
the cradle; mother and father were weeping.
"Restrain your tears," she said, "I myself will
heal the child." Straightway she thrice touched
the doorposts, one after the other, with arbutus
leaves; thrice with arbutus leaves she marked the
threshold. She sprinkled the entrance with water
(and the water was drugged), and she held the
raw inwards of a sow just two months old. And
thus she spoke: "Ye birds of night, spare the
child's inwards: a small victim falls for a small

OVID

cor pro corde, precor, pro fibris sumite fibras.
    hanc animam vobis pro meliore damus."
sic ubi libavit, prosecta sub aethere ponit,
    quique adsint sacris, respicere illa vetat;
165 virgaque Ianalis de spina ponitur alba,
    qua lumen thalamis parva fenestra dabat.
post illud nec aves cunas violasse feruntur,
    et rediit puero, qui fuit ante, color.
pinguia cur illis gustentur larda Kalendis,
170   mixtaque cum calido sit faba farre, rogas ?
prisca dea est aliturque cibis, quibus ante solebat,
    nec petit ascitas luxuriosa dapes.
piscis adhuc illi populo sine fraude natabat,
    ostreaque in conchis tuta fuere suis.
175 nec Latium norat, quam praebet Ionia dives,
    nec quae Pygmaeo sanguine gaudet, avem;
et praeter pennas nihil in pavone placebat,
    nec tellus captas miserat ante feras.
sus erat in pretio, caesa sue festa colebant:
180   terra fabas tantum duraque farra dabat.
quae duo mixta simul sextis quicumque Kalendis
    ederit, huic laedi viscera posse negant.
arce quoque in summa Iunoni templa Monetae
    ex voto memorant facta, Camille, tuo:
185 ante domus Manli fuerat, qui Gallica quondam
    a Capitolino reppulit arma Iove.
quam bene, di magni, pugna cecidisset in illa,
    defensor solii, Iuppiter alte, tui !
vixit, ut occideret damnatus crimine regni:

---

    a Francolin (*attagen*).
    b Crane. The Cranes were said to wage war on the
Pygmies.   *c* See i. 637.
   d M. Manlius Capitolinus, 390 B.C.

child. Take, I pray ye, a heart for a heart, entrails
for entrails. This life we give you for a better
life." When she had thus sacrificed, she set the
severed inwards in the open air, and forbade those
present at the sacrifice to look back at them. A
rod of Janus, taken from the white-thorn, was placed
where a small window gave light to the chambers.
After that, it is said that the birds did not violate
the cradle, and the boy recovered his former colour.

169 You ask why fat bacon is eaten on these
Calends, and why beans are mixed with hot spelt.
She is a goddess of the olden time, and subsists upon
the foods to which she was inured before ; no
voluptuary is she to run after foreign viands. Fish
still swam unharmed by the people of that age,
and oysters were safe in their shells. Latium knew
not the fowl that rich Ionia supplies,[a] nor the bird
that delights in Pygmy blood[b] ; and in the peacock
naught but the feathers pleased, nor had the earth
before sent captured beasts. The pig was prized,
people feasted on slaughtered swine : the ground
yielded only beans and hard spelt. Whoever eats
at the same time these two foods on the Calends of
the sixth month, they affirm that nothing can hurt his
bowels.

183 They say, too, that the temple of Juno Moneta
was founded in fulfilment of thy vow, Camillus, on
the summit of the citadel[c] : formerly it had been
the house of Manlius, who once protected Capitoline
Jupiter against the Gallic arms.[d] Great gods, how
well had it been for him if in that fight he had fallen
in defence of thy throne, O Jupiter on high ! He
lived to perish, condemned on a charge of aiming at

331

OVID

190   hunc illi titulum longa senecta dabat.
    lux eadem Marti festa est, quem prospicit extra
      appositum Tectae porta Capena viae.
    te quoque, Tempestas, meritam delubra fatemur,
      cum paene est Corsis obruta classis aquis.
195 haec hominum monumenta patent. si quaeritis astra,
      tunc oritur magni praepes adunca Iovis.

2. [AF]

Postera lux Hyadas, Taurinae cornua frontis,
    evocat, et multa terra madescit aqua.

3. BC

Mane ubi bis fuerit Phoebusque iteraverit ortus
200   factaque erit posito rore bis uda seges,
hac sacrata die Tusco Bellona duello
    dicitur et Latio prospera semper adest.
Appius est auctor, Pyrrho qui pace negata
    multum animo vidit, lumine captus erat.
205 prospicit a templo summum brevis area Circum,
    est ibi non parvae parva columna notae :

---

    a Probably a colonnade rising along the side of the Appian
way.
    b Dedicated by L. Corn. Scipio, 259 B.C., after expelling
the Carthaginians from Corsica.
    c True evening rising was on June 3.
    d Vowed by Appius Claudius Caecus in 296 B.C., when he
as consul conquered the Etruscan and Samnite united forces.
    e After the defeat of 280 B.C., Pyrrhus offered honourable
332

the crown : that was the title that length of years
reserved for him.

191 The same day is a festival of Mars, whose
temple, set beside the Covered Way,[a] is seen afar
without the walls from the Capene Gate. Thou, too,
O Storm, didst deserve a shrine, by our avowal,
what time the fleet was nearly overwhelmed in
Corsican waters.[b] These monuments set up by men
are plain for all to see : if you look for stars, the bird
of great Jupiter with its hooked talons then rises.[c]

IV. Non.   2nd

197 The next day calls up the Hyades, which form
the horns of the Bull's forehead ; and the earth is
soaked with heavy rain.

III. Non.   3rd

199 When twice the morning shall have passed, and
twice Phoebus shall have repeated his rising, and
twice the crops shall have been wetted by the fallen
dew, on that day Bellona is said to have been
consecrated in the Tuscan war,[d] and ever she comes
gracious to Latium. Her founder was Appius, who,
when peace was refused to Pyrrhus, saw clearly in
his mind, though from the light of day he was cut
off.[e] A small open space commands from the temple
a view of the top of the Circus. There stands a little
pillar of no little note. From it the custom is to hurl

terms of peace : but Appius Claudius the Blind had himself
carried into the Senate, and persuaded them to refuse.

hinc solet hasta manu belli praenuntia mitti,
　　in regem et gentes cum placet arma capi.

4. CC

Altera pars Circi Custode sub Hercule tuta est :
210　　quod deus Euboico carmine munus habet.
　　muneris est tempus, qui Nonas Lucifer ante est :
　　　si titulum quaeris, Sulla probavit opus.

5. D NON

Quaerebam, Nonas Sanco Fidione referrem,
　　an tibi, Semo pater ; tum mihi Sancus ait :
215 " cuicumque ex istis dederis, ego munus habebo :
　　nomina terna fero : sic voluere Cures."
　　hunc igitur veteres donarunt aede Sabini
　　　inque Quirinali constituere iugo.

6. EN

Est mihi (sitque, precor, nostris diuturnior annis)
220　　filia, qua felix sospite semper ero.
　　hanc ego cum vellem genero dare, tempora taedis
　　　apta requirebam, quaeque cavenda forent :
　　tum mihi post sacras monstratur Iunius Idus
　　　utilis et nuptis, utilis esse viris,

---

a The *fetialis*, or sacred herald, advanced to the enemy
boundary, and threw over it a spear with the solemn words
of declaration. See Livy i. 32. When war was declared
against Pyrrhus, a soldier of Pyrrhus was caught, and compelled to buy a patch of land, and there a pillar was set up
334

by hand a spear, war's harbinger, when it has been resolved to take arms against a king and peoples.[a]

Pr. Non. 4th

[209] The other part of the Circus is protected by Guardian Hercules: the god holds office in virtue of the Euboean oracle.[b] The time of his taking office is the day before the Nones. If you ask about the inscription, it was Sulla who approved the work.

Non. 5th

[213] I inquired whether I should refer the Nones to Sancus, or to Fidius, or to thee, Father Semo ; then Sancus said to me : "To whomsoever of them thou mayest give it, the honour will still be mine : I bear the three names : so willed the people of Cures." Accordingly the Sabines of old bestowed on him a shrine, and established it on the Quirinal hill.[c]

VIII. Id. 6th

[219] I have a daughter, and I pray she may outlive me ; I shall always be happy while she survives. When I would give her to a son-in-law, I inquired what times were suitable for weddings and what should be avoided. Then it was shown to me that June after the sacred Ides is good for brides and good for bridegrooms, but the first part of this month was

before Bellona's temple. This was taken to represent the enemy territory in future declarations of war.

[b] The Sibylline Books ; the Sibyl being of Cumae, founded by Euboea.

[c] See App. p. 429.

225 primaque pars huius thalamis aliena reperta est;
    nam mihi sic coniunx sancta Dialis ait :
" donec ab Iliaca placidus purgamina Vesta
    detulerit flavis in mare Thybris aquis,
non mihi dentosa crinem depectere buxo,
230   non ungues ferro subsecuisse licet,
non tetigisse virum, quamvis Iovis ille sacerdos,
    quamvis perpetua sit mihi lege datus.
tu quoque ne propera. melius tua filia nubet,
    ignea cum pura Vesta nitebit humo."

7. FN

235 Tertia post Nonas removere Lycaona Phoebe
    fertur, et a tergo non habet Ursa metum.
tunc ego me memini ludos in gramine Campi
    aspicere et dici, lubrice Thybri, tuos.
festa dies illis, qui lina madentia ducunt,
240   quique tegunt parvis aera recurva cibis.

8. GN MENTI · IN · CAPIT

Mens quoque numen habet. Mentis delubra videmus
    vota metu belli, perfide Poene, tui.
Poene rebellaras, et leto consulis omnes
    attoniti Mauras pertimuere manus.
245 spem metus expulerat, cum Menti vota senatus
    suscipit, et melior protinus illa venit.

---

   a See vi. 713 note. The Flamen Dialis and his wife were
subjected to many strange taboos.
   b Because Arctophylax, the Bearward, had set. Arcturus
was identified with Arcas, grandson of Lycaon, whose
daughter was Callisto. Lycaon is here put for him.

found to be unsuitable for marriages; for the holy wife of the Flamen Dialis spoke thus to me : " Until the calm Tiber shall have carried down to the sea on its yellow current the filth from the temple of Ilian Vesta, it is not lawful for me to comb down my hair with a toothed comb, or cut my nails with iron, or touch my husband, though he is the priest of Jupiter, and though he was given to me for life. Thou, too, be in no hurry ; thy daughter will better wed when Vesta's fire shall shine on a clean floor." [a]

VII. Id.   7th

[235] On the third morn after the Nones it is said that Phoebe chases away (the grandson of) Lycaon, and the Bear has none behind her to fear.[b] Then I remember that I saw games held on the sward of the Field of Mars, and that they were named thine, O smooth Tiber. The day is a festival for those who draw their dripping lines and hide their bronze hooks under little baits.

VI. Id.   8th

[241] The mind also has its divinity. We see that a sanctuary was vowed to Mind during the terror of thy war, thou treacherous Carthaginian. Thou didst renew the war, thou Carthaginian, and, thunderstruck by the consul's death, all dreaded the Moorish bands. Fear had driven out hope, when the Senate made vows to Mind,[c] and straightway she came better disposed. The day on which the vows were

---

[a] After the defeat at Lake Trasimene, 217 B.C.

337

aspicit instantes mediis sex lucibus Idus
illa dies, qua sunt vota soluta deae.

9. H VEST FER · VESTAE

Vesta, fave ! tibi nunc operata resolvimus ora,
250   ad tua si nobis sacra venire licet.
in prece totus eram : caelestia numina sensi,
laetaque purpurea luce refulsit humus.
non equidem vidi (valeant mendacia vatum)
te, dea, nec fueras aspicienda viro ;
255 sed quae nescieram, quorumque errore tenebar,
cognita sunt nullo praecipiente mihi.
dena quater memorant habuisse Parilia Romam,
cum flammae custos aede recepta dea est,
regis opus placidi, quo non metuentius ullum
260   numinis ingenium terra Sabina tulit.
quae nunc aere vides, stipula tum tecta videres,
et paries lento vimine textus erat.
hic locus exiguus, qui sustinet atria Vestae,
tunc erat intonsi regia magna Numae.
265 forma tamen templi, quae nunc manet, ante fuisse
dicitur, et formae causa probanda subest.
Vesta eadem est et terra : subest vigil ignis utrique :
significant sedem terra focusque suam.
terra pilae similis nullo fulcimine nixa,
270   aëre subiecto tam grave pendet onus.
[ipsa volubilitas libratum sustinet orbem,
quique premat partes, angulus omnis abest,
cumque sit in media rerum regione locata
et tangat nullum plusve minusve latus,
275 ni convexa foret, parti vicinior esset,

---

[a] See iv. 732, and Appendix, p. 430.
[b] Numa.   [c] See Appendix, p. 431.

paid to the goddess is separated from the coming
Ides by six intermediate days.

V. Id.   9th

[249] O Vesta, grant me thy favour ! In thy service
now I ope my lips, if it is lawful for me to come to
thy sacred rites. I was wrapt up in prayer ; I felt
the heavenly deity, and the glad ground gleamed with
a purple light. Not indeed that I saw thee, O goddess
(far from me be the lies of poets !), nor was it meet
that a man should look upon thee ; but my ignorance
was enlightened and my errors corrected without
the help of an instructor. They say that Rome had
forty times celebrated the Parilia [a] when the goddess,
Guardian of Fire, was received in her temple ; it was
the work of that peaceful king, than whom no man
of more god-fearing temper was ever born in Sabine
land.[b] The buildings which now you see roofed
with bronze you might then have seen roofed with
thatch, and the walls were woven of tough osiers.
This little spot, which now supports the Hall of
Vesta, was then the great palace of unshorn Numa.
Yet the shape of the temple, as it now exists, is
said to have been its shape of old, and it is based
on a sound reason.[c] Vesta is the same as the
Earth ; under both of them is a perpetual fire ; the
earth and the hearth are symbols of the home. The
earth is like a ball, resting on no prop ; so great a
weight hangs on the air beneath it. Its own power
of rotation keeps its orb balanced ; it has no angle
which could press on any part ; and since it is placed
in the middle of the world and touches no side more
or less, if it were not convex, it would be nearer to

339

nec medium terram mundus haberet onus.
arte Syracosia suspensus in aëre clauso
    stat globus, immensi parva figura poli,]
et quantum a summis, tantum secessit ab imis
280   terra ; quod ut fiat, forma rotunda facit.
par facies templi : nullus procurrit in illo
    angulus ; a pluvio vindicat imbre tholus.
cur sit virginibus, quaeris, dea culta ministris ?
    inveniam causas hac quoque parte suas.
285 ex Ope Iunonem memorant Cereremque creatas
    semine Saturni, tertia Vesta fuit ;
utraque nupserunt, ambae peperisse feruntur,
    de tribus impatiens restitit una viri.
quid mirum, virgo si virgine laeta ministra
290   admittit castas ad sua sacra manus ?
nec tu aliud Vestam quam vivam intellege flammam,
    nataque de flamma corpora nulla vides.
iure igitur virgo est, quae semina nulla remittit
    nec capit et comites virginitatis amat.
295 esse diu stultus Vestae simulacra putavi,
    mox didici curvo nulla subesse tholo :
ignis inextinctus templo celatur in illo,
    effigiem nullam Vesta nec ignis habet.
stat vi terra sua : vi stando Vesta vocatur,
300   causaque par Grai nominis esse potest.
at focus a flammis et quod fovet omnia, dictus ;
    qui tamen in primis aedibus ante fuit.
hinc quoque vestibulum dici reor : inde precando

ᵃ The orrery of Archimedes, which Cicero tells us was
brought to Rome by Marcellus, the conqueror of Syracuse,
212 B.C.

ᵇ ἵστημι, ἑστάναι, confused with ἑστία.

ᶜ Ovid takes *vestibulum* as from Vesta, guessing that the

some part than to another, and the universe would not have the earth as its central weight. There stands a globe hung by Syracusan art in closed air, a small image of the vast vault of heaven, and the earth is equally distant from the top and bottom.[a] That is brought about by its round shape. The form of the temple is similar : there is no projecting angle in it ; a dome protects it from the showers of rain.

[283] You ask why the goddess is tended by virgin ministers. Of that also I will discover the true causes. They say that Juno and Ceres were born of Ops by Saturn's seed ; the third daughter was Vesta. The other two married ; both are reported to have had offspring ; of the three one remained, who refused to submit to a husband. What wonder if a virgin delights in a virgin minister and allows only chaste hands to touch her sacred things ? Conceive of Vesta as naught but the living flame, and you see that no bodies are born of flame. Rightly, therefore, is she a virgin who neither gives nor takes seeds, and she loves companions in her virginity.

[295] Long did I foolishly think that there were images of Vesta : afterwards I learned that there are none under her curved dome. An undying fire is hidden in that temple ; but there is no effigy of Vesta nor of the fire. The earth stands by its own power ; Vesta is so called from standing by power (vi stando) ; and the reason of her Greek name may be similar.[b] But the hearth (focus) is so named from the flames, and because it fosters (fovet) all things ; yet formerly it stood in the first room of the house. Hence, too, I am of opinion that the vestibule took its name ; [c] it

hearth stood there, as it did not. But he goes on as if he took it from *ve* and *stare*, " to stand apart."

OVID

praefamur Vestam, quae loca prima tenet.
305 ante focos olim scamnis considere longis
mos erat et mensae credere adesse deos;
nunc quoque, cum fiunt antiquae sacra Vacunae,
ante Vacunales stantque sedentque focos.
venit in hos annos aliquid de more vetusto:
310 fert missos Vestae pura patella cibos.
ecce coronatis panis dependet asellis,
et velant scabras florida serta molas.
sola prius furnis torrebant farra coloni
(et Fornacali sunt sua sacra deae):
315 suppositum cineri panem focus ipse parabat,
strataque erat tepido tegula quassa solo.
inde focum observat pistor dominamque focorum,
et quae pumiceas versat asella molas.
praeteream referamne tuum, rubicunde Priape,
320 dedecus? est multi fabula parva ioci.
turrigera frontem Cybele redimita corona
convocat aeternos ad sua festa deos.
convocat et satyros et, rustica numina, nymphas;
Silenus, quamvis nemo vocarat, adest.
325 nec licet et longum est epulas narrare deorum:
in multo nox est pervigilata mero.
hi temere errabant in opacae vallibus Idae,
pars iacet et molli gramine membra levat,
hi ludunt, hos somnus habet, pars brachia nectit
330 et viridem celeri ter pede pulsat humum.
Vesta iacet placidamque capit secura quietem,
sicut erat, positum caespite fulta caput.
at ruber hortorum custos nymphasque deasque
captat et errantes fertque refertque pedes.

---

a See Appendix, p. 432. *b* See ii. 525.
c Told already in i. 391–440.

is from there that in praying we begin by addressing
Vesta, who occupies the first place : it used to be
the custom of old to sit on long benches in front of
the hearth and to suppose that the gods were present
at table ; even now, when sacrifices are offered to
ancient Vacuna,*a* they stand and sit in front of her
hearths. Something of olden custom has come down
to our time : a clean platter contains the food offered
to Vesta. Lo, loaves are hung on asses decked with
wreaths, and flowery garlands veil the rough millstones. Husbandmen used formerly to toast only
spelt in the ovens, and the goddess of ovens has
her own sacred rites *b* : the hearth of itself baked the
bread that was put under the ashes, and a broken
tile was laid on the warm floor. Hence the baker
honours the hearth and the mistress of hearths and
the she-ass that turns the millstones of pumice.

319 Shall I pass over or relate thy disgrace, rubicund
Priapus ? It is a short story, but a very merry one.*c*
Cybele, whose brow is crowned with a coronet of
towers, invited the eternal gods to her feast. She
invited also the satyrs and those rural divinities, the
nymphs. Silenus came, though nobody had asked
him. It is unlawful, and it would be tedious, to
narrate the banquet of the gods : the livelong night
was passed in deep potations. Some roamed at
haphazard in the vales of shady Ida ; some lay and
stretched their limbs at ease on the soft grass ; some
played ; some slept ; some, arm linked in arm, thrice
beat with rapid foot the verdant ground. Vesta lay
and careless took her peaceful rest, just as she was,
her head low laid and propped upon a sod. But the
ruddy guardian of gardens courted nymphs and
goddesses, and to and fro he turned his roving

335 aspicit et Vestam : dubium, nymphamne putarit
    an scierit Vestam, scisse sed ipse negat.
spem capit obscenam furtimque accedere temptat
    et fert suspensos corde micante gradus.
forte senex, quo vectus erat, Silenus asellum
340   liquerat ad ripas lene sonantis aquae.
ibat, ut inciperet, longi deus Hellesponti,
    intempestivo cum rudit ille sono.
territa voce gravi surgit dea ; convolat omnis
    turba, per infestas effugit ille manus.
345 Lampsacus hoc animal solita est mactare Priapo
    fata : " asini flammis indicis exta damus."
quem tu, diva, memor de pane monilibus ornas ;
    cessat opus, vacuae conticuere molae.

Nomine quam pretio celebratior arce Tonantis,
350   dicam, Pistoris quid velit ara Iovis.
cincta premebantur trucibus Capitolia Gallis :
    fecerat obsidio iam diuturna famem.
Iuppiter ad solium superis regale vocatis
    " incipe ! " ait Marti.   protinus ille refert :
355 " scilicet ignotum est, quae sit fortuna meorum,
    et dolor hic animi voce querentis eget.
si tamen, ut referam breviter mala iuncta pudori,
    exigis : Alpino Roma sub hoste iacet.
haec est, cui fuerat promissa potentia rerum.
360   Iuppiter ? hanc terris impositurus eras ?

---

    a This refers to the capture of Rome by the Gauls, 390 B.C.,
and the siege of the Capitol.   The besieged threw out loaves
of bread, to show they were not in want.

steps. He spied Vesta too; it is doubtful whether
he took her for a nymph or knew her to be Vesta;
he himself said that he knew her not. He conceived
a wanton hope, and tried to approach her furtively;
he walked on tiptoe with throbbing heart. It
chanced that old Silenus had left the ass, on which
he rode, on the banks of a babbling brook. The
god of the long Hellespont was going to begin,
when the ass uttered an ill-timed bray. Frightened
by the deep voice, the goddess started up; the
whole troop flocked together; Priapus made his
escape between hands that would have stopped
him. Lampsacus is wont to sacrifice this animal to
Priapus, saying: "We give to the flames the inwards of the tell-tale ass." That animal, goddess,
thou dost adorn with necklaces of loaves in memory
of the event: work comes to a stop: the mills are
empty and silent.

³⁴⁹ I will explain the meaning of an altar of Baker
Jupiter, which stands on the citadel of the Thunderer
and is more famous for its name than for its value.
The Capitol was surrounded and hard pressed by
the fierce Gauls: the long siege had already
caused a famine. Having summoned the celestial
gods to his royal throne, Jupiter said to Mars,
"Begin." Straightway Mars made answer: "For-
sooth, nobody knows the plight of my people, and
this my sorrow needs to find utterance in complaint.
But if thou dost require me to declare in brief the
sad and shameful tale: Rome lies at the foot of the
Alpine foe.ᵃ Is this that Rome, O Jupiter, to which
was promised the domination of the world? is this
that Rome which thou didst purpose to make the

iamque suburbanos Etruscaque contudit arma,
    spes erat in cursu : nunc lare pulsa suo est.
vidimus ornatos aerata per atria picta
    veste triumphales occubuisse senes :
365 vidimus Iliacae transferri pignora Vestae
    sede : putant aliquos scilicet esse deos.
at si respicerent, qua vos habitatis in arce,
    totque domos vestras obsidione premi,
nil opis in cura scirent superesse deorum
370   et data sollicita tura perire manu.
atque utinam pugnae pateat locus ! arma capessant
    et, si non poterunt exsuperare, cadant.
nunc inopes victus ignavaque fata timentes
    monte suo clausos barbara turba premit."
375 tunc Venus et lituo pulcher trabeaque Quirinus
    Vestaque pro Latio multa locuta suo est.
" publica " respondit " cura est pro moenibus istis,"
    Iuppiter " et poenas Gallia victa dabit.
tu modo, quae desunt fruges, superesse putentur
380   effice, nec sedes desere, Vesta, tuas.
quodcumque est solidae Cereris, cava machina
       frangat,
    mollitamque manu duret in igne focus."
iusserat, et fratris virgo Saturnia iussis
    annuit. et mediae tempora noctis erant,
385 iam ducibus somnum dederat labor : increpat illos
    Iuppiter et sacro, quid velit, ore docet :
" surgite et in medios de summis arcibus hostes

---

a The Vestals buried some of their sacred things, and
carried away what they could : these included relics brought
from Troy. See below, l. 451, and Livy v. 40-41.
346

mistress of the earth? Already she had crushed her neighbours and the Etruscan hosts. Hope was in full career, but now she is driven from her own hearth and home. We have seen old men decked in embroidered robes—the symbol of the triumphs they had won—cut down within their bronze-lined halls. We have seen the pledges of Ilian Vesta removed from their proper seat [a]: plainly the Romans think that some gods exist. But if they were to look back to the citadel in which ye dwell, and to see so many of your homes beleaguered, they would know that the worship of the gods is of no avail, and that incense offered by an anxious hand is thrown away. And would that they could find a clear field of battle! Let them take arms, and, if they cannot conquer, then let them fall! As it is, starving and dreading a coward's death, they are shut up and pressed hard on their own hill by a barbarous mob." Then Venus and Quirinus, in the pomp of augur's staff and striped gown, and Vesta pleaded hard for their own Latium. Jupiter replied, "A general providence is charged with the defence of yonder walls. Gaul will be vanquished and will pay the penalty. Only do thou, Vesta, look to it that the corn which is lacking may be thought to abound, and do not abandon thy proper seat. Let all the grain that is yet unground be crushed in the hollow mill, let it be kneaded by hand and roasted by fire in the oven." So Jupiter commanded, and the virgin daughter of Saturn assented to her brother's command. It was the hour of midnight: now sleep had overcome the wearied leaders. Jupiter chode them, and with his sacred lips informed them of his will. "Arise and from the topmost battlements cast

OVID

mittite, quam minime tradere voltis, opem ! "
somnus abit, quaeruntque novis ambagibus acti,
390   tradere quam nolint et iubeantur opem.
esse Ceres visa est ; iaciunt Cerealia dona,
    iacta super galeas scutaque longa sonant.
posse fame vinci spes excidit. hoste repulso
    candida Pistori ponitur ara Iovi.

395 Forte revertebar festis Vestalibus illa,
    qua Nova Romano nunc via iuncta foro est.
huc pede matronam vidi descendere nudo :
    obstipui tacitus sustinuique gradum.
sensit anus vicina loci iussumque sedere
400   alloquitur quatiens voce tremente caput :
" hoc, ubi nunc fora sunt, udae tenuere paludes ;
    amne redundatis fossa madebat aquis.
Curtius ille lacus, siccas qui sustinet aras,
    nunc solida est tellus, sed lacus ante fuit.
405 qua Velabra solent in Circum ducere pompas,
    nil praeter salices cassaque canna fuit ;
saepe suburbanas rediens conviva per undas
    cantat et ad nautas ebria verba iacit.
nondum conveniens diversis iste figuris
410   nomen ab averso ceperat amne deus.

---

^a The Via Nova was as old as the time of the kings. Like
the Via Sacra (these were the only roads in Rome called *via*),
it began from the Porta Mugonia, the old gate of the Palatine
(near the arch of Titus), and ran along the N. slope of the
Palatine, behind the House of the Vestals, and descended by
a staircase to the Velabrum, lately made (*nunc*).

^b See Appendix, p. 436.

^c A place in the Forum, then dry, where in ancient times a
gulf had appeared, which could not be filled until the most
precious thing of Rome should be cast in. Marcus Curtius

348

into the midst of the foe the last resource which ye
would wish to yield." Sleep left them, and moved
by the strange riddle they inquired what resource
they were bidden to yield against their will. They
thought it must be corn. They threw down the
gifts of the Corn-goddess, which, in falling, clattered
upon the helmets and long shields of the foe. The
hope that the citadel could be reduced by famine
now vanished : the enemy was repulsed and a white
altar set up to Baker Jupiter.

395 It chanced that at the festival of Vesta I was
returning by that way which now joins the New
Way to the Roman Forum.ᵃ Hither I saw a matron
coming down barefoot : amazed I held my peace
and halted. An old woman of the neighbourhood
perceived me, and bidding me sit down she addressed me in quavering tones, shaking her head.
" This ground, where now are the forums,ᵇ was once
occupied by wet swamps : a ditch was drenched
with the water that overflowed from the river.
That Lake of Curtius,ᶜ which supports dry altars,
is now solid ground, but formerly it was a lake.
Where now the processions are wont to defile through
the Velabrum to the Circus, there was naught but
willows and hollow canes ; often the roysterer, returning home over the waters of the suburb, used to
tip a stave and rap out tipsy words at passing sailors.
Yonder god (Vertumnus),ᵈ whose name is appropriate
to various shapes, had not yet derived it from

leapt in fully armed on horseback, crying that arms and
valour were the most precious thing for Rome. The gulf
then filled up (362 B.C.).
ᵈ See Appendix, p. 438.

349

hic quoque lucus erat iuncis et harundine densus
    et pede velato non adeunda palus.
stagna recesserunt et aquas sua ripa coercet,
    siccaque nunc tellus : mos tamen ille manet."
415 reddiderat causam. " valeas, anus optima ! " dixi
    " quod superest aevi, molle sit omne, tui."

Cetera iam pridem didici puerilibus annis,
    non tamen idcirco praetereunda mihi.
moenia Dardanides nuper nova fecerat Ilus
420   (Ilus adhuc Asiae dives habebat opes) :
creditur armiferae signum caeleste Minervae
    urbis in Iliacae desiluisse iuga.
cura videre fuit, vidi templumque locumque :
    hoc superest illic, Pallada Roma tenet.
425 consulitur Smintheus lucoque obscurus opaco
    hos non mentito reddidit ore sonos :
" aetheriam servate deam, servabitis urbem :
    imperium secum transferet illa loci."
servat et inclusam tenet Ilus summa in arce,
430   curaque ad heredem Laomedonta redit.
sub Priamo servata parum : sic ipsa volebat,
    ex quo iudicio forma revicta sua est.
seu genus Adrasti, seu furtis aptus Ulixes,
    seu pius Aeneas eripuisset eam,
435 auctor in incerto, res est Romana : tuetur

---

    a The famous Palladium, the Luck of Troy, which fell
from heaven as described here, and so long as it was preserved, Troy was safe. Ulysses and Diomedes stole it (see
Ovid, *Met.* xiii. 335-356) ; but the Roman belief was, that it
remained until Aeneas brought it to Italy, and that it was
kept in the temple of Vesta at Rome.
    b Apollo Smintheus, the Mouse Apollo, named for having
destroyed a plague of mice.

damming back the river (*averso amne*). Here, too,
there was a grove overgrown with bulrushes and
reeds, and a marsh not to be trodden with booted
feet. The pools have receded, and the river confines
its water within its banks, and the ground is now
dry ; but the old custom survives." The old woman
thus explained the custom. " Farewell, good old
dame," said I ; " may what remains of life to thee
be easy all ! "

417 The rest of the tale I had learned long since
in my boyish years ; yet not on that account may I
pass it over in silence. Ilus, descendant of Dardanus,
had lately founded a new city (Ilus was still rich and
possessed the wealth of Asia) ; a celestial image of
armed Minerva is believed to have leaped down on
the hills of the Ilian city.ᵃ (I was anxious to see it :
I saw the temple and the place ; that is all that is
left there ; the image of Pallas is in Rome.) Smin-
theusᵇ was consulted, and in the dim light of his
shady grove he gave this answer with no lying lips :
" Preserve the heavenly goddess, so shall ye preserve the city. She will transfer with herself the
seat of empire." Ilus preserved the image of the
goddess and kept it shut up on the top of the
citadel ; the charge of it descended to his heir
Laomedon. In Priam's reign the image was not
well preserved. Such was the goddess's own will
ever since judgement was given against her in the
contest of beauty. Whether it was the descendant
of Adrastus,ᶜ or the guileful Ulysses, or pious Aeneas
who carried her off, the doer of the deed is uncertain ; the thing is now at Rome : Vesta guards

ᶜ Diomedes.

Vesta, quod assiduo lumine cuncta videt.
heu quantum timuere patres, quo tempore Vesta
    arsit et est tectis obruta paene suis !
flagrabant sancti sceleratis ignibus ignes,
440   mixtaque erat flammae flamma profana piae.
attonitae flebant demisso crine ministrae :
    abstulerat vires corporis ipse timor.
provolat in medium, et magna " succurrite ! " voce
    " non est auxilium flere " Metellus ait.
445 " pignora virgineis fatalia tollite palmis :
    non ea sunt voto, sed rapienda manu.
me miserum ! dubitatis ? " ait. dubitare videbat
    et pavidas posito procubuisse genu.
haurit aquas tollensque manus, " ignoscite," dixit
450   " sacra ! vir intrabo non adeunda viro.
si scelus est, in me commissi poena redundet :
    sit capitis damno Roma soluta mei."
dixit et irrupit. factum dea rapta probavit
    pontificisque sui munere tuta fuit.
455 nunc bene lucetis sacrae sub Caesare flammae :
    ignis in Iliacis nunc erit usque focis,
nullaque dicetur vittas temerasse sacerdos
    hoc duce nec viva defodietur humo.
sic incesta perit, quia quam violavit, in illam
460   conditur, et Tellus Vestaque numen idem.

---

[a] 241 B.C.
[b] L. Caecilius Metellus, Pontifex Maximus.
[c] The sacred things on which the safety of Rome depended : the Palladium, the conical image (*acus*) of the Mother of the Gods, the earthen chariot which had been brought from Veii, the ashes of Orestes, the sceptre of Priam, the veil of Iliona, and the sacred shields (*ancilia*).

it, because she sees all things by her light that never fails.

[437] Alas, how alarmed the Senate was when the temple of Vesta caught fire, and the goddess was almost buried under her own roof [a]! Holy fires blazed, fed by wicked fires, and a profane flame was blent with a pious flame. Amazed the priestesses wept with streaming hair; fear had bereft them of bodily strength. Metellus [b] rushed into their midst and in a loud voice cried, "Hasten ye to the rescue! There is no help in weeping. Take up in your virgin hands the pledges given by fate; it is not by prayers but by deed that they can be saved. Woe's me, do ye hesitate?" said he. He saw that they hesitated and sank trembling on their knees. He took up water, and lifting up his hands, "Pardon me, ye sacred things, [c]" said he, "I, a man, will enter a place where no man should set foot. If it is a crime, let the punishment of the deed fall on me! May I pay with my head the penalty, so Rome go free!" With these words he burst in. The goddess whom he carried off approved the deed and was saved by the devotion of her pontiff.

[455] Ye sacred flames, now ye shine bright under Caesar's rule; the fire will now be for ever on the Ilian hearths, and it will not be on record that under his leadership any priestess defiled her sacred fillets, and none shall be buried in the live ground. [d] That is the doom of her who proves unchaste; because she is put away in the earth which she contaminated, since Earth and Vesta are one and the same deity.

---

[d] The *infula* and *vitta* were torn from an unfaithful Vesta before she was buried alive.

OVID

Tum sibi Callaico Brutus cognomen ab hoste
    fecit et Hispanam sanguine tinxit humum.
scilicet interdum miscentur tristia laetis,
    nec populum toto pectore festa iuvant :
465 Crassus ad Euphraten aquilas natumque suosque
    perdidit et leto est ultimus ipse datus.
" Parthe, quid exultas ? " dixit dea " signa remittes,
    quique necem Crassi vindicet, ultor erit."

10. AN

At simul auritis violae demuntur asellis,
470   et Cereris fruges aspera saxa terunt,
navita puppe sedens " Delphina videbimus," inquit
    " humida cum pulso nox erit orta die."

11. B MATR · N

Iam, Phryx, a nupta quereris, Tithone, relinqui,
    et vigil Eois Lucifer exit aquis :
475 ite, bonae matres (vestrum Matralia festum)
    flavaque Thebanae reddite liba deae.
pontibus et magno iuncta est celeberrima Circo
    area, quae posito de bove nomen habet :
hac ibi luce ferunt Matutae sacra parenti
480   sceptriferas Servi templa dedisse manus.
quae dea sit, quare famulas a limine templi
    arceat (arcet enim) libaque tosta petat,

---

[a] A tribe of north-west Spain (Galicia) conquered by
Dec. Junius Brutus, 138–137 B.C.
   [b] At Carrhae, 53 B.C.   [c] See v. 580.
   [d] Correct for true evening rising ; apparent, May 26.
   [e] Mater Matuta, wrongly identified with Ino.
   [f] Forum Boarium.

⁴⁶¹ Then did Brutus win his surname from the Gallaecan *a* foe, and dyed the Spanish ground with blood. To be sure, sorrow is sometimes blent with joy, nor are festivals a source of unmingled gladness to the people: Crassus lost the eagles, his son, and his soldiers at the Euphrates, and perished last of all himself.*b* "Why exult, thou Parthian?" said the goddess; "thou shalt send back the standards, and there will be an avenger who shall exact punishment for the slaughter of Crassus."*c*

IV. Id.   10th

⁴⁶⁹ But as soon as the long-eared asses are stripped of their violets, and the rough millstones grind the fruits of Ceres, the sailor, sitting at the poop, says, "We shall see the Dolphin, when the day is put to flight and dank night has mounted up."*d*

III. Id.   11th

⁴⁷³ Now, Phrygian Tithonus, thou dost complain that thou art abandoned by thy spouse, and the watchful Morning Star comes forth from the eastern waters. Go, good mothers (the Matralia is your festival), and offer to the Theban goddess *e* the yellow cakes that are her due. Adjoining the bridges and the great Circus is an open space of far renown, which takes its name from the statue of an ox *f* : there, on this day, it is said, Servius consecrated with his own sceptered hands a temple to Mother Matuta. Who the goddess is, why she excludes (for exclude she does) female slaves from the threshold of her temple, and why she calls for toasted cakes,

OVID

Bacche, racemiferos hedera redimite capillos,
    si domus illa tua est, dirige vatis opus.
485 arserat obsequio Semele Iovis: accipit Ino
    te, puer, et summa sedula nutrit ope.
intumuit Iuno, raptum quod paelice natum
    educet: at sanguis ille sororis erat.
hinc agitur furiis Athamas et imagine falsa,
490   tuque cadis patria, parve Learche, manu.
maesta Learcheas mater tumulaverat umbras
    et dederat miseris omnia iusta rogis.
haec quoque, funestos ut erat laniata capillos,
    prosilit et cunis te, Melicerta, rapit.
495 est spatio contracta brevi, freta bina repellit
    unaque pulsatur terra duabus aquis:
huc venit insanis natum complexa lacertis
    et secum e celso mittit in alta iugo.
excipit illaesos Panope centumque sorores,
500   et placido lapsu per sua regna ferunt.
nondum Leucothea, nondum puer ille Palaemon
    verticibus densi Thybridis ora tenent.
lucus erat; dubium Semelae Stimulaene vocetur:
    Maenadas Ausonias incoluisse ferunt.
505 quaerit ab his Ino, quae gens foret: Arcadas esse
    audit et Evandrum sceptra tenere loci.
dissimulata deam Latias Saturnia Bacchas
    instimulat fictis insidiosa sonis:

---

^a See iii. 715, note. Ino is sister of Semele, and wife of
Athamas. In consequence of Juno's resentment, Athamas
went mad, and murdered his son Learchus; upon which Ino
cast herself into the sea, with her other son Melicertes, from
the Isthmus of Corinth. Panope and the other sea-nymphs
caught her; and the two became sea-divinities with the
names of Leucothea and Palaemon. See *Met.* iv. 512-519.
^b See i. 469.

do thou, O Bacchus, whose locks are twined with clustered grapes and ivy, (explain and) guide the poet's course, if the house of the goddess is also thine. Through the compliance of Jupiter with her request Semele was consumed with fire:[a] Ino received thee, young Bacchus, and zealously nursed thee with the utmost care. Juno swelled with rage that Ino should rear the son who had been snatched from his leman mother; but that son was of the blood of Ino's sister. Hence Athamas was haunted by the furies and by a delusive vision, and, little Learchus, thou didst fall by thy father's hand.[g] His sorrowful mother committed the shade of Learchus to the tomb and paid all the honours due to the mournful pyre. She, too, after tearing her rueful hair, leaped forth and snatched thee, Melicertes, from thy cradle. A land there is, shrunk with narrow limits, which repels twin seas, and, single in itself, is lashed by twofold waters. Thither came Ino, clasping her son in her frenzied embrace, and hurled herself and him from a high ridge into the deep. Panope and her hundred sisters received them scatheless, and smoothly gliding bore them through their realms. They reached the mouth of thick-eddying Tiber before Ino had yet received the name of Leucothea and before her boy was called Palaemon. There was a sacred grove; it is doubtful whether it should be called the grove of Semele or the grove of Stimula: they say that it was inhabited by Ausonian Maenads. Ino inquired of them what was their nation; she learned that they were Arcadians and that Evander was king of the place.[b] Dissembling her godhead, the daughter of Saturn slily incited the Latian

OVID

" o nimium faciles, o toto pectore captae !
510   non venit haec nostris hospes amica choris.
fraude petit sacrique parat cognoscere ritum ;
    quo possit poenas pendere, pignus habet."
vix bene desierat, complent ululatibus auras
    Thyades effusis per sua colla comis,
515 iniciuntque manus puerumque revellere pugnant.
    quos ignorat adhuc, invocat illa deos :
" dique virique loci, miserae succurrite matri ! "
    clamor Aventini saxa propinqua ferit.
appulerat ripae vaccas Oetaeus Hiberas :
520   audit et ad vocem concitus urget iter.
Herculis adventu, quae vim modo ferre parabant,
    turpia femineae terga dedere fugae.
" quid petis hinc " (cognorat enim) " matertera
    Bacchi ?
an numen, quod me, te quoque vexat ? " ait.
525 illa docet partim, partim praesentia nati
    continet, et furiis in scelus isse pudet.
rumor, ut est velox, agitatis pervolat alis,
    estque frequens, Ino, nomen in ore tuum.
hospita Carmentis fidos intrasse penates
530   diceris et longam deposuisse famem ;
liba sua properata manu Tegeaea sacerdos
    traditur in subito cocta dedisse foco.
nunc quoque liba iuvant festis Matralibus illam :
    rustica sedulitas gratior arte fuit.
535 " nunc," ait " o vates, venientia fata resigna,

---

        [a] Hercules, burnt on his pyre on Mount Oeta.
    [b] Ino.   [c] Juno.
        [d] See i. 461. Tegea is in Arcadia.

Bacchanals by glozing words : " Too easy souls !
O blinded hearts ! This stranger comes no friend
to our assemblies. Her aim is treacherous, she
would learn our sacred rites. Yet she has a pledge
by which we can ensure her punishment." Scarce
had she ended, when the Thyads, with their locks
streaming down their necks, filled the air with their
howls, and laid hands on Ino, and strove to pluck
the boy from her. She invoked the gods whom
still she knew not : " Ye gods and men of the land,
succour a wretched mother ! " The cry reached
the neighbouring rocks of the Aventine. The
Oetaean hero[a] had driven the Iberian kine to the
river bank ; he heard and hurried at full speed
towards the voice. At the approach of Hercules
the women, who but a moment before had been
ready to use violence, turned their backs shamefully
in womanish flight. " What would'st thou here, O
sister of Bacchus' mother[b] ? " quoth Hercules, for
he recognized her ; " doth the same deity[c] who
harasses me harass thee also ? " She told him her
story in part, but part the presence of her son
induced her to suppress ; for she was ashamed to
have been goaded into crime by the furies. Rumour
—for she is fleet—flew far on pulsing wings, and thy
name, Ino, was on many lips. It is said that as a
guest thou didst enter the home of loyal Carmentis
and there didst stay thy long hunger.[d] The Tegean
priestess is reported to have made cakes in haste
with her own hand and to have quickly baked them
on the hearth. Even to this day she loves cakes
at the festival of the Matralia. Rustic civility was
dearer to her than the refinements of art. " Now,"
said Ino, " reveal to me, O prophetess, my future

qua licet.   hospitiis hoc, precor, adde meis."
parva mora est, caelum vates ac numina sumit
   fitque sui toto pectore plena dei;
vix illam subito posses cognoscere, tanto
540   sanctior et tanto, quam modo, maior erat.
" laeta canam.   gaude, defuncta laboribus Ino,"
   dixit " et huic populo prospera semper ades.
numen eris pelagi, natum quoque pontus habebit.
   in vestris aliud sumite nomen aquis:
545 Leucothea Grais, Matuta vocabere nostris;
   in portus nato ius erit omne tuo,
quem nos Portunum, sua lingua Palaemona dicet.
   ite, precor, nostris aequus uterque locis!"
annuerat, promissa fides.   posuere labores,
550   nomina mutarunt: hic deus, illa dea est.
cur vetet ancillas accedere, quaeritis?   odit,
   principiumque odii, si sinat illa, canam.
una ministrarum solita est, Cadmeï, tuarum
   saepe sub amplexus coniugis ire tui.
555 improbus hanc Athamas furtim dilexit; ab illa
   comperit agricolis semina tosta dari.
ipsa quidem fecisse negat, sed fama recepit.
   hoc est, cur odio sit sibi serva manus.
non tamen hanc pro stirpe sua pia mater adoret:
560   ipsa parum felix visa fuisse parens.
alterius prolem melius mandabitis illi:
   utilior Baccho quam fuit ipsa suis.

---

[a] See Appendix, p. 440.
[b] Ino.   Compare ii. 628, iii. 853.

fate, so far as it is lawful; I pray thee, add this
favour to the hospitality I have already received."
A brief pause ensued, and then the prophetess
assumed her heavenly powers, and all her bosom
swelled with majesty divine. Of a sudden you could
hardly know her again; so holier, so taller far was
she than she had been but now. "Glad tidings I
will sing: rejoice, Ino, thy labours are over," said
she. "O come propitious to this people evermore! Thou shalt be a divinity of the sea: thy son,
too, shall have his home in ocean. Take ye both
different names in your own waters. Thou shalt be
called Leucothea by the Greeks and Matuta by
our people: thy son will have all authority over
harbours; he whom we name Portunus[a] will be
named Palaemon in his own tongue. Go, I pray
ye, be friendly, both of ye, to our country!" Ino
bowed assent, she gave her promise. Their troubles
ceased: they changed their names: he is a god and
she a goddess.

551 You ask why she forbids female slaves to
approach her? She hates them, and the source of
her hatred, with her leave, I will tell in verse. One
of thy handmaids, daughter of Cadmus,[b] used often to
submit to the embraces of thy husband. The caitiff
Athamas loved her secretly, and from her he learned
that his wife gave toasted seed-corn to the husbandmen. She herself, indeed, denied it, but rumour
affirmed it. That is why she hates the service of a
woman slave. Nevertheless let not an affectionate
mother pray to her on behalf of her own offspring:
she herself proved to be no lucky parent. You
will do better to commend to her care the progeny
of another; she was more serviceable to Bacchus

hanc tibi, " quo properas ? " memorant dixisse,
    Rutili,
" luce mea Marso consul ab hoste cades."
565 exitus accessit verbis, flumenque Toleni
    purpureum mixtis sanguine fluxit aquis.
proximus annus erat : Pallantide caesus eadem
    Didius hostiles ingeminavit opes.

Lux eadem, Fortuna, tua est auctorque locusque ;
570   sed superiniectis quis latet iste togis ?
Servius est, hoc constat enim, sed causa latendi
    discrepat et dubium me quoque mentis habet.
dum dea furtivos timide profitetur amores,
    caelestemque homini concubuisse pudet
575 (arsit enim magno correpta cupidine regis
    caecaque in hoc uno non fuit illa viro),
nocte domum parva solita est intrare fenestra ;
    unde Fenestellae nomina porta tenet.
nunc pudet, et voltus velamine celat amatos,
580   oraque sunt multa regia tecta toga.
an magis est verum post Tulli funera plebem
    confusam placidi morte fuisse ducis,
nec modus ullus erat, crescebat imagine luctus,
    donec eum positis occuluere togis ?
585 tertia causa mihi spatio maiore canenda est,
    nos tamen adductos intus agemus equos.
Tullia coniugio sceleris mercede parato
    his solita est dictis extimulare virum :

---

[a] P. Rutilius Lupus, slain by the Marsians at the river
Tolenus, 90 B.C. In 89 B.C. L. Porcius Cato was slain by
the same tribe. T. Didius served in the Marsic war.
   [b] Pallantis, for Aurora.
   [c] King Servius Tullius dedicated a temple to Fortune and
one to Matuta on the same day and place. The muffled
image was probably Fortune herself.   [d] Unknown.

than to her own children. They relate that she said
to thee, Rutilius, " Whither dost thou hasten ? On
my day in thy consulship thou shalt fall by the hand
of a Marsian foe." Her words were fulfilled, and
the stream of the Tolenus flowed purple, its water
mingled with blood.*a* When the next year was come,
Didius, slain on the same day,*b* doubled the forces
of the foe.

569 The same day, Fortune, is thine, and the same
founder, and the same place.*c* But who is yonder
figure that is hidden in robes thrown one upon the
other ? It is Servius : so much is certain, but
different causes are assigned for his concealment,
and my mind, too, is haunted by a doubt. While
the goddess timidly confessed her furtive love, and
blushed to think that as a celestial being she should
mate with a mere man (for she burned with a deep,
an overmastering passion for the king, and he was
the only man for whom she was not blind), she was
wont to enter his house by a small window (*fenestra*) ;
hence the gate*d* bears the name of Fenestella (" the
Little Window "). To this day she is ashamed and
hides the loved features beneath a veil, and the
king's face is covered by many a robe. Or is the
truth rather that after the murder of Tullius the
common folk were bewildered by the death of the
gentle chief, there were no bounds to their grief,
and their sorrow increased with the sight of his
statue, until they hid him by putting robes on him ?

585 A third reason must be expounded in my
verse at greater length, though I will rein in my
steeds. Having purchased her marriage at the
price of crime, Tullia used to incite her husband

" quid iuvat esse pares, te nostrae caede sororis
590   meque tui fratris, si pia vita placet ?
vivere debuerant et vir meus et tua coniunx,
    si nullum ausuri maius eramus opus.
et caput et regnum facio dotale parentis :
    si vir es, i, dictas exige dotis opes.
595 regia res scelus est.   socero cape regna necato,
    et nostras patrio sanguine tingue manus."
talibus instinctus solio privatus in alto
    sederat : attonitum volgus ad arma ruit.
hinc cruor et caedes, infirmaque vincitur aetas :
600   sceptra gener socero rapta Superbus habet.
ipse sub Esquiliis, ubi erat sua regia, caesus
    concidit in dura sanguinulentus humo.
filia carpento patrios initura penates
    ibat per medias alta feroxque vias.
605 corpus ut aspexit, lacrimis auriga profusis
    restitit.   hunc tali corripit illa sono :
" vadis, an expectas pretium pietatis amarum ?
    duc, inquam, invitas ipsa per ora rotas."
certa fides facti : dictus Sceleratus ab illa
610   vicus, et aeterna res ea pressa nota.
post tamen hoc ausa est templum, monumenta
        parentis,
    tangere : mira quidem, sed tamen acta loquar.
signum erat in solio residens sub imagine Tulli ;
    dicitur hoc oculis opposuisse manum,
615 et vox audita est " voltus abscondite nostros,
    ne natae videant ora nefanda meae."

by these words : " What boots it that we are well matched, thou by my sister's murder, and I by thy brother's, if we are content to lead a life of virtue ? Better that my husband and thy wife had lived, if we do not dare attempt some greater enterprise. I offer as my dower the head and kingdom of my father : if thou art a man, go to, exact the promised dower. Crime is a thing for kings. Kill thy wife's father and seize the kingdom, and dye our hands in my sire's blood." Instigated by such words, he, private man though he was, took his seat upon the lofty throne ; the mob, astounded, rushed to arms. Hence blood and slaughter, and the weak old man was overpowered : his son-in-law (Tarquin) the Proud snatched the sceptre from his father-in-law. Servius himself, at the foot of the Esquiline hill, where was his palace, fell murdered and bleeding on the hard ground. Driving in a coach to her father's home, his daughter passed along the middle of the streets, erect and haughty. When he saw her father's corpse, the driver burst into tears and drew up. She chode him in these terms : " Wilt thou go on, or dost thou wait to reap the bitter fruit of this thy loyalty ? Drive, I say, the reluctant wheels across his very face ! " A sure proof of the deed is the name of the street called Wicked after her ; the event is branded with eternal infamy. Yet after that she dared to touch the temple, her father's monument : strange but true the tale I'll tell. There was a statue seated on a throne in the likeness of Tullius : it is said to have put its hand to its eyes, and a voice was heard, " Hide my face, lest it should see the execrable visage of my own daughter." The statue was covered by a robe

veste data tegitur, vetat hanc Fortuna moveri
et sic e templo est ipsa locuta suo :
" ore revelato qua primum luce patebit
620   Servius, haec positi prima pudoris erit."
parcite, matronae, vetitas attingere vestes :
sollemni satis est voce movere preces,
sitque caput semper Romano tectus amictu,
qui rex in nostra septimus urbe fuit.
625 arserat hoc templum, signo tamen ille pepercit
ignis : opem nato Mulciber ipse tulit.
namque pater Tulli Volcanus, Ocresia mater
praesignis facie Corniculana fuit.
hanc secum Tanaquil sacris de more peractis
630   iussit in ornatum fundere vina focum :
hic inter cineres obsceni forma virilis
aut fuit aut visa est, sed fuit illa magis.
iussa foco captiva sedet : conceptus ab illa
Servius a caelo semina gentis habet.
635 signa dedit genitor tunc cum caput igne corusco
contigit, inque comis flammeus arsit apex.

Te quoque magnifica, Concordia, dedicat aede
Livia, quam caro praestitit ipsa viro.
disce tamen, veniens aetas, ubi Livia nunc est
640   porticus, immensae tecta fuisse domus ;

---

^a Ovid seems to allude to the opinion that this was a
statue of Chastity or Modesty.

^b In the great conflagration of 213 B.C.

^c Ocresia, or Ocrisia, was the wife of a prince of Corniculum
named Tullius. When Tarquin took that city, the wife was
given as a handmaid to Tanaquil. She was with child and
Servius was her son. But his great fortunes suggested the
magical story here told. When the boy was young, his head
was once seen to be aflame, and this was taken for an omen
(Livy, i. 39).

lent for the purpose : Fortune forbade the garment
to be moved, and thus she spoke from her own
temple : " That day on which the statue of Servius
shall be laid bare by unmuffling his face will be
the first day of modesty cast to the winds."[a] Ye
matrons, refrain from touching the forbidden
garments ; enough it is to utter prayers in solemn
tones. Let him who was the seventh king in our
city always keep his head covered with Roman
drapery. This temple was once burnt,[b] yet the fire
spared the statue : Mulciber himself rescued his
son. For the father of Tullius was Vulcan, his
mother was the beautiful Ocresia of Corniculum.[c]
After performing with her the sacred rites in due
form, Tanaquil ordered Ocresia to pour wine on the
hearth, which had been adorned. There among
the ashes there was, or seemed to be, the shape of
the male organ ; but rather the shape was really
there. Ordered by her mistress, the captive Ocresia
sat down at the hearth. She conceived Servius,
who thus was begotten of seed from heaven. His
begetter gave a token of his paternity when he
touched the head of Servius with gleaming fire, and
when on the king's hair there blazed a cap of flame.

[637] To thee, too, Concordia, Livia dedicated a
magnificent shrine, which she presented to her dear
husband. But learn, thou age to come, that where
Livia's colonnade now stands, there once stood a
palace huge.[d] The single house was like the fabric

[d] Bequeathed by Vedius Pollio to Augustus, who destroyed it and built this colonnade on the site, and named
it after Livia, 7 B.C.

urbis opus domus una fuit, spatiumque tenebat,
  quo brevius muris oppida multa tenent.
haec aequata solo est, nullo sub crimine regni,
  sed quia luxuria visa nocere sua.
645 sustinuit tantas operum subvertere moles
  totque suas heres perdere Caesar opes.
sic agitur censura et sic exempla parantur,
  cum iudex, alios quod monet, ipse facit.

12. CN   13. D EID · N

Nulla nota est veniente die, quam dicere possis.
650   Idibus Invicto sunt data templa Iovi.
et iam Quinquatrus iubeor narrare minores.
  nunc ades o coeptis, flava Minerva, meis.
" cur vagus incedit tota tibicen in urbe ?
  quid sibi personae, quid stola longa volunt ? "
655 sic ego.   sic posita Tritonia cuspide dixit :
  (possim utinam doctae verba referre deae !)
" temporibus veterum tibicinis usus avorum
  magnus et in magno semper honore fuit.
cantabat fanis, cantabat tibia ludis,
660   cantabat maestis tibia funeribus :
dulcis erat mercede labor.   tempusque secutum,
  quod subito gratae frangeret artis opus . . .¹
adde quod aedilis, pompam qui funeris irent,
  artifices solos iusserat esse decem.
665 exilio mutant urbem Tiburque recedunt.

---

¹ *There seems to be a lacuna here.*

ᵃ See iii. 809 for the greater Quinquatrus.
ᵇ Athena, who by one account was a daughter of Poseidon
and the Tritonian lake in Libya.

of a city; it occupied a space larger than that
occupied by the walls of many a town. It was
levelled with the ground, not on a charge of treason,
but because its luxury was deemed harmful. Caesar
brooked to overthrow so vast a structure, and to
destroy so much wealth, to which he was himself
the heir. That is the way to exercise the censorship; that is the way to set an example, when the
judge does himself what he warns others to do.

PR. ID. 12th. ID. 13th

649 The next day has no mark attached to it which
you can note   On the Ides a temple was dedicated
to Unconquered Jupiter. And now I am bidden to
tell of the Lesser Quinquatrus.ᵃ Now favour my
undertaking, thou yellow-haired Minerva. " Why
does the flute-player march at large through the
whole city? What mean the masks? What means
the long gown? " So did I speak, and thus did
Tritonia ᵇ answer me, when she had laid aside her
spear—would that I could report the very words of
the learned goddess! " In the times of your
ancestors of yore the flute-player was much employed
and was always held in great honour. The flute
played in temples, it played at games, it played at
mournful funerals. The labour was sweetened by
its reward; but a time followed which of a sudden
broke the practice of the pleasing art. . . . Moreover, the aedile had ordered that the musicians
who accompanied funeral processions should be ten,
no more. The flute-players went into exile from

exilium quodam tempore Tibur erat !
quaeritur in scaena cava tibia, quaeritur aris ;
    ducit supremos naenia nulla toros.
servierat quidam, quantolibet ordine dignus,
670   Tibure, sed longo tempore liber erat.
rure dapes parat ille suo turbamque canoram
    convocat ; ad festas convenit illa dapes.
nox erat, et vinis oculique animique natabant,
    cum praecomposito nuntius ore venit,
675 atque ita ' quid cessas convivia solvere ? ' dixit
    ' auctor vindictae nam venit ecce tuae.'
nec mora, convivae valido titubantia vino
    membra movent : dubii stantque labantque pedes.
at dominus ' discedite ' ait plaustroque morantes
680   sustulit : in plaustro scirpea lata fuit.
alliciunt somnos tempus motusque merumque,
    potaque se Tibur turba redire putat.
iamque per Esquilias Romanam intraverat urbem,
    et mane in medio plaustra fuere foro.
685 Plautius, ut posset specie numeroque senatum
    fallere, personis imperat ora tegi,
admiscetque alios et, ut hunc tibicina coetum
    augeat, in longis vestibus esse iubet ;
sic reduces bene posse tegi, ne forte notentur

---

    [a] The flute-players, enraged at some ordinance of the Twelve
Tables, seceded to Tibur, and refused to return. Livy says
that the magistrates made them drunk, and got them back
to Rome in wagons (ix. 30. 5-10) ; Ovid and Plutarch
ascribe the feat to a freedman (Plutarch, *Quaest. Rom.* 55).
    [b] The *vindicta* was the rod with which the freedman had
been touched in the ceremony of manumission. The
messenger pretends that the freedman's old master is coming,
possibly to reclaim him as a slave.
    [c] Censor 312 B.C., his colleague being Appius Claudius,

the city and retired to Tibur*: once upon a time
Tibur was a place of exile! The hollow flute was
missed in the theatre, missed at the altars; no dirge
accompanied the bier on the last march. At Tibur
there was a certain man who had been a slave, but
had long been free, a man worthy of any rank. In
his country place he made ready a banquet and
invited the tuneful throng; they gathered to the
festal board. It was night, and their eyes and
heads swam with wine, when a messenger arrived
with a made-up tale, and thus he spoke (to the
freedman): 'Break up the banquet without delay,
for see here comes the master of thy rod*!' Immediately the guests bestirred their limbs, reeling
with heady wine; their shaky legs or stood or
slipped. But the master of the house, 'Off with
you all!' says he, and when they dawdled he
packed them in a wain that was well lined with
rushes. The time, the motion, and the wine allured
to slumber, and the tipsy crew fancied that they
were on their way back to Tibur. And now the
wain had entered the city of Rome by the
Esquiline, and at morn it stood in the middle of
the Forum. In order to deceive the Senate as to
their persons and their number, Plautius* commanded
that their faces should be covered with masks; and
he mingled others with them and ordered them to
wear long garments, to the end that women flute-
players might be added to the band. In that way he
thought that the return of the exiles could be best

whose action drove the flute-players into exile, according to
Livy. Ovid suggests that one of the censors helped them
to evade the law. *Plautius* is a conjection for ms. *callidus*
or *Claudius*.

OVID

690   contra collegae iussa redisse sui.
    res placuit, cultuque novo licet Idibus uti
        et canere ad veteres verba iocosa modos."
    haec ubi perdocuit, " superest mihi discere " dixi
        " cur sit Quinquatrus illa vocata dies."
695 " Martius " inquit " agit tali mea nomine festa,
        estque sub inventis haec quoque turba meis.
    prima, terebrato per rara foramina buxo
        ut daret, effeci, tibia longa sonos.
    vox placuit : faciem liquidis referentibus undis
700 vidi virgineas intumuisse genas.
    ' ars mihi non tanti est ; valeas, mea tibia ' dixi :
        excipit abiectam caespite ripa suo.
    inventam satyrus primum miratur et usum
        nescit ; at inflatam sensit habere sonum
705 et modo dimittit digitis, modo concipit auras.
        iamque inter nymphas arte superbus erat :
    provocat et Phoebum.   Phoebo superante pependit ;
        caesa recesserunt a cute membra sua.
    sum tamen inventrix auctorque ego carminis huius.
710 hoc est, cur nostros ars colat ista dies."

        14. E E[N]   15. F Q · ST · D · F

Tertia lux veniet, qua tu, Dodoni Thyone,
    stabis Agenorei fronte videnda bovis.

    ᵃ Appius Claudius.
    ᵇ Ovid thought this implied five days ; see iii. 809.
    ᶜ Marsyas.
    ᵈ One of the Hyades, also called nymphs of Dodona.
Their true morning rising was on May 6 ; apparent, June 9.
372

concealed, lest they should be censured for having
come back against the orders of his colleague.[a] The
plan was approved, and now they are allowed to
wear their new garb on the Ides and to sing merry
words to the old tunes."

693 When she had thus instructed me, " It only
remains for me to learn," said I, " why that day
is called Quinquatrus.[b] " " A festival of mine,"
quoth she, " is celebrated under that name in the
month of March, and among my inventions is
also the guild of flute-players. I was the first, by
piercing boxwood with holes wide apart, to produce
the music of the long flute. The sound was
pleasing; but in the water that reflected my face
I saw my virgin cheeks puffed up. ' I value not
the art so high; farewell, my flute!' said I, and
threw it away; it fell on the turf of the river-bank.
A satyr [c] found it and at first beheld it with wonder;
he knew not its use, but perceived that, when he
blew into it, the flute gave forth a note, and with
the help of his fingers he alternately blew out and
drew in his breath. And now he bragged of his
skill among the nymphs and challenged Phoebus;
but, vanquished by Phoebus, he was hanged and his
body flayed of its skin. Yet am I the inventress
and foundress of this music; that is why the profession keeps my days holy."

XVII. KAL. IVL. 15th

711 The third day will come, on which thou, O
Thyone [d] of Dodona, wilt stand visible on the brow of

haec est illa dies, qua tu purgamina Vestae,
  Thybri, per Etruscas in mare mittis aquas.

715 Si qua fides ventis, Zephyro date carbasa, nautae.
  cras veniet vestris ille secundus aquis.

16. GC   17. HC   18. AC

At pater Heliadum radios ubi tinxerit undis,
  et cinget geminos stella serena polos,
tollet humo validos proles Hyriea lacertos :
720   continua Delphin nocte videndus erit.
scilicet hic olim Volscos Aequosque fugatos
  viderat in campis, Algida terra, tuis ;
unde suburbano clarus, Tuberte, triumpho
  vectus es in niveis, Postume, victor equis.

19. BC

725 Iam sex et totidem luces de mense supersunt,
  huic unum numero tu tamen adde diem :
sol abit a Geminis, et Cancri signa rubescunt ;
  coepit Aventina Pallas in arce coli.

20. CC

Iam tua, Laomedon, oritur nurus ortaque noctem
730   pellit, et e pratis uda pruina fugit :

---

  ^a Father of Europa.
  ^b Swept out yearly on this day. See App. p. 425.
  ^c Helios, ἥλιος, " the Sun."
  ^d Orion. See v. 493-536. Ovid is right for one star of
Orion as to the day, but wrong in placing it at evening
instead of morning.
  ^e In 431 B.C., A. Postumius Tubertus, dictator, defeated
the Aequians and Volscians at Mount Algidus.
  ^f Father of Tithonus.

Agenor's *a* bull. It is the day on which thou, O
Tiber, dost send the filth of Vesta's temple down the
Etruscan water to the sea.*b*

XVI. Kal. 16th

715 If any trust can be put in the winds, spread your
canvas to the West Wind, ye mariners; to-morrow it
will blow fair upon your waters.

XV. Kal. 17th. XIV. Kal. 18th

717 But when the father of the Heliades *c* shall have
dipped his rays in the billows, and heaven's twin
poles are girdled by the stars serene, the offspring
of Hyrieus *d* shall lift his mighty shoulders above the
earth : on the next night the Dolphin will be visible.
That constellation once indeed beheld the Volscians
and the Aequians put to flight upon thy plains, O
land of Algidus ; whence thou, Postumius Tubertus,*e*
didst win a famous triumph over the neighbouring
folks and didst ride victorious in a car drawn by
snow-white horses.

XIII. Kal. 19th

725 Now twice six days of the month are left, but to
that number add one day ; the sun departs from the
Twins, and the constellation of the Crab flames red :
Pallas begins to be worshipped on the Aventine hill.

XII. Kal. 20th

729 Now, Laomedon,*f* thy son's wife rises, and
having risen she dispels the night, and the dank

375

reddita, quisquis is est, Summano templa feruntur,
   tum, cum Romanis, Pyrrhe, timendus eras.

Hanc quoque cum patriis Galatea receperit undis,
   plenaque securae terra quietis erit,
735 surgit humo iuvenis telis afflatus avitis
   et gemino nexas porrigit angue manus.
notus amor Phaedrae, nota est iniuria Thesei :
   devovit natum credulus ille suum.
non impune pius iuvenis Troezena petebat :
740   dividit obstantes pectore taurus aquas.
solliciti terrentur equi frustraque retenti
   per scopulos dominum duraque saxa trahunt.
exciderat curru lorisque morantibus artus
   Hippolytus lacero corpore raptus erat
745 reddideratque animam, multum indignante Diana.
   " nulla " Coronides " causa doloris " ait ;
" namque pio iuveni vitam sine volnere reddam,
   et cedent arti tristia fata meae."
gramina continuo loculis depromit eburnis
750   (profuerant Glauci manibus illa prius,
tunc cum observatas augur descendit in herbas,
   usus et auxilio est anguis ab angue dato),

ᵃ A sort of nocturnal Jupiter, god of the nightly sky,
especially in his capacity of a hurler of lightning.
   ᵇ Probably 278 B.C.
   ᶜ Anguitenens (Ophiuchus). Evening rising, April 19 ;
but this is within a few days of its true morning setting at
Alexandria.
   ᵈ See *Met*. xv. 497-529. Phaedra, wife of Theseus, made
advances to his son Hippolytus, which were repulsed. She
accused him of having made advances to her, and he prayed
to his father Poseidon, to punish Hippolytus. Poseidon sent
a bull out of the sea to frighten Hippolytus's horses, and the
young man was killed.   ᵉ Aesculapius.

hoar-frost flees from the meadows. The temple is
said to have been dedicated to Summanus,[a] whoever
he may be, at the time when thou, Pyrrhus, wast
a terror to the Romans.[b]

XI. Kal. 21st

733 When that day also has been received by
Galatea in her father's waters, and all the world is sunk
in untroubled sleep, there rises above the horizon the
young man blasted by the bolts of his grandsire and
stretches out his hands, entwined with twin snakes.[c]
Familiar is the tale of Phaedra's love, familiar, too,
the wrong that Theseus did, when, too confiding, he
did curse his son to death.[d] Doomed by his piety,
the youth was journeying to Troezen, when a bull
cleft with his breast the waters in his path. Fear
seized the startled steeds ; in vain their master held
them back, they dragged him along the crags and
flinty rocks. Hippolytus fell from the car, and, his
limbs entangled by the reins, his mangled body
was whirled along, till he gave up the ghost, much
to Diana's rage. "There is no need for grief,"
said the son of Coronis,[e] "for I will restore the
pious youth to life all unscathed, and to my leech-
craft gloomy fate shall yield." Straightway he
drew from an ivory casket simples that before had
stood Glaucus' ghost[f] in good stead, what time
the seer went down to pluck the herbs he had
remarked, and the snake was succoured by a snake.

[f] The story is told by Apollodorus, iii. 3. 1 (see the Loeb
edition by J. G. Frazer, vol. i. p. 311). Glaucus, as a boy,
was drowned in a jar of honey ; and his father restored him
by using a herb which he saw a serpent use for a fellow-
serpent.

pectora ter tetigit, ter verba salubria dixit :
  depositum terra sustulit ille caput.
755 lucus eum nemorisque sui Dictynna recessu
  celat : Aricino Virbius ille lacu.
at Clymenus Clothoque dolent : haec, fila reneri,
  hic, fieri regni iura minora sui.
Iuppiter exemplum veritus direxit in ipsum
760 fulmina, qui nimiae noverat artis opem.
Phoebe, querebaris : deus est, placare parenti :
  propter te, fieri quod vetat, ipse facit.

21. DC

Non ego te, quamvis properabis vincere, Caesar,
  si vetet auspicium, signa movere velim.
765 sint tibi Flaminius Trasimenaque litora testes
  per volucres aequos multa monere deos.
tempora si veteris quaeris temeraria damni,
  quintus ab extremo mense bis ille dies.

22. EC

Postera lux melior : superat Masinissa Syphacem,
770 et cecidit telis Hasdrubal ipse suis.

23. FC. 24. GC

Tempora labuntur, tacitisque senescimus annis,
  et fugiunt freno non remorante dies.

---

^a See iii. 263.   ^b Pluto.
  ^c One of the three Fates.
  ^d 217 B.C. Flaminius set the omens at defiance.
  ^e Hasdrubal, son of Gisco, and Syphax were defeated by
Masinissa and Scipio, 203 B.C.
  ^f Hasdrubal, brother of Hannibal, fell fighting at the
378

Thrice he touched the youth's breast, thrice he spoke healing words; then Hippolytus lifted his head, low laid upon the ground. He found a hiding-place in a sacred grove and in the depths of Dictynna's own woodland; he became Virbius of the Arician Lake.[a] But Clymenus[b] and Clotho[c] grieved, she that life's broken thread should be respun, he that his kingdom's rights should be infringed. Fearing the example thus set, Jupiter aimed a thunderbolt at him who knew the resources of a too potent art. Phoebus, thou didst complain. But Aesculapius is a god, be reconciled to thy parent: he did himself for thy sake what he forbids others to do.

X. Kal. 22nd

753 However great thy haste to conquer, O Caesar, I would not have thee march, if the auspices forbade. Be Flaminius and the Trasimenian shores thy witnesses that the kind gods give many warnings by means of birds. If you ask the date of that ancient disaster, incurred through recklessness, it was the tenth day from the end of the month.[d]

IX. Kal. 23rd

769 The next day is luckier: on it Masinissa defeated Syphax,[e] and Hasdrubal fell by his own sword.[f]

VIII. Kal. 24th

771 Time slips away, and we grow old with silent lapse of years; there is no bridle that can curb the

Metaurus, 207 B.C.; perhaps this refers to the son of Gisco, who took poison after the defeat of Syphax.

quam cito venerunt Fortunae Fortis honores !
   post septem luces Iunius actus erit.
775 ite, deam laeti Fortem celebrate, Quirites :
   in Tiberis ripa munera regis habet.
pars pede, pars etiam celeri decurrite cumba,
   nec pudeat potos inde redire domum.
ferte coronatae iuvenum convivia lintres,
780   multaque per medias vina bibantur aquas.
plebs colit hanc, quia qui posuit, de plebe fuisse
   fertur et ex humili sceptra tulisse loco.
convenit et servis, serva quia Tullius ortus
   constituit dubiae templa propinqua deae.

25. HC 26. AC

785 Ecce suburbana rediens male sobrius aede
   ad stellas aliquis talia verba iacit :
" zona latet tua nunc, et cras fortasse latebit :
   dehinc erit, Orion, aspicienda mihi."
at si non esset potus, dixisset eadem
790   venturum tempus solstitiale die.

27. BC 28. CF

Lucifero subeunte Lares delubra tulerunt
   hic, ubi fit docta multa corona manu.
tempus idem Stator aedis habet, quam Romulus olim
   ante Palatini condidit ora iugi.

---

[a] True morning rising of middle star was on June 21 ;
apparent, July 13. The summer solstice was on June 24.
[b] In a battle between Romans and Sabines, the Romans
were driven back ; but Romulus prayed Jupiter to stay their
flight, and vowed a temple in case of success to Jupiter the
Stayer, which he afterwards built on the spot (Livy i. 12).

flying days. How quickly has come round the festival of Fors Fortuna! Yet seven days and June will be over. Come, Quirites, celebrate with joy the goddess Fors! On Tiber's bank she has her royal foundations. Speed some of you on foot, and some in the swift boat, and think no shame to return tipsy home from your ramble. Ye flower-crowned skiffs, bear bands of youthful revellers, and let them quaff deep draughts of wine on the bosom of the stream. The common folk worship this goddess because the founder of her temple is said to have been of their number and to have risen to the crown from humble rank. Her worship is also appropriate for slaves, because Tullius, who instituted the neighbouring temples of the fickle goddess, was born of a slave woman.

VII. KAL. 25th. VI. KAL. 26th

785 Lo, returning from the suburban shrine, a maudlin worshipper thus hails the stars : " Orion, thy belt is now invisible, and perhaps it will be invisible to-morrow : after that it will be within my ken." But if he had not been tipsy, he would have said that the solstice would fall on the same day.[a]

V. KAL. 27th

791 Next morn the Lares were given a sanctuary on the spot where many a wreath is twined by deft hands. At the same time was built the temple of Jupiter Stator, which Romulus of old founded in front of the Palatine hill.[b]

OVID

29. DF

795 Tot restant de mense dies, quot nomina Parcis,
   cum data sunt trabeae templa, Quirine, tuae.

30. EC

Tempus Iuleis cras est natale Kalendis :
   Pierides, coeptis addite summa meis.
dicite, Pierides, quis vos adiunxerit isti,
800   cui dedit invitas victa noverca manus.
sic ego.   sic Clio : " clari monumenta Philippi
   aspicis, unde trahit Marcia casta genus,
Marcia, sacrifico deductum nomen ab Anco,
   in qua par facies nobilitate sua est.
805 [par animo quoque forma suo respondet ; in illa
   et genus et facies ingeniumque simul.]
nec quod laudamus formam, tu turpe putaris :
   laudamus magnas hac quoque parte deas.
nupta fuit quondam matertera Caesaris illi.
810   o decus, o sacra femina digna domo ! "
sic cecinit Clio.   doctae assensere sorores;
   annuit Alcides increpuitque lyram.

---

[a] See ii. 511, February 17.   There appears to have been only one temple, dedicated by L. Papirius Cursor in 293 B.C., rebuilt by Augustus 16 B.C. ; but on which day does not appear.

[b] Juno, who reluctantly gave Hercules a place in the temple of the Muses.

[c] L. Marcius Philippus restored the temple of Hercules Musarum, in the time of Augustus.   His daughter Marcia was wife of P. Fabius Maximus.   Compare Ovid, *Ex Ponto*, i. 127-142, iii. 1. 75-78.   The Marcian family claimed to be

III. KAL. 29th

795 When as many days of the month remain as the Fates have names, a temple was dedicated to thee, Quirinus, god of the striped gown.[a]

PR. KAL. 30th

797 To-morrow is the birthday of the Kalends of July. Pierides, put the last touches to my undertaking. Tell me, Pierides, who associated you with him to whom his stepmother was forced to yield reluctantly.[b] So I spoke, and Clio answered me thus: "Thou dost behold the monument of that famous Philip from whom the chaste Marcia is descended, Marcia who derives her name from sacrificial Ancus, and whose beauty matches her noble birth.[c] In her the figure answers to the soul; in her we find lineage and beauty and genius all at once. Nor deem our praise of figure base; on the same ground we praise great goddesses. The mother's sister of Caesar was once married to that Philip.[d] O glorious dame! O lady worthy of that sacred house!" So Clio sang. Her learned sisters chimed in; Alcides bowed assent and twanged his lyre.

descended from King Ancus Marcius, and added the surname Rex to their family name.

[a] Atia, mother of Augustus, appears to have married Marcius Philippus after the death of C. Octavius. Atia was niece of Julius Caesar. Some think that Atia had a younger sister, also Atia, who was confused with the elder.

APPENDIX

The year of ten months (i. 28).—According to Roman tradition, Romulus instituted a year of ten months, with a total of 304 days; the months began with March and ended with December. Afterwards two months, January and February, were added, making a total of 355 days, approximately a lunar year. O. E. Hartmann thought that in the old days the time from mid-winter to spring, during which the labours of the husbandmen were for the most part suspended, and nature herself appeared to be dormant, if not dead, was looked on as a period of rest, and was therefore excluded from the calendar, the object of which was to regulate the activities of the people during the remainder of the year. This explanation I regard as probably the true one. Analogies had suggested the explanation to me, before I learnt that it had been anticipated. The calendar in that form must date from a prehistoric age, when the Latins were still a rude people, subsisting mainly by agriculture. To all appearances our remote ancestors recognized only lunar months, which they allowed to run on without attempting to fit them into the solar year.

Take the Negro tribes of S. Nigeria, described by Mr. P. Amaury Talbot. " Time was measured by the moon. . . . This lunar month was divided into weeks of four or eight days in the west. . . . The subdivisions into weeks in all likelihood originated chiefly from the necessity of differentiating between the days on which the various markets were held. . . . The fitting of the weeks into months is by no means perfect. . . . As a rule, those months from about Nov.-Dec. to Jan.-Feb., when no

o 385

work was being done, were thought negligible and hardly included. In fact, the word translated by our ' year' more often meant the season. . . . There was usually no thought about the number of months in the year." Among the Yoruba of this region the three months February, March, April, are generally given no specific name.

The African calendar resembles the old Roman in its system of an eight-day week based on the recurrence of markets; these market-days correspond exactly to the *nundinae*. On Roman market-days, as on the Jewish Sabbath, all ordinary work in the fields was strictly forbidden: the same rule is observed on the market-days in S. Nigeria.

The parallel with Rome is not confined to Africa. We may follow it, for example, to New Zealand. An English missionary (Rev. W. Yate) in the early part of the nineteenth century, described their customs from personal observation. "Nine months of the year, a great portion of the natives are employed on their grounds; and there are only two months in which they can say they have nothing to do. . . . These two months are not in the calendar: they do not reckon them: nor are they in any way accounted of. ' It is a time,' the natives say, ' not worthy to be reckoned: as it is only spent in visiting, feasting, talking, playing and sleeping.'" In the Triobrand Islands, to the east of New Guinea, most mature men can count up to eight months and sometimes up to ten, only a few specially trained can enumerate correctly twelve months. The period of nameless months is the time when work in the gardens is finished. There are some indications that in other parts of the world the original calendar reckoned only ten months in the year. Such a system is found among the Chams of Indo-China, and in some islands of the Indian Archipelago. A division of the year into ten parts, we can hardly call them months, is found also among peoples who earn a precarious subsistence by hunting, fishing, and collecting wild fruits and roots.

APPENDIX

There is some ground for thinking that the Anglo-Saxons at one time recognized, or at least named, only ten months of the year : for according to Bede they had only one name for December and January, and only one name for June and July.

Janus (i. 89).—Some of the most eminent authorities have agreed in deriving the name from *ianua*, " a door." But there are difficulties in the way. In the first place, so far from Janus being called after *ianua*, " a door," it appears probable, if not certain, that *ianua* was called after him ; and if that was so, it seems to follow that Janus led a separate and independent life before he came to be especially associated with doors. The reason for thinking so is this. The word *ianua* as applied to a door has nothing to correspond to it in any Indo-European language : but the regular word for door is the same in all the languages of the Aryan family from India to Ireland. Why, when the Romans were in possession of this good old name for a door, did they invent another and call it *ianua* ? The word has the appearance of being an adjectival form derived from the noun Ianus. I conjecture that it may have been customary to set up an image or symbol of Janus at the principal door of the house in order to place the entrance under the protection of the great god that, as we shall see immediately, Janus appears originally to have been. A door thus guarded might be known as the *ianua foris*, that is a Januan door, and the phrase might in time be abridged into *ianua*, the noun *foris* being understood but not expressed.

There seems to be good reason to think that the original form of the god's name was Dianus, the initial DI having been corrupted into J, just as the original Diovis and Diespiter were corrupted into Jovis and Jupiter. Similarly the name of Diana, which is the feminine form of Dianus, appears to have been corrupted in vulgar pronunciation into Jana : for Varro tells us that in reference to the days of the month country people spoke of the waxing and waning Jana, where educated folk would seemingly have

APPENDIX

said Diana, meaning the moon. In Greek it is certain that the original DI was similarly corrupted into Z, as is proved by the name of Zeus, for the original DI reappears in the genitive, dative, and accusative DIOS, DII, DIA. Similarly ZAN, an old form of Zeus, stands for an original DIAN, which answers exactly to the Latin DIANUS, JANUS. Further, at Dodona, his most ancient sanctuary, Zeus shared his temple with Dione, in whom the learned mythologist Apollodorus discerned the first wife of Zeus, the wife whom that fickle and faithless god afterwards exchanged for Hera. His Italian counterpart gave proof of much greater conjugal fidelity by always keeping to his first wife, Juno, whose old name, to judge by that of her Greek counterpart Dione, must have been Diono. Compared with the kindred Sanscrit name Dyaus, the old German Zio, and so forth, all these names are ultimately derived from an Indo-European root DI, meaning "bright"; and as the Sanscrit Dyaus, the Greek Zeus, and the Latin Jupiter were undoubtedly personifications of the sky, a very strong presumption is raised that Janus also, whose name cannot without violence be separated from theirs, was in origin also a god of the sky, a simple duplicate of Dyaus, Zeus, and Jupiter. The ancients themselves seem to have been sensible of the kinship, not to say identity, of Janus and Jupiter. An inscription records the dedication of an offering to Jupiter Dianus, as if Jupiter and Dianus (Janus) were one and the same. And we know from the good testimony of Varro that some of the ancients identified Janus with the sky; in the fourteenth book of his *Divine Antiquities* that most learned of Roman antiquaries affirmed that among the Etruscans in particular the name Janus was used as equivalent to the sky. We shall do well to acquiesce in this opinion of some ancient authorities, strongly supported as it is by the conclusions of modern philology.

But why was Janus regularly represented with two heads? The question is perhaps even more difficult to answer than that of the original nature of the deity.

APPENDIX

Elsewhere I have conjectured that this curious mode of representation originated in a custom of placing an image of the god at gates and doors as a sort of divine sentinel to guard them from the passage of evil powers, and in support of this conjecture I have cited the double-headed idol which the Bush negroes of Surinam regularly set up as a guardian at the entrance of a village. The idol consists of a block of wood with a human face rudely carved on each side; it stands under a gateway composed of two uprights and a cross-bar. Beside the idol generally lies a white rag intended to keep off the devil; and sometimes there is also a stick which seems to represent a bludgeon or weapon of some sort. Further, from the cross-bar dangles a small log which serves the useful purpose of knocking on the head any evil spirit who might attempt to pass through the gateway. Clearly this double-headed fetish at the gateway of negro villages in Surinam bears a close resemblance to the double-headed images of Janus, which, grasping a staff in his right hand and a key in his left, stood sentinel at Roman archways (*iani* i. 95, 99), and it seems reasonable to suppose that in both cases the heads facing two ways are to be similarly explained as expressive of the vigilance of the guardian god, who kept his eye on spiritual foes both before and behind, and stood ready to bludgeon them on the spot.

Lupercalia (ii. 267).—The priesthood of the Luperci included two colleges, the Quinctiales or Quinctilii, and the Fabiani or Fabii. In 44 B.C. a third college, called the Julii, was established by Julius Caesar. The sanctuary which was the centre of the sacred functions of the Luperci was known as the Lupercal; it appears to have been situated at the south-west foot of the Palatine hill. It was traditionally said to have been a great cave at the foot of the hill, with springs of water welling up under the rocks, and overarched by a thick grove of oaks. In that sylvan scene the she-wolf is said to have suckled Romulus and Remus. In the Lupercal there formerly grew a fig-tree called the Ficus Ruminalis.

APPENDIX

According to the testimony of the ancients the Lupercalia was essentially a purificatory rite. In particular it was a purification of the ancient city on the Palatine, of which the boundary, as it was believed to have been fixed by Romulus, continued to be marked out by stones down to Imperial times. At their annual festival the Luperci appear to have run round the boundary of the ancient city. Certainly they started from the Lupercal and made a circuit, in the course of which they ran up the Sacred Way and down again, which Christians in the time of Augustine absurdly interpreted as a reminiscence of the Deluge, the Luperci representing the sinners who on that occasion ran up and down the mountains as the waters of the Flood rose or fell. Moreover, Dionysius of Halicarnassus expressly affirms that in the time of Romulus the Lupercalia were celebrated by young men, who, starting from the Lupercal (which he calls the Lyceum), ran round the village on the Palatine, clad only in girdles made from the skins of the sacrificial victims; and he adds that the rite was a traditional purification observed by the villagers in the time of Romulus and continued down to the writer's own day. The skins of which the girdles were made were those of goats which had been sacrificed. At the festival the Luperci also sacrificed a dog, which was deemed a purificatory rite. With strips of the skins of the sacrificed goats the Luperci struck at all whom they met, but especially at women, who held out both hands to receive the blows, persuaded that this was a safe mode of securing offspring and an easy delivery. The goatskin with which they were struck was called Juno's cloak, a name which becomes intelligible when we remember that in her great temple at Lanuvium the goddess was represented clad in a goatskin as in a cloak. Hence it is not surprising to read, that according to a certain Anysius in his treatise on the months, the rites performed by the Luperci in February aimed at promoting the growth of the crops; for in the minds of many people at an early stage of culture the fertility of women is closely

APPENDIX

bound up with the fertility of the earth, and the same causes which promote or hinder the one are thought to promote or hinder the other, a vital connexion being supposed to subsist between the union of the human sexes on the one hand and the fruitfulness of the ground on the other. A hint of this connexion is perhaps given by the part which the Vestal Virgins played at the Lupercalia. Between the 7th and 14th of May, on alternate days, the three eldest Vestals collected ears of spelt in reapers' baskets, and with their own hands roasted and ground them. From this spelt, mixed with salt, they provided the sacrificial meal on three days of the year, namely at the Lupercalia on January 15, at the festival of Vesta (the Vestalia) on June 9, and on the Ides (13th) of September. The name of Creppi or Crepi popularly applied to the Luperci appears to be an old form of *capri*, "he-goats," and to have been suggested by the goatskins which they wore and which they carried in their hands.

By far the most famous celebration of the Lupercalia was that which fell on the 15th of February, 44 B.C., exactly one month before the assassination of Caesar. The dictator was then at the height of his power and at the summit of human glory. A golden throne had been set for him on the Rostra, and there, clad in the gorgeous costume of a general at his triumph, he sat watching the antics of the Luperci in the Forum below. It chanced that his friend Mark Antony was his colleague in the consulship and also Master of the new college of Julian Luperci. In that capacity Antony, naked and glistening with oil after the fashion of the Luperci, came running into the Forum, the crowd opening to let him pass. He made straight for the Rostra, and being hoisted on to the platform by his colleagues, he advanced to Caesar, and offered to place on the dictator's head a diadem twined with laurel. In the crowd there was some slight applause but more hissing. When Caesar pushed the bauble away, the crowd applauded. Again Antony presented the crown, and again Caesar refused it, whereupon the whole multitude

391

APPENDIX

broke into a tumult of applause. Caesar frowned, and standing up from his golden chair he pulled his robe from his neck and offered his throat to anyone who pleased to cut it. His friends placed the crown on one of his statues, but when the tribunes tore it down, the spectators cheered them. According to Cicero, who may have witnessed the scene, Antony was drunk as well as naked when he attempted to crown Caesar king of Rome.

According to Ovid, the god whom the Luperci served was Faunus, a deity of the woodlands and of cattle, whose festival fell on the 5th of December, when the flocks and herds skipped in his honour on the greensward, and in the forest the fallen leaves " yellow, and black, and pale, and hectic red," made a soft carpet for the light footsteps of the amorous god as he pursued the nymphs among the trees. He was thought to keep the wolves from the lambs, a function appropriate to the Lupercalia, if, as some have thought, the prime aim of that festival was to guard the flocks and herds from the prowling wolf. But according to Livy the god whom the Luperci honoured was named Inuus. The ancients identified this Inuus with the Greek god Pan, and both of them with Faunus ; otherwise little or nothing is known about him, except that in Italy he was honoured, sometimes with yearly, sometimes with monthly festivals. An image of the supposed god, whatever he may have been called, stood in the Lupercal ; it represented the deity in the costume of the Luperci, that is, naked with a girdle of goatskin about his loins.

The primitive character of the ritual and of the ideas implied in it suggests that originally the Lupercalia was rather a magical than a religious rite, and hence that it did not involve a reference to any particular deity, but was simply one of those innumerable ceremonies whereby men have attempted, in all ages and in all countries, by their own efforts, without divine assistance, to repel the powers of evil and so to liberate the powers of good, thus promoting the fertility at once of man, of beast, and of the earth. These ceremonies commonly take the form of

APPENDIX

a periodic, generally of an annual, expulsion of evils, which are usually conceived in the form of demons or ghosts; having forcibly driven out these dangerous intruders, the community fancies itself safe and happy for the time being, till the recurrence of the old troubles seems to require a fresh application of the old remedy. Viewed in their essential character as a riddance of evil, such ceremonies are properly called purifications; and the ancients, as we have seen, commonly explained the Lupercalia as a purification, in which they appear to have been substantially right. The late W. Warde Fowler, our genial and learned interpreter of Roman religion, happily compared the Lupercalia to the annual custom of "beating the bounds," which is still kept up in some parts of England; and he suggested that the peeled wands carried by the bound-beaters at Oxford on Ascension Day may once have been used in the same way as the thongs of goatskin wielded by the Luperci on their rounds. The theory has much to commend it, and its author may have been quite right in describing the Lupercalia as "at the same time a beating of the bounds and a rite of purification and fertilization."

Mannhardt proposed to explain the title *lupercus*, "wolf-goat," as signifying the union of two priestly colleges, of which the one personated wolves and the other goats, and of which the members called themselves accordingly Wolves and Goats respectively. Under these two names, according to him, the priests represented the Spirit of Vegetation in animal form, for down to this day in European folk-lore both wolves and goats are very often conceived to be embodiments of the Corn-spirit. In point of fact, as we have seen, the Luperci were divided into two colleges, the Quinctiales and the Fabii, of which the Quinctiales were associated with Romulus and the Fabii with Remus.

This ingenious theory, though it is not free from difficulties, seems open to less serious objections than either of its rivals, and we may provisionally acquiesce

393

in it till a better has been suggested. It has, indeed, been objected to it that the festival appears to have been a purely pastoral one, and that it was recognized as such by the ancients; for Cicero refers contemptuously to the college of the Luperci as " a sort of wild and thoroughly pastoral and rustic brotherhood of regular Wolves (*germanorum Lupercorum*), which was formed in the woods before the institution of civilized life and law "; and Plutarch, speaking of the Lupercalia, observes that " many write that it was of old a festival of shepherds, and it somewhat resembles the Arcadian Lycaea." To this it may be retorted that in the ancient accounts of the festival which have come down to us there are references to the crops but none to the flocks and herds. Therefore, so far as the balance of evidence is concerned, it inclines rather against than in favour of the pastoral theory of the Lupercalia. However, the two apparently inconsistent theories are reconciled by the view that the festival was one of purification, which, by ridding the community of the evil powers of barrenness and disease that had infested it in the past year, set free the kindly powers of nature to perform their genial task of promoting the fertility alike of women, of cattle, and of the fields.

Regifugium (ii. 685).—The ceremony called the Flight of the King is marked on February 24. All that we know about the ritual is contained in a statement of Plutarch, who says that after offering an ancient sacrifice in the Comitium, the King of the Sacred Rites fled hastily from the Forum. The ancients appear to have generally interpreted the ceremony as an annual celebration of the flight of Tarquin the Proud. In modern times, scholars are generally agreed in rejecting the old explanation, but they are by no means agreed as to what to substitute for it. On the analogy of certain Greek rites, in which the sacrificer fled after the sacrifice, it has been suggested that the animal sacrificed by the king in the Comitium was a holy animal, and that his flight was a sort of apology for the sacrilegious sacrifice which he had offered. This theory was first proposed tentatively by Lobeck. Another suggestion is that the sacrifice was a sin-offering, and that the victim, regarded as a scapegoat to which the sin had been transferred, became an object of fear and abhorrence from which the sacrificer sought to save himself by flight. On this theory the sacrifice was one of the purificatory rites from which the month of February took its name.

I formerly conjectured that the rite may have been a survival of a race which in ancient times the real king of Rome had annually to run for the purpose of proving his physical fitness to discharge the duties of his office. But since the Flight of the King on February 24 always followed after the intercalary month, which was regularly inserted after February 23, I have been led, in the course of this work, to suggest a somewhat different explanation of the rite in question, namely, that the king who fled from the Comitium may originally have been a temporary king who was invested with a nominal authority during the intercalary period, whether of a month or of eleven or twelve days, while the power of the real king was in abeyance; and that at the end of his brief and more or less farcical reign he was obliged to take to his heels lest a worse thing should befall him. The theory fits in with the view, which seems to be widespread, that an intercalary period is an abnormal time during which ordinary rules do not hold and consequently the ordinary government is suspended and replaced by the temporary sway of a mock king, who at the end of his nominal reign has sometimes to pay with his life for his brief tenure of a crown. On this view the king who fled from the Comitium on February 24 may be compared with the mock King of the Saturnalia who held sway during the festival of Saturn in December; and the analogy between the two would be still closer if we suppose that the mock King of the Saturnalia originally personated Saturn himself and was put to death in the character of the god at the end of a month's reign of revelry and licence; for we are expressly informed that such a mode of celebrating the Saturnalia was actually observed by the Roman soldiers at Durostorum in Lower Moesia in the early years of the fourth century of our era, before the establishment of Christianity by Constantine. If that was so, we must apparently conclude that the rude soldiers on the frontiers of the empire retained or revived, in all their crude barbarity, the original features of the festival which had long been effaced in the civilized society of the capital, leaving behind them only a tradition of Saturn's earthly reign and of the human victims that had been immolated on his altars. But if the representative of Saturn was formerly put to death at the Saturnalia, it may well be that the Flight of the mock King on February 24 was a mitigation of an older custom which compelled him to end his life with his reign. If the analogy here suggested between the King of the Saturnalia and the King of the Sacred Rites (the Sacrificial King) should prove to be well founded, we should be confronted with the curious coincidence of the reign of a mock king at the end both of the old and of the new Roman year, the King of the Sacred Rites reigning at the end of the old Roman year in February and the King of the Saturnalia reigning at the end of the new Roman year in December. How this duplication, if such indeed it was, is to be explained, it would be premature to speculate. As both ceremonies probably had their root in the necessity of regulating the course of the agricultural year for the benefit of farmers, we might suppose that the duplication either sprang from the union of two peoples with two different calendars, which were combined in the new system, or that it originated in successive attempts to bring the calendar more into accord with the conflicting claims of science and religion. As any systematic attempt to harmonize the solar and lunar years by intercalation betokens a fairly advanced state of culture, we must apparently conclude that an Intercalary King, who mediated, as it were, between Sun and Moon, was a later invention than a human Saturn who gave his life to quicken the crops. But these are hardly more than idle guesses.

Mars (iii. 1).—Though Mars has been most commonly conceived both in antiquity and in modern times as a god of war, there are good grounds for thinking that originally this was not his only nor even his principal function. In his treatise on farming, Cato the Elder, a pattern Roman of the olden time, puts into the mouth of the farmer a prayer to Father Mars that he would ward off disease, bad weather, and other calamities from the farm; that he would cause the fruits of the earth, the corn, the vines, and the copses to grow and prosper; that he would keep the shepherds and the cattle safe; and that he would bestow health and strength on the farmer himself, his family and household; and in order to induce the deity to grant his prayer, the farmer begged Father Mars to accept the sacrifice of a pig, a sheep and a bull, which were first led in procession round the fields. Further, Cato instructed the farmer how to make a vow and an offering to Mars Silvanus for the cattle, in order that the animals should be well and strong. Thus we may safely conclude that Mars was the god to whom above all others the Roman farmer looked for help in promoting the growth of the crops and preserving the health of man and beast. We can therefore understand why the Arval Brethren, whose special function was " to make the fields bear fruit," should have addressed their solemn prayers principally to Mars. Scholars differ as to the exact way in which this side of his nature is to be reconciled with his warlike character. Perhaps the view of William Ramsay comes as near the truth as any. He wrote: " We must bear in mind that when Italy was portioned out among a multitude of small independent tribes, many of them differing from each other in origin and language, forays must have been as common among neighbouring states as they were in the days of our ancestors on the English border and the Highland frontier. The husband-man would be compelled to grasp the sword with one hand while he guided the plough with the other, and would be often forced to peril life and limb to save the produce of his toil from the spoiler. In such a state of society it is little wonderful that the Deity of the rustic should have presented a mixed character, and have been worshipped as one who could protect his votaries from every form of danger to which they were exposed."

Ovid was unquestionably right in believing that the worship of Mars had been common to the Latin and other Italian peoples before the foundation of Rome.

Under the month of March the rustic calendars record "a sacred rite in honour of Mamurius" (*Sacrum Mamurio*), and under March 14 the calendar of Philocalus records the Mamuralia, that is, the festival of Mamurius. In their songs the Salii, that is, the Leapers or Dancers (from *salire*, "to leap," "to dance"), made mention of a certain Mamurius Veturius, which Varro interpreted to mean *memoria vetus*, "old memory." But a legendary or mythical explanation of the words was given by Ovid himself later on in this book. To this tale a remarkable addition is made by Joannes Lydus, a writer of the sixth century A.D. He tells us that, lest the shields (*ancilia*) which had fallen from heaven should be worn out by constant use, the craftsman Mamurius made other shields in their likeness, and that misfortunes followed the disuse of the ancient shields; so Mamurius was beaten with rods and driven out of the city, in memory whereof on the Ides of March (March 15) a man, wrapped up in goatskins, was led about and beaten with long slender rods. From this account, combined with the mention of Mamurius Veturius in the Song of the Salii, we may infer, with some probability, that every year, in the month of March, a man wrapped up in goatskins and called Mamurius Veturius was beaten with rods by the Salii and driven out of the city. The day appears from the entry in the calendar of Philocalus to have been the fourteenth, which went by the name of Mamuralia, and not the fifteenth, as stated by Joannes Lydus. Now Mamurius was associated with the

Oscan land ; perhaps he was thought to be driven away to the Oscan land to die, for Propertius prayed that the Oscan earth might lie light on the cunning hands of Mamurius, who wrought in bronze, and Mamers was the Oscan form of Mars. Further, as we have seen, Varro explained the name *Veturius* as equivalent to *vetus*, " old." Hence it is a plausible conjecture that Mamurius Veturius means " the Old Mars," and that the ceremony of driving his personal representative out of Rome on the 14th of March, that is on the eve of the full moon (the Ides) of the first month, was intended to assist the growth of vegetation in the new year, at the commencement of spring, by getting rid of the withered vegetation of the old year ; for Mars, as we have seen, was originally a deity of vegetation as well as of war. Thus interpreted the ceremony is analogous to the Slavonic ceremony of " Carrying out Death " in spring.

The original twelve Salii or dancing priests are said to have been instituted by Numa to minister to Mars Gradivus, the Marching Mars. Afterwards twelve more Salii were appointed by King Tullus Hostilius. The original twelve Salii were called the Palatine Salii, because their chapel was on the Palatine hill. The later twelve Salii were called the Colline or Agonalian or Agonensian Salii ; their chapel was on the Quirinal hill ; hence they were also known as the Quirinal Salii. All the Salii wore embroidered tunics, girt with bronze belts, purple-edged cloaks, and high conical caps ; they had swords girt at their sides, and each man bore in his right hand a spear, or rather staff or truncheon, and in his left hand one of the sacred shields (*ancilia*). Thus arrayed they used to go through the city for many days in the month of March, visiting the Forum, the Capitol, and many other places both public and private, dancing solemnly in measured time, chanting their ancient hymns, and clashing their staves against their shields. In March the festival lasted for thirty days. In the city there were stations (*mansiones*), where the Salii halted on their march, probably for the night, and stored their arms. At these stations the Salii refreshed themselves after their labours by banqueting in a style of magnificence which became proverbial. In ordinary times, when the shields were not in use, they were kept in the sacristy (*sacrarium*) of Mars ; when war was declared, the general in command entered the sacristy, moved the shields, and said, " Mars, awake ! " It is said that before the Cimbrian war, when for the second time in her history Rome was put in deadly peril by the Gauls, the shields in the sacristry were heard to stir and clang, as if impatient for the signal to march. However, it does not appear that the shields were ever carried with the army to battle, though the Salii themselves were free to perform military service abroad.

The Salii were not peculiar to Rome. Similar colleges of dancing priests bearing the same name were found in other Italian cities, for example, at Tibur, where they served Hercules instead of Mars, at Anagnia, and in cities beyond the Po, such as Patavium (Padua) and Sicinum.

I have suggested that the dancing procession of the armed Salii in March may have been intended to rout out and expel the demons that had accumulated in the city during the past year, especially the demons of blight and infertility, who might otherwise check the growth of the crops in spring. At the time of sowing the seed the Khonds, a wild tribe of India, drive out the " evil spirits, spoilers of the seed," from every house in the village ; the expulsion is effected by young men, who beat each other and strike the air violently with long sticks. At Whydah in West Africa, when the king's lands were to be hoed and sowed, the people went to the fields singing and dancing, half of them carrying their farm-tools and half of them " armed as in a day of battle." Arrived at the scene of their labours they worked to the sound of musical instruments, and returning at evening danced before the king's palace. A French traveller has described how at Timbo in Guinea men hoed the ground for sowing to the chant of women, while between the diggers and the singers a man armed with a musket danced, brandishing his weapon, and two others danced pirouetting and smiting the earth with their hoes; and we are told that "all that is necessary for exorcizing the spirits and causing the grain to grow." On the first day when the Barundi of East Africa begin to hoe the fields, a sorcerer dances in front of them with cries and gesticulations "to ban the spirits and bless the sowing."

If this interpretation of the Salii is correct, their dances were not war-dances in the ordinary sense of the word, and their weapons were not directed against any human foes. They waged war on demons: it was against these invisible enemies that they carried their arms: it was these dreadful beings that they essayed to terrify by the clash of their batons on their shields. The skin-clad man whom they beat and probably drove out of the city was, on this hypothesis, only an embodiment of the legion of spirits swarming in the air, especially the outworn spirit of vegetation of the past year, who was driven away that he might make room for a youthful and vigorous successor, the new Mars, who was thought to be born on the 1st of March. The view that the weapons they carried and the clangour they made were directed against spiritual, not human foes, can be supported by analogies in many parts of the world, where swords are brandished, guns fired, metal clashed, and drums beaten for the purpose of expelling evil spirits. To take a single example, the Eghap, a tribe of the Central Cameroons in West Africa, believe that illness is caused by the ghosts of persons who have left no relatives behind them. Hence during a time of sickness these troublesome spirits are driven away; and as it is believed that the only people whom the spirits fear are the old men who play the sacred instruments, the operation of banishing ghosts falls to the lot of these venerable musicians. "When all the preparations have been made, the sacred instrument men gather in the head-chief's compound. Here three of them play lustily on drums

401

for about fifteen minutes. At a given signal all of them spring into the air and rush through the narrow opening of the mat fence surrounding the head-chief's compound, bellowing like cattle. They beat the fencing, stamp on the ground, and strike the drums with great vigour. All those people in the town who are supposed to be controlled by evil spirits rush about in great agitation, foaming at the mouth, with their eyes wide open and staring. In the market-place the men who are supposed to drive the evil ghosts away divide into five sections. At the head of each is a drummer, followed first by a man with a whisk, and then by a number of men armed with spears. A dance is then held, in which the performers spring high into the air, some of them with stalks of elephant-grass (*mbere*) in their hands to drive the ghosts away. No one is allowed to leave his compound while this is going on, and complete silence reigns over the town. Whatever appears, whether human beings or animals, will be at once caught by the evil ghosts."

In harmony with this theory of the Salii we may conjecture that the leaps from which the Salii took their name were supposed to promote the growth of the crops by sympathetic magic; it cannot be without significance that in their hymns these dancing priests named, and probably invoked, Saturn, the god of sowing. We may surmise that the people in the streets, and especially farmers from the country, watched their dances with eager curiosity and prognosticated the height of the corn at the next harvest from the height of their leaps into the air. In some parts of Europe, especially in Germany and Austria, it is or was till lately customary to dance or leap high for the express purpose of making the crops grow correspondingly tall; the leaps are executed sometimes by the sower on the field, sometimes by other persons, at certain seasons, such as Candlemas and Walpurgis Night (the eve of May Day), but especially on Shrove Tuesday. Indeed in some places men used to assemble in bands for the purpose of thus fostering the growth of

APPENDIX

the crops by their leaps and antics. This was the case, for example, at Grub in the Swiss canton of the Grisons. The peasants there " assembled in some years, mostly at the time of the summer solstice, disguised themselves as maskers so as to be unrecognizable, armed themselves with weapons defensive and offensive, took every man a great club or cudgel, marched in a troop from one village to another, and executed high leaps and strange antics. They ran full tilt at each other, struck every man his fellow with all his might, so that the blow resounded, and clashed their great staves and cudgels. These foolish pranks they played from a superstitious notion, that their corn would thrive the better." These Swiss *Stopfer* correspond exactly to the Roman *Salii*, if my view of that ancient Italian priesthood is correct.

Nemi (iii. 271).—The priest of Diana in her sacred grove (*nemus*) at Nemi bore the title of King of the Grove (*Rex Nemorensis*). He had to be a runaway slave; he succeeded to the dignity by slaying his predecessor in single combat; and he held office till he was himself slain by his successor. But before he fought the priestly king in office, a candidate for the priesthood had to break a branch from a tree in the sacred precinct, and public opinion in antiquity identified this branch with the Golden Bough, which, at the Sibyl's bidding, Aeneas plucked and carried with him as a sort of passport on his journey to the world of the dead. Once when the King of the Grove had occupied his unenviable throne for many years, the ferocious madman Caligula sent a stronger man to attack him, professing that the king's reign had lasted too long. The strange rule of this priestly kingdom naturally attracted the attention of the Greek writers.

This is all we know about the priesthood of Diana at Nemi. The only hope of explaining both the title and the rule seems to lie in the discovery of analogous customs elsewhere, which, being better known and more fully reported, may throw a light on the mysterious priesthood of Nemi. Now it has been the belief of peoples in many

403

parts of the world, that kings are possessed of a divine or magical character, in virtue of which not only the welfare of their subjects, but the course of nature, including particularly the fertility of the ground, of cattle, and of women, are bound up with the life of the ruler and will suffer serious damage, or even perish, if his strength fails through illness or old age, and that the most fatal consequences would surely follow if he were allowed to die a natural death. To avert these dangers various measures are adopted. Sometimes the king's reign is limited to a period during which he may reasonably be expected to retain his bodily and mental vigour, at the end of which he is put to death in order to avert the disasters which are expected to ensue from the failure of his natural powers. Sometimes without putting a fixed term to his reign and his life, his people allow him to reign till symptoms of old age or serious illness warn them of his threatened dissolution, which accordingly he is obliged to anticipate either by suicide or by submitting to execution. Sometimes, again, he is suffered to reign and to live so long as he can give proof of undiminished health and strength by repelling any armed attacks made upon him by candidates for the throne; but should he succumb in the combat, he is immediately succeeded in office by his slayer, who reigns in his stead until he is in his turn slain by his successor. I have suggested that the King of the Grove at Nemi was a king of this sort and held office under this last tenure, and in support of this suggestion I have adduced a number of parallels drawn from various parts of the world, particularly India and Africa. The evidence has been set forth in the *Golden Bough* and I need not repeat or recapitulate it here.

But here I may be allowed to cite some confirmatory evidence which has come to my knowledge since the *Golden Bough* was published. The custom of killing divine or semi-divine kings to prevent them from dying a natural death is particularly common in Africa. Thus in the Jukun kingdom of Kororofa, a pagan state of Northern Nigeria,

APPENDIX

" the most striking thing is the semi-divine character of the Jukun king. His person is charged with a spiritual force which makes it dangerous for anyone to be touched by him. If he even touched the ground with his hands or uncovered foot the crops would be ruined, and it was no doubt due to this blasting power of his *mana* that in former times the chief spoke to his subjects from behind a screen, a custom which Ibn Batuta records was also followed by the early kings of Bornu. The Jukun king is indeed a demi-god, and with a view to the transmission of his divine spirit unimpaired he was ceremonially slain at the end of seven years." However, the king was by no means always permitted to live out the full term of seven years. "The king of the Jukun was only allowed to rule for seven years, and if during that period he fell ill, or even sneezed or coughed, or fell off his horse, he might be put to death, the duty of slaying him devolving on the head councillor."

According to Mr. H. R. Palmer, " There was a king made every two years. When a king had reigned two years it was considered that he had enjoyed power long enough, and he was compelled to fight with the senior member of the royal family, who came forward and challenged him to fight until one of them was killed. The descent of the kingship did not go from the reigning king to one of his sons, but to any of the children of any deceased king. The would-be successor, at about the season of the great feast, used to come into the king's mess suddenly and walk round and then go out. Of course under ordinary circumstances this would have been a great affront, but the king understood from this that from that time forward he must guard himself. At the first opportunity after this the successor attacked the king. If he killed him, the fight was over for a time ; if he did not kill him, another of his relations came forward and challenged the king in the same way. This went on until someone did kill the king."

Anna Perenna (iii. 523).—The feast of Anna Perenna

APPENDIX

was celebrated at the first milestone on the Flaminian Way. Hence the place would seem to have been near the site of the present Porta del Popolo, the northern gate of Rome, and not far from the river. Here, apparently between the Flaminian and the Salarian roads, the goddess had a fruitful grove which was visible from the Janiculum. Martial, who mentions this, says that the grove " delights in virgin blood," an obscure allusion which has hitherto not been explained. Macrobius tells us that in the month of March people went to Anna Perenna to sacrifice both publicly and privately in order that they might pass the year and many other years in prosperity ; and to the same effect Joannes Lydus says that on the Ides (the 15th) of March public prayers were offered that the year might be healthy. Taken in conjunction with the custom, mentioned by Ovid (lines 531-534), of praying that the wassailers might live as many years as they had quaffed cups of wine, these statements furnish a clue to the nature of the festival and of the goddess herself. As Anna she is a feminine personification of the year (*annus*) ; as Perenna she is a personification of the endless procession of the years ; hence we need not wonder that she is conceived as an old, old woman. The festival was a New Year festival ; for March was the first month of the old Roman year, and the Ides of March was the first full moon of the New Year, a very appropriate day for good wishes and prayers for that and for many years to follow. The celebration of the festival, as described by Ovid, was a thoroughly popular one. The pairing of sweethearts, lying on the grass, trolling out ribald staves, and drinking themselves drunk, points to customs like those formerly observed on May Day and Midsummer Eve in many parts of Europe, when the licence accorded to the sexes was a relic of magical rites performed for the purpose of maintaining the fertility of nature alike in the greenwoods and the fields, in man and beast. In this licence we may perhaps detect the true explanation of Martial's allusions to " the virgin blood " in which the grove of the goddess

406

APPENDIX

delighted. It was a day of Valentines, and into the tents and leafy huts on the greensward of the grove many a girl may have gone in a maid who came out a maid no more.

Nerio (iii. 675).—This custom Ovid explains by a story of the love of Mars for Minerva. According to the tale which he now unfolds, the god fell in love with Minerva and desired to marry her. So he begged the aged Anna Perenna, now raised to the godhead, to persuade the coy goddess to crown his wishes. Anna promised her help and professed to have elicited a promise of marriage from Minerva. But this was only a sham ; for when all the preparations for the wedding had been made, and the bride was conducted to the bridal chamber, the bridegroom lifted the veil to salute her, but discovered, to his chagrin, that she was not Minerva but the old crone Anna herself.

In this story Minerva has probably taken the place of Nerio, an old goddess, whom ancient Roman writers, quoted by Aulus Gellius, explicitly described as the wife of Mars. The first author cited by Gellius is Plautus, who wrote either at the end of the third century or at the beginning of the second century B.C. Plautus wrote (*Truc.* 515) : " Mars arriving from abroad salutes his wife Nerio." Plautus could hardly have used this language if the belief that Nerio was the wife of Mars had not been familiar to his audience. Again, the old comic dramatist Licinius Imbrex, quoted by Aulus Gellius, wrote : " I would not have you called Neaera but Nerio, since you have been given in marriage to Mars." Once more Aulus Gellius quotes from the third book of the *Annals* of his namesake Cnaeus Gellius a passage in which Neria (another form of Nerio) is plainly mentioned as the wife of Mars. Cnaeus Gellius wrote in the second century B.C. The passage in question contains a prayer to Mars supposed to have been uttered by Hersilia, the wife of Romulus, on the occasion when she was interceding with the Sabine king Tatius to pardon the Romans for having carried off the Sabine women, of whom she herself was one. The prayer runs thus : "Neria (wife) of Mars, I beseech thee, grant us peace, that we may enjoy true and happy marriages, because it fell out by the advice of thy husband that they (the Romans) should carry off us virgins, for the purpose of getting children for themselves and their people, and posterity for the fatherland." In this prayer for marriage, appropriately addressed by a human to a divine wife, the words "thy husband" (*tuus coniux*) refer, of course, to Mars, as Aulus Gellius observes, adding very justly, "whereby it appears that the expression of Plautus was not a poetical flourish, but that it was a tradition that Nerio was by some said to be the wife of Mars." It is true that Aulus Gellius himself, writing in the second century A.D., preferred to explain Nerio, not as the wife, but merely as "the force, power, majesty" of Mars ; but no weight can be attached to this explanation, since it is merely an etymological guess based on a fanciful derivation of Nerio from the Greek *neuron* through the Latin *nervus*. Further, in a passage of Martianus Capella on the uxoriousness of the gods the love of Mars for his wife Nerio is mentioned in terms which agree so closely with those in which Ovid describes the passion of Mars for Minerva that both authors would seem to have drawn on the same source, in which Nerio, not Minerva, was represented as the wife of Mars. Lastly, the assumed substitution of Minerva for Nerio in the story of Mars's wooing is confirmed by a note of the old scholiast Porphyrion on Horace, which runs thus : "There is a religious scruple about marrying in the month of May and also in March, in which a contest concerning marriage was held wherein Mars was vanquished by Minerva, and having maintained her virginity she was called Neriene." Here, as Warde Fowler observed, Neriene is clearly equivalent to Nerio, and "this looks much like an attempt to explain the occurrence of two female names, Minerva and Nerio, in the same story ; the original heroine Nerio having been supplanted by the later Minerva." Varro also coupled

APPENDIX

Minerva and Nerienes, which Aulus Gellius tells us was a vocative form of Nerio, though in the old books the nominative of the name was Nerio. Now from the work of Joannes Lydus on the Roman calendar we know that on the twenty-third of March there was a festival of Mars and Nerine, and that Nerine was no other than Nerio is put beyond a doubt by the explanation of the author, who says that Nerine was the Sabine name of a goddess whom people identified with Athena (Minerva) or Aphrodite (Venus), " for Nerine is manliness and the Sabines call manly men Nerones." This ceremony in honour of Mars and Nerine (Nerio) on the twenty-third of March is in all probability the " contest concerning marriage " in the month of March which is mentioned by Porphyrion ; and taken in conjunction with the present passage of Ovid we may conclude that it represented a marriage of Mars to Nerio, in which the god was beguiled by the substitution of a withered hag for a young and blooming bride. From a variety of indications H. Usener ingeniously argued that the marriage of Mars and Nerio was celebrated at Rome in March in the New Year, while Anna represented the old wife of the god in the Old Year which had just run its course.

Mr. Warde Fowler rejected the marriage of Mars and Nerio, together with the marriage of all the genuine old Roman gods, believing that the view of their conjugal relations was a later interpretation created by the influence of Greek mythology, in which the marriage of the deities was a commonplace. But in arriving at this conclusion he was obliged to set aside a considerable body of ancient evidence to the contrary, including the direct and explicit testimony of the greatest of Roman antiquaries, Varro himself, who, as quoted by St. Augustine, declared that " in the matter of the generations of the gods the peoples lean to the opinion of the poets rather than to that of natural philosophers ; and therefore his ancestors, that is, the old Romans, believed in the sex and generations of the gods and established their marriages." For my part

409

APPENDIX

I think it safer to accept than to reject the testimony of the ancients on a point concerning which they were necessarily much better informed than we are.

This incident in the loves of Mars and Minerva (or rather Nerio) strikingly resembles a wide-spread practice which is known to students of folk-lore by the name of " the False Bride." It is a common custom among Slavonic, Teutonic, and Romance peoples, as also among the Esthonians, that when a bridegroom or his representative comes to fetch the bride from her home, a false bride is substituted for the real one, another woman, frequently an ugly old one, or a little girl, or even a man being palmed off on him as the bride. In Brittany the substitutes are first a little girl, then the mistress of the house, and lastly the grandmother. In the Samerberg district of Bavaria, a bearded man in woman's clothes personates the bride ; in Esthonia, the bride's brother or some other young man. Sometimes the substitution takes place already at the betrothal, and sometimes only at the wedding-feast. The custom is not restricted to Europe. Among the Beni-Amer in North-East Africa, when women with a camel are sent to fetch the bride, her people often substitute a false bride for the true one, and it is only when the procession is well outside the village that the substitute reveals herself and runs back laughing.

The most probable explanation of the custom seems to be that it is an attempt to protect the bride against the evil eye and evil spirits by substituting a dummy on which they can safely wreak their spite. This explanation is confirmed by a custom said to be observed at a marriage in Java. A traveller in that island tells us that " among other apartments we saw the ' family bridal chamber,' in which we noticed two painted wooden figures, one of a man and the other of a woman, standing at the foot of the ' family nuptial couch.' These figures, as we were told, are called Lorobonyhoyo, or the youth and maiden, and are placed there to cheat the devil, who, according to

410

APPENDIX

their belief, during the wedding night hovers round the bed, with the view of carrying off one of the happy pair. These figures, however, are their protection, for, deceived by their resemblance, he carries them off instead of the sleeping lovers." In harmony with this view the Germans of Western Bohemia, in whose marriage customs the False Bride figures prominently, believe that the " Old Bride " will always carry away the bad luck from the true bride out of the house.

The Parilia (iv. 721).—The festival of the Parilia on the 21st of April is marked PAR in the Caeretan, Maffeian, and Praenestine calendars. The name is derived from that of the divinity Pales, in whose honour the festival was celebrated. Hence the more correct, though less usual, form of the name of the festival was Palilia. Ovid treats Pales as a goddess, and so did Festus, Virgil, Tibullus, the author of the *Culex*, Florus, and Probus. But according to others, including Varro, Pales was male, and as a male he is noticed by Arnobius and Martianus Capella. Connected with Pales was probably the goddess Palatua, the guardian of the Palatine hill, whose worship was conducted by a special flamen of her own (*flamen Palatualis*), and must, therefore, have been of great antiquity, since none but the genuine old Roman deities could boast of the services of a flamen. At the festival of the Septimontium or the Seven Hills a sacrifice called Palatuar was offered to her. If Pales was originally a male deity, Palatua may have been his female counterpart or wife.

As Ovid relates a little further on (lines 807 *sqq.*), the festival of the Parilia or Palilia was believed to be older than the foundation of Rome, and it was supposed that the first foundations of the city were laid on the very day of the festival, so that the 21st of April was henceforth celebrated as the birthday of Rome. The day was naturally a popular holiday, especially for the young. Athenaeus describes how a learned discussion was suddenly interrupted by a great uproar, in which the shrill music of fifes, the clash of cymbals, and the rub-a-dub of drums were blent with singing into a confused hubbub of sound ; it was the people in the street rejoicing at the coming of the Parilia, though by that time, in the third century A.D., the old name Parilia had been changed to Romaea, that is, the Roman Festival, on account of its association with the birth of Rome. It was not lawful to sacrifice any animal at the Parilia : no blood might be shed on that happy day.

Numa is said to have been born, by some divine chance, on the very day on which Rome was founded.

The festival was essentially a rustic rite observed by shepherds and husbandmen for the good of their flocks and herds. This is well brought out by Ovid in the following account which he gives of the ritual and the prayers that accompanied it ; and the same truth was recognized by Varro and other ancient writers. In Eastern Europe many analogous rites have been performed down to recent times, and probably still are performed, for the same purpose, by shepherds and herdsmen on St. George's Day, the 23rd of April, only two days after the Parilia, with which they may well be connected by descent from a common festival observed by pastoral Aryan peoples in spring. The ceremonies appear to be mainly designed to guard the flocks and herds against wolves and witches, the two great foes of whom the herdsman stands most in dread, and of the two the witches are perhaps even more dreaded than the wolves. Many peoples of Eastern Europe, including the Esthonians, Russians, and Ruthenians, drive their cattle out to pasture for the first time on St. George's Day after their long confinement during the winter : on the eve of that day witches resort to many tricks to steal the milk of the cattle ; and many accordingly are the precautions which the herdsman takes to defeat their infernal machinations. Among these precautions are the kindling of bonfires at cross-roads, and the fumigating of the cattle with sulphur or *asafoetida*. Even in England it seems to have been formerly the custom to kindle bonfires on St. George's Day, as we gather from Shakespeare :

> *Bonfires in France I am forthwith to make,*
> *To keep our great St. George's feast withall.*

St. George is regarded as the patron of wolves as well as of cattle ; hence it is naturally held that he can protect the flocks and herds against the ravages of wolves, his creatures. He has probably displaced an old pastoral deity or deities, of whom Pales may have been one. Another may possibly have been Pergrubius, to whom the heathen Prussians and Lithuanians used to sacrifice on St. George's Day. He appears to have been a Lithuanian god of the spring, who caused the grass and the corn to grow and the trees to burst into leaf ; however, nothing is said of his relation to cattle, and so far his analogy to St. George breaks down, though his festival fell on the saint's day. In Russia St. George's Day is celebrated as a national as well as an ecclesiastical festival ; and the popular songs devoted to it serve to prove, by their mythical character, " that the Christian hero, St. George, has merely taken the place of some old deity, light-bringing or thunder-compelling, who used to be honoured at this time of the year in heathen days. It is not a slayer of dragons and protector of princesses who appears in these songs, but a patron of farmers and herdsmen, who preserves cattle from harm, and on whose day, therefore, the flocks and herds are, for the first time after the winter, sent out into the open fields."

The October Horse (iv. 733).—Ovid means that the materials used in fumigation will be supplied by the Vestal Virgins ; and of these materials he mentions three, the blood of a horse, the ashes of a calf, and beanstalks. The " ashes of a calf " are explained by the ritual observed at the Fordicidia on the 15th of April, which the poet has already described. On that day pregnant cows were sacrificed to Earth ; the unborn calves were torn from them and burned by the senior Vestal Virgin, and the ashes kept by her to be used for the purification of the people at the Parilia. It is these ashes which the worshipper is now bidden to procure from Vesta, that is, from the Vestal Virgins or from the senior member of the college. The reason why the ashes of unborn calves were employed in the ritual is not hard to divine. Since a principal object of the festival, as we learn from the shepherd's prayer (lines 771-772), was to ensure the fecundity of the flock, and since sheep were fumigated (lines 739-740) as well as the shepherds, it seems plain that the smoke from ashes of the calves was supposed to fertilize, by sympathetic magic, the ewes and doubtless the cows, though curiously enough Ovid speaks only of sheep.

The blood of the horse, which was also employed in the fumigations at the Parilia, was procured in a curious fashion. On the 15th of October in every year a chariot-race was run in the Field of Mars (*Campus Martius*) at Rome. Stabbed with a spear, the right-hand horse of the victorious team was then sacrificed to Mars for the purpose of ensuring good crops, and its head was cut off and adorned with a string of loaves. Thereupon the inhabitants of two wards—the Sacred Way and the Subura—contended with each other who should get the head. If the people of the Sacred Way got it, it was fastened to a wall of the King's House (*Regia*), which stood on the Sacred Way; if the people of the Subura got it, they fastened it to the Mamilian tower, which stood in the Suburan ward and took its name from the Mamilian family. The horse's tail was cut off and carried to the King's House with such speed that the blood dripped on the hearth of the house. This blood the King caught in a vessel and kept, or handed it over to the Vestal Virgins, whose house adjoined his own, to be burned, and fumigate by its smoke the sheep and shepherds at the Parilia. In this account the King is the Sacrificial King of republican times, though no doubt in the regal period it was the monarch himself who received the blood of the horse.

The rite was intended to procure a good crop, as indeed was explicitly stated by Festus; hence the decoration of the

APPENDIX

horse's head with a string of loaves, and hence the use of its blood at the Parilia, where its smoke, like that from the ashes of unborn calves, was probably regarded as a fertilizing agent to get the ewes and cows with young. It is true that, in its application to the blood of a horse and the ashes of calves, the conception involved a certain confusion of the processes of animal and vegetable fertilization, but such confusion is habitual, if not universal, in ancient and primitive thought.

The question why beanstalks formed the third ingredient in the fuel kindled to make a smoke at the Parilia, is less easy to answer. In antiquity beans were the subject of such a tangle of superstitions that it is seldom or never possible to single out the separate threads and follow them up to their starting-point in the muzzy brain of primitive man.

On St. George's Day (April 23), which is the modern equivalent of the Parilia, Southern Slavonian peasants crown their cows with wreaths of flowers to guard them against the witches; in the evening the wreaths are taken from the cows and fastened to the door of the cattle-stall, where they remain throughout the year till the next St. George's Day.

With the offerings (line 745) and the prayer that accompanied them at the Parilia we may compare the ritual which herdsmen in the Highlands of Scotland used to observe, and the prayers which they used to utter at Beltane, the festival which is the Celtic analogue of the Italian Parilia. Thomas Pennant, who travelled in the Highlands in 1769, describes as follows the ceremony of Beltane, or Bel-tien as he calls it. "On the first of May, the herdsmen of every village hold their Bel-tien, a rural sacrifice. They cut a square trench on the ground, leaving the turf in the middle : on that they make a fire of wood, on which they dress a large caudle of eggs, butter, oatmeal and milk : and bring besides the ingredients of the caudle, plenty of beer and whisky : for each of the company must contribute something. The rites begin with spilling some of the caudle on the ground, by way of libation : on that every one takes a cake of oatmeal, upon which are raised nine square knobs, each dedicated to some particular being, the supposed preserver of their flocks and herds, or to some particular animal, the real destroyer of them : each person then turns his face to the fire, breaks off a knob, and flinging it over his shoulders, says, ' This I give to thee, preserve thou my horses ; this is to thee, preserve thou my sheep ; and so on.' After that they use the same ceremony to the noxious animals : ' This I give to thee, O fox ! spare thou my lambs ; this to thee, O hooded crow ! this to thee, O eagle ! ' When the ceremony is over, they dine on the caudle ; and after the feast is finished, what is left is hid by two persons deputed for that purpose ; but on the next Sunday they reassemble, and finish the reliques of the first entertainment."

In this account of the Beltane festival the spilling of the caudle (composed partly of milk) on the ground answers to the offering of milk to Pales, and the Highland herdsman's prayer to the being who preserved his flocks and herds corresponds to the prayer which the Italian shepherd addressed to Pales, as we learn from the following verses of Ovid. Tibullus tells us that it was his wont to purify his shepherd every year and to sprinkle Pales with milk, referring no doubt to the libation of milk to the goddess at the Parilia. Perhaps Ovid's expression, " when the viands have been cut up," is explained by the Beltane custom, described by Pennant, of breaking a cake of oatmeal in pieces and throwing the bits over the shoulder as offerings to the preservers or destroyers of the flocks and herds. Among the viands so cut up at the Parilia were no doubt included the millet cakes mentioned by Ovid in a previous line. These the Italian shepherd, like the Highland herdsman, may have broken and thrown over his shoulder as an offering to Pales. Certainly the cakes were an important feature of the festival ; for the shepherd ends his prayer with a promise that next year he " will make great cakes for Pales, the shepherds' mistress " (lines 775-776). The oatmeal cakes with nine knobs offered by the Highland herdsmen at Beltane remind us of the cakes with twelve knobs which the Athenians, or some of them, sacrificed in different months to Apollo and Artemis, Zeus the Farmer (Zeus Georgos), Poseidon, Cronus, Hercules, and Theios, whoever Theios may have been.

The Mundus (iv. 821).—Plutarch says that, under the direction of the wise men whom Romulus fetched from Etruria, a trench was dug round the place afterwards called the Comitium, and that first-fruits of all things which are deemed good and necessary were deposited in the trench; and finally all the people brought small portions of soil from their old habitations, threw them into the trench, and mixed them up together. This concluding part of the ceremony was doubtless a symbolical way of transferring the old homes to the new, and of ensuring union and harmony among the citizens by mingling soil brought from all the places where they had dwelt before. It is to this part of the ceremony that Ovid alludes in the words " earth fetched from the neighbouring soil." It is said to be a Hindoo custom to bury earth from the parental homestead in the foundations of a new house. We may also compare a custom observed by the natives of the Northern territories of the Gold Coast in West Africa. "The practice of nearly every family in this country is for the headman to hold a horn containing earth from the sacred place of his ancestors, no matter how far away that is. Thus the story of the family's original home is preserved with great truth. To it sacrifices are made, and thus the Earth-god of the homeland is appeased."

The throwing of fruits of the earth and other useful objects into the trench at the foundation of the city was, we cannot doubt, a sacrifice intended to secure the stability of the walls and the prosperity of the city, either magically by the intrinsic virtue of the things themselves, or religiously by appeasing the spirits of the earth, who were naturally disturbed by the digging of the trench. Sacri-

P

fices offered at the foundation of edifices, such as houses, bridges, and city gates, have been exceedingly common all over the world ; the victims sacrificed have often been human beings. The sacrifices offered by the Romans at the laying of foundations would seem to have been bloodless.

It is to be remembered that the digging of the trench, here described by Ovid, was supposed (as the poet has just reminded us) to have taken place at the festival of the Parilia, which, as we have seen, has some points of analogy with Beltane, the festival formerly held by Scottish herdsmen on May Day. It will be remembered that a feature of the Beltane celebration was the cutting of a square or round trench, in which the herdsmen sacrificed, prayed, and partook of a sacrificial meal. This trench seems to form another link between the Parilia and Beltane. Now the original trench dug at the foundation of the city, on the day of the Parilia appears to have been square, being in fact identical with what was called Square Rome (*Quadrata Roma*), which, as described by Festus, was a place " in front of the temple of Apollo on the Palatine, where are laid up the things which are wont to be employed for the sake of a good omen at the founding of a city ; it is so called because it was originally fortified with a stone wall in a square form." The description answers well to that which Ovid and Plutarch give of the trench dug by Romulus at the foundation of Rome to receive the foundation sacrifices, except that Plutarch describes the trench as carried in a circle round the Comitium ; but Plutarch was certainly wrong as to the situation of the trench, and he may have been equally wrong as to its shape.

Perhaps we can explain Plutarch's mistake in regard to the shape. For he tells us that the trench was called the *mundus* or sky (Olympus is the word he uses to translate the Latin *mundus*), and that the furrow marking out the boundary of the new city was traced in a circle round the *mundus*, as centre. Yet in another passage Plutarch mentions Square Rome, but applies the name in a wider

APPENDIX

sense to the whole city founded by Romulus, and it was apparently in this wider sense that the term Square Rome was generally employed, as by Dionysius of Halicarnassus and Solinus, who says that the city founded by Romulus " was first called Square Rome because it was laid out in a quadrangle. It begins at the wood which is in Apollo's area, and it ends on the brow of the hill at the staircase of Cacus, where was the hut of Faustulus. Romulus dwelt there." Yet the use of the name Square Rome to designate a particular place on the Palatine persisted down to the year A.D. 204 at the least. We may perhaps reconcile the testimonies of Festus and Plutarch on this point by supposing that Square Rome was a square subterranean chamber supposed to represent the trench dug by Romulus at the foundation of the city, while the *mundus* was a circular aperture in the middle of the floor, which gave access to a lower vault or crypt, and down which the offerings could be cast into the vault. This accords well with a statement of Festus, quoting Ateius Capito, that the *mundus* was opened only on three days in the year, namely, on the day after the festival of Vulcan (which fell on the 23rd of August), and again on the 5th of October and the 8th of November. The reason for keeping the *mundus* closed all the rest of the year, according to Festus, or rather his authority, Ateius Capito, was that the lower part of the structure (what I have called the vault or crypt) was sacred to the deified spirits of the dead (*di manes*), who would naturally be able to issue forth and roam about the city if the aperture were uncovered. Hence the three days on which the *mundus* stood open, and hell was let loose, were " religious " days : no public business might be transacted on them, and no battle fought with an enemy.

In 1914 Giacomo Boni discovered on the Palatine a subterranean structure which he identified with the *mundus*, and the identification appears to be generally regarded as at least probable. The structure is situated under the north-eastern portion of the peristyle of the

APPENDIX

Flavian palace, and consists of " a chamber with a beehive roof, the sides of which are lined with *cappellaccio* (the soft dark tufa used in the earliest buildings of Rome) ; in the centre of it a circular shaft descends to two underground passages lined with cement : these diverge, but meet again in another chamber with a domed roof (cut in the rock), of which only half is preserved, the rest having been destroyed by Domitian's foundations."

From Mr. Ashby's account it appears that the discoverer, Boni, identified the upper chamber with the *mundus*. But perhaps we should rather identify the upper chamber with Square Rome and the circular shaft with the *mundus* ; the lower chamber, to which the shaft gives access, would then be the abode of the dead, and we should have to suppose that the hatches were battened down on the ghosts by keeping the mouth of the shaft closed throughout the year, except on the three days when the hatches were unbarred and the unquiet spirits were let loose to squeak and gibber about the streets.

W. Warde Fowler propounded a theory that the *mundus* was a receptacle in which the corn-seed was stowed at harvest, and from which it was brought out for the sowing, but in support of this view, which has no ancient authority, he adduced only somewhat vague analogies. On the other hand he may well have been right in his assumption (equally destitute, however, of ancient authority), that the *mundus* was closed by the stone called *lapis manalis*, which may mean " the ghost stone " ; for we are told by Festus that the stone " was esteemed the Gate of Hell (*Ostium Orci*) through which the souls of the underground folk, who are called ghosts (*manes*), pass to the folk above." Such a stone would be admirably fitted to bottle up the ghosts at the bottom of the *mundus* by inserting it, like a stopper, in the mouth of the shaft.

Robigalia (iv. 907).—The festival of the Robigalia in honour of the god or goddess Mildew (*Robigus* or *Robigo*), for there was some difference of opinion as to the sex of the deity, is recorded under the twenty-fifth of April

420

APPENDIX

in the Esquiline, Caeretan, Maffeian, and Praenestine calendars; and the date of the festival is further confirmed by the testimony of Festus, Pliny, and Servius. A note in the Praenestine calendar, probably indited by Verrius Flaccus, gives some additional information: " The festival of Robigus takes place at the fifth milestone on the Claudian Way, lest mildew (robigo) should harm the corn. A sacrifice is offered and games are held by runners both men and boys." According to Pliny, the festival was instituted by Numa in the eleventh year of his reign, and the reason for holding it on the twenty-fifth of April was because at that season the crops were attacked by mildew. That Mildew, whether you call him Robigus or her Robigo, was a deity, and that he or she could protect the crops against the mildew from which he or she took his or her name, of that no reasonable man appears to have entertained a doubt. " The Robigalia," says the grave Varro, " is named after Robigus; while the crops are in the field sacrifices are offered to this god, lest mildew should attack the crops." To the same effect Festus, or rather his late epitomizer Paulus, says that " the Robigalia is a festival on the twenty-fifth day of April, on which they sacrificed to their god Robigus, who, they thought, could ward off mildew." The only question that could fairly be asked was whether the deity was male or female, a god (Robigus) or a goddess (Robigo). Ovid makes a goddess of Mildew (Robigo), and in this he is supported by Columella, and followed by the Christian Fathers Tertullian, Lactantius, and Augustine. But the weight of ancient authority is in favour of the view that Mildew was really a god (Robigus) rather than a goddess (Robigo); so at least thought, or reported, Varro, Verrius Flaccus, Festus, Aulus Gellius, and Servius.

We learn from Ovid that the victims sacrificed to Mildew (Robigus or Robigo) at the Robigalia were a dog and a sheep (lines 908, 935-936). Columella describes the canine victim more exactly as a sucking puppy, whose blood and bowels served to propitiate the malignant goddess Mildew

421

(Robigo), in order that she might not blight the green crops.

But the god or goddess Mildew was not by any means the only enemy with whom the crops had to wrestle, and whose favour was sought by the sacrifice of a dog. Another formidable foe of the farmer was Sirius or the Dog-star, and what could be more natural than to appease the wrath of the Dog-star by the sacrifice of a dog? And this in fact was done. Every year a sacrifice, called the Doggy Sacrifice (*sacrum canarium*), was offered at Rome by the public priests, because at the rising of the Dog-star the heat of the summer was most intense and sickness was rife. However, it would seem that the sacrifice was not offered at the moment of the rising of the Dog-star, which, as we have seen, took place on the second of August; for in the books of the pontiffs it was laid down as a rule that the days for taking the omens from dogs (*augurio canario agendo*), which presumably coincided with the days on which the dogs were sacrificed, " should be fixed before the corn has sprouted from the sheath, but not before it is in the sheath." This points to a day in spring, and certainly not in the torrid heat of an Italian August. If, as Warde Fowler says, this stage in the growth of the corn takes place in Italy at the end of April or the beginning of May, the Doggy Sacrifice must have been offered about the same time as the Robigalia, but it need not have coincided with it, except by accident; for whereas the Doggy Sacrifice was clearly a movable feast, the date of which was determined by the pontiffs from year to year according to the state of the crops, the Robigalia was always nailed down to the twenty-fifth of April. The Doggy Sacrifice was offered not far from a gate at Rome which was called in consequence the Puppy's Gate (*Porta Catularia*), because there " red bitches were sacrificed to appease the Dog-star, which is hostile to the corn, in order that the yellowing corn may reach maturity."

The situation of the Puppy's Gate at Rome is otherwise unknown; it appears to be mentioned by no other ancient writer. The same may be said of the grove of Mildew mentioned by Ovid, where he saw the rites of the Robigalia performed.

The Good Goddess (v. 148).—The nature of the Good Goddess appears to have been a matter of some uncertainty both in ancient and modern times. Cornelius Labeo regarded her as an Earth-goddess, identical with Maia, Fauna, Ops, and Fatua ; he affirmed that her character as an Earth-goddess was proved by the secret rites observed in her honour, and that she was invoked in the books of the pontiffs under the titles Good, Fauna, Ops, and Fatua. On the whole, this view of the Good Goddess as an Earth-goddess, invoked by women for the sake of procuring offspring and ensuring the fertility of the ground, has been adopted by modern writers on Roman religion. Her identification with the old Roman goddess Maia, who gave her name to the month of May, may have arisen from the accident that both were worshipped on May Day. According to Festus, the Good Goddess was also called Damia, her priestess bore the title of Damiatrix, and a secret sacrifice in her honour was known as *Damium*. This points to an identification or confusion of the Good Goddess with the Greek goddess Damia, a divinity of growth and fertility akin to Demeter. The affinity of the Good Goddess to Demeter comes out in other ways. The victim offered to the Good Goddess was a sow, and tame serpents seem to have been kept in her temple. Similarly, pigs were the victims regularly offered to Demeter, and in her sacred vaults or chasms there were serpents which consumed the pigs thrown into them at the women's festival of the Thesmophoria. Once a year the Roman women celebrated by night secret rites in honour of the Good Goddess ; the celebration took place in the house of the consul or praetor for the year, and all men had to quit the house for the occasion, because no male might be present at the rites ; the Vestal Virgins assisted at the ceremony. In the year 62 B.C., while the women were celebrating these mysteries in the house of Julius Caesar,

APPENDIX

who was then praetor, the notorious profligate Publius Clodius made his way into their midst disguised as a lute-girl, but he was discovered and ejected. The affair created a great scandal, and Caesar in consequence divorced his wife Pompeia, with whom Clodius was in love.

Lemuria (v. 421).—The Lemures were the wandering spirits of the dead, conceived especially as mischievous and dangerous to the living. In this sense, the word seems nearly equivalent to *larvae*, whereas *manes* is so far distinct that it seems generally to signify the benevolent and worshipful spirits of the dead. The ghosts who visited the houses on the three days of the festival (see 491-2) were the spirits of kinsfolk departed this life (443). From this it appears that the three days of the Lemuria were All Souls' Days, on which the spirits of the dead were supposed to revisit their old homes : they were received with a mixture of reverence and fear, and after they had picked up the black beans thrown to them, they were politely, but firmly, turned out of doors. The ghosts were supposed to accept the beans as a substitute for the living members of the family, whom otherwise they would have carried off, being either envious of the living or feeling lonesome in the other world. The Romans threw beans into graves " for the safety of men," probably in the hope that the dead would accept the offering and leave the living alone. The reason which induced ghosts to accept beans as substitutes is not manifest, but beans were supposed to belong in a special way to the dead, and for that reason the Flamen Dialis might not touch or name them, much less might he eat them: his sanctity would have been profaned by any contact, direct or indirect, with the dead.

In many parts of the world it is a common notion that he spirits of the dead revisit the living on one day or on several days of the year ; they return in particular to their old homes, and are received with respect by their kinsfolk, who after entertaining them hospitably, dismiss them more or less forcibly to the Land of the Dead, where it is hoped they will remain peaceably till the same time

APPENDIX

next year. They are believed to be very touchy, and capable, if offended, of afflicting the living with all kinds of misfortune. The use of beans finds a curious parallel in the use of beans at the expulsion of demons in Japan. The head of the family, clad in his finest robes, goes through all the rooms at midnight, carrying a box of roasted beans. From time to time he scatters a handful on a mat, pronouncing a form of words which means " Go forth demons ! enter riches ! "

The Argei (v. 621).—Dionysius of Halicarnassus (i. 38. 3) says, that down to his own time, on the Ides of May, " after offering the preliminary sacrifices according to the laws, the Pontiffs, and with them the Virgins who guard the eternal fire, and the praetors, and all the citizens who may lawfully attend the rites, fling effigies made in human form, thirty in number, from the sacred bridge into the stream of the Tiber, and the effigies they call Argei." Varro : " The Argei are twenty-seven effigies of men made of rushes. . . ." The name Argei or Argea was also applied to a number of chapels distributed over the four regions of Rome : twenty-seven, if we accept a probable emendation of Varro's text. The number twenty-seven (thrice nine) had a mystic significance in Greek or Roman ritual. A procession went to the twenty-seven chapels on March 16 and 17 (iii. 791) ; it is a plausible conjecture that on these days the puppets were carried to the chapels, and left there till May 14 or 15, when they were brought forth, carried again in solemn procession through the streets to the Sublician Bridge, and cast by the Vestals into the Tiber. With regard to the origin and signification of the custom, the ancients seem to have been as much in the dark as we are. Some believed the rite to have been a substitute for human sacrifices. Another theory was that in ancient times men over sixty years of age used to be thrown from the bridge into the river ; and in support of this view the proverb *Sexagenarios de ponte* was quoted. So rooted in the Roman mind was the association of sexagenarians with a bridge and a watery death, that an

appropriate word was coined to describe them, *Depontani* !
—W. Mannhardt proposed to regard the puppets as
representing the dying spirit of vegetation in the spring,
who at the beginning of summer was carried out to burial
and thrown into the river, in order that revived by the
water, he might return in fresh vigour next year, to animate
the crops and other fruits of the earth. This ingenious
theory he supported by many parallel customs of modern
European peasants, in which the outworn spirit of Vegetation is certainly thus represented by puppets thrown
into water. But he admitted that the date was not a
very suitable one for the death and burial of the Spirit of
Vegetation, who at that season might rather be thought
to be in the very flower of his age. To meet this objection,
he was driven to conjecture that the custom may originally
have been celebrated in the height of summer, perhaps on
Midsummer Day ; the shift of date he thought may have
occurred under the old unreformed calendar, when the
times were out of joint. But this is a mere conjecture,
unsupported by evidence. The theory is open to other
objections ; and so far as I can see, there is little or nothing
to suggest that the ceremony had anything to do with
vegetation. The puppets were made of rushes ; the case
would have been different if they had been made of corn-
stalks. There was little in the Vestals and Pontiffs to
connect them with the Spirit of Vegetation. The old bridge
over the Tiber is hardly a place where we should expect
to meet the Spirit of Vegetation. On the whole then, I
find no sufficient reason for regarding the ceremony as a
fertility rite.

But the description of Plutarch, "the greatest of
purifications" (*Q. Rom.* 86), suggests an interpretation
which can be supported by world-wide analogies. In many
parts of the world it has been customary to set apart a day
or several days every year for the public expulsion of all
the evils which are supposed to have accumulated in the
country and the town during the past year. Often these
evils are personified as demons or ghosts ; where the people

dwell beside a river or sea, the demons are often sent away in boats which are allowed to drift down stream or out to sea. Sometimes they are supposed to be embodied in effigies, which are cast out with great ceremony. Here I will quote only a single example.

" At Old Calabar, on the coast of Guinea, the devils and ghosts are, or used to be, publicly expelled once in two years. Among the spirits thus driven from their haunts are the souls of all the people who have died since the last lustration of the town. About three weeks or a month before the expulsion, which, according to one account, takes place in the month of November, rude effigies representing men and animals, such as crocodiles, leopards, elephants, bullocks and birds, are made of wicker-work or wood, and being hung with strips of cloth and bedizened with gewgaws, are set before the door of every house. About three o'clock in the morning of the day appointed for the ceremony the whole population turns out into the streets, and proceeds with a deafening uproar and in a state of the wildest excitement to drive all lurking devils and ghosts into the effigies, in order that they may be banished with them from the abodes of men. For this purpose bands of people roam through the streets knocking on doors, firing guns, beating drums, blowing on horns, ringing bells, clattering pots and pans, shouting and hallooing with might and main ; in short, making all the noise it is possible for them to raise. The hubbub goes on till the approach of dawn, when it gradually subsides and ceases altogether at sunrise. By this time the houses have been thoroughly swept, and all the frightened spirits are supposed to have huddled into the effigies or their fluttering drapery. In these wicker figures are also deposited the sweepings of the houses and the ashes of yesterday's fires. Then the demon-laden images are hastily snatched up, and carried in tumultuous procession down to the brink of the river, and thrown into the water to the tuck of drums. The ebb-tide bears them away seaward, and thus the town is swept clean of ghosts and devils for another two years."

427

APPENDIX

Now if we could assume that the Argei represented the accumulated demons of the whole year, the resemblance between the Roman and African customs would be close, and Plutarch would be justified in describing the ceremony as " the greatest of purifications." The three days of the Lemuria ended on May 13, that is, on the very day before the Argei were thrown into the water. The immediate sequence suggests that while the Lemuria was the private expulsion of ghosts, the ceremony of the Argei was the public expulsion of the same uncanny visitors on the following day.

But there is another and simpler explanation of the Argei which deserves to be considered. May they not have been offerings to the River-god, to pacify him, and to induce him to put up with the indignity of having a bridge built across his stream? There is much to be said for this explanation, which I suggested many years ago, and which I still incline to think the most probable. We can easily imagine the indignation which a river-god must feel at the sight of a bridge, and of people passing dry-shod across it, who in the course of nature would have been drowned at the ford. Thus the deity is robbed of his prey; and he naturally puts in a claim for compensation. That claim the Romans may have attempted to satisfy by throwing, once a year, the puppets in human shape from the offending bridge, one puppet for every ward in the city, trusting that the river-god would graciously accept them instead of live men and women, and that thus contented, he would not rise in flood, and come in person to snatch his prey from the streets and houses of Rome. On this hypothesis, nothing could be more fitting than that the offering should be under the auspices of the pontiffs, whose very name, signifying " bridge-makers," marked them out as the culprits responsible for the sacrilege, and therefore as the penitents bound to atone for it. The bridge which the pontiffs are traditionally said to have built was the very same Sublician Bridge from which the puppets were thrown; the tradi-

APPENDIX

tion of the construction was presumed in the song of the Salii, one of the oldest documents of the Latin language. The bridge was the first ever built at Rome; its custody and maintenance were committed to the pontiffs, who had to perform certain solemn rites and sacrifices whenever it stood in need of repairs.

The belief that the spirit of a river demands a sacrifice of one or more human victims each year persists in some parts of Europe till this day. Similar conceptions meet us in many parts of the world; to this day, or down at all events to recent times, bridges have been the object of superstitious fear, not only in Africa and India, but even in the more backward parts of Europe.

Semo Sancus (vi. 213).—The worship of Semo Sancus Dius Fidius was cared for by a special company of priests, who bore the title of Bidental; and as *bidental* was the name given to a place struck by lightning, at which an expiatory sacrifice of two-year-old sheep (*bidentes*) had been offered, we may infer that the Bidental priests were charged with the duty of offering such sacrifices. Semo is apparently the singular form of a noun which occurs in the plural form *Semunis* in the song of the Salii. The statue of Semo Sancus, which Justin Martyr and Tertullian took for that of Simon the Magician, has been found at Rome, with the inscription which Tertullian, or his informant, misread: *Sanco sancto Semon. deo* [*sic*, for *Dio*] *Fidio sacrum decuria sacerdotum bidentalium.* Thus to make sure that the god received his full title, the priests called him sanctus as well as sancus. It was natural that he should be invoked in oaths or asseverations to attest the truth of the statement: *Me Dius Fidius* or *Medius Fidius.* It was a rule of domestic ritual, that he who would swear by Dius Fidius should go out into the *compluvium*, the unroofed place in the middle of the house, where he could swear under the open sky; and the god's temple had a hole in the roof through which the sky could be seen. If Dius Fidius was a sky-god who wielded the lightning, it was very natural that those who took his name on their lips should do so in the open air, where the deity could see them and smite them to the ground with his thunderbolt if they took his name in vain. On the bronze tablets discovered at Gubbio (Iguvium) there is mention of a god Fisos Sansios or Fisous Sansios, who was probably no other than Fidius Sancus in a dialectically different form. Dius is probably connected with the nouns Djovis and Jupiter : in other words, the people originally swore by the Sky-god under the special title of Fidius, as the guardian of good faith : but in time they came to look upon him as a distinct deity. Thus we seem bound to recognize a process of multiplying gods, by creating special gods for the discharge of special functions, which had previously been performed by a single god of all work. No people, perhaps, carried this principle further than the Romans ; and if only they had had time to apply it consistently to their chief god Jupiter, they might have ended by stripping him of his multifarious duties, and entrusting them to a number of deputy-deities, who, we cannot doubt, would have discharged them quite as efficiently. Thus, gradually retiring from the active control of affairs in this sublunary sphere, Jupiter might at last have become little more than a sleeping partner in a divine firm, whose august name might still be read on the golden plate of the celestial door, and whose existence everyone acknowledged in theory, though nobody troubled about him in practice. To this state of dignified and somnolent repose the great Sky-god has in fact been reduced almost all over Africa at the present day.

The worship of Vesta (vi. 257).—There seems every reason to believe that the worship of Vesta, in other words, the institution of a Common Hearth with a sacred and perpetual fire burning on it, was very much older than the oldest of her temples in Rome. When we compare Vesta with the Greek Hestia, whose very name, etymologically linked with Vesta, means simply " Hearth," and who like Vesta was worshipped in the Prytaneum, that is, in the Prince's house, where a perpetual fire burned on the hearth,

APPENDIX

we can hardly doubt that the institution dates from a remote prehistoric period when the ancestors of the Greeks and Romans dwelt together and worshipped the fire which burned on the hearth of the King's house. For the temple of Vesta was situated beside the Regia or King's house, and was never a temple in the strict sense of the word, for it had never been consecrated by the augurs. So in Greece the Common Hearth appears never to have been placed in a temple, but regularly in a prytaneum, that is the house of the prytanis or prince. The maintenance of a perpetual fire in it was probably at first a matter rather of practical convenience than of religious ritual. When a fire has to be laboriously kindled by rubbing two sticks against each other, it is very convenient to keep a fire constantly burning. That this mode of kindling fire by the friction of wood was formerly in vogue amongst the Romans, we know from the rule, that whenever the Vestal fire was accidentally extinguished, the Vestal Virgins were whipped by the Pontifex Maximus, and compelled to rub a board of lucky wood with a borer till it took fire. We may further suppose that the Vestal Virgins represented the King's unmarried daughters, who may have been charged with the duties of keeping the fire always alight on the hearth, fetching water, grinding corn, and baking cakes, to be eaten by the family as well as to be offered to the Goddess of the Hearth.

The Pontifex Maximus seems to have possessed paternal power over them, and he appears in certain respects to have succeeded to the place and functions of the old King, though in other respects these were inherited by the Rex Sacrificulus.

Among the Damaras or Hereros of S.W. Africa the sacred fire, which is kept constantly burning, is regularly tended by the King's eldest unmarried daughter. The round shape of the temple of Vesta is explained most naturally as the ancient form of house which the Italians are known to have inhabited in prehistoric ages. The prehistoric villages disinterred in North Italy show these round huts, which appear to have been constructed of wattle and daub, or branches. In the cemetery of Alba Longa, the ashes are deposited in urns which obviously represent round huts, constructed of clay, brushwood, or other perishable stuff. At Rome itself funeral urns of the same type were found. In view of all this evidence it is reasonable to assume that the first temple of Vesta at Rome was a round hut of the same sort. Two such huts were sedulously preserved at Rome itself. One of these was the hut of Romulus on the Palatine (iii. 183) ; the other was the hut of Faustulus, preserved in the temple of Jupiter (*Mythographi Graeci*, p. 149).

Vacuna (vi. 307).—Writing from his home in the Sabine hills an immortal letter, instinct with love of the country, to a city friend who did not share his rural tastes, Horace concludes by saying that he had dictated the letter " behind Vacuna's mouldering fane." On this passage his old scholiast Porphyrion remarks that Vacuna was a Sabine goddess of uncertain form and nature ; some thought that she was Bellona, others Minerva, and others Diana. In the first book of his lost work, *The Antiquities of Divine Things*, Varro identified her with Victory. The statement that she was a Sabine goddess is confirmed by several inscriptions found in the Sabine country, for they contain dedications to her. One of them, found near Reate, records the vow of two persons to Vacuna for the return of a certain L. Acestus from Africa. Another, also found near Reate, records the vow of a certain Esuvius Modestus for the health of his father. The latter vow suggests that Vacuna was a medical goddess, endowed with healing power.

Now we know from Pliny that Vacuna had a grove in the Sabine country near to the river Avens (the modern *Velino*) and to Reate, and that in the territory of Reate there was a lake called the lake of Cutilia or Cutiliae, which Varro regarded as the navel or central point of Italy, and in which there was a wood and a floating island. Seneca tells us that he had seen the island, and that.

though it was clothed with grass and trees, it never remained stationary, but floated hither and thither with every breath of wind. This property he attributed in part to the weight of the water, which he describes as medicated. The lake of Cutilia, with its moving island, is mentioned by Varro, and is described by Dionysius of Halicarnassus and Macrobius, who confirm Seneca's account of the floating island, except that according to Dionysius only grass and some inconsiderable bushes grew on it, and the island stood not more than a foot above the level of the lake. Dionysius tells us further that the natives regarded the lake as bottomless and as sacred to Victory (Nike), and that in consequence they surrounded the water with fillets and allowed nobody to approach it except at certain times of the year, when religious rites were performed. At these times sacrifices were offered on the floating island by persons who might lawfully do so. Now since in this part of his work, which describes the first settlement of the aborigines in the heart of Italy, Dionysius is professedly following the *Antiquities* of Varro, it becomes highly probable that the goddess of the lake, whom Dionysius calls Victory, was no other than Vacuna, whom Varro, as we saw, identified with Victory.

Strabo informs us that the water of Cutilia was cold, and that people drank it and sat in it for the healing of disease. He does not indeed mention the lake but only the waters at Cutiliae (Cutilia), which was a town on a hill near the lake. This water at Cutilia in the Sabine country is described by Pliny as so excessively cold that it almost seemed to bite the drinker, yet as extremely salubrious for the stomach, the sinews, and indeed the whole body; further he says that it was of a nitrous quality and purgative in its effect. The same statement had previously been made by Vitruvius, from whom Pliny may have borrowed it. Celsius recommended standing " in cold medical springs like those at Cutiliae " as a remedy for looseness of the bowels.

The purgative effect of the water of Cutilia was ex-

433

perienced with fatal results by the Emperor Vespasian. Being a native of the Sabine country, for he was born at a small village near Reate, it was his habit to pass the hot months of the Italian summer among his native mountains at Cutilia and in the country about Reate. In the last year of his life (A.D. 79), being troubled with a slight indisposition in Campania, he returned in haste to Rome, and from there rode or was carried up to the scenes of his youth at Cutilia and the neighbourhood. There, as a remedy for the sickness which increased upon him, he took frequent draughts of the ice-cold water, and though they had no effect in abating his malady, he continued to discharge his imperial duties lying in bed, where he gave audience to embassies. But at last he was seized with a fit of diarrhœa so violent that he almost swooned. Feeling the hand of death upon him, he said, " An emperor should die standing." So saying, he struggled to his feet and, with the support of his attendants, died standing like an emperor and a soldier.

The Emperor was not the only victim of the cold water cure, which had been made fashionable by Antonius Musa, physician to Augustus. Having recalled his imperial master from the gates of death by cold baths and copious draughts of cold water in the style of Doctor Sagrando, the Roman doctor blossomed out into fame : the Emperor rewarded him liberally : the Senate showered money and honours on him : his admirers subscribed for a portrait-statue of the good physician, which was set up beside that of his divine prototype Aesculapius. Cold water now became the rage and the last word in medical science. The fashionable doctor compelled poor Horace, shivering and shuddering, to submit to cold douches in the depth of winter, when he longed for the sunshine and the myrtle-groves of Baiae. But Musa tried his nostrum once too often when he applied it to the youthful Marcellus, the hope of Rome and perhaps the destined heir of the empire ; for the young man succumbed to the cure.

On the whole it appears that for a time the cold medicinal

springs of Cutilia in the Sabine hills were resorted to by the sick, who both drank the water and bathed in it for the sake of their health. Perhaps, on the days when sacrifices were offered to the goddess on the island, and the holy lake was opened to the public, the patients were allowed to plunge into its healing water, like the impotent folk at the pool of Bethesda ; and as the curative property of the pool at Jerusalem was ascribed to an angel who went down at a certain season into the pool and troubled the water, so we may suppose that at Cutilia the sick who survived the cold plunge attributed their deliverance to the divine Lady of the Lake, the goddess Vacuna. From Ovid we learn that, when sacrifices were offered to Vacuna, people stood and sat in front of her sacred hearth. If the present view of Vacuna is correct, we may suppose that these worshippers were the visitors to the Spa who had benefited by the waters, and who testified their gratitude to the goddess for their cure by joining in a thanksgiving service. And when we remember the purgative effect of the water, and the melancholy fate of Vespasian, we shall perhaps not go far astray if we conjecture that the name and the function of Vacuna, the goddess of the water, had reference *ad evacuandum alvum.* In that case we need not wonder that Horace, who had suffered from her, allowed her shrine at the back of his house in the country to fall into decay. Yet long after the poet's ashes had been laid beside those of his friend Maecenas on the Esquiline, the Emperor Vespasian, who had even less reason than Horace to be grateful to Vacuna, appears to have repaired the ruined shrine ; for in the valley of the Digentia, which flowed through or near Horace's farm, and at the village of Rocca Giovine, there was found an inscription recording that the Emperor Vespasian had restored at his own expense the temple of Victory, which had fallen into ruin through long lapse of time. When we bear in mind that Vacuna was identified with Victory by Varro, we need not hesitate to believe that this ruined temple of Victory was no other than

APPENDIX

" the mouldering fane of Vacuna " mentioned by Horace. In after ages, when the memory of Vacuna and her drastic water had faded from the minds even of the learned, the poet Ausonius used her name as a synonym for leisure, evidently deriving her name from *vacare* in the sense of " to be at leisure."

Cloaca (vi. 401).—The low ground in the centre of Rome, surrounded by hills from which the water runs down into it, must have been very swampy in the old days before it was drained by the wonderful system of stone sewers, which dates from the regal period and has survived in part to the present time. Dionysius of Halicarnassus tells us that when the Sabine king Tatius first occupied the Capitoline and Quirinal hills, the valley at the foot of the Capitol was occupied partly by a wood and partly by a lake formed by the streams which poured down from the surrounding hills. The king cut down the wood and filled up a great part of the lake, and so formed the Roman Forum, which was probably in origin rather a market than a place of public assembly, like the Cattle Market (*Forum Boarium* or *Bovarium*), the Vegetable Market (*Forum Holitorium*), the Fish Market (*Forum Piscarium*), and so forth. Varro speaks of " the marshy place which was then in the Forum before the sewers were made." Even when Rome had risen to the height of her glory as mistress of the world, the extent and solidity of these vast drainage works, testifying to the engineering skill and enterprise of earlier ages, excited the wonder and admiration of Greeks and Romans alike.

The existing remains of the ancient Roman sewers are of various dates and various styles. The sewers of Republican or regal date are built of squared blocks of tufa or peperino : the oldest of them are roofed over with triangular tops formed of courses of stones on level beds, each course projecting over the one below. This archaic mode of construction, which probably preceded the invention of the arch, is exemplified in the great beehive tombs of prehistoric Greece, and at Rome the lowest

APPENDIX

dungeon of the Mamertine prison, known as the Tullianum, where the Catalinarian conspirators were strangled, is built in the same primitive style of masonry and in the same circular shape. But most, apparently, of the Republican or regal sewers are roofed with regular arches of solid masonry. Under the Empire great sewers were formed of concrete faced with bricks and covered with semicircular vaults also of concrete. Smaller drains were commonly roofed with large tiles set leaning together in a triangular form. The Great Sewer (*Cloaca Maxima*) starts in the valley of the Subura, at the foot of the Carinae, the elevated spur of the Esquiline, on which now stand the churches of S. Pietro in Vincoli and S. Francesco di Paolo. It then crosses the Forum, passing under the south end of the Basilica Julia. Thence it runs under the ancient Tuscan street (*vicus Tuscus*) and the valley of the Velabrum, till it reaches the Tiber near the little round temple in the Forum Boarium. In 1890 a piece of the sewer more than 200 yards long was cleared out between the Forum of Augustus and the Roman Forum. It is here built of massive blocks of peperino (*lapis Gabinus*); it is 10 feet 6 inches wide, and about 14 feet high to the crown of the vault. Its floor is paved with polygonal blocks of lava, like a Roman street. At its exit on the Tiber the arch of the sewer is nearly 11 feet wide and more than 12 feet high, and is formed of three rings of peperino blocks. A considerable piece of this great sewer is now to be seen near the church of S. Giorgio in Velabro. The larger part of this section belongs to the Republican period, but some of the restorations are of later date.

As the original construction of these great arched sewers was unanimously referred by the Romans to their two Etruscan kings, the Tarquins, it is natural to suppose that the use of the arch in architecture was borrowed by the Romans from Etruria. Indeed, some good modern scholars have held that the invention of the true arch, built of wedge-shaped blocks of stone (*voussoirs*) fitted together in a segment of a circle, must be attributed to

437

the Etruscans, who in that case proved themselves the masters both of the Greeks and the Romans in this important branch of architecture. The Etruscan origin of the great Roman sewers is confirmed by the existence of an exactly similar sewer built of stone at the Etruscan city of Graviscae, by the sea near Tarquinii. It is 14 feet wide, and ends, like the Great Sewer at Rome, in a massive quay wall some 20 feet high. Other ancient sewers of the same sort exist in Etruria. In recent years the excavations conducted by Mr. Woolley for the British Museum at Ur of the Chaldees have proved that the principle of the arch was familiar to the ancient inhabitants of Mesopotamia at a time which long preceded, not only the foundation of Rome, but the settlement of the Etruscans in Italy. Hence it is probable that the Etruscans brought the knowledge of the arch with them from their old home in Asia, where they may have borrowed it, directly or indirectly, from Babylonia.

Vertumnus or Vortumnus (vi. 409).—Some Roman antiquaries looked on Vortumnus as an Etruscan deity. Varro even affirmed that Vortumnus was the chief god of Etruria, and that at Rome his image was set up in the Tuscan Street on account of his Tuscan origin. Similarly Propertius represents the god as declaring in so many words that he was an Etruscan and came from Etruria, having deserted the Etruscan city of Volsinii during the wars. But we know that there was a temple of Vortumnus on the Aventine, which appears to have been dedicated on the 13th of August, and the temple contained a picture of M. Fulvius Flaccus in his triumphal robes. Since M. Fulvius Flaccus was consul in 264 B.C. and celebrated a triumph in the same year for his victory over the Volsinians, we may suppose with some degree of probability that the temple was erected by the victorious general, not only to commemorate his success, but also to secure the divine favour by transferring the chief god of the conquered foe from Volsinii to Rome. Now in the days of the independence of Etruria, the federal council of the

APPENDIX

league regularly met at the shrine of a goddess named Voltumna, where measures of war and peace were concerted. This shrine of Voltumna appears to have been at or near Volsinii, for down to the time of Constantine an annual assembly was held at Volsinii, accompanied by the celebration of theatrical performances and gladiatorial combats. This suggests that the goddess Voltumna was the wife, or, at all events, the female counterpart, of Vortumnus, and that the pair were the patron deities of Volsinii, from which they took their name and to which they stood in much the same relation in which Athena stood to Athens. If that was so, the proper form of the god's name would seem to have been Voltumnus rather than Vortumnus.

If Vortumnus was indeed an Etruscan deity in name and origin, the similarity of his name, especially in the form Vertumnus, to Latin is deceptive, and the account which the Roman poets gave of his power of shape-shifting must be dismissed as based on nothing better than the false etymology which would explain the name Vertumnus as equivalent to Turner, from *vertere*, " to turn." We have seen that Propertius and Ovid proposed to derive the god's name from his exploit in turning back the flooded Tiber. But no sooner has he suggested this explanation than Propertius propounds another. Perhaps, says he, speaking in the god's name, " I am called Vertumnus because I receive the fruit of the turning year " (*annus vertens*). For it seems that the first fruits of the season were offered to Vertumnus. In the right hand of his image, or perhaps rather in a basket which he held out to his worshippers, might be seen the first purple grapes of the vintage, the first yellow ears of corn at harvest, sweet blushing cherries, autumn plums, apples and pears, and mulberries reddening in summer days; there, too, in the basket lay the dark-green cucumber and swelling gourd, and there, or wreathed about his face, drooped every flower that bloomed in the meadows. This fancy Ovid took up and told, in charming verses worthy of Herrick,

APPENDIX

how Vertumnus, the god of the turning year, wooed and won the love of Pomona, the goddess of fruit, who dwelt demure in her loved orchard, barred against the wanton crew of amorous rural deities, till Vertumnus found his way into her heart. But the goddess was coy, and the god justified his name by turning into many shapes before she yielded. Now he presented himself to her in the guise of a reaper, with his basket of corn-ears on his arm; now he was a haymaker, fresh from tossing the hay in the meadow, with a wisp of grass wound round his brows; now he was a ploughman with an ox-goad in his hand, as if he had just unyoked the weary oxen on the furrowed field; again he showed himself as a pruner of vines with his pruning-knife; or he carried a ladder on which to climb the fruit-trees and pluck the ripening apples from the boughs; he even took the shape of a fisherman with his rod and of a soldier with his sword. But all in vain; the shy goddess still said no, till at last he doffed his disguises and appeared in his own proper form, as the sun breaks through clouds to shine in undimmed radiance. Thus Vertumnus won Pomona's love. In this description of the god's successive transformations Ovid clearly borrowed much of his imagery from Propertius, who enumerates an even greater variety of personages into which this Italian Proteus could convert himself at will, among them a girl in Coan silk, a tipsy reveller, a hunter, a fowler, a charioteer, a circus-rider, a pedlar, a shepherd, and one who carried baskets of roses on summer's dusty ways. More briefly, Tibullus alludes to the thousand varied garbs which Vertumnus could assume, and every one of which sat well on him. Thus, if we accept the evidence of the poets, Vertumnus was a sort of heavenly harlequin.

Portunus (vi. 547).—Portunus was a genuine old Latin god; Virgil calls him Father Portunus, and represents him as giving a shove to one of the galleys in the race instituted, with other games, by Aeneas in honour of his father Anchises. The antiquity of his worship is indicated by the circumstance that it was in charge of a special

APPENDIX

flamen (*Flamen Portunalis*), one of whose duties, oddly enough, was to anoint the arms of the god Quirinus with ointment drawn from a special vessel, coated with pitch, called a *persillum*. A festival called the Portunalia was held in his honour on the seventeenth of August; it is mentioned in many ancient calendars, of which three (the Amiternine, the Valensian, and the Allifanine) add a note explaining that the Portunalia was a festival celebrated in honour of Portunus at the Aemilian bridge. Hence, when Varro tells us that "the Portunalia is named after Portunus, to whom on that day a temple was dedicated in the port of Tiber (*in portu Tiberino*) and a festival instituted," we may assume that "the port of the Tiber," and with it the temple of Portunus, was at Rome near the Aemilian bridge, and not at the mouth of the Tiber, at Ostia, as Th. Mommsen supposed.

As to the nature and functions of Portunus the ancients seem to have hesitated whether to derive his name from *portus*, "port," "harbour," or from *porta*, "gate," and consequently whether to regard him as the guardian deity of harbours or of gates. Ovid clearly takes the former view, for he says (line 546) that Portunus was given all authority over harbours. Cicero seems to have been of the same mind, for he derived the name of Portunus from *portus*, "port"; and Virgil apparently adopted the same opinion, for in his description of the race between the galleys he makes Portunus help the winning galley "into port." Consistently with this etymology, Virgil's old commentator Servius, in a note on this passage, describes Portunus as "a marine god who presides over harbours." On the other hand, Festus, or rather his abbreviator Paulus, informs us that the guardianship of the key was thought to be with Portunus, who was supposed to hold a key in his hand and was thought to be "the god of gates." A scholiast on Virgil says that Portunus was usually painted holding a key in his hand. Varro combined both etymologies and functions, for he described Portunus as "the guardian of harbours and gates." In favour of the con-

APPENDIX

nexion of Portunus with gates rather than with harbours
it has been pointed out that the temple of Janus, who in
one at least of his aspects was certainly a god of gates,
was dedicated on the same day as the temple of Portunus,
that is, on August 17. Taking this along with his emblem
the key, which was also an emblem of Janus, we may
perhaps conclude with Wissowa that Portunus was
primarily a god of gates (*portarum*) and only secondarily
a god of harbours (*portuum*). There seems to be reason
to think that originally *portus* and *porta* differed only in
sound, not in sense.

The site of the Aemilian bridge, near which stood the
temple of Portunus, is not certain, but it seems to have
coincided roughly with that of the modern Ponte Rotto,
now removed. In the flat ground on the left bank of the
Tiber at this point there are two well-preserved ancient
temples which have been converted into churches under
the names of S. Maria Egiziaca and S. Maria del Sole,
and the former has been conjecturally identified by Huelsen
with the temple of Mother Matuta. The same eminent
topographer would identify the church of S. Maria del
Sole with the temple of Portunus.

INDEX

Acastus, cleansing of Peleus by, ii. 40

Acca mourns Remus, iv. 854, v. 453

Achates meets Anna, iii. 604

Achelous, ii. 43

Achilles, Homer's poems on, ii. 119; and Chiron, v. 390

Acmonides, one of the Cyclopes, iv. 288

Actium, victory of, 31 B.C., i. 711

Actorides cleansed by Peleus, ii. 39

Adonis, red anemones from, v. 227

Aegeus and Medea, ii. 41

Aemilian Bridge, the, temple of Portunus at, p. 441; site of, p. 442

Aeneas, Vestal fire brought to Rome by, i. 527; introduces All Souls' Days, ii. 543; lands in Latium, ii. 680, iv. 251*; Augustus' descent from, iii. 425; offers hospitality to Anna, iii. 601; born of Venus and Anchises, iv. 37; Greek beliefs brought to Italy by, iv. 78; fire allows escape of, iv. 799; his war with Turnus, iv. 879, and his appeal to Jupiter, iv. 892; the Palladium brought to Rome by, vi. 434; and the Golden Bough, p. 403; games instituted by, p. 440

Aesculapius, restores Hippolytus, vi. 746; Jupiter's thunderbolt at, vi. 759; reference, i. 291

Aethra, mother of the Hyades, v. 171

Africa, parallel to rites of Salii in, pp. 400-401; killing of divine kings in, pp. 404-405; expulsion of devils, p. 427; Sky-god of, p. 430; sacred fire in, p. 431

African calendars, pp. 385-386

Agamemnon, v. 307

Aganippe, v. 7

Agenor, father of Europa, vi. 712

Agonal, derivation of, i. 318, v. 721

Agrippa, son of Tiberinus, iv. 49

Aitia (Callimachus) *Fasti* suggested by, p. xxiv

Alba Longa, funeral urns at, p. 432; reference, iv. 43

Albula, River (the Tiber), ii. 389, v. 646

Alcides. See Hercules

Alcmaeon, son of Amphiaraus, ii. 43

Alcyone of the Pleiades, iv. 173

Algidus, Mt., Battle of, vi. 722

All Souls' Days, introduction and rites of, ii. 548; the Lemuria as, p. 424

Almo, God of the river, father of Lara, ii. 601; the river, iv. 337

Amalthea the Naiad, hides Jupiter, v. 115; Horn of, v. 128

Ampelus, legend of, iii. 409

Amphitrite, v. 731

Amulius, uncle of Silvia, Romulus and Remus ordered to be drowned by, iii. 35, 49, iv. 53; killed by Romulus, iii. 67, iv. 809

Anchises, marries Venus, iv. 35, 123; games in honour of, p. 440

Ancilia, Numa receives, from Jupiter, iii. 377; Mamurius' copies of, p. 398

Ancus Marcius, King, vi. 803

Anglo-Saxon Calendar, the, p. 387

443

INDEX

INDEX

INDEX

INDEX

447

INDEX

448

INDEX

INDEX

Ida, Mt., Cybele on, iv. 249, 264
Idas fights Pollux, v. 699, 713
Ilia (see Silvia), mother of Romulus and Remus
Ilus founds Troy, vi. 419
Imbrex, Licinius, on Nerio, p. 407
Inachian Cow (Isis) as Anna Perenna, iii. 657
India, Bacchus in, iii. 720, 729; parallel to Salii in, p. 400
Ino, wife of Athamas, and the toasted seeds, ii. 628, vi. 553; plots against Phrixus and Helle, iii. 853; nurses Bacchus, vi. 485; Juno's resentment against, vi. 487, 507; becomes Leucothea, vi. 501, 545; attacked by Thyads, vi. 514; saved by Hercules, vi. 521; entertained by Carmentis, vi. 529; becomes Matuta, vi. 545
Inuus, god honoured by the Luperci, p. 392
Io as the Bull constellation, v. 619
Iris, purple, v. 223
Isis, daughter of Inachus, goose sacrificed to, i. 454
Ivy, its connexion with Bacchus, iii. 767

Janiculum, i. 246
January, added to ancient calendar, i. 33, p. 385; the first month in the year, ii. 48
Janus, opener of the year, i. 64; form of, i. 69, pp. 388-389, and reason, i. 133; derivation from Chaos, i. 104; changing functions of, i. 116; omens connected with, i. 171; figured on the *As*, i. 231; repulses the Sabines, i. 268; the gate in peace and war, i. 277; gives the nymph Crane control of hinges, vi. 119; rod of, white-thorn, vi. 129, 165; derivation from door, p. 387; original form of name, p. 387; connexion with Jupiter, p. 388; similarity of function to Portunus, p. 442; references, iii. 881, v. 424
Japan, use of beans for demons in, p. 425
Jason, i. 491

Jerome cited on death of **Ovid**, p. xvii n.
Jove. See Jupiter
Juba, defeat of, by Caesar, **iv.** 380
Jukun, King of the, magical character of, pp. 404-405
Julia Augusta, deification of, **i.** 536
Julii, college of the Lupercii, p. 389; Mark Antony Master of, p. 391
Julius Caesar, Pontifex Maximus, i. 530; reform of calendar by, iii. 156; murder of, iii. 697; descent from Venus, iv. 124; defeats Juba, iv. 379; Augustus avenges death, v. 573; college of the Luperci founded by, p. 389; refuses the crown, pp. 391-392; the Thesmophoria held at house of, 62 B.C., p. 423; divorces Pompeia, p. 424
Julus, sire of the Julian house, iv. 39
July, interpolation in *Fasti* to explain, p. xviii
June, month of the young, i. 41, v. 73, vi. 88; derived from Juno, vi. 26; in calendars of neighbouring towns, vi. 58; from Juventas, vi. 75; from junction of Sabines and Romans, vi. 96; weddings in, vi. 223
Juno, guardian of the Calends, i. 55; aids the Sabines, i. 265; punishes Callisto, ii. 177; Lara informs of Jupiter and Juturna, ii. 605; worshipped in Sparta and Mycenae, iii. 83; Sabine wives assemble in temple of, iii. 205; temple to, on Mt. Esquiline, iii. 246; dislike of the Bull, iv. 720; judgement of Paris, vi. 16, 44, 99; claims June, vi. 26; in temple of Jupiter, vi. 34, 52, 73; sister and wife of Jupiter vi. 27; daughter of Saturn, vi. 29, 285; worship of, by Rome, vi. 51, and other towns, vi. 58; resents Ino, vi. 487, 507; derivation from Diono, p. 388
Juno Lucina, origin of belief in her power to aid women in childbed,

451

INDEX

INDEX

INDEX

Maori calendar, the, p. 386

Marcellus, Musa's cold-water treatment of, p. 434

March, the first month, i. 39, iii. 135, p. 385; named from Mars, iii. 4

Marcia, daughter of L. Marcius Philippus, vi. 802

Mark Antony as Master of the Luperci offers Julius Caesar the crown, pp. 391-392

Mars, the first month given to, by Romulus, i. 39, iii. 73; father of Romulus, i. 39, iii. 39, iv. 57, v. 465, p. 481; as the Marching God (*Gradivus*), ii. 861; possesses Silvia, iii. 21; early worship of, iii. 79, p. 398; months in foreign calendars named after, iii. 87; reason for festival kept by Matrons, iii. 170; loves Minerva, iii. 681, p. 407; Anna Perenna beguiles, iii. 685, p. 407; Venus' month next to that of, iv. 130; and Sterope, iv. 172; birth of, v. 229; as the Avenger visits temple built by Augustus, v. 550; festival of, in June, vi. 191; appeals to Jupiter regarding Gallic siege of Rome, 390 B.C., vi. 354; as God of War, p. 397; God of Agriculture and Vegetation, pp. 397-399; prayer to, by Hersilia, p. 407; Nerio as wife of, pp. 407-409; sacrifice of October horse to, p. 414

Marsyas, first flautist, iv. 703

Martial on Anna Perenna, p. 406

Masinissa defeats Syphax, iv. 769

Matralia, the mothers' festival, vi. 475

Matrons, festival of (Matronalia), reasons for being in March, iii. 170; worship of Juno Lucina at, iii. 247

Matuta, festival of (Matralia), vi. 479; identified with Ino (*q.v.*), vi. 545; her dislike of slaves, vi. 551; temples to, vi. 480, 569, p. 442; goddess of mothers, vi. 559

Mavors, Father, iv. 828, vi. 53

May, the third month, i. 41; derivations of, v. 1; as Majesty, v. 25; as the month of the Elders,

v. 74, 427, vi. 88; from Maia of the Pleiades, v. 84, vi. 35; ill luck to wed in, v. 490, p. 408

Medea, the Phasian witch, ii. 42; Jason's wife, ii. 627

Medusa, iii. 451, v. 8

Megalesia, feast of Cybele, iv. 182; reason for being the first games, iv. 357

Meleager, v. 305

Melicertes, son of Ino, vi. 494; becomes Palaemon, vi. 501, 547, and Portunus, vi. 547

Melite (Malta), Anna at, iii. 567

Merchants, Mercury worshipped by, v. 671

Mercury, and Lara, ii. 608; son of Maia, v. 88; worship of, v. 90, brought to Latium by Evander, v. 100; gives mother's name to May, v. 103; worshipped by thieves, v. 104, 690, and merchants, v. 671; explains Lemuria, v. 447; entertained by Hyrieus, v. 496; attributes of, v. 663; temple of, v. 669; explains origin of Twins constellation, v. 698

Merkel, R., edition of *Fasti* by, p. xxv

Merope of the Pleiades, marriage to Sisyphus, iv. 175

Metamorphoses, the (Ovid), pp. xi, xvii

Metanira, wife of Celeus, iv. 539

Metellus, L. Caecilius, saves sacred things from temple of Vesta, vi. 444

Metellus, Q. Caecilius, founds temple to Cybele, iv. 348, 351

Mezentius helps Turnus and is slain, iv. 881

Mildew. See Robigalia

Mind, sanctuary to, vi. 241

Minerva, warlike aspects of, iii. 5, 809; goddess of arts and crafts, iii. 176, 815; Mars in love with, iii. 681, p. 407; Capta, shrine of, iii. 837; sacrifices to, iii. 850; birth of, v. 231; armed figure of, at Troy (the Palladium), vi. 421, is brought to Rome, vi. 424, 435; explains the rite of the flute-players, vi. 652; inventor

454

INDEX

INDEX

INDEX

INDEX

INDEX

INDEX

460

INDEX

hastens the sunset on April 15th, iv. 673; celebration of, by the common wenches, iv. 865; brought to Rome, iv. 875; temple of, near the Colline Gate, iv. 871; pleads to Jupiter for Rome, vi. 375; Nerine identified with, p. 409. See also Dione

Verticordia (changer of the Heart), name for Venus, iv. 160

Vertumnus, the Etruscan god of Volsinii, vi. 409, pp. 438-439; Roman derivation of name, p. 439; functions of, pp. 439-440; Ovid's verses on, p. 440

Vespasian, Emperor, fatal results of water at Cutilia, vi. 434, 435

Vesta, temple of, ii. 69, vi. 227, its annual cleansing, vi. 227, 713, rites connected with, vi. 295, and incident of fire at, vi. 437; March rites of, iii. 141; Augustus' connexion with, as Pontifex Maximus, iii. 421; refers to murder of Julius Caesar, iii. 698; at the founding of Rome, iv. 828; day dedicated to, iv. 949. vi. 249, vi. 391; Numa introduces worship of, vi. 259; connexion with Earth, vi. 263, 460; daughter of Ops and Saturn, vi. 286; and Priapus, vi. 319; pleads for Rome, vi. 376; origin of worship, p. 430; connexion with the king, pp. 430-431; shape of temples of, pp. 431-432

Vestal fire brought to Rome, i. 528

Vestal Virgins, fumigating materials for Parilia provided by, iv. 639, pp. 413-414; cast the Argei, v. 621, pp. 425, 426; in the siege of Rome, 390 B.C., vi. 365; punishment of, for unchastity, vi. 457;

in the Lupercalia, p. 391; at the Thesmophoria, p. 423

Vestibule, derivation of, vi. 303

Via Nova, the, vi. 396

Victor, a title of Jupiter, iv. 621

Victory (Nike), identification of Vacuna with, pp. 432, 433, 435

Vinalia, the, iv. 863; a festival of Venus, iv. 877, but belongs to Jupiter, iv. 878

Vindicta, the, vi. 676

Virbius, Hippolytus becomes, vi. 756

Virgil, Ovid's contemporary, p. ix; on Portunus, p. 441

Vitruvius on the water of Lake Cutilia, p. 433

Volsinii, Voltumnus the god of, pp. 438-439

Voltumna, wife of Voltumnus, p. 439

Vortumnus. See Vertumnus

Vulcan, worshipped in Lemnos, iii. 82; crown given to Venus by, iii. 514; day of, v. 725; father of Servius Tullius, vi. 627

Walpurgis Night, p. 402

Week, the Roman, i. 54; the African, pp. 385-386

Whitethorn used against witches, vi. 129, 165

Wissowa on Portunus, p. 442

Woodpecker, iii. 37

Woolley, Mr., excavations at Ur of the Chaldees by, p. 438

Yate, Rev. W., on the Maori calendar, p. 386

Zephyr weds Flora, v. 201, 319

Zeus, corrupted from Dios, p. 388

Printed in Great Britain by R. & R. CLARK, LIMITED, *Edinburgh*

THE LOEB CLASSICAL LIBRARY

VOLUMES ALREADY PUBLISHED

LATIN AUTHORS

AMMIANUS MARCELLINUS. J. C. Rolfe. 3 Vols.

APULEIUS : THE GOLDEN ASS (METAMORPHOSES). W Adlington (1566). Revised by S. Gaselee.

ST. AUGUSTINE : CITY OF GOD. 7 Vols. Vol. I. G. E. McCracken. Vol. II. W. M. Green. Vol. III. D. Wiesen. Vol. IV. P. Levine. Vol. V. E. M. Sanford and W. M. Green. Vol. VI. W. C. Greene.

ST. AUGUSTINE : CONFESSIONS OF. W. Watts (1631). 2 Vols.

ST. AUGUSTINE : SELECT LETTERS. J. H. Baxter.

AUSONIUS. H. G. Evelyn White. 2 Vols.

BEDE. J. E. King. 2 Vols.

BOETHIUS : TRACTS AND DE CONSOLATIONE PHILOSOPHIAE. Rev. H. F. Stewart and E. K. Rand.

CAESAR : ALEXANDRIAN, AFRICAN AND SPANISH WARS. A. G. Way.

CAESAR : CIVIL WARS. A. G. Peskett.

CAESAR : GALLIC WAR. H. J. Edwards.

CATO AND VARRO : DE RE RUSTICA. H. B. Ash and W. D. Hooper.

CATULLUS. F. W. Cornish : TIBULLUS. J. B. Postgate ; and PERVIGILIUM VENERIS. J. W. Mackail.

CELSUS : DE MEDICINA. W. G. Spencer. 3 Vols.

CICERO : BRUTUS AND ORATOR. G. L. Hendrickson and H. M. Hubbell.

CICERO : DE FINIBUS. H. Rackham.

CICERO : DE INVENTIONE, etc. H. M. Hubbell.

CICERO : DE NATURA DEORUM AND ACADEMICA. H. Rackham.

CICERO : DE OFFICIIS. Walter Miller.

CICERO : DE ORATORE, etc. 2 Vols. Vol. I : DE ORATORE, Books I and II. E. W. Sutton and H. Rackham. Vol. II : DE ORATORE, Book III ; DE FATO ; PARADOXA STOICORUM ; DE PARTITIONE ORATORIA. H. Rackham.

CICERO : DE REPUBLICA, DE LEGIBUS, SOMNIUM SCIPIONIS. Clinton W. Keyes.

1

THE LOEB CLASSICAL LIBRARY

CICERO : DE SENECTUTE, DE AMICITIA, DE DIVINATIONE. W. A. Falconer.

CICERO : IN CATILINAM, PRO MURENA, PRO SULLA, PRO FLACCO. Louis E. Lord.

CICERO : LETTERS TO ATTICUS. E. O. Winstedt. 3 Vols.

CICERO : LETTERS TO HIS FRIENDS. W. Glynn Williams. 3 Vols.

CICERO : PHILIPPICS. W. C. A. Ker.

CICERO : PRO ARCHIA, POST REDITUM, DE DOMO, DE HARUSPICUM RESPONSIS, PRO PLANCIO. N. H. Watts.

CICERO : PRO CAECINA, PRO LEGE MANILIA, PRO CLUENTIO, PRO RABIRIO. H. Grose Hodge.

CICERO : PRO CAELIO, DE PROVINCIIS CONSULARIBUS, PRO BALBO. R. Gardner.

CICERO : PRO MILONE, IN PISONEM, PRO SCAURO, PRO FONTEIO, PRO RABIRIO POSTUMO, PRO MARCELLO, PRO LIGARIO, PRO REGE DEIOTARO. N. H. Watts.

CICERO : PRO QUINCTIO, PRO ROSCIO AMERINO, PRO ROSCIO COMOEDO, CONTRA RULLUM. J. H. Freese.

CICERO : PRO SESTIO, IN VATINIUM. R. Gardner.

[CICERO] : RHETORICA AD HERENNIUM. H. Caplan.

CICERO : TUSCULAN DISPUTATIONS. J. E. King.

CICERO : VERRINE ORATIONS. L. H. G. Greenwood. 2 Vols.

CLAUDIAN. M. Platnauer. 2 Vols.

COLUMELLA : DE RE RUSTICA, DE ARBORIBUS. H. B. Ash, E. S. Forster, E. Heffner. 3 Vols.

CURTIUS, Q. : HISTORY OF ALEXANDER. J. C. Rolfe. 2 Vols.

FLORUS. E. S. Forster ; and CORNELIUS NEPOS. J. C. Rolfe.

FRONTINUS : STRATAGEMS AND AQUEDUCTS. C. E. Bennett and M. B. McElwain.

FRONTO : CORRESPONDENCE. C. R. Haines. 2 Vols.

GELLIUS. J. C. Rolfe. 3 Vols.

HORACE : ODES AND EPODES. C. E. Bennett.

HORACE : SATIRES, EPISTLES, ARS POETICA. H. R. Fairclough.

JEROME : SELECT LETTERS. F. A. Wright.

JUVENAL AND PERSIUS. G. G. Ramsay.

LIVY. B. O. Foster, F. G. Moore, Evan T. Sage, A. C. Schlesinger and R. M. Geer (General Index). 14 Vols.

LUCAN. J. D. Duff.

LUCRETIUS. W. H. D. Rouse.

MARTIAL. W. C. A. Ker. 2 Vols.

MINOR LATIN POETS : from PUBLILIUS SYRUS TO RUTILIUS NAMATIANUS, including GRATTIUS, CALPURNIUS SICULUS,

2

THE LOEB CLASSICAL LIBRARY

NEMESIANUS, AVIANUS, with "Aetna," "Phoenix" and other poems. J. Wight Duff and Arnold M. Duff.
OVID : THE ART OF LOVE AND OTHER POEMS. J. H. Mozley.
OVID : FASTI. Sir James G. Frazer.
OVID : HEROIDES AND AMORES. Grant Showerman.
OVID : METAMORPHOSES. F. J. Miller. 2 Vols.
OVID : TRISTIA AND EX PONTO. A. L. Wheeler.
PETRONIUS. M. Heseltine : SENECA : APOCOLOCYNTOSIS. W. H. D. Rouse.
PHAEDRUS AND BABRIUS (Greek). B. E. Perry.
PLAUTUS. Paul Nixon. 5 Vols.
PLINY : LETTERS. Melmoth's translation revised by W. M. L. Hutchinson. 2 Vols.
PLINY : NATURAL HISTORY. 10 Vols. Vols. I-V and IX. H. Rackham. Vols. VI-VIII. W. H. S. Jones. Vol. X. D. E. Eichholz.
PROPERTIUS. H. E. Butler.
PRUDENTIUS. H. J. Thomson. 2 Vols.
QUINTILIAN. H. E. Butler. 4 Vols.
REMAINS OF OLD LATIN. E. H. Warmington. 4 Vols. Vol. I (Ennius and Caecilius). Vol. II (Livius, Naevius, Pacuvius, Accius). Vol. III (Lucilius, Laws of the XII Tables). Vol. IV (Archaic Inscriptions).
SALLUST. J. C. Rolfe.
SCRIPTORES HISTORIAE AUGUSTAE. D. Magie. 3 Vols.
SENECA : APOCOLOCYNTOSIS. Cf. PETRONIUS.
SENECA : EPISTULAE MORALES. R. M. Gummere. 3 Vols.
SENECA : MORAL ESSAYS. J. W. Basore. 3 Vols.
SENECA : TRAGEDIES. F. J. Miller. 2 Vols.
SIDONIUS : POEMS AND LETTERS. W. B. Anderson. 2 Vols.
SILIUS ITALICUS. J. D. Duff. 2 Vols.
STATIUS. J. H. Mozley. 2 Vols.
SUETONIUS. J. C. Rolfe. 2 Vols.
TACITUS : DIALOGUS. Sir Wm. Peterson ; and AGRICOLA AND GERMANIA. Maurice Hutton.
TACITUS : HISTORIES AND ANNALS. C. H. Moore and J. Jackson. 4 Vols.
TERENCE. John Sargeaunt. 2 Vols.
TERTULLIAN : APOLOGIA AND DE SPECTACULIS. T. R. Glover ; MINUCIUS FELIX. G. H. Rendall.
VALERIUS FLACCUS. J. H. Mozley.
VARRO : DE LINGUA LATINA. R. G. Kent. 2 Vols.
VELLEIUS PATERCULUS AND RES GESTAE DIVI AUGUSTI. F. W. Shipley.

THE LOEB CLASSICAL LIBRARY

VIRGIL. H. R. Fairclough. 2 Vols.
VITRUVIUS : DE ARCHITECTURA. F. Granger. 2 Vols.

GREEK AUTHORS

ACHILLES TATIUS. S. Gaselee.
AELIAN : ON THE NATURE OF ANIMALS. A. F. Scholfield.
  3 Vols.
AENEAS TACTICUS, ASCLEPIODOTUS AND ONASANDER. The
  Illinois Greek Club.
AESCHINES. C. D. Adams.
AESCHYLUS. H. Weir Smyth. 2 Vols.
ALCIPHRON, AELIAN AND PHILOSTRATUS : LETTERS. A. R.
  Benner and F. H. Fobes.
APOLLODORUS. Sir James G. Frazer. 2 Vols.
APOLLONIUS RHODIUS. R. C. Seaton.
THE APOSTOLIC FATHERS. Kirsopp Lake. 2 Vols.
APPIAN'S ROMAN HISTORY. Horace White. 4 Vols.
ARATUS. Cf. CALLIMACHUS.
ARISTOPHANES. Benjamin Bickley Rogers. 3 Vols. Verse
  trans.
ARISTOTLE : ART OF RHETORIC. J. H. Freese.
ARISTOTLE : ATHENIAN CONSTITUTION, EUDEMIAN ETHICS,
  VIRTUES AND VICES. H. Rackham.
ARISTOTLE : THE CATEGORIES. ON INTERPRETATION. H. P.
  Cooke ; PRIOR ANALYTICS. H. Tredennick.
ARISTOTLE : GENERATION OF ANIMALS. A. L. Peck.
ARISTOTLE: HISTORIA ANIMALIUM. A. L. Peck. 3 Vols. Vol. I.
ARISTOTLE : METAPHYSICS. H. Tredennick. 2 Vols.
ARISTOTLE : METEOROLOGICA. H. D. P. Lee.
ARISTOTLE : MINOR WORKS. W. S. Hett. " On Colours,"
  " On Things Heard," " Physiognomics," " On Plants,"
  " On Marvellous Things Heard," " Mechanical Problems,"
  " On Indivisible Lines," " Situations and Names of
  Winds," " On Melissus, Xenophanes, and Gorgias."
ARISTOTLE : NICOMACHEAN ETHICS. H. Rackham.
ARISTOTLE : OECONOMICA AND MAGNA MORALIA. G. C.
  Armstrong. (With Metaphysics, Vol. II.)
ARISTOTLE : ON THE HEAVENS. W. K. C. Guthrie.
ARISTOTLE : ON THE SOUL, PARVA NATURALIA. On BREATH.
  W. S. Hett.

THE LOEB CLASSICAL LIBRARY

ARISTOTLE: PARTS OF ANIMALS. A. L. Peck; MOTION AND PROGRESSION OF ANIMALS. E. S. Forster.

ARISTOTLE: PHYSICS. Rev. P. Wicksteed and F. M. Cornford. 2 Vols.

ARISTOTLE: POETICS; LONGINUS ON THE SUBLIME. W. Hamilton Fyfe; DEMETRIUS ON STYLE. W. Rhys Roberts.

ARISTOTLE: POLITICS. H. Rackham.

ARISTOTLE: POSTERIOR ANALYTICS. H. Tredennick; TOPICS. E. S. Forster.

ARISTOTLE: PROBLEMS. W. S. Hett. 2 Vols.

ARISTOTLE: RHETORICA AD ALEXANDRUM. H. Rackham. (With Problems, Vol. II.)

ARISTOTLE: SOPHISTICAL REFUTATIONS. COMING-TO-BE AND PASSING-AWAY. E. S. Forster; ON THE COSMOS. D. J. Furley.

ARRIAN: HISTORY OF ALEXANDER AND INDICA. Rev. E. Iliffe Robson. 2 Vols.

ATHENAEUS: DEIPNOSOPHISTAE. C. B. Gulick. 7 Vols.

BABRIUS AND PHAEDRUS (Latin). B. E. Perry.

ST. BASIL: LETTERS. R. J. Deferrari. 4 Vols.

CALLIMACHUS: FRAGMENTS. C. A. Trypanis.

CALLIMACHUS: HYMNS AND EPIGRAMS, AND LYCOPHRON. A. W. Mair; ARATUS. G. R. Mair.

CLEMENT OF ALEXANDRIA. Rev. G. W. Butterworth.

COLLUTHUS. *Cf.* OPPIAN.

DAPHNIS AND CHLOE. *Cf.* LONGUS.

DEMOSTHENES I: OLYNTHIACS, PHILIPPICS AND MINOR ORATIONS: I-XVII AND XX. J. H. Vince.

DEMOSTHENES II: DE CORONA AND DE FALSA LEGATIONE, C. A. Vince and J. H. Vince.

DEMOSTHENES III: MEIDIAS, ANDROTION, ARISTOCRATES, TIMOCRATES, ARISTOGEITON. J. H. Vince.

DEMOSTHENES IV-VI: PRIVATE ORATIONS AND IN NEAERAM. A. T. Murray.

DEMOSTHENES VII: FUNERAL SPEECH, EROTIC ESSAY, EXORDIA AND LETTERS. N. W. and N. J. DeWitt.

DIO CASSIUS: ROMAN HISTORY. E. Cary. 9 Vols.

DIO CHRYSOSTOM. 5 Vols. Vols. I and II. J. W. Cohoon. Vol. III. J. W. Cohoon and H. Lamar Crosby. Vols IV and V. H. Lamar Crosby.

DIODORUS SICULUS. 12 Vols. Vols. I-VI. C. H. Oldfather. Vol. VII. C. L. Sherman. Vol. VIII. C. B. Welles. Vols. IX and X. Russel M. Geer. Vols XI and XII. F. R. Walton. General Index. Russel M. Geer.

THE LOEB CLASSICAL LIBRARY

DIOGENES LAERTIUS. R. D. Hicks. 2 Vols.

DIONYSIUS OF HALICARNASSUS : ROMAN ANTIQUITIES. Spelman's translation revised by E. Cary. 7 Vols.

EPICTETUS. W. A. Oldfather. 2 Vols.

EURIPIDES. A. S. Way. 4 Vols. Verse trans.

EUSEBIUS : ECCLESIASTICAL HISTORY. Kirsopp Lake and J. E. L. Oulton. 2 Vols.

GALEN : ON THE NATURAL FACULTIES. A. J. Brock.

THE GREEK ANTHOLOGY. W. R. Paton. 5 Vols.

THE GREEK BUCOLIC POETS (THEOCRITUS, BION, MOSCHUS). J. M. Edmonds.

GREEK ELEGY AND IAMBUS WITH THE ANACREONTEA. J. M. Edmonds. 2 Vols.

GREEK MATHEMATICAL WORKS. Ivor Thomas. 2 Vols.

HERODES. *Cf.* THEOPHRASTUS : CHARACTERS.

HERODOTUS. A. D. Godley. 4 Vols.

HESIOD AND THE HOMERIC HYMNS. H. G. Evelyn White.

HIPPOCRATES AND THE FRAGMENTS OF HERACLEITUS. W. H. S. Jones and E. T. Withington. 4 Vols.

HOMER : ILIAD. A. T. Murray. 2 Vols.

HOMER : ODYSSEY. A. T. Murray. 2 Vols.

ISAEUS. E. S. Forster.

ISOCRATES. George Norlin and LaRue Van Hook. 3 Vols.

ST. JOHN DAMASCENE : BARLAAM AND IOASAPH. Rev. G. R. Woodward, Harold Mattingly and D. M. Lang.

JOSEPHUS. 9 Vols. Vols. I-IV. H. St. J. Thackeray. Vol. V. H. St. J. Thackeray and Ralph Marcus. Vols. VI and VII. Ralph Marcus. Vol. VIII. Ralph Marcus and Allen Wikgren. Vol. IX. L. H. Feldman.

JULIAN. Wilmer Cave Wright. 3 Vols.

LONGUS : DAPHNIS AND CHLOE. Thornley's translation revised by J. M. Edmonds ; and PARTHENIUS. S. Gaselee.

LUCIAN. 8 Vols. Vols. I-V. A. M. Harmon. Vol. VI. K. Kilburn. Vols. VII and VIII. M. D. Macleod.

LYCOPHRON. *Cf.* CALLIMACHUS.

LYRA GRAECA. J. M. Edmonds. 3 Vols.

LYSIAS. W. R. M. Lamb.

MANETHO. W. G. Waddell ; PTOLEMY : TETRABIBLOS. F. E. Robbins.

MARCUS AURELIUS. C. R. Haines.

MENANDER. F. G. Allinson.

MINOR ATTIC ORATORS. 2 Vols. K. J. Maidment and J. O. Burtt.

NONNOS : DIONYSIACA. W. H. D. Rouse. 3 Vols.

THE LOEB CLASSICAL LIBRARY

OPPIAN, COLLUTHUS, TRYPHIODORUS. A. W. Mair.

PAPYRI. NON-LITERARY SELECTIONS. A. S. Hunt and C. C. Edgar. 2 Vols. LITERARY SELECTIONS (Poetry). D. L. Page.

PARTHENIUS. *Cf.* LONGUS.

PAUSANIAS: DESCRIPTION OF GREECE. W. H. S. Jones. 5 Vols. and Companion Vol. arranged by R. E. Wycherley.

PHILO. 10 Vols. Vols. I-V. F. H. Colson and Rev. G. H. Whitaker. Vols. VI-X. F. H. Colson. General Index. Rev. J. W. Earp.
Two Supplementary Vols. Translation only from an Armenian Text. Ralph Marcus.

PHILOSTRATUS: THE LIFE OF APOLLONIUS OF TYANA. F. C. Conybeare. 2 Vols.

PHILOSTRATUS: IMAGINES; CALLISTRATUS: DESCRIPTIONS. A. Fairbanks.

PHILOSTRATUS AND EUNAPIUS: LIVES OF THE SOPHISTS. Wilmer Cave Wright.

PINDAR. Sir J. E. Sandys.

PLATO: CHARMIDES, ALCIBIADES, HIPPARCHUS, THE LOVERS, THEAGES, MINOS AND EPINOMIS. W. R. M. Lamb.

PLATO: CRATYLUS, PARMENIDES, GREATER HIPPIAS, LESSER HIPPIAS. H. N. Fowler.

PLATO: EUTHYPHRO, APOLOGY, CRITO, PHAEDO, PHAEDRUS. H. N. Fowler.

PLATO: LACHES, PROTAGORAS, MENO, EUTHYDEMUS. W. R. M. Lamb.

PLATO: LAWS. Rev. R. G. Bury. 2 Vols.

PLATO: LYSIS, SYMPOSIUM, GORGIAS. W. R. M. Lamb.

PLATO: REPUBLIC. Paul Shorey. 2 Vols.

PLATO: STATESMAN, PHILEBUS. H. N. Fowler: ION. W. R. M. Lamb.

PLATO: THEAETETUS AND SOPHIST. H. N. Fowler.

PLATO: TIMAEUS, CRITIAS, CLITOPHO, MENEXENUS, EPISTULAE. Rev. R. G. Bury.

PLOTINUS. A. H. Armstrong. 6 Vols. Vols. I-II.

PLUTARCH: MORALIA. 15 Vols. Vols. I-V. F. C. Babbitt. Vol. VI. W. C. Helmbold. Vol. VII. P. H. De Lacy and B. Einarson. Vol. IX. E. L. Minar, Jr., F. H. Sandbach, W. C. Helmbold. Vol. X. H. N. Fowler. Vol. XI. L. Pearson, F. H. Sandbach. Vol. XII. H. Cherniss, W. C. Helmbold. Vol. XIV. P. H. De Lacy and B. Einarson.

PLUTARCH: THE PARALLEL LIVES. B. Perrin. 11 Vols.

POLYBIUS. W. R. Paton. 6 Vols.

THE LOEB CLASSICAL LIBRARY

PROCOPIUS : HISTORY OF THE WARS. H. B. Dewing. 7 Vols.
PTOLEMY : TETRABIBLOS. *Cf.* MANETHO.
QUINTUS SMYRNAEUS. A. S. Way. Verse trans.
SEXTUS EMPIRICUS. Rev. R. G. Bury. 4 Vols.
SOPHOCLES. F. Storr. 2 Vols. Verse trans.
STRABO : GEOGRAPHY. Horace L. Jones. 8 Vols.
THEOPHRASTUS : CHARACTERS. J. M. Edmonds ; HERODES, etc. A. D. Knox.
THEOPHRASTUS : ENQUIRY INTO PLANTS. Sir Arthur Hort. 2 Vols.
THUCYDIDES. C. F. Smith. 4 Vols.
TRYPHIODORUS. *Cf.* OPPIAN.
XENOPHON : ANABASIS. C. L. Brownson.
XENOPHON : CYROPAEDIA. Walter Miller. 2 Vols.
XENOPHON : HELLENICA. C. L. Brownson. 2 Vols.
XENOPHON : MEMORABILIA AND OECONOMICUS. E. C. Marchant. SYMPOSIUM AND APOLOGY. O. J Todd.
XENOPHON : SCRIPTA MINORA. E. C. Marchant and G. W. Bowersock.

VOLUMES IN PREPARATION

GREEK AUTHORS

ARISTIDES : ORATIONS. C. A. Behr.
HERODIANUS. C. R. Whittaker.
LIBANIUS : SELECTED WORKS. A. F. Norman.
MUSAEUS : HERO AND LEANDER. T. Gelzer and C. H. Whitman.
THEOPHRASTUS : DE CAUSIS PLANTARUM. G. K. K. Link and B. Einarson.

LATIN AUTHORS

ASCONIUS : COMMENTARIES ON CICERO'S ORATIONS. G. W. Bowersock.
BENEDICT : THE RULE. P. Meyvaert.
JUSTIN–TROGUS. R. Moss.
MANILIUS. G. P. Gould.
PLINY : LETTERS. B. Radice.

DESCRIPTIVE PROSPECTUS ON APPLICATION

CAMBRIDGE, MASS.   LONDON
HARVARD UNIV. PRESS   WILLIAM HEINEMANN LTD